DIDIER COLIN

DICTIONARY
of symbols, myths and legends

HACHETTE
Illustrated

Layout and typesetting: Graph'M
Illustrations: Thierry Aubert, François Charles, Fanny Ruelle/Graph'M
Photographs: Jean Riby/Graph'M
Editorial: Sophie Rey-Lilienfeld
English edition design: Chris Bell

© Hachette Livre (Hachette Pratique) 2000
This edition published by
Hachette Illustrated UK, Octopus Publishing Group,
2–4 Heron Quays, London E14 4JP

English translation produced by Wendy Allatson
and Sue Rose for JMS Books LLP
Translation © Octopus Publishing Group

A CIP catalogue for this book is available from the British Library

ISBN: 1 84430 025 0

Printed by Tien Wah, Singapore

From the real world to the language of life

The language of symbols is the language of dreams. It is a language that our forebears learned to decipher long before the invention of the subconscious, that pure product of the real world. The language of symbols is a living language based on close observation of the natural world and its phenomena, some of which, as we now know, have changed over the ages. The landscapes of our modern world are very different from those of our ancestors. During the course of its history, the Earth has suffered at least four major cataclysms attributable to various causes. While some rendered life on its surface virtually impossible during the course of the past 200 million years, all significantly modified the climate and geology of the planet.

Although the doctrine of catastrophism associated with the French naturalist Georges Cuvier (1769–1837) was soon abandoned in favour of the principle of geological time, some areas of advanced modern research (e.g. the neocatastrophic school) are currently expanding and developing the theory advanced by Cuvier in his *Discours sur les révolutions de la surface du globe* ('Discourse on the Revolutions of the Globe'). Cuvier believed that the great climatic and geological changes that took place during certain geological eras and periods in the earth's history may well have been provoked by cataclysmic occurrences. Furthermore, far from there being no reason to suppose that such events will never recur, there is in fact every reason to believe that they *will* recur, in similar forms or as a result of processes of which we are not even remotely aware. For example, although it is a well-known fact that the visible and invisible matter of the real world as we know it consists of atoms, and that the earth is continuously bombarded with countless cosmic rays (protons and helium nuclei emitted by the sun, stars and galaxies), we still do not know how to estimate the short- and long-term interactions and influences, the subtle and potential relationships between these phenomena.

In this sense we are still little more than observers, increasingly interventionist it is true, but observers nonetheless. However, we can certainly draw a great many conclusions from our observations, which enable us to influence and in some cases control natural phenomena. Some of these phenomena are hostile, others are less dangerous but still perceived as hostile. Whatever their nature, we still seek to control them and turn them to our advantage or profit. From this, it seems we are forced to conclude that the human race is the most interventionist species the earth has ever known, and also the most destructive, since human beings are not – or no longer – content to observe life, they wish – and are able – to control it. The human race has issued a new challenge to biological death, the fate that has dogged it since it first came into being and which is a certainty for life on earth, and possibly for life in the universe, since stars and galaxies also come into being and die. And that challenge is the ability to create life and extend it indefinitely.

Powerless to comprehend the meaning of life or its origins, the human race believed it had been created by gods, and then by one all-powerful God, to the point where this God was embodied in a living god prepared to sacrifice his earthly existence in order to gain eternal life. This revolution in individual consciousness was accomplished in less than ten thousand years, while the human species seems to have existed and made little progress for almost half a million years!

However, regardless of whether we are believers or atheists, as we enter the third millennium, we do so alone. If a god, or God, exists within us, we should expect nothing from him. The increasing tendency to believe 'scientifically' in the probable existence of not only another life but also another – extraterrestrial – intelligence is the result of human anguish. This anguish stems from the belief – not yet at a wholly global level, but rather latent, muted and final – that we are alone on earth, alone in the universe, from the moment of our conception to the point at which our bodies disintegrate. We therefore scan the vastness of the cosmos in an attempt to define its limits, for our scientists argue that if the real world has its limits, the universe must also have limits – at least that is how we 'see' the world. We record shock waves that, again according to science, are the incontrovertible proof of the original explosion, the famous big bang that resulted in the creation of the universe. And we do this because we feel isolated and because we are afraid of being alone.

More than ever before, we are aware of the transient nature of our life on earth.

It is a solitary journey, whose length may have been extended (at least in the richer countries of the world), but during which time is in increasingly short supply – on the one hand because the pace of our social life is quickening and on the other because occupations, information and entertainment distract us from ourselves.

If we are to believe the scientists, the human race has emerged laboriously from a state of wild, primordial animality and freed itself from the implacable laws of nature by following a long and quite exceptional process of evolution that has enabled it to control its environment. Human beings have got the measure of the real, material world, a world that is external to them and that they recognize as such, from which they accept that they originated, whose limits they know and whose components they dissect and analyse on a daily basis. Even when forced to admit that this world is temporal, they are not discouraged. What is more, as if to prove to themselves that the world they manipulate at will is the only real world, they have found a way of realizing their dreams, which means that the world in which we live is filled with objects, instruments, accessories and even materials that do not exist. Every day, our television and cinema screens transmit images of the world that are either unreal or distorted, or coarse and violent, as well as streams of watered-down dreams, illusions and unreal adventures. We know, however, which is the dream and which the reality because dreams have become a product to be consumed to excess.

However, this one-sided view of life to which we all more or less willingly subscribe tends to ride roughshod over our emotions, possibly because they are regarded as too simplistic. This tends to give rise to a sort of latent disenchantment which surfaces every time we are confronted with difficulties that isolate us and force us to rely or act on our own initiative. Those individuals who organize and orient themselves exclusively in relation to a world in which everything seems to be worked out for them in advance and which therefore does away with the need to develop their curiosity, imagination or personality, no longer have the slightest suspicion of the existence of another, inner life. This other life only assumes its full meaning through permanent contact, a continuous dialogue between itself and the external world. Without this contact or dialogue, which leads to ongoing and useful questions being asked on both sides, everything remains static.

This is the paradox towards which we are inexorably drawn by our desire to control the real world, a world on which we are currently focusing all our conscious desires and efforts. The more we find out about its structures and principles, the more we can dominate and replicate them, and the more our lives and future depend on that world. The atoms and cells that govern the real world are subject to immutable rules. So, even when we acquire the means to modify genetic structure in order to improve the real world (by making it what we regard as healthier, purer and more balanced), whether we like it or not we are playing by these rules since the rules of the real world are inescapable. The victory of human beings over a real world whose limits they have defined and in which they can see and understand only these limits is an illusion based on abstractions. This leads to disenchantment with a life that is ultimately absurd, devoid of sense, lacking in motivation, with no potential for development and no hope, unless it is the hope of living longer, being more attractive, having a higher IQ, never being ill, having everything to hand and so on. But then what would be left for us to achieve, what would be the purpose of it all? Happiness, well-being, gratification of the senses perhaps? We don't really know and no one really asks the question any more since it is not regarded as relevant.

Being 'relevant' is the magic phrase, the key to this real world. What is happening right now is all that seems real. The past is a dream whose only value is to assess the progress made by humanity. As for the future, it is already mapped out since the human race controls the real world and therefore its own destiny. Of course, old terrors sometimes resurface, horrors dating from the time when men and women were victims of their own ignorance and at the mercy of events and the elements – the horrors of war, epidemic, famine and the apocalypse. But these are considered necessary fears, salutary memories that should never be forgotten and should be kept in mind the better to cling to the real world and convince ourselves of its vital reality.

Are we really aware of the choice we have made to live in a real world whose mysteries will one day – sooner or later, but without a shadow of a doubt – all be solved? Are we really willing to live in a world that is not only devoid of mysteries, but also of any form of outlet or release? Are we prepared to live in a world where there will be nothing left to invent, imagine, understand, discover, find or dream? The real world described above is just such a world.

This does not mean that we should live in the past or move forward either blindly or looking backwards. But we should be allowed to ask ourselves whether we have not, at some point in our history, taken a wrong turning or simply exaggerated one of our discoveries and made it an end in itself. Are we not inclined to reject a whole way of life out of hand, on the pretext that we have dis-covered another, apparently easier, way of life which in reality suits a handful of people much better? However, there is a different approach to life that in no way excludes the life of the real world. It is also based on a close observation of life, not the life of the world whose limits have been clearly and finally defined, but of the world as it manifests itself to us, as it expresses itself in all its possible, innumerable, varied and continually renewed forms. In order to interact with these multiple forms of life, some of which seemed totally alien to them, human beings developed a language based on a close observation of nature. Through this language, they were not only able to communicate with life in all its forms but also with themselves. In so doing, their spirits were able to emerge from the original chaos into which they had been plunged, of which there are accounts in all the ancient cosmogonies of the world.

This is, of course, the language of symbols, which is at the origin of all languages, including those that we use to define the great principles that govern the real world. In other words, mathematics, alphabets, signs, figures and letters – in short, everything that enables us to name and classify living creatures and inanimate objects, to organize the real world according to our concept of it – are based on the language of symbols.

However, the uniqueness of this language is that it lies deep within our emotions, in the heart of every man and woman on earth, and is so deeply rooted in the collective memory that we all speak it without realizing it.

The language of symbols is universal. It is a language common to all human beings, whatever their culture, race or mother tongue, and may even be a language shared with animals, plants, stones, the elements and – why not? – atoms and cells.

The language of symbols is the language of life in all its forms. It is the language that is used each night by men and women in their dreams, but it is also used by anything that dreams, breathes, hopes, loves and suffers – in other words, lives – here on earth. It is a receptive and living language, which is continuously incorporating thoughts, ideas, new concepts and new forms of life, which is sufficiently flexible to stretch into the past and towards the future, and sufficiently malleable to assume all the appearances of visible and invisible, real and imaginary life.

The language of symbols stems from the inner life of human beings. It is the link that connects them with the external world. In absolute terms, it is the embodiment of the world. If you want to understand how it works, it is no longer enough to immerse yourself in the natural world. Today, this natural world is rarely pure, free and wild since the human race has forged nature in its own image in an attempt to impose its own idea of the 'real' world. Instead, you need to withdraw to a place where nature mirrors the myriad twists and turns of the contradictory ideas, thoughts and feelings that continually assail your mind. For, like our minds, nature is in a constant state of flux between peace and turmoil.

How can we hope to understand what is going on within us, who we are and where we come from if we are not in touch with the natural world from which we spring, of which we are made, and with which we are so deeply and closely linked? Nature is our true mother, the mother of each and every one of us, deified in the past as the mythical mother-goddess. Whatever her name, her language is the language of life, the language of symbols.

It is only by living within the womb of our mother and speaking her language that we can one day hope to be born or, more accurately, cease to die – but not by seeking to create life or extend it artificially. To live in the intimacy of this eternal womb that gives and takes life at will, in accordance with immutable and universal cycles, all we have to do is immerse ourselves in the daily world of our dreams. The term 'dreams' refers not only to the dreams we have when we are asleep but also to those we have when we believe we are awake. We usually have this second type of dream when we are disturbed by uncontrollable thoughts and ideas that tempt us to escape, speculate, imagine, believe or love.

All these dreams have meaning but while some may be relatively unimportant others are laden with illuminating revelations. Whichever they are, the meaning of our dreams is never concealed from us – we simply don't know how to decipher them. All we need to do is rediscover the language of symbols – the language of life – and use it to understand the meaning of a dream that has come to us in sleep or that obsesses us during our waking hours.

As its name suggests, this *Dictionary of Symbols, Myths and Legends* is a practical guide to the interpretation of the symbols, myths and legends that help us to understand and communicate with ourselves. As well as revealing their various meanings and historical origins, it aims to help the reader to decipher personal messages in the signs and symbols that form this language and which are so often interrelated.

What is more important than one's self? What is richer, more amazing or more wonderful than the universe that each of us contains within us? This book invites you to discover this hidden treasure. The list of symbols, myths and legends is far from exhaustive and you will certainly find in other works information that has been omitted here, either deliberately or inadvertently. But as you become increasingly absorbed by the language of symbols, you will begin to realize that it is not only an instrument of revelation and self-knowledge but also a link between human beings.

And, hopefully, as you turn the pages of this book, you will rediscover this link that unites us closely with our fellow human beings and use this instrument whose language is life.

A

'A' is the first letter of the alphabet and the first of the five vowels. It corresponds to *aleph* (literally, 'ox'), the first letter of the Hebrew alphabet, which was the source for *alpha*, the first letter of the Greek alphabet.

Originally, this letter was represented by a circle surmounted by a crescent, a diagrammatic and symbolic representation of the horned head of a buffalo or an ox and, later, the crowned head of a king.

Gradually, the written form of the letter was rotated to the right by 45 degrees and lost one of its horns or one side of its crown, which gave it its present form.

'A' is the symbol of primordial and original strength, energy, unity, eternity, initiative, creation and free will that cannot be contained or conditioned. It is also the symbol of the link between terrestrial elements (the head) and celestial powers (the horns or crown).

The letter 'A' corresponds to the figure '1', the symbol of perfection, accomplishment and achievement. In personal terms, it symbolizes the beginning and the end, the start and the comple-tion of an event, situation or undertaking, something that is sufficient unto itself, a return to the point of departure, the end of one life cycle and the beginning of another. It represents innate, perfect and absolute knowledge, a new beginning, a creation or a birth.

'A' also symbolizes the assets, financial resources and potential wealth at your disposal, which can be turned turn to good advantage. Or it may represent an association, relationship, marriage, friendship or grouping that you are about to form, enter into or that is central to your concerns. Finally, it may announce success in a particular area of your life.

Abbey

An abbey represents unity of life. It is a privileged place where those who have chosen to share and contribute to its communal lifestyle can achieve material independence and devote themselves wholeheartedly to meditation and religious reflection. However, as well as being places of intense spiritual activity, abbeys were also centres for commercial exchanges and a focal point around which villages gradually grew up. The abbey is therefore a symbol of union, of work achieved by communal effort, a rallying point, a centre for academic and commercial exchanges, material prosperity and spiritual wealth. It is also a symbol of temporal and political power exercised in a closed environment. For example, the head of a family, a company leader or a politician can be represented by an abbey in their capacity as head of their own particular 'abbey' or community.

Being in an abbey means gathering together or gathering other people around you. Conversely, being in a monastery means isolating yourself. The appearance of an abbey in your dreams always corresponds to a period of intense intellectual, social, material and spiritual activity in your life.

Adam

See Paradise, page 410

Air

The air we breathe keeps us alive. This makes it both vital and fatal, magical and ambiguous.

In astrology, the precise moment used to draw up an astronomic map or birth chart is the moment when the newborn baby takes its first complete breath or inspiration–expiration. This rhythm of life is also the rhythm of death. The breath that enables a child to live freely and independently of the umbilical cord, by using its lungs and respiratory system, is based on a continuous binary movement. Taking your first breath means living and being independent, while breathing your last means expiring and dying.

Breath has always been closely linked with the soul. Both are invisible and impalpable but they are not one and the same thing. Breath is rather the vehicle of the soul.

Air, whether it is breath or wind, is impregnated with the scents and smells, warmth and cold of the spaces it fills and within which it moves. If you place your hand in front of your

mouth, you can feel the warmth of your breath each time you breathe out. In this respect, air is the sustenance of the gods, since it is by breathing that the organism produces the warmth of its inner life or fire. Similarly, when the wind blows, it is not the wind we see and hear, but the branches of the trees bending and moving and the leaves rustling.

Breathing is therefore a spontaneous, instinctive and vital action that enables us to take in air, live and move. But breath is not air, it is part of the act of breathing. Wind is not air either. It is caused by a displacement of air that is in turn produced by the earth's rotation on its axis. Therefore, if breath and wind are both vehicles of the invisible but very real and omnipresent air around us, without which all forms of life would be impossible, breath can equally well be the vehicle of the soul that makes each of us different from our fellows, unique, intelligent and free. It could even be regarded as the symbolic proof of the existence of the soul.

Breath is also the vehicle of thought, the mind, sounds, the voice, words and speech. Again, these are all invisible things that are manifested within the real world through the medium of air. Just as, according to the principles of Chinese astrology, wood makes fire manifest (by supplying the raw material for flames), so air qualifies fire.

Air is the same for everyone, but breath is unique. When you inspire or inhale, you take in the air everyone else is breathing or, if you prefer, everyone around you is breathing the same air as you. But when you expire or exhale, you breathe out air that is unique to you, air that has been filtered through your lungs and, as it were, 'personalized'. However, although the lungs control the respiratory process, the skin also breathes through its pores. It is sustained by the breath of life. This is why people born under the Air signs (Gemini, Libra, Aquarius) often have fine, sensitive skin and can be very 'touchy'.

The airway tree is a tree of life. The lungs are connected to the right and left bronchi (branches) that join at the base of the trachea (trunk). When you examine the system formed by the lungs, bronchi and trachea, it looks rather like an inverted tree. There is an obvious symbolic analogy between the airway tree and the two forms of the world tree: the tree of life (see page 498) – the horizontal centre of the world and the source of life – and the tree of the knowledge of good and evil – the vertical centre of the world linking heaven and earth – which stood in the Garden of Eden. Like both forms of the world tree, the airway tree is the origin of individual consciousness but also implies a movement between life and death, between inspiration and expiration (or expiry). The tree of life is therefore also a tree of death. Nor should we forget the heart, lying coiled between the lungs, whose binary movement of diastole (dilation of the heart and arteries) and systole (contraction of the heart and arteries) passes continually between life and death. The beating of the heart is the rhythm of life and death. Without it, all life would be impossible.

However, respiration is an act of life, the manifestation of an act of will that originates in the lower back, in the area of the kidneys, which are also binary in nature. The lower back is the seat of balance, strength and power. In French, the expression 'avoir

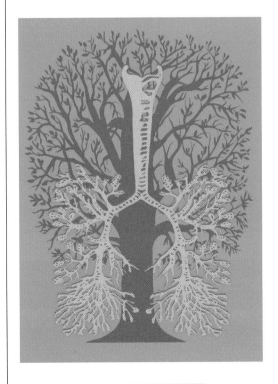

les reins solides' ('to have a strong back') is used in its figurative sense ('to be on a sound footing') when describing a well-balanced person who has acquired a certain degree of self-control or who enjoys a certain level of material comfort. Like all parts of the body that fulfil a vital function, the kidneys also breathe. They are the organs of genital respiration, in the lower part of the body, while the lungs are the organs of pulmonary respiration, in the upper part of the body. Those who control their strength and desires, in the lower back or kidney area, control their breathing and mind in the pulmonary or lung area. This control is achieved by the use of the muscles of the diaphragm, which separates the thorax from the abdomen and enables the respiratory system to open up and expand.

The respiratory exercises used in Hatha Yoga ('union of force') promote breathing control and develop the airway tree, the tree of life within us. They also make us aware of its rhythm since air, breathing and respiration are all forms of rhythm. We each have our own rhythm. Regulating our breathing and respiration means getting into our rhythm, learning to live in time to our own rhythm.

Etymologically speaking, rhythm means movement, cadence and harmony but it is also a way of being. By learning to control the air within us and regulate our breathing, we can discover our personal rhythm and our way of being.

Airplane

Like the automobile, the airplane is a symbol of the modern world but is also associated with ancient Greek mythology. Icarus and his father Daedalus were imprisoned in the Labyrinth by King Minos of Crete, but escaped by making wings which they attached to their shoulders with

Airplane
Albatross

wax (see *Labyrinth*, page 306). Daedalus told Icarus not to fly too low or too high, but Icarus did not heed his father's warning and flew too close to the sun with the result that the wax melted and he fell into the sea. This myth was obviously not particularly encouraging for the early pioneers of aviation but they persevered nonetheless and finally enabled human beings to achieve one of their oldest dreams – to fly like a bird.

If you dream about a plane, you should keep the ideas of flight (i.e., escape), pride and presumption that are central to this myth very much in mind. You should also consider whether you feel the need to escape at the time you have the dream, or whether you are taking a detached view of things – possibly too detached – and in so doing are distancing yourself from the reality of your everyday life.

Albatross

This huge and very beautiful seabird is particularly graceful in flight. Its name originates from the Arabic *al jattaz* ('pelican'), which became *alcatraz* in Portuguese, the name of the former prison perched, like a bird, high on a rock in San Francisco Bay.

The English word 'albatross' (French *albatros*) incorporates the Latin root *albus*, meaning 'white'.

The albatross rears one fledgling at a time, sitting on the single egg for three months in its cliff-top nest. It is a truly spectacular glider and in windy weather achieves flight speeds of up to 80km (50 miles) per hour without flapping its wings, by simply using the air currents. It is also one of the few birds that can sleep while flying, or rather gliding, an almost unheard-of phenomenon.

In the past, the albatross was greatly respected by mariners who regarded it as a bird of good omen, the harbinger of good tidings and fair weather. Killing an albatross was thought to bring bad luck, as illustrated by Samuel Taylor Coleridge's poem *The Rime of the Ancient Mariner*. As the guide and symbol of souls and spiritual freedom, it was commonly believed that the souls of mariners lost at sea were reincarnated in the body of an albatross and, in this way, were able to reach heaven.

Almond, almond tree

Because it is enclosed in a pod, the almond symbolizes the soul incarnate encased within a mortal shell. The walnut has the same symbolic meaning for the same reason.

By extension, the almond is a symbol of the eternal and immortal nature of the soul, the divine light contained within each human being. This light is contained within us as if within a pod or shell that only needs to be opened up for the soul to be liberated, illuminated and transcendent. The almond therefore corresponds to the self-fulfilment that occurs in its own good time, when the time is ripe, just as when the almond has ripened the pod cracks and breaks open or falls away. In the Middle Ages, this imagery was often used in the Christian churches of Western Europe to illustrate the concept of the abandonment or loss of the mortal shell that would free the soul, of the death of the 'original human being' represented by Adam and the emergence of the 'new human being' glorified by the divine light, i.e. the demigod. Christ and the Virgin were often depicted surrounded by an almond-shaped area of light known as the mandorla.

From an etymological point of view, the word 'almond' is a distortion of *amandala*, derived from the classical Latin *amygdala* and the Greek *amagdala*, meaning 'tonsil'. This is presumably a reference to its shape.

The almond also has symbolic connotations with the female genitalia since it often represents the vulva. In this sense, it corresponds to the Hindu term *yoni*, meaning 'vulva' or 'womb', represented by an almond or nut divided in two. Because ground, bitter almonds are thought to have aphrodisiac properties, the almond is also the symbol of creative energy. In some regions of Europe it has long been believed (and still is in some areas!) that if a girl falls asleep under an almond tree, she may wake up pregnant.

The almond tree, which flowers in the early spring, is a symbol of renewal and rebirth. For the Hebrews, the almond tree (*shoqed*) represented a revelation or a Coming, and revealed the resemblance between mortals and God who had made mortals in his image: 'When [...] the almond tree shall flourish [...] man goeth to his long home ...' (Ecclesiastes 12: 5–6).

Finally, it should be remembered that according to western esoteric tradition, the almond represents something obscure, hidden, secret, mysterious and concealed deep within us. Eating almonds, therefore, signifies initiation into the knowledge of secrets and mysteries.

Amber

The word 'amber' is derived from the Arabic term *anbar*, used to refer to 'ambergris', a solid substance formed in the intestine of the sperm whale and used to fix the scent of the fine perfumes sold by Arab merchants throughout medieval Europe. The Greek *êlektron* ('brilliant', or 'gold-and-silver alloy') referred to the yellow amber – fossil tree resin between 40 and 60 million years old – that is still gathered today, mainly on the shores of the Baltic Sea.

The Greek word gave rise to the modern term 'electricity', an association that stems from the discovery of the magnetic properties of yellow amber, in the 6th century BC, by the Greek astronomer, philosopher and mathematician Thales of Miletus. Thales described amber beads and amulets as 'current capacitors' that charged themselves by absorbing the excess magnetism produced by the person wearing or telling the amulets or beads. In ancient times, amber was therefore widely regarded as a beneficent and protective stone because of its ability to absorb 'negative waves'. Yellow amber was also associated with the lynx because of the belief that the resin was formed from the animal's solidified urine. It was thought to confer the gift of second sight on the wearer because the lynx was reputed to have extremely acute vision.

In ancient Chinese legends, amber contained the tiger's soul, while Greek mythology tells of the amber tears shed by the Heliads, the daughters of sun-god Helios, as they mourned Phaethon, the beloved brother who had driven the sun-chariot through the sky for a day with such disastrous consequences. In a Christian legend inspired by the Greek myth, amber tears were shed by the birds on the day of Christ's crucifixion.

Amber was also associated with ambrosia, the nectar of the gods and the drink of immortality offered to them by Hera, sister-wife of Zeus and the most powerful of the Olympian goddesses. She was also guardian of the garden of the Hesperides ('daughters of evening'), the nymphs who guarded the tree bearing golden apples that Gaia gave to Hera on the occasion of her marriage to Zeus.

According to Pliny the Elder, amber was a cure for fevers, blindness, deafness and other infirmities. In the 16th century, it was customary to use amber to cure stomach and throat ailments and, in the early 20th century, amber necklaces were still worn to cure throat irritations and swollen glands. The curative properties of amber inspired pipe-makers to make amber pipes in the belief that they would prevent infections of the mouth.

In the zodiac, amber is associated with the sign of Capricorn and, as a symbol of longevity, magnetism and light, it can only be beneficial.

Androgyne to twins
from unity to duality

In the beginning there was the androgyne and in the end there will be the androgyne. In the meantime, there are twins. This formulation seems to capture the spirit of the universal myths of the androgyne and twins, which are based on principles, fundamentals and interpretations that intersect, coincide and sometimes even merge. They also relate to the belief in the existence of the astral body that can be regarded as the etheric double of the individual, which formed the basis for the image of the angel in the minds of our forebears.

The androgyne can be regarded as a single entity, an original being that is both male

and female, not a hermaphrodite but a legendary being of undifferentiated sex. By contrast, twins are two distinct but identical beings whose only difference lies in the fact that one is male and the other female. Thus the star sign Gemini (the twins) is represented by a boy and girl, while twins of legend and fable are represented by two individuals who look the same, of course, and are sometimes both male or both female, but with one of the two always more masculine and one more feminine than the other. Whatever the combination, there is never the slightest

ambiguity or ambivalence in either the mythical or symbolic principle of the androgyne or the twins. It is always a question of explaining or understanding that the two are in fact one, but that each has their double.

So what exactly is an androgyne? As so often happens in the history of the human race, the interpretation of this wonderful universal myth – found in Egypt, Greece, China, in a number of African tribes and the Inca and Aztec cultures, to name but a few – was gradually distorted. The European term was derived from Latin via the Greek *androgynos* (*aner, andros* man + *gyne* woman). However, in other parts of the world and in more primitive cultures, especially in Africa, the word used for androgyne usually meant 'woman-man', a nuance that speaks volumes about our modern civilizations where, like it or not, the male has always tended to be regarded as dominant. The term was used in 14th-century Europe to describe a metal alloy and, in the 16th century, to refer to an individual who had both male and female sexual organs. Thus the meaning of 'androgyne' gradually became synonymous with 'hermaphrodite'.

In the 19th century, many Romantic writers were fascinated

from an esoteric and, it has to be said, confused contemporary interpretation of the cabbala, according to which Adam was originally male and female.

However, this is not an accurate derivation of the myth of the androgyne, which is closely associated with another universal myth – the creation myth of the cosmic egg. A number of cosmogonies throughout the world – including the Mesopotamian, Egyptian, Greek, Phoenician, Celtic, Chinese, Indian, Tibetan and Japanese cosmogonies – explain the creation and life of the world in terms of the cosmic egg. These cosmogonies subscribe to the theory that creation derives from a cosmic egg and, in many cases, that it was from this same egg that the first human being of undifferentiated sex was born. In his *Tao te ching*, Lao Tzu (*fl.* 6th century BC) writes:

> *These two are the same*
> *But diverge in name as they*
> *   issue forth.*
> *Being the same they are called*
> *   mysteries,*
> *Mystery upon mystery –*
> *The gateway of the manifold*
> *   secrets.*

> Translated from the Chinese by D.C. Lau, Penguin Classics, 1963.

by the concept and used it as a pretext to give free rein to their idealistic fantasies while also investing it with homosexual or narcissistic connotations. You only have to think of such characters as Théophile Gautier's Mademoiselle de Maupin, Honoré de Balzac's Séraphïta and Achim von Arnim's Isabella von Äegypten and, albeit later, Virginia Woolf's Orlando. In spite of the unquestionable talent of these great writers whose works have become European classics, it seems they were not particularly well acquainted with the myth of the androgyne. They drew their inspiration mainly

From this it can be deduced that the androgyne is not only the original human being but also the summation of all human beings, which brings us to the great principle of unification on which all world religions are based. This is essentially what the myth of the androgyne is all about.

While the androgyne symbolizes the unification of humanity and perfect, original harmony regained, twins, on the other hand, represent division, opposition and the embodiment of duality. Myths and legends about twins often reveal rivalry and fratricidal disputes. The first that springs to mind is the myth of the Dioscuri, Castor and Polydeuces (or Pollux), the sons of Zeus and Leda. However, it is not always mentioned that Leda gave birth to two sets of male-female twins – Helen and Polydeuces and Clytemnestra and Castor – in two separate eggs (possibly because Zeus had visited Leda in the guise of a swan), an echo of the cosmic egg.

While the myth of the Dioscuri is a perfect illustration of the male-female ambivalence of twins, it has none of the rivalry and very obvious duality found in the biblical myth of Cain and Abel or the Native American myth of the good twin of the morning and the evil twin of the evening, or the myth of Romulus and Remus, the legendary founders of Rome.

The twin myth was also widely found in Greek mythology – for example, the myths of Heracles (Hercules) and his twin brother Iphicles, and Eteocles and Polyneices, the sons of Oedipus. There are also the

Mash.Tab.Ba, the 'great twins' of Sumerian mythology, better known today as the star sign Gemini. However, the most beautiful twin myth, the one that comes close to the myth of the androgyne, is undoubtedly the Egyptian myth of Isis and Osiris.

Anemone

The name of the anemone or windflower (especially *A. nemorosa*) derives from the Greek *anemos* ('wind') and from the fact that its flowers appear to be blown open by the wind. The term pasqueflower – from the Old French *pasque* (Easter) – is applied to such spring-flowering varieties as *A. pulsatilla*, *A. patens* and *A. pratensis*. According to the Greek poet Bion of Smyrna (*fl.* 100 BC) the anemone was the flower of Adonis. In his 'Lament for Adonis' he tells how the goddess Aphrodite (the Roman Venus) shed as many tears as Adonis lost drops of blood from the wounds inflicted by a boar. A rose sprang up from each of the goddess's tears, and a blood-red anemone from each of Adonis's drops of blood. When associated with the lilies of the field and the lilies of the valley mentioned in the biblical 'Song of Songs', the anemone can either symbolize the soul receptive to spiritual life or the ephemeral beauty of the body.

An anemone in your dreams can equally well mean religious or spiritual aspirations or a passionate, sensual or carnal temptation. The fact that the fresh flower is harmful (*A. nemorosa* causes blistering of the skin), while an infusion calms the nerves, is indicative of this dual meaning of destructive passion and salutary tranquillity. The anemone is also often a symbol of ephemeral emotions, joys and passions.

Angel

Angels can be regarded as mediums or intermediaries between God and mortals. They are God's messengers or representatives. According to the Bible, the angels form a 'heavenly host' and as such fulfil a protective function, for example guarding the people of Israel when they crossed the Red Sea, watching over the servant of Abraham and over Jacob, and delivering Tobit from his blindness. In short, angels are found everywhere in the Bible – they are the voice and hand of God.

However, although angels are often represented by beneficent images, they also have their darker, more malevolent side. Satan is a fallen angel, Izra'il is the Islamic angel of death, and, according to the Bible, the Apocalypse is announced by the exterminating angel.

An angel in a dream can therefore herald good or bad news, depending on the context in which it appears. But whatever the context or the news, it symbolizes a revelation, the discovery of a fact or a situation to which your attention is particularly drawn or which requires consideration. The supernatural aspect of the angel – which is both wonderful and terrifying – should be seen as the representation of a warning, rather than a piece of advice.

Animal

Human beings have always been surrounded by two apparently magical worlds – the animal and vegetable kingdoms – invested with many beliefs and superstitions. Etymologically, the term 'animal' – any living organism characterized by voluntary movement – is derived from the Latin *animalis* ('living, breathing') and *anima* ('breath', 'air' or 'wind') (see *Air*, page 19). The association that seems to have existed between the soul and the animal for thousands of years probably derives from the age-old belief that the human spirit could be reincarnated in the body of an animal. It is possible that the belief in the transmigration of the human soul into the body of an animal predates the concept of successive reincarnations of the soul in other human bodies.

For our forebears, the belief that the human soul could inhabit the body of a sacred or deified animal (e.g. the eagle or the lion) was the ultimate sign of the immortality of the soul and the merits acquired by the individual during life on earth. In other words, the eternal embodiment of the individual in question was thought to be the majestic eagle or lion they had resembled during their life. It was most probably this belief that gave rise to the theories of reincarnation and metempsychosis. Similarly, warriors and tribal chiefs were often compared to an animal during their lifetime, and that animal became their symbol, fetish and totem. They often had visions of the totem animal and identified with it during certain rites of initiation.

A number of myths from cultures throughout the world tell of human beings who had the power to change themselves into a particular animal. In *La Poussière du Monde* – 'The Dust of the World' (NIL éditions, 1997) – Jacques Lacarrière states that assuming the form of a gazelle or tiger, a dove or falcon is more than the simple expression of a whim or an unfulfilled desire. It is a particularly spectacular way of declaring an inner lightness or darkness and a nostalgia for missed or wasted incarnations. He goes on to say that, in the 11th century, asking a Sufi (a member of a Muslim mystical and pantheist sect) about his favourite animal was not without its dangers and terrifying consequences since, rather than giving a straightforward answer like any non-initiate, he might well assume the form of the animal before the questioner's very eyes! Lacarrière concludes that the choice of animal is therefore crucial. Choosing to be a dove means choosing the path of innocence since the dove is the symbol of peace, whereas choosing to be a falcon means electing to follow the path of voracity by becoming a bird of prey.

For humans, the diversity of the animal kingdom has always represented the great cosmic, material and spiritual forces of nature. It has also provided an endless supply of living symbols and images with which to identify. Depending on the animal chosen by – or which chose – a particular individual, that person's status was enhanced or diminished in the eyes of the community. But even so, the

analogy and resemblance between the individual and the animal were obvious to all and sundry. Even today, there is a tendency, when observing and identifying the physical traits and characteristics of certain people, to associate them with the appearance and behaviour of particular animals.

Furthermore, a great many popular expressions refer directly or indirectly to the animal kingdom: to be at bay (stag), to bury one's head in the sand (ostrich), to sing like a bird, to be as stubborn as a mule, as cunning as a fox, as artful as a monkey, as happy as a lark, as proud as a peacock, as strong as an ox, as hungry as a horse, as weak as a kitten, to be eagle-eyed, doe-eyed, crocodile tears … the list is endless.

In this context, it is impossible not to refer to the collection of Greek fables which, although set in the animal kingdom, reflect human relations, behaviour and foibles. These fables, written in the 6th century BC and commonly known as Aesop's fables, were probably inspired by ancient Sumerian tales written over a thousand years earlier. The tradition was perpetuated by the 17th-century French poet, Jean De La Fontaine, whose fables were based on the Greek Aesopic tradition.

More recently, an original theory was developed from beliefs related to the 'Christian cabbala' that flourished during the Renaissance; in this theory, each animal species had a 'collective soul', in much the same way that the human body is made up of numerous cells each with their own individual consciousness but no meaning or *raison d'être* when taken separately. The 'collective soul' of each species was thought to have a spiritual body that combined all the experiences of each individual member of the family and influenced the behaviour and life of those members currently living on earth.

The presence of a real or symbolic, wild or domestic animal in your life or dreams should not be ignored (see under the heading for the animal in question).

Anniversary

*See Year, new year
(annual, anniversary), page 550*

Ant

According to Greek mythology, Myrmex (the Greek word for 'ant') angered Athena, the goddess of war, by claiming the invention of the plough, generally attributed to the goddess. Athena took her revenge by transforming Myrmex into an ant. However, Zeus, in his mercy, reversed the spell cast by Athena and, at the same time, transformed all the ants in the anthill into a people known as the Myrmidons. They became the symbol of organized work, achieved by united effort for the good of the community and, by analogy, the symbol of honesty, abnegation and solidarity since the ant cannot exist outside its community. In the tale of 'The Ant and the Grasshopper', which appears in both the Aesop cycle and the fables of Jean De La Fontaine (see *Animal*, page 31), the ant illustrates the grasshopper's lack of foresight and its own lack of generosity. However, in reality, neither could survive on its own.

For this reason, the appearance of a single ant in a dream is often a sign that the dreamer is dangerously isolated.

However, a dream about an anthill is just as worrying since it represents a form of mental activity that, although extremely organized and apparently healthy and balanced when observed from the outside, is nonetheless the expression of a mind that is so logical and coherent, so inward looking and focused on a single, precise objective that it denies itself all possibility of development, of opening up to the world and life. As a result, ants in a dream reflect too strong an attachment to the physical world and material possessions, which will only prove frustrating for the dreamer's sensitivity and imagination.

Aphrodite

See Inanna, Ishtar, Astarte, Aphrodite and Venus, page 274

Apple

It seems likely that Christians substituted the apple for the fig, the probable fruit in the Garden of Eden. If we refer to the text of Genesis in the Bible, the name of the forbidden fruit is not mentioned, although Adam and Eve wore fig leaves, not vine leaves, to cover themselves after

tasting this fruit (Genesis 3: 3, 7; and see *Fig tree*, page 184 and *Apple tree*, page 36). However, Christians were not the only ones to transpose the apple and the fig. In India, some authors transformed the tree of life into an apple tree, instead of the fig tree linking earth to heaven mentioned in the *Upanishads*. This was called 'the tree of bliss' and was therefore the equivalent of the tree of the knowledge of good and evil in Eden (see page 498).

However, in India, as in Europe, this symbolic transposition was not the result of any confusion or ignorance with regard to the original texts. It was done deliberately by certain authors who thought the apple much more universal than the fig. Our distant ancestors, the neolithic gatherers, who ate a great deal of fruit, were certainly very fond of crab apples. This version of the original fruit also clearly shows the influence of Greek culture.

The apple plays a key role in many Greek myths. It is associated with the adventures, misadventures and exploits of some of the most illustrious gods and demi-gods in mythology. One of these legends, which per-

fectly illustrates the analogy that can be drawn between the vine and the apple tree, concerns Dionysus: the story, and the beliefs associated with it for the three centuries preceding the birth of Christ, had a profound influence on early Christianity, as did the myth of Orpheus. According to this legend, Dionysus, Greek god of vines, wine and ecstasy, created the apple to give to Aphrodite. This symbolic gesture – which inverted the roles in the story of Adam and Eve, since it was the man who offered the apple to the woman, not the other way around – thus acquired an erotic connotation. However, the apple is not only the fruit of love, according to the Greeks. In another myth, Eris or Strife, the sister and companion of Ares, threw a golden apple inscribed 'For the Fairest', onto the table at a wedding celebration. Paris, who had to choose between Hera, Athena and Aphrodite, awarded this 'apple of discord' to the latter. Lastly, at the wedding of Zeus and Hera, Gaia, the earth, presented the bride with some golden apples, symbols of fertility, which were later guarded, then hidden by the

Hesperides, goddesses of the night. These apples formed the 11th Labour of Hercules (see *Hercules*, page 224).

The numerous legends revolving around the apple make it easy to understand how this fruit became the symbol of carnal love, discord and fertility and why it aroused so many desires. These contradictory emotions are therefore associated with the apple and should be taken into account when it appears in a dream. It should also be remembered that, in the age-old tale of Snow White, the young woman falls into a deep sleep similar to death after taking a bite of a poisoned apple. The apple has some very ambiguous symbolic qualities indeed.

Apple tree

From this tree came the sensual, abundant fruit that was viewed by Christians as being synonymous with sin, replacing the original fruit which is believed to be a fig (see *Fig tree*, page 184). The fruit of wisdom and revela-

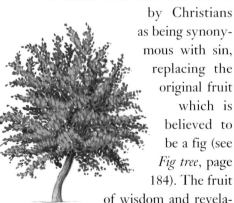

tion became that of wrongdoing and original sin, and the fig tree of the Garden of Eden, probably situated in the valleys of the Tigris and Euphrates rivers, became a blossoming apple tree with the serpent and tempter curled around its trunk. Thus, because generally accepted ideas die hard and seem more compelling than historical truth, the apple tree has prevailed in the Garden of Eden for centuries, and Eve has always tempted Adam to eat an apple. In the Gardens of the Hesperides, the golden apples offered immortality to anyone who tasted their sweet flesh (see page 251). It is hardly surprising, therefore, that the apple should have been assimilated to the fruit of good and evil and that the apple tree should have been regarded as the tree of life.

Aquarius
(sign of)

See Zodiac, page 581

Arcadia
(the hind of)

See Hercules, page 233

Apple tree
Aquarius
Arcadia
(the hind of)
Aries
Ash tree

Aries
(sign of)

See Zodiac, page 553

Ash tree

The ash tree, which can sometimes reach dizzying heights, was a symbol of grandeur for our ancestors. However, this did not appear to deter them from cutting off the smaller branches to feed to their goats, which were particularly fond of the leaves. It was also believed that the properties of the leaves effectively immunized these reputedly frail animals against disease.

The Celts used the wood of the ash to make spears, lances and arrows, while the druids – like the shamans of certain North American tribes – invoked the ash in order to bring rain during periods of drought.

Above all, the tree plays a major role in Scandinavian and Norse mythology where it is Yggdrasill ('Ygg's horse'), the world tree. Ygg is another name for Odin, the father of the gods, who hanged himself on the world tree. In this case, the horse is a metaphor for the gallows, and Odin sacrifices himself for knowledge, thereby learning the runes. Odin was also the god of poets, fallen warriors, war and ecstasy. According to the *Edda* – a body of literature that includes heroic and mythological poems (the *Poetic Edda*) recounting the creation and history of the Germanic world – Yggdrasill, a giant ash, is planted in the centre of the world, which it dominates and covers with its huge branches that touch and reach into the sky. The tree has three equally amazing roots. The first extends into Asgard, the home of the gods, the second into Jötunheim, the land of the ice-giants that populated the earth before man was created, while the third extends into Niflheim ('the misty region'), the underworld that is the equivalent of Hades for the Greeks and the hereafter for the Egyptians.

But beneath this third root lies the well known as Hvergelmir ('roaring kettle'), the source of all life, the source of the world that feeds all the springs and rivers of the earth. Thus, according to the mythology of the *Edda*, the ash is the origin of life, the axis of the world, the tree of life (see page 498).

Ashes

Ashes are the product of fire or, more precisely, of the combustion of inflammable materials. Since ashes are all that remain of fire, they are symbolically associated with the image of death and the body of the deceased, just as fire is a symbolic representation of life being consumed.

Certain early cultures used to cremate their dead, before it became customary to bury them, and the ashes of the dead assumed a magical and sacred quality. They were regarded as the physical representation of what remained of the deceased – their soul or their spirit, or even their symbol, a tutelary animal or tree – that was blown by the wind over the surface of the earth, sometimes

haunting certain regions. Ashes therefore have a sacred quality associated with the rite of passage from the world of the living to the world of the dead. This implies that death is not an end, but a transition, a transformation, and that the soul of the person who was so dearly loved and respected on earth is eternal.

For all these reasons, dreaming about ash or ashes often means it is time for you to consider certain aspects, experiences and events in your life on another level, to detach yourself from certain material considerations and allow yourself to feel freer and lighter. Or it may be time to realize that the great importance you attach to something at the time you have the dream is entirely relative, because this 'something' can easily be reduced to ashes.

Ass

The ass has always had a bad reputation. As the symbol of ignorance, obstinacy, wickedness, laziness and lust, it was for a long time associated with the forces of darkness and evil. For the ancient Egyptians, who believed in life in the hereafter, an encounter with a red ass (see *Red*, page 429) could prove fatal for the *ka* (see page 460). The Greeks, who adopted a number of ancient Egyptian gods, often represented Seth, the Egyptian god of chaos who murdered his brother Osiris, as an ass. In medieval Europe, the Devil was sometimes depicted as a naked man with the head and hooves of an ass.

In the 12th century, in a mixture of religious worship and theatre, there was even a special festival dedicated to the ass which often coincided with Christmas, the day of the winter solstice, symbolizing the death and rebirth of the sun and light or, in Christian terms, the death and resurrection of Christ. The Christian image of the ass – its role in the Nativity, the flight into Egypt and Christ's entry into Jerusalem – is reminiscent of the ass ridden by the Meso-potamian prophet Balaam when, ordered by the Moabite king Balak to place a malediction on the people of Israel and drive them from the plains of Moab, he was charged by Yahweh to go and bless his people in his name.

In Greek mythology, Dionysus, the son of Zeus – whose name means 'twice born' and whose myth no doubt inspired the writers of the life of Christ – often rode an ass. These three images of the ass are there-fore completely different. As a symbol of humility, simplicity, poverty, self-denial, asceticism, truth, revelation, initiation and wisdom, it possesses all the virtues. Thus, symbolically and in absolute terms, the ass has two opposing natures – ignorance and

wisdom – and either knows nothing or everything.

So, if you dream about an ass, how can you tell whether it is a good or a bad omen? Unfortunately, this is not always easy. Usually, you have to take account of the circumstances and context of your dream. If you are riding an ass, it is a symbol of humility, perceptiveness and revelation. If you are pulling it along by the bridle, it is a sign of living from hand to mouth (from the French 'tirer le diable par la queue' meaning 'to pull the devil by the tail') and your dream is a sign of the difficulties, constraints and obstacles that lie ahead. An ass with its ears pricked often means you can expect a beneficial happening or event, while an ass with drooping ears symbolizes a stagnant and unhealthy situation, obstinacy, stubbornness, a refusal to accept change or development. An ass can be a sign of good news, of renewal and change in your life. Alternatively, it can symbolize sterility or an offence or infidelity that you have committed or of which you are the victim. Whatever it means, it nearly always tells you something you need to know and which should not be ignored.

Astarte

See Inanna, Ishtar, Astarte, Aphrodite and Venus, page 274

Athena, Cybele and Hecate

Athena, Cybele and Hecate are the goddesses of war, destruction and death respectively. As such, they are the personifications of three eternal, temporal dramas that seem to haunt, obsess and continually prey upon the human mind, which, while it can be incredibly strong, can also be extremely fragile and impressionable.

Athena, goddess of war. War appears, first and foremost, as a form of collective hysteria, a sort of emotional flare-up. It blinds the human mind so effectively that men and women commit the most terrible atrocities in the firm belief that they are defending a just cause or combating the forces of evil, embodied by their enemies. But in war, each side is the other's enemy and, even though we are often inclined to fight for a cause that seems more just than another, can we really believe in the existence of a just war or that a cause, however noble, merits the sacrifice of thousands and even millions of lives? Isn't there rather a sort of fatal drive in human societies that could equally well be a form of outlet or release and whose most violent and dramatic manifestation is war? This would appear to be borne out by the Greek legend in which Athena accidentally kills her girl companion Pallas in a friendly hand-to-hand combat using a lance and shield. According to Robert Graves in *The Greek Myths* (Penguin, 1960), the name Athena ('queen of heaven') is inspired by that of the Sumerian goddess Anatha, but can also be identified with the Egyptian goddess Neith, a warlike divinity whose attributes were the bow, shield and arrows.

In other words, if we consider Athena (the Roman goddess Minerva) as the Greek goddess of war *par excellence* and within the context of the story of her accidental killing of Pallas, we can conclude that Greek mythologists saw war as a game that turned sour. However, this is not a combat between two men,

but between two women, who undoubtedly represent emotions that, like certain forces of nature, can sometimes erupt and overflow, destroying everything in their path.

Cybele, the goddess of destruction. It would have been possible to choose the great Egyptian goddess Sekhmet ('she who is powerful') – whose body gave off a fiery glow, whose hot breath was the hot desert wind and who had the power to spread disease, epidemics and death among mortals – or Kali – the fierce and terrifying goddess whose Sanskrit name means 'black' (see *Isis and Kali*, page 281) – to represent the forces of destruction.

However, these forces are better represented by Cybele ('she of the hair' or 'she of the axe') in the sense that she was associated with the blood of sacrifice and the cult of ecstasy which, like war, are also forms of outlet or release. Admittedly these 'outlets' disrupt social order, but they are also catalysts that accelerate

the urge for death, which co-exists with the urge for life – two forces inherent in life and all living beings which can, however, assail the human mind alternately and separately.

Some thousand years before the Kaaba – containing the black stone given by the angel Gabriel to Abraham – stood in Mecca and became the most sacred place of Muslim pilgrimage, Cybele was symbolized and worshipped, especially by the Romans, in the form of the sacred black stone of the Phrygian mother-goddess. This stone represented the place where life is born and dies to be reborn. Life, death and rebirth are the three great principles of Cybele, who gives life generously, but takes it just as easily so that human beings can be reborn. She excites the senses so that the body exults and the soul is delivered from the weight of the flesh.

In the 4th century AD, the festival of Christmas was established, replacing the festival of the New Year that had previously coincided with the winter solstice (21 December) and the 'rebirth' of the sun. Until then, Cybele had been honoured at the Saturnalia, the famous orgiastic winter festival celebrated from 17 to 24 December, during which men and women gave free rein to their instincts and indulged their senses.

Hecate, goddess of destiny, life and death. Greek mythologists undoubtedly drew their inspiration for the goddess Hecate from Heket, the frog-headed Egyptian goddess and female complement of the ram-god Khnum. While Khnum created the first humans on his potter's wheel, Heket fashioned the child in the womb and gave it life (symbolized by the *ankh*). By following the legendary and mythical trajectory of Hecate, it becomes clear that she possesses many powers, the greatest being the power to grant or take life at will. She is a magician-goddess, skilled in the art of sorcery and spells, able to entwine and unravel the Fates. She is the mistress of destinies, able to foresee, predict and direct the will of all living beings. In other words, Hecate has assimilated all the powers of nature, which she embodies and controls, and over which she exercises power. She therefore possesses the knowledge of the mysteries of nature, which contain all the creative and destructive forces of life. It is to this knowledge that the modern scientist aspires, like a sorcerer's apprentice or a disciple of Hecate, playing with life and death without understanding the consequences and inventing tools that are more destructive than creative. If we were to analyse the history of the 20th century, we would probably be forced to conclude that, increasingly ignorant of the forces of nature that it claims to have conquered,

the human race has in fact destroyed more lives than it has ever saved.

Atlantis

In two of his *Dialogues*, written in 347 BC, Plato refers to the legend of the island kingdom of Atlantis, ruled by King Atlas. Its capital Basileia (the Greek word for 'kingdom') was built on a layout of three concentric circles with a cross radiating from the outer edge of the central circle (see page 100). This layout – the diagrammatic representation of earth and water – formed the basis for the design of what is still know as the Cross of Atlantis. In an account begun in *Timaeus* and developed in *Critias*, Plato tells how, during a voyage to the Nile Delta, the Athenian lawgiver Solon (7th–6th century BC) encountered Egyptian priests who told him the tale of the legendary war between the Athenians and the people of Atlantis.

According to these priests, Atlantis was an island situated in the Atlantic Ocean, just beyond the Pillars of Hercules (Straits of Gibraltar). In other words, the legendary island would have lain south-west of modern-day Spain and north-west of Morocco. According to Plato: '[...] there was an island outside the channel which your countrymen tell me you call the Pillars of Heracles. This island was larger than Libya and Asia together, and from it seafarers, in those times, could make their way to the others [...]. In this Atlantic island had arisen a great and wonderful monarchy, which was mistress of the whole island, as well as of many others [...]. Its monarchs, moreover, within the straits, held Libya as far as the Egyptian border, and Europe as far as Tyrrhenia [Italy].' (*Timaeus*, translated by A.E. Taylor, Methuen, 1929.) Whether or not the island existed, it certainly fired the imagination of Plato's contemporaries and its factual or legendary history remained engraved on the collective memory long after his time. Even today, archaeologists, geologists, historians and theologians are still trying to solve the mystery of Atlantis.

The real or imaginary tale of the kingdom of Atlantis is linked to the myth of a golden age, a paradise lost, but it also echoes the story of the great flood since, according to Plato, the island sank into the sea following one of the natural disasters common to these regions.

Augeas (stables of)

See Hercules, page 237

Aura, aureole

The aura is the subtle or etheric body that surrounds the gross or earthly body. In Latin, *aura* – derived from *aer*, the root of 'aero' and 'air' – means 'breath', 'air' or 'wind'. The subtle body is also known as the 'auric body' or 'etheric double'. It takes the form of an oval-shaped area of light and often appears in Romanesque religious art surrounding the figure of Christ. In this context, it is called a mandorla (see *Almond*, page 24) and symbolizes a being bathed in divine light. It is also a representation of the cosmic egg from which light and life emerged (see *Egg*, page 168).

The aureole or halo could be described as a superior form

of aura. It derives from the Latin *aureola* ('gold crown') and refers to the circle of gold light or radiance above or behind the heads of angels and saints in the religious art of the Western and Eastern Christian churches. Thus the aura is based on an ethereal, etheric but innate principle that is common to all living beings, while the aureole is divine and sacred in nature and emanates from the superior faculties of the mind and spirit. The concept of aura and aureole can be compared to that of the chakras (energy centres) that form the basis of the doctrine of yoga. The aura would correspond to the six principal chakras located along the spinal cord and the aureole to the seventh chakra above the crown of the skull.

Some people appear to be able to see the aura, which has been described as a concentration of electromagnetic energies produced by the vital functions of the individual and which may be scientifically visualized and fixed by means of radiography or spectrography. Research and studies are currently being carried out in this field with a view to one day being able to detect different colour zones, thereby revealing an individual's vital and organic strengths and weaknesses. It appears that, in ancient times, this phenomenon was already widely used by certain physicians to carry out diagnoses and prepare remedies.

Automobile

There is a strong tendency, when considering myths and symbols, to use antiquity as a reference point. However, the history of symbols is still being written. For example, the automobile, a relatively recent invention, is associated with a great many symbols which, although they originated with such ancient

vehicles as the cart or chariot, are particularly representative of the preoccupations and landscapes of our modern societies.

The principal symbols associated with the automobile are those of the mind and body – the body being represented by the vehicle and the mind by the driver – resulting in the overall symbolism of a controlled mind having the power to drive and direct the body. Driving means controlling yourself, acting autonomously, being independent and responsible for your own actions and decisions.

The automobile is also associated with the universal symbol of the solar wheel (see *Circle*, page 100) since it runs on four wheels and is driven by a fifth, the steering wheel. Finally, it has an engine or motor. 'Motor' is derived from the Latin noun *motor* ('a mover') and the verb *movere* ('to move'), words that also underlie the ideas of 'emotion' and 'motivation'. Thus, the person sitting behind the wheel symbolizes the individual in control of their thoughts and desires, controlling and directing the bodily vehicle or physical being, moving from place to place and therefore developing and evolving through their feelings and emotions. Furthermore, the road often represents the path of life or destiny on which crossroads signify a choice of direction or a decision to be made, and road signs indicate the rules to be observed or advice to be taken. Red traffic lights symbolize either a delay, obstacle or constraint, while a 'green light' means the driver can move on and is free to go where he or she wants to.

Dreaming of an accident doesn't mean you are going to be involved in a road accident and should not be seen as a bad omen. It usually predicts a psychological or moral shock, a sudden realization, or quite simply means that, when you had the dream, you had taken a wrong turning.

Axe

The axe is thought to have first appeared in Europe during the palaeolithic period, somewhere between 35,000 and 9500 BC. It was as much a tool as a weapon but was almost certainly

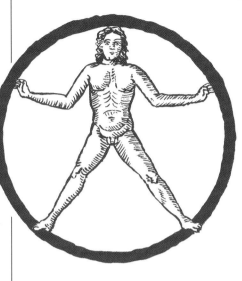

used as a tool before it was conceived as an instrument of battle. The axe was often the attribute of the gods of thunder and lightning, an expression of their anger, but was also used in fertility rites and rituals, especially to invoke rain during periods of drought. The tomahawk used by Native Americans was a fighting axe with a stone or iron head, as Europeans found out to their cost when they began to colonize this wild and beautiful continent. The axe used to fell trees was also a symbol of death.

If you dream about an axe, it is the 'cutting' aspect that should remain uppermost in your mind since it is usually an allusion, not to a death, but to some form of necessary break or rupture in your life. A dream about the rhythmic and repetitive blows of an axe can also represent an imminent fact or event of which repeated early warnings have not yet been recognized by the dreamer.

Axis

The tree, mountain and staff are all symbolic representations of the axis of the world that links one point with another, that is heaven and earth or the upper world and the underworld. The tree is of course the tree of life, the cosmic tree, whose roots plunge deep into the centre of the earth and whose branches reach up to heaven (see *Tree of life*, page 498). The mountain is the sacred mountain, the place where heaven and earth meet, a place of revelation and spiritual elevation, the mother-mountain often regarded as the navel of the world (see *Mountain*, page 348). The staff is the stick, cane or wand of the master, the magician, the prophet, the pilgrim and the Hermit, the IXth card in the Major Arcana of the divinatory Tarot cards (see *Rod, staff* page 433). The staff guides and supports, it is the guardian of the world and of mankind.

But the most representative figure of the axis of the

world is Everyman, the pillar of the world, the centre of all things, around whom everything revolves (see *Circle*, page 100). In personal terms, being on an axis means feeling balanced, in control of our destiny as well as ourselves. In general terms it means being located in the centre or at the heart of a situation of which, in some way, we are in control or for which we are responsible, since its evolution depends on us.

The appearance of an axis (tree, mountain or staff) in a dream always represents your share of responsibility in the development of the events of your life.

Bamboo

In China, bamboo – once the principle material used in the construction of light buildings – was also used in divination. For the Buddhists, it represented the culmination of the initiatory and spiritual quest, because its sturdiness and smooth, erect habit give it a quality of perfection.

Its symbolic significance has no equivalent in the West. In Europe, bamboo is simply an exotic plant representing distant and unknown lands and, by analogy, its appearance in a dream should be interpreted as such.

This association with far-off and exotic lands may explain the popular French expression 'coup de bambou', dating from the 16th century, used to refer to someone who has 'a touch of sunstroke', is 'round the bend' or 'shattered'. Dreaming about bamboo can be a sign of madness or excessive fatigue – but perhaps only for the French ....

Baptism

Baptism can be associated with the concept of taking a bath (see *Bath, bathing*, page 52), since both are acts of purification. However, there is one fundamental difference. When you take a bath, you

are responsible for cleansing and purifying yourself, whereas when you are baptized, you are being purified and purged of your sins, at least in the Christian sense of the term.

Although the baptism of Christ is described as an immersion, most baptisms carried out today involve aspersion, the sprinkling of holy water. Symbolically, immersion represents a person's merging into the depths of their own being or 'inner sea', from which they emerge revived and restored. As such, it symbolizes the 'overturning of consciousness' represented by Aquarius (the Water Carrier) (see *Zodiac*, page 581).

A bath is therefore an act of free will while baptism has all the appearance of a rite of initiation, of the passage from one mental state to another. It is through baptism that consciousness is overturned, reoriented and liberated.

In a dream, attending a baptism means we are witnessing a new situation that is about to occur in our life or, at a deeper level, that we are on the point or in the process of experiencing an inner revolution, or approaching a major turning point in our life. It is a sign not so much of birth as of rebirth. A sick or infirm person who dreams of a baptism is witnessing their almost certain recovery in the real world.

Barn owl

See Owl, page 406

Barrel

The barrel is not only a symbol of wealth and prosperity, but also of the gradual accumulation of knowledge that leads to wisdom when used judiciously. However, the barrel rarely indicates how its contents are to be used – that is up to its owner and what they do with it is their own business. In this respect, the barrel can be compared to the human body and its contents to the soul within. Alternatively, the latter can be regarded as a symbolic representation of fate, the former as the manifest being who cannot exist without fate, and he who makes use of the contents of the barrel, in other words his fate, is therefore the human being exerting his free will. Thus, wine, beer or mead – manmade drinks worthy of the gods – which are left to settle, mature or ferment in barrels, may cause ecstasy or inebriation, depending on the quantity drunk and the drinker's state of mind or inner strength. As legend has it, an enlightened member of the order of whirling dervishes was once condemned to death by orthodox Muslims for drinking wine, which is forbidden in this religious tradition. When asked by his judges why he had flouted this interdiction, scorned the commandments of Muhammad and dishonoured his tribe, he replied simply: 'If I drink a glass of wine, and my consciousness is submerged by it, then I am drunk. If I drink a glass of wine, and it pours into

the ocean of my consciousness, then I am set free.' (see *Wine*, page 539). Wine, a sacred product that comes from the earth, like the spring whose invigorating waters never stop flowing and are always replenished, can be drunk by anyone. The barrel symbolizes both the fertile, productive earth and, owing to its shape and its contents, the pregnant woman.

When a barrel appears in a dream, therefore, it is often a sign that events or circumstances are in a process of gestation and that they will soon bring about a complete change in the dreamer's life. This change is likely to be promising, although everything will depend on how the dreamer deals with it. A dream of a wine cellar or granary full of barrels is a sign of abundance and wealth. However, once again, the question must be asked whether the riches that are symbolically at the dreamer's disposal are being put to use and, if so, how.

Bat

This hybrid creature, part-mouse, part-bird, has existed since the dawn of time. Its general appearance and habits – hanging upside down, sleeping during the day and hunting by

night – mean that the bat has never been particularly popular in Europe. In China, however, this peaceable and useful creature (it feeds on mosquitoes) is associated with happiness, perseverance and faith.

Dreaming about a bat can be interpreted in one of two ways. It can either be associated with the symbolism of the Hanged Man – the XIIth card in the Major Arcana of the Tarot – who hangs head downwards, or it can represent uncontrollable (usually sexual) urges or dark, insane and obsessive ideas that haunt the dreamer.

Bath, bathing

Bathing is a symbol of purification and regression, since it is often symbolically associated with life in the womb. The English word 'bath' is related to the Old Norse *bath* and the Swedish *bada* ('to clean with warm water'), while the term 'balneology' and the adjectives 'balneal' and 'balneary' derive from the Latin *balneum* and the Greek *balaneion*. The Greek *balanos*, from which the French *bain* is derived, refers to any kind of plug or stopper, and especially the plug used to stop the hole in a bath tub, whose Greek name *balaneiomphalos* means 'having a bulge in the centre'. In ancient Greece, the *omphalos* was regarded as the centre, the belly or navel of the world and the *omphalos* of Delphi was the Temple of Apollo that stood on the navel of the earth. Taking a bath means literally and figuratively cleansing and purifying yourself, gathering your strength and reviving yourself. It is a symbolic return to one's origins, the waters of the

womb or the primordial waters from which all life emerged (see *Water*, page 528).

Dreaming about taking a bath reveals a need for purification, for a return to your origins. A cold bath is stimulating, while a warm bath is comforting.

Bean, broad

Not only does the broad bean have a number of symbolic points in common with the egg (see page 168), but it is also associated with all aspects of gestation, anything that is about to be born, be created or appear but which is at present in the embryonic stage. For the ancient Egyptians, it was a symbol of resurrection and for the Greeks, a representation of the soul. Interestingly, the festivals of Osiris, in Egypt, and Dionysus, in Greece – two divinities associated with the myth of resurrection – were held on or around 6 January, the twelfth day of the Christian festival of Christmas, celebrating the birth of Christ, who is also associated with the myth of resurrection, and his manifestation to the Magi. The tradition of inserting a bean (nowadays a symbolic porcelain one) into the *galettes des Rois* (cakes eaten in France on Twelfth Night) is no doubt a

legacy of the broad beans that our early ancestors slipped into the special bread baked for the festivals of Osiris and Dionysus. The person served with the piece of bread or cake containing the bean was 'crowned' king, i.e. they became immortal – symbolically, of course – like Osiris, Dionysus and, later, Christ.

Beard

In ancient times, a beard was often regarded as a symbol of virility, courage, physical strength, moral fortitude and wisdom, although it was also an ornamental attribute that did not necessarily reflect these virtues. Even so, most gods, demigods and mythical figures were depicted with beards.

In China, heroes were always bearded to reinforce the distinction between them and ordinary mortals since the Chinese were generally reputed to have scant facial hair. A very long beard was usually a sign of great wisdom and a deep under-

standing of people and things, as well as a symbol of detachment from the material world. This is why hermits were always depicted with long beards.

Conversely, saints were often depicted as short-haired and beardless, to indicate that they had been elevated above the human condition. When Christianity was in its infancy, in the early years AD, Jesus was represented as a young man with short hair and no beard.

Whatever the symbolism of mythology and legend, in our dreams a beard tends to be more often a sign of deceit and dissimulation rather than a symbol of virility or wisdom, unless, of course, it is a long, white beard. A man who sees himself in a dream with an unkempt beard has an excess of energy that he tends to suppress but which runs the risk of overflowing and submerging him. A woman who dreams of herself with a beard may tend to be rather intransigent, or it may

indicate that she is suffering from a 'virility complex'. Dreaming about a bearded man always has a dual symbolic significance and has to be interpreted according to your circumstances at the time of the dream. It can indicate that you will be the victim of lies or slander spread by a hypocritical and malicious person, or that someone from among your friends or family will make or help you see yourself or your situation more clearly.

Finally, dreaming that you are shaving is always a sign of a voluntary sacrifice or deprivation, and of the triumph of truth.

Bee

The bee or honeybee is a symbol of the soul, resurrection, work accomplished by communal effort, and self-fulfilment. Bees have often been used to represent the soul leaving the body or as the resuscitating breath of God entering the mouth of a dead person. It was also once commonly believed that bees died in winter and were reborn in spring.

In ancient Greece, the priestesses of the Eleusinian mysteries were known collectively as 'the bees' because they formed an intelligent entity working for the survival and prosperity of the community and producing the nectar of the gods – the honey-based ambrosia. The bee also featured in one of the names of the pharaoh of ancient Egypt – *nesw-bit* – meaning 'he of the sedge and the bee' ('king of Upper and Lower Egypt'). In France, the bee was the emblem of the Merovingian king Childeric, and Napoleon I chose it to decorate his coronation cloak.

If a bee appears in your dream, it is a sign of death and rebirth, renewal and regeneration. It also represents disinterested devotion to the accomplishment of a communal enterprise, a highly developed sense of community, or

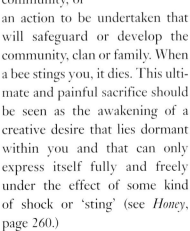

an action to be undertaken that will safeguard or develop the community, clan or family. When a bee stings you, it dies. This ultimate and painful sacrifice should be seen as the awakening of a creative desire that lies dormant within you and that can only express itself fully and freely under the effect of some kind of shock or 'sting' (see *Honey*, page 260.)

Beech tree

During the Middle Ages, the beech was thought to have magical powers. It was known as the 'fairy tree' due to the widespread belief that, after dark, the fairies sang and danced inside a magic circle that they drew around its solid and sturdy trunk.

It was under a beech tree known as the Fairy Tree, near Domrémy, that Joan of Arc heard her famous voices, as she herself told Pierre Cauchon, bishop of Beauvais, during her interrogation on 24 February 1430. In ancient Greece, the beech was an oracular tree and was also dedicated to Zeus, who protected it from storms and lightning. According to the *Edda* – a body of Scandinavian and Norse literature consisting of heroic epics and mythological poems recounting the creation and history of the Germanic world – Alvilda, Hetha and Visna, warrior-women who are sometimes wrongly identified with Odin's daughters, the Valkyries – maidens who chose dead warriors for Valhalla (Old Norse

Valkyrja, 'chooser of the slain') – lived in a beech wood on the island of Rügen, in the Baltic Sea. Here they were safe from the potentially destructive rages of Odin, the father of the gods, who, like Zeus in Greece, caused the thunder to roll and lightning to fall upon the earth.

Finally, it was from the trunk of the beech, which apparently enjoys divine protection and never seems to be struck by lightning, that the famous Yule log was hewn (although the Celts burnt a fir tree). Nowadays, the log that was traditionally burnt in the hearth at Christmas during the Middle Ages is more likely to be found on our plates, in the form of a delicious cake.

Beer

While butter was regarded as the unguent of eternal youth, beer was the drink of immortality, the beverage of the gods, in civilizations as far apart as ancient Egypt and Celtic Europe. Beer flowed freely when the peoples of northern Europe celebrated the winter solstice (the Celtic 'night of the silver pine'), on 21 December, and the spring equinox ('night of the gorse bush'), on 21 March. However, it was above all on the festival of Samhain ('summer'send'), celebrated on 1 November (New Year's Day in the Celtic calendar), that excessive amounts of this brew were consumed. Samhain was one of the most important festivals in the Celtic calendar, when the gods became visible and played tricks on mortals who believed that getting drunk put them on an equal footing with the gods. Beliefs and aspirations may have changed, but mortals still drink beer in an attempt to bolster their confidence and give themselves 'Dutch courage'.

As a general rule, dreaming about beer tends to refer more to the fermentation process that produces it than the state of drunkenness induced by the beer. In this sense it can be a sign of something about to happen, a situation that is currently developing – i.e. 'brewing' or 'fermenting' – or a change taking place in a state of mind or mental outlook.

Bell

In Europe and the Far East, the bell was regarded as a musical instrument that could invoke divinities and the spirits of the natural world. The sound of the bell could be heard for miles around, which led people to believe that it also had the power

to fly and was invested with a divine quality. As a result, the bell – like the African tom-tom – was one of the first instruments of communication between human beings and, since it was rung to announce good or bad news, it became associated with beliefs concerning good fortune and misfortune.

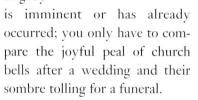

Depending on its tone and the sounds made when it is rung, the bell announces a happy event or that a tragedy is imminent or has already occurred; you only have to compare the joyful peal of church bells after a wedding and their sombre tolling for a funeral.

The bell appears as one of the three instruments – the bell, book and candle – used in excommunications and other such ecclesiastical ceremonies. On a lighter note, it has found its way into such popular expressions as 'sound as a bell', meaning 'in perfect condition', and 'to ring a bell', 'to sound familiar'.

You have to take all this into account when interpreting a dream about a bell. However, it usually announces a piece of news, which can be good or bad, depending on the circumstances and especially the context in which it appears. In all cases, it represents a warning and is putting you on your guard.

Belt, girdle

Nowadays we think of a belt as merely something used to hold up trousers or as an accessory worn around the waist. However, in early antiquity, the belt was regarded as a sacred object that symbolized the union of the forces of heaven and earth and invested the wearer with magical powers.

Dreaming about a belt often has nothing to do with having limited financial means, as the popular expression 'to tighten your belt' might suggest. It rather represents a certain harmony between intelligence and instinct, mind and body.

Birch, silver (tree)

There was once a beautiful tree that grew in abundance on the plains of Siberia. The inhabitants of these cold, northern regions made it their sacred tree, carving between 7 and 12 horizontal notches across its trunk to symbolize the cosmic ladder linking earth and heaven.

For the Russians, it symbolized a girl of marriageable age and they called it the tree of springtime. They also believed its bark concealed the spirit of the forest which had the power to ward off harmful spirits and the evil eye. Placing its white hand (its bark) on the heads of those who had been afflicted would relieve them of their sufferings or punish them, depending on the circumstances.

The Gauls made torches from its twigs and branches that they lit at marriage ceremonies as an omen of good fortune. In this way, they invoked Guilledouce, the solitary fairy who can sometimes be glimpsed in birch woods clad in her short dress of leaves and mosses.

Some traditions associate the silver birch with the moon, and its wood was used to make the famous brooms on which, as everyone knows, witches flew to their sabbaths. Others associated it with Jupiter and invested it with that planet's protective and beneficial virtues.

In the early 20th century, the branches of the silver birch were used to make the famous birch rod, the cane used by schoolmasters to punish their pupils.

Bird

See Scales to feathers (from), page 443

Bird-of-paradise

This beautiful bird is around 30cm (12in) in length and lives in the tropical forests of Indonesia, New Guinea and northern Australia. The male has magnificent yellow, red and blue plumage with a blue or black neck, depending on the species, and a brown or russet body. It feeds mainly on fruit and seeds, but it also eats small animals occasionally. It was called the bird-of-paradise by European explorers and settlers because of its exotically beautiful multicoloured plumage.

The legends associated with the bird-of-paradise are lost in the mists of time, although traces of them can still be found in the mythologies of the Australian aborigines and the tribes of New Guinea and neighbouring islands. These relate, for example, that this bird can fly day and night without rest, that it feeds solely on the perfume of flowers and that it is a child and messenger of the sun.

Birds of the Stymphalian Marshes

See Hercules, page 240

Black

Black, like white (see page 536), is not actually a colour. However, it is often contrasted with white, as good is with evil, darkness with light and death with life. Black has therefore, perhaps unjustly, acquired a bad reputation. Does black have a meaning?

This appears self-evident for those of us who like things to be straightforward. However, white is just as often used to conjure up the idea of death as black. Black has sometimes been regarded as an empty space, the abyssal void being represented by either white or black, while primeval chaos, the source of all life, was symbolized by black. Similarly, in ancient Egypt, black was associated with the fertility and abundance of the earth and with life, probably both because of the black soil and the black clouds swollen with fertilizing rain. In the West, though, black is commonly associated with mourning, death, barrenness and sadness.

Consequently, although black can often conjure up gloomy thoughts, distress, sadness, melancholy, mourning, wickedness, cruel thoughts and intentions, dark, obscure and disturbing objects, birds or animals that bring bad luck (the crow and the blackbird are black, for example, and seeing a black cat can be considered unlucky), there is no denying that black has an ambiguous symbolic value. Black is never completely black, particularly when you consider the fact that light appears in the most profound darkness, the blackest night. This aspect should always be remembered when black appears in one of your dreams.

Blackbird

The blackbird (*Merula turdus*) is commonly found throughout Europe and North Africa. Because it lives just as happily in the countryside, woods and forests as it does in the cities, it seems much more adaptable and far less vulnerable than many other birds. Blackbirds living in woods or forests are more timid than those found in the city, so the former build their nests in treetops while the latter build them randomly anywhere.

A mating pair of blackbirds will produce two or three broods of four or five eggs in the spring.

Although we usually associate the swallow with spring because of the well-known proverb 'One swallow does not make a summer', the black-bird should also be given its due, because this bird is often the first to announce the coming of spring with the short, rather repetitive phrases of its melodious fluting song.

Blind man

Symbolically, the 'blind man' has lost or sacrificed his ability to see the external world in favour of developing his inner sight. But 'to blind yourself to the truth' also means to lie to yourself, delude yourself and refuse to see reality. You can therefore be blind and perceptive or be sighted and obtuse. Someone who is blind *to* appearances understands the deeper and concealed meaning of things, whereas someone who is blinded *by* appearances trusts in those appearances and fails to see what is going on beneath the surface.

Dreaming that you are going blind should be interpreted as you (the dreamer) telling yourself to step back from the world of appearances, which seems to be taking up too much of your life, and to develop your faculties of discernment, your intuitions and a more reflective, subtle and deeper insight into people and things.

A blind person, who often carries a white stick, can be compared with the Hermit, the IXth card in the Major Arcana of the divinatory Tarot cards. They both find their way through the darkness of the external world using a staff or stick and the lantern of their mind or insight.

Dreaming about a blind man with a stick or cane in his hand often implies the need for awareness or realization. In this sense, it can represent a revelation that will be made to, or a discovery made by, the dreamer.

Blood

Blood is life. It serves as a vehicle for the soul: 'But flesh with the life thereof, which is the blood thereof, shall ye not eat. And surely your blood of your lives will I require; at the hand of every beast will I require it, and at the hand of man; at the hand of every man's brother will I require the life of man.' (Genesis 9: 4–5.) This is how Jehovah addressed the sons of Noah when establishing the new order after the flood. And if theologians question the link between the soul and blood, they have not read this passage from Genesis properly, since it leaves little room for doubt. According to this text, even the animals must be accountable to God for man's soul and any human blood they have spilled. The soul and blood were therefore inextricably linked in the minds of our forebears who believed that the body drained of blood no longer had a soul. Blood is also credited with regenerative and purifying properties. It is the seat of the next generation and of the race. We commonly talk of our children as our flesh and blood. Blood is an agent of transmission and our children's blood contains unique properties and qualities that we ourselves have inherited from our parents. Therefore blood ties are also ties that bind an individual to the soul of his or her family.

These considerations should all be taken into account when a dream features blood so prominently that we remember it clearly. Many of us have an uncontrollable fear of blood that, apart from these symbolic representations and the beliefs associated with them, is linked to the fact that, without the 6 to 7 litres (10 to 12 pints) of blood

flowing in our arteries and veins, we would die.

Instinctively, therefore, we all know that life and blood are intimately linked. Any human being who loses his blood loses his life. For this reason, dreaming of blood always has a profound impact. However, even when, at the very worst, you dream that your blood is pouring out of you, this should not be seen as a sign of imminent death. It either signals a loss of energy or a necessary purification that may concern your psychological or physical health. An injury or open wound oozing with blood does not mean that you will be the victim of an accident, but either that you are likely to have to make a sacrifice, or else that your feelings may be hurt by the attitudes or behaviour of someone close to you.

Blue

Through its association with water, blue is connected with the spiritual life, the soul, purity, depth and crystal. It is also linked to the sky, the firmament, heaven, the infinite, the absolute and diamonds. White and blue therefore have a number of points in common, with the obvious difference that blue is a true colour.

In this respect, it is interesting to note that, in the past, washerwomen and housewives used powdered cobaltine or 'dolly blue' to add extra whiteness to their laundry. The product is still used as a whitener today and gave rise to the expression 'to blue the laundry'. The link between blue and white is found in its Germanic origins – Old Norse *blár*, Old High German *blāo* and the Middle Dutch *blā* which also meant 'pallid or 'pale'.

Similarly, although ghosts often appear dressed in white, immortal mythical gods and demons are frequently represented with a blue head and body, especially in India.

Be that as it may, the appearance of blue in a dream is almost always a good omen, in the sense that it often reveals a state of grace, a relationship with the superior spirit that lies dormant within each and every one of us, and the spiritual aspirations of which

we are more or less aware or which preoccupy us during our waking hours. Blue should always be associated with well-being, gentleness, harmony, and pure and profound sentiments. It calms fever, passions and tensions, wards off fate and absorbs evil. Blue is therefore a beneficial colour. It is also the colour of love.

Boar, the Erymanthian

See Hercules, page 235

Boar, wild

As its Latin name, *Porcus singularis*, suggests, this wild pig lives a solitary life. The Celts used to hunt the wild boar: not only were they fond of its flesh, but they also regarded it as a divine and sacred food. Thus, on the night of Samhain, a festival marking the end of summer and the last day of the year – a precursor of the festival of Halloween (see *Fairies*, page 176) – the Celts sacrificed a boar to their god Lug, also known as Samildanach. His name meant 'skilled in all the arts' and he was a master warrior, champion, poet, sorcerer, physician, blacksmith and carpenter. A temple was erected to him in a Roman town called Lugdunum, which over the years became known more simply as Lyon, in France.

A symbol of unbridled primordial instincts, the boar was also identified with the Hindu god Vishnu and was one of his attributes or avatars. This animal is renowned not only for its ability to cause a great deal of damage, but also for its remarkable sense of smell that enables it to find truffles buried in the ground. The wild boar has appeared in numerous myths throughout the world (see *The Erythmanthian boar* page 235).

The appearance of a wild boar in a dream is often a sign that the dreamer may be about to succumb to an uncontrollable urge or commit some violent, instinctive and reckless act. However, it may also emphasize the fact that the dreamer needs to trust his instincts if he is to find whatever it is he is seeking,

particularly in a period of doubt, worry or uncertainty.

Boat

In ancient times, the boat was often represented as the vehicle that transported the bodies of the dead into the hereafter. It was also associated with the sun's chariot since, in certain regions of the world, the sun often sank below a horizon that lay beyond the sea.

The boat therefore corresponds to both birth and death and can be compared to the cradle and the coffin, or even the ark. It is also a symbol of destiny and the path of life, but the oars used to row it introduce the concept of free will.

The boat therefore has great symbolic significance but this significance varies depending on whether you dream of a boat with or without oars. Rowing implies effort, but also that you are in control of your own destiny. The French phrase 'mener sa barque' ('to call the tune') conveys this admirably. On the other hand, dreaming that you are adrift in a boat without oars often reveals a lack of free will or a tendency to let things slide and allow yourself to be carried along by events.

Bones
(skeleton)

Bones have always been thought to have magical properties, primarily because of their endurance and strength. As a result, the skeleton was often regarded as a representation of the eternal, immortal and imperishable aspect of the individual. If a shadow was the visible manifestation of the soul (see page 460), then the skeleton and the bones that form it were seen by our forbears as the seat of the soul, the part of man's body that contains the essence of the human soul. The Bible story about the creation of Eve, for example, relates that she was born from one of Adam's bones, thus from his skeleton.

Based on this belief, which was subsequently taken literally, the Christians saw the skeleton as the seat of the soul. For a long period in the Middle Ages, the bones of the saints were regarded as precious relics and coveted for the beneficial effect they were supposed to confer on those who possessed them.

The magical power of human bones was also exploited in many primitive societies, where it was thought that individuals could appropriate the forces, gifts or talents of a dead person by possessing their bones and carrying them around. For this reason, there is nothing morbid about dreaming of bones since this simply suggests that you are about to inherit or acquire new powers, gifts or talents, occasionally even property.

Book

A book symbolizes memory, knowledge and wisdom. *Liber*, the original Latin noun (from which we get 'library'), referred to the thin layer between the wood and the bark (Latin *cortex*) used by the Egyptians as a writing material before papyrus. Nevertheless, when a book appears in a dream, it should always be remembered that another word is derived from its Latin name: the verb 'deliver', which originally meant to 'liberate, set free'. In fact, *livre* ('book' in French), *liber* and *libre* ('free' in

French) share the same etymology and origin. For this reason, it was believed that the goal of a book was to deliver, to free people from ignorance. Although this may not always be the case today, it almost always holds true in dreams.

When a book appears in a dream or plays a prominent role, this is often a sign of a realization, a discovery or revelation that will set you free or allow you to free yourself from some of the chains holding you captive. Seeing or consulting an open book in a dream is often an indication that you should read your own thoughts to gain a better understanding of yourself.

Bottle

From wine skin to stoppered bottle and wine flask, the bottle has nearly always been a good omen. Emptying the dregs of a bottle or drinking the last glass or last drops of the liquid contained in a bottle has always been considered a sign of future luck and good fortune, or the promise of love or marriage. If an air bubble forms a ring in the neck of a bottle, after filling a glass with the liquid it contains or drinking from the bottle, it is regarded as the sign of imminent good news. If several bubbles or rings form, it is a sure sign of several pieces of good news. A message in a bottle, although essentially a distress signal, can also be interpreted in a positive light as an act of hope on the part of the person sending it. Last but not least, the contents of the bottle quench the thirst and often cause drunkenness.

From this, it can be concluded that the bottle and its contents, which are closely associated and sometimes become synonymous, quench the thirst of mortals and put them on an equal footing with the gods (see *Beer*, page 56). For certain ancient peoples, especially the Greeks and Celts, drunkenness was a privilege and was recognized as a gift from the gods.

Seeing one or more full bottles in a dream is a promise of

future happiness in your life, in the sense that your desires, wishes and aspirations will be fulfilled. A partly empty bottle means that joy and happiness still lie in store, while an empty bottle signifies that you have discovered all you need to know. Finally, a cellar filled with bottles represents the full extent of the potential knowledge and wealth at your disposal and with which you can 'quench your thirst'. But in order to do this, you must first go down into the 'cellar' and plumb the very depths of your personality.

Box

This evergreen shrub, which thrives on chalky soils, was chosen to replace the palm fronds – branches from the palm trees and date palms – that the crowd cut to celebrate Christ's entry into Jerusalem, a week before Passover. Since then, Christians have celebrated Palm Sunday, the Sunday before Easter, by offering sprigs of box as a symbol of immortality and eternity. Because of its strength and robustness, box wood was used to make flutes, pipes and spinning tops. For this reason, it is also a symbol of perseverance and steadfastness.

Brain
(right and left
sides of the)

Today the terms 'right' and 'left' are widely used in politics. In Britain the political term 'Right' probably dates from the 18th century, when it was used to designate the right-wing members of Parliament who sat on the right side of the Speaker in the House of Commons (in France it referred to the conservative deputies to the right of the president of the National Assembly). Similarly, the 'left' was used to

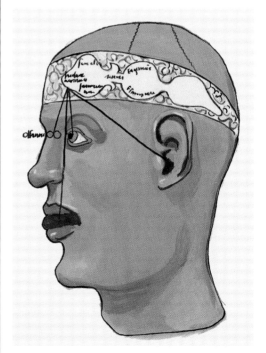

The brain according to Grégoire Reish (16th century).

refer to the more progressive deputies who sat to the left of the speaker (president). In this instance, however, the terms could be considered purely fortuitous or an example of the subconscious word games described by Sigmund Freud in *Jokes and their relation to the subconscious*. (Translated from the German under the general editorship of James Strachey; present volume edited by Angela Richards. Harmondsworth: Penguin, 1991.)

The word 'right' derives from the Latin *rectus*, which means 'ruled', 'straight' or 'in a straight line' when used literally, and 'straightforward, 'honest' and 'upright' when used figuratively. What is straight therefore has a certain straightforwardness about it. There may well be a connection between the English word 'left' and the Latin *laevus* but the associated adjectives 'sinister' and 'sinistral' are definitely derived from the Latin *sinister* which literally means 'left' or 'on the left hand'. It was used figuratively to mean 'wrong', 'perverse' and 'unfavourable' since the left-hand side was regarded by Roman augurers and soothsayers as unlucky. The Greeks also believed that a sign coming from the left was ill-fated. This is why, in the past, left-handed people were often regarded with suspicion (which gave rise to the current meaning of 'sinister'), while in France, the term *sénestre* was widely used to refer to the left hand or a left-handed person until the 15th century. Its counterpart *destre* – derived from the Latin *dexter*, which has more ancient Indo-European origins – meant the 'right hand' or 'on the right' and, by extension, 'upright' and 'normal'. It was also associated with good omens since the Greeks and Romans both believed that signs from the right were favourable in the sense of the now little-used English term 'dexter' meaning 'favourable', 'auspicious' or 'propitious'.

But all values are relative and the Etruscans believed exactly the opposite. For them, omens that came from the left were perceived as favourable and they used the same word for 'favourable' and 'coming from the left'. However, the Greeks and Romans appear to have had the last word on the subject.

The concept of 'left' and 'right' are important when considering the brain, which has now been scientifically proven to comprise two hemispheres, the right and left hemispheres. In human beings, there is a subtle inverse relationship between the two hemispheres of the brain and the right and left sides of the body. This means that what we may refer to in simple terms as the right hemisphere of the brain controls the left side of the body, while the left hemisphere controls the right side of the body. In other words, when you use your right hand, it is operated by the left side of your brain, and when you use your left hand, it is operated by the right side of your brain.

In symbolic terms, according to the sacred tree of the sephiroth (see *Tree of life according to the cabbala*, page 501), the right side of the brain corresponds to *binah* ('intelligence'), the third sephira. This sephira is associated with the mother, the feminine principle, and controls *chesed* ('grace' or 'mercy'), the fourth sephira, situated in the area of the left shoulder, and, lower down, *netzach* ('victory', 'triumph' or 'power'), the seventh sephira, situated in the area of the left hip. Thus, the right side of the brain, symbolized by *binah*, represents the feminine potential of all human beings regardless of their sex.

Similarly, the left side of the brain corresponds to *chokmah* ('wisdom'), the second sephira. This sephira is associated with the father, the masculine principle, and it controls *geburah*

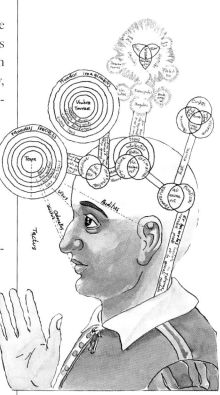

The brain according to Robert Fludd's **Utriusque cosmi historia,** *Vol. II (1619).*

('strength'), the fifth sephira, situated in the area of the right shoulder, and, lower down, *hod* ('honour' or 'glory'), the eighth sephira, situated in the area of the right hip. Thus the left side of the brain, symbolized by *chokmah*, represents the masculine potential of all human beings regardless of their sex.

It is therefore possible to conclude that the right hand and all of the right side of the body are controlled by feminine intelligence (*binah*), and that the left hand and the whole of the left side of the body are controlled by masculine wisdom (*chokmah*). It is also true that every well-balanced human being is able to make the most of his or her feminine and masculine components, without either predominating, once again regardless of their sex.

To achieve this balance and harmony within us, we have to distance ourselves from our prejudices regarding the feminine and masculine principles, which always incline us, whatever anyone says, to prioritize the latter to the detriment of the former. In so doing, we are unconsciously adopting a stereotypical and oversimplified form of feminine behaviour. In other words, all men and women who believe that the masculine principle dominates the feminine principle are the victims of their feminine component – in suppressed and unbalanced form, not properly integrated.

It is this inner personal harmony to which all human beings aspire. This is the great principle set out in the cabbala, but it is also expressed in different forms in many other mystical texts. According to the cabbala, it is the principle of unification that can make all human beings both intelligent (*binah*) and wise (*chokmah*).

Branch

In much of the Middle East, in ancient times, it was the custom for the assembled crowds to cheer and wave palm branches as their hero or king rode by. Palm branches are still associated with honorary titles and awards, such as the Palme d'or, a trophy awarded for the best film at the Cannes film festival. The Greeks and Romans also awarded palms to winners, so palms and branches are always symbols of victory and honour. However, in the story of the life of Jesus, when the latter triumphantly entered Jerusalem riding on a donkey, symbolizing his great humility, and was greeted by his disciples throwing palm branches, this glorious day, Palm or Passion Sunday, was a prelude to his crucifixion. Branches also play a deceptive role in *Macbeth*, when Malcolm orders his soldiers to carry them before them, to disguise their advance. It seems as if Birnam Wood is moving, in fulfilment of the witches' promise that Macbeth will not be defeated 'till Birnam wood do come to Dunsinane'. (*Macbeth*, act 5, scene v). Thus, for the past two thousand years, a meteoric rise in social status has unavoidably been seen in conjunction with the inevitable fall that ensues. As a result, a dream in which branches play an important role is often ambiguous and should be interpreted as an omen of short-lived victory or success.

Bread

It is easy to understand why bread is associated with certain beliefs, myths and mysteries. Scientifically speaking, from a biological, chemical and physical point of view, there is nothing mysterious about bread. Nevertheless, the ingredients used to make it and the recipe employed still retain a certain magic and, although bread is no longer necessarily a staple, it is still a welcome, even inevitable, addition to any meal virtually anywhere in the world.

However, if you dream of a loaf of bread, you should focus on the alchemical process it suggests – the quasi-magical transformation that was a key source of inspiration for priests and sorcerers in ancient times. They saw bread as a gift from the gods and a marvellous representation of the spiritual transformation that is required of mankind. As a result, it was often compared to man's body, while the leaven used to make it rise was seen as symbolizing the soul, since it acted from within, bringing about a metamorphosis by sacrificing and transforming itself.

Likewise, the grain that makes bread can been seen as a symbol of the soul that enriches, changes and improves human beings who can and must become the equals of gods themselves, even aspiring to something other than godhead that only they can achieve. First, the seeds are planted in the ground to become ears of wheat that are plucked or scythed. Once the grain is harvested, it is hulled and ground into flour which, with the addition of water, salt and leaven, forms a dough that is kneaded and moulded as the bread-maker vigorously turns it this way and that. The dough is then left to rest and slowly rises. Once risen, it is placed in the oven and cooked, becoming crusty on the outside and soft on the inside. Grain, water, salt and leaven are all very real ingredients that have great symbolic significance.

This is because bread is the fruit of man's labour. He grows and harvests its ingredients by the sweat of his brow; it nourishes him and transforms him. This is how we should interpret a dream in which bread plays an important or key role: we reap what we sow and it nourishes us as well. Bread clearly symbolizes the rich fruits of the land but, more than that, it represents essential food that man has produced by his own hand and, by extension, the metamorphosis or transmutation so dear to the alchemists that must take place within him to transform his soul.

Breath

People rarely dream about breath, because it is such an abstraction. Nevertheless, it is not unusual for something that may seem abstract, or perhaps so ordinary that it generally escapes notice in everyday life, to assume great significance in a dream. This may be the case with breath. For example, in one case-history, the subject regularly woke up in the middle of the night for many years after a recurring dream in which he had sensed a disturbing, although not hostile, presence and felt its warm, perfectly even breath on the back of his neck. The breath and the spirit are inextricably linked, if only in the Latin *spiritus*, 'spirit', which translated the Greek *pneuma*, 'breath', itself derived from the verb *pneim*, 'to breathe' or 'blow', which was already a translation of the Hebrew *ruah*. *Pneuma* was therefore used by the ancients both to refer to breath and the spirit, particularly the breath that came from God and returned to God, in other words, the Holy Spirit or the Holy Ghost. This can be seen by the popular expression 'to give up the ghost', which means 'to return one's breath or spirit to God', and in the saying 'he or she has breathed their last'. Certain philologists see an analogy between the letter E, which was originally written slanting, and the figure of a man standing with his two arms raised to heaven to catch his breath. The fifth letter-number of the cabbala, *hé* (lattice window), is related to

breath, in other words, the actions of breathing in and breathing out which form the complete cycle of respiration and the rhythm of life. This letter-number also corresponds to the letter E of Western alphabets. However, it is interesting to note that the confusion between the concepts of the soul and the spirit with regard to breath continues to this day.

Breath is either an exhalation or an inhalation. It relates both to the act of breathing out and the act of breathing in or inspiration that has preceded it. Thus breath reveals the presence of existing life and there is nothing abstract about it.

To dream that you can feel a breath on you, as in the example cited above, is a good omen – there is nothing sinister about it. It is just your own spirit that is calling you to order, conveying a message, a piece of advice or a truth, or telling you something important.

Bridge

The bridge is a crossing point, a link between two banks and therefore between two worlds, in other words, by extension and by analogy, between earth and heaven, terrestrial life and the

beyond, the visible world and the invisible world, between men and gods or, simply, between life and death. The symbolic meaning of the bridge can be likened to that of the rainbow, which is also a bridge between heaven and earth and, in the Bible, the symbol of the treaty of alliance between Jehovah and Noah and his descendants (see *Noah's Ark*, page 359). Thus, treaty and union are the two keywords that relate to the bridge. However, since a bridge can also represent the journey taken by man during his life on earth, it can be seen as a transitional zone between life before life and life after life.

For this reason, when a bridge plays a vital role in a dream, it often reveals that the dreamer is in a state of transition, either physically or with regard to personal, inner and spiritual development. He or she may be on the point of taking an important step, of entering a new phase of life, just as we cross a bridge to get from one side of the river to the other.

Buckle, boss

The word 'buckle' is derived from the Old French *bocle* ('shield boss') and the Latin *buccula*, meaning 'little cheek' or 'cheek strap of a helmet'. The Old French *bocler* (from *bocle*) gave rise to the term 'buckler', a small round shield worn on the forearm. Later, 'buckle' was used to refer to the ring or loop used to hold the buckler or shield and through which the soldier put his arm. From this point on, the English terms 'ring' and 'loop' appear to have been used for a number of things translated by the modern French *boucle*. Thus the English 'ear-ring' is the equivalent of the French *boucle d'oreille*, while a loop in a river or road is also translated by *boucle*. Even in modern terms, 'to loop the loop' has a direct equivalent – 'boucler la boucle'!

Because the ear-ring often shared the same symbolism of attachment as the ring, the engagement ring, wedding ring or slave's ring, dreaming that you are wearing an ear-ring can have a dual significance – attachment or alienation. Also, the fact that the ear-ring is usually attached to the ear lobe, which is sometimes pierced, means that we should be more attentive to what people are saying to us or to what a particular person – to whom we are attached in one way or another – wants to say or may say to us. Alternatively, it can mean that we ought to be more receptive and listen to what is going on within us.

Butter

The Greek word for butter, *bouturon*, was also the word for an unguent believed to have certain properties, including the ability to bestow, if not immortality, at least eternal youth. For the ancient Greeks, Celts and peoples of India, butter was regarded as a magical and sacred substance. Today, this function has been superseded by the regenerative beauty creams – supposed to prevent the skin from ageing by slowing the rate of cell degeneration – that have made the fortunes of cosmetics companies.

Dreaming about butter sometimes puts us in touch with the deeper and unchanging layers of our personality, linked to the eternal and immortal soul.

Butter can also be a reference to the churning process, which involves agitating or stirring cream to make butter. In this sense, it has associations with combat, tumult, dispute, confusion, agitation, and the completion or accomplishment of a task or action. Dreaming about butter can therefore correspond to a period of dispute and confusion, the successful completion of a task or project, profitable transactions (the French 'faire son beurre' means 'to make a packet'), or the accomplishment of an action that will bring about change or renewal in your life.

Butterfly

In some respects, the symbolic significance of the butterfly is similar to that of bread (see page 71), because it too is a symbol of the soul and a representation of its metamorphosis. It is common knowledge, after all, that the butterfly starts life without wings. By means of an amazing and complex process, it develops from a larva to a caterpillar, from a caterpillar to a chrysalis, and then from a chrysalis to what is called the *imago*, a biological term that describes a sexed adult insect that has completed all the various stages of its

metamorphosis. Although the Latin *imago* originally meant 'image', it also referred to an appearance, a vision, even a ghost.

As a result, the ancients regarded the *imago* or butterfly as an image, an aspect of the human soul. Furthermore, the metamorphoses of the butterfly, which progresses from a larva to a beautiful insect heralding fine weather and summer warmth, also allude to birth, life and death, childbirth, a succession of inevitable deaths that are essential if the earthbound caterpillar is to gain wings and take flight.

So, although the butterfly represents the soul, it is also a representation of its freedom and its release from physical ties. We know today that one tiny butterfly antenna contains over 40,000 nerve fibres, around 35,000 of which transmit signals from the olfactory cells to the brain, while the remaining 5,000 broadcast sensory messages. It can therefore be said that once the larva has metamorphosed into a butterfly, it attains a state close to perfection at its stage of evolution.

For this reason, although hesitation, uncertainty, lightness, happiness and vacillating ideas, thoughts or feelings are sometimes associated with the butterfly's flight, dreaming about a butterfly is primarily a sign that the dreamer wishes to attain a certain goal, a state of perfection, deliverance or freedom.

Buzzard

This huge bird of prey (*Buteo buteo*), with broad wings and dark brown plumage, is particularly popular with farmers since it feeds mainly on the rats and field mice that devastate their crops. However, some buzzards also feed on fish, other small birds and even frogs.

Some species are sedentary, others migratory, but all females lay a clutch of between two and five eggs every year, in a nest that is usually built in a tree or on a cliff, near the ground. This is one of the main reasons why the buzzard population is currently in decline while the rodent population is flourishing.

When watching its prey, the bird's head remains perfectly still, a characteristic that has been incorporated into the popular expressions of some cultures and has become associated with stupidity, fixed ideas and stubbornness. However, as is so often the case with any predator, the buzzard has been perceived in different ways by the peoples of different regions. Some regarded the buzzard as a benign bird that drove out the 'demons' responsible for destroying their crops, while others saw it as a bird of ill omen that attacked henhouses and especially young chicks. Even so, it has never been a bird of myth and legend.

Caduceus

In ancient Greece, the caduceus (Doric Greek *karukeion*) was originally the staff of the herald, the official messenger on the battlefield or in the diplomatic world, who convened assemblies and announced the laws and decisions passed by the Senate. In India, it was the staff of the bard, the singer or the poet. Its symbolism is deeply rooted in these two cultures.

However, it was the Greeks who made the caduceus the attribute of the god Hermes (the Roman god Mercury), and the staff of the herald and bard became a wand surmounted by a pair of wings and entwined by two serpents, that formed a sort of spiral representing the opposing forces of good and evil, positive and negative energies. This magical attribute assumed the significance of a sceptre in the hands of Hermes, symbolizing his power to maintain the balance between the forces of creation and destruction around a staff that represented the axis of the world. It was these opposing forces that had given rise to the primordial chaos from which all life had emerged but into which it could equally well disappear forever.

However, there is no doubt that the symbol of the caduceus existed in India – where it has been found carved on tablets dating from the third millennium BC – long before the god Hermes appeared on Mount Olympus. In India, it symbolized the Brahmanic staff representing the kundalini (cosmic energy) circulating along the 'tree' of the chakras (the psychic-energy centres of the body) and sushumna (the central channel carrying kundalini energy). When we bear in mind that a similar insignia – the staff of Asklepios (Aesculapius), the attribute of the Greco-Roman god of medicine – is still used today by doctors and pharmacists throughout the world, it becomes clear that the staff of the bard and the herald is a universal symbol that has been revered for some five thousand years!

However, it should also be remembered that the true magic and power possessed by Hermes, Asklepios and the Brahmin, and symbolized by the caduceus and staff, are the magic and power of the soul. Thus, in absolute terms, the two serpents and the wings on the caduceus represent the energies revealed or created by the forces of the soul moving within the body. When these energies move and work in harmony, the soul and body also work in harmony, with the forces of the body reinforcing those of the spirit and in turn regenerated by the forces of the soul.

The balance and harmony of the soul and body are to the advantage of the spirit, which renders the soul immortal. However, the spiritual dimension has tended to be overshadowed by the cult of cure, and more recently by the cult of health so dear to our modern civilizations, which have forgotten that physical health can never be fully achieved independently of spiritual health. Today, it has become so widely accepted that health relates exclusively to the body that the two have become virtually synonymous. Yet the caduceus and its association with the international symbol of medicine has a totally different symbolism. Perhaps one day we will learn to reinvest it with its original significance.

Be that as it may, you are unlikely to dream about a caduceus – you are much more likely to dream about one or more serpents. If these serpents are

intertwined or fighting, they always symbolize your primordial energies, your physical and moral health, your mental and physical energies. They are questioning your biological and psychological balance and, as such, are related to the caduceus.

Calendar

Throughout the world, unconnected cultures with no links to each other and therefore unable to learn from each other, felt the need to measure time by establishing temporal reference points that corresponded to terrestrial and celestial natural phenomena. This need was probably prompted by the necessities of

day-to-day living and, histori-cally, it appears to have devel-oped at approximately the same time in different cultures.

However, the fascination of the calendar lies in the fact that it is a wonderful tool for marking the rhythm, the perpetual cycle, the constant renewal and points of convergence between natural phenomena and the events and circumstances that marked the lives of clans, tribes and, more exceptionally, individuals.

A dream about a calendar can therefore mean that a cyclical event that has already occurred in your life is about to recur. Furthermore, since the calendar is directly related to the concept of time, it sometimes appears in a dream to make you more aware of the use you are making of your time, of the time remaining to do something important or necessary, or the time needed to achieve a particular goal or accomplish a desire.

Camel

As the symbol of moderation, restraint, endurance, equanimity and simplicity, the camel was sometimes associated by Christ-ians with the wisdom and humility of Christ. However, the imagery attributed to the camel is ambivalent since it is also regarded as a representation of presumption, obstinacy, impu-rity and bad temper.

Over and above these traits of character, it should be remembered that the camel is the ideal, if not the only, mount on which to cross a desert. Dream-ing about a camel can therefore predict providential aid that will help you through a difficult period in your life.

Cancer (sign of)

See Zodiac, page 561

Candlestick

The candlestick is the holder for a candle. The terms 'candle', 'candlestick' and 'candelabrum' derive from the Latin *candela* ('candle'), from *candere* 'to be of a shining white', 'to shine', 'to glit-ter' and, by extension, 'to glow with heat'. The terms 'candour' (Latin *candor*, 'dazzling white', 'whiteness', 'clarity', 'simplicity') and 'candid' (Latin *candidus*, 'shining white') are also derived from *candere*.

The Christian festival of Candlemas ('festival of candles'),

celebrated on 2 February, is the day on which the church candles are blessed. It is the Feast of the Purification of the Virgin Mary and of the Presentation of Christ in the Temple and is commemorated by holding lighted candles. Originally, however, it was a Roman festival dedicated to Pluto, god of the Underworld, and to the dead. During the festival, men and women held lighted candles as they kept watch, prayed, sang and invoked the gods, in order to protect the souls of the dead. The festival was held in the month of Februarius, 'the cleansing month'.

However, the most magical and sacred candlestick, the symbol of divine and eternal light, is the seven-branched candelabrum or *menorah* (Hebrew, meaning 'candlestick'). Although there are several references to it in the Bible, it appears to have originated in Mesopotamia where, according to the Babylonian

astral religion, it was the representation of the seven stars governing the zodiac. In the Bible, the prophet Zechariah referred to it in his fifth 'vision of the night': 'And the angel that talked with me came again, and waked me, as a man that is wakened out of his sleep, and said unto me, What seest thou? And I said, I have looked, and behold a candlestick all of gold, with a bowl upon the top of it, and his seven lamps thereon, and seven pipes to the seven lamps, which are upon the top thereof.' (Zechariah 4: 1–3.)

According to the Christian cabbalists of the Renaissance, the menorah represented the hierarchy of the terrestrial and celestial worlds. The central branch represented Everyman, while the three left-hand branches, working from the centre outwards, symbolized the animal, vegetable and mineral kingdoms. The three right-hand branches, again starting from the centre, symbolized the angels, the archangels and God. According to this esoteric principle, mankind is therefore placed at the centre of creation.

A dream about a lighted candle in a candlestick often has great spiritual significance. It can represent a message of hope from the dreamer to him- or herself or predict an imminent revelation or, quite simply and more practically, a good idea. If, on the other hand, the candle is not alight, it symbolizes a certain refusal to be frank and open or to communicate and exchange ideas and opinions, but can also represent a form of hypochondria, latent depression or persistent despair. The appearance of a candelabrum, with its candles lit, is always a sign of prosperity, happiness, personal development and advancement.

Capricorn
(sign of)

See Zodiac, page 578

Carpet, rug

A carpet was once thought of as a magical object, endowed with certain powers, both because of its shape, whether it be square, rectangular, circular or octagonal, and because of the symbols woven into its pattern, which include sacred and protective birds, beneficial trees, like the cypress, palm, fig and the tree of life, and beneficial

flowers and fruit. One of its legendary attributes was the ability to fly, to take off and soar skywards through the clouds, carrying its passengers to far-off, fabled and fantastic lands in search of adventure, escape or the thrill of exploring unknown worlds. Although it was also said to bring peace, happiness, knowledge, prosperity or wealth to its owner, it could sometimes be the harbinger of violence, destruction and rebellion. Indeed, if you knew the powers that were once attributed to a carpet or rug, by the threads with which it was woven, the hands that made it, the words spoken during its weaving, the materials and colours used, you would not look at, buy or walk on it again without taking certain precautions.

Thus, walking on a rug or carpet that features prominently in a dream often symbolizes the dreamer's entry into another world that could be considered dangerous if it is unknown or covered with magic signs. Any carpet is potentially magical and able to carry us, symbolically speaking, to another world, causing us to lose touch with our own reality. In one case, an individual dreamed that he was walking on a rug that was unrolled in a street he used daily; shortly afterwards he completely changed direction in life, moving to a new area and making a new circle of friends.

The carpet protects or enchants. However, it is also a symbolic representation of the garden, the original, perfect and idyllic garden from which all souls were banished and to which they long to return. Belief systems from all over the world agree on this point: everyone carries a garden within, a paradise, a marvellous microcosm that is the mirror image of the macrocosm, the universe in which we live. The carpet is therefore a symbolic representation of this inner garden on which man, who consecrates the ground on which it is laid, kneels to pray. A dream of a prayer rug indicates that you feel at peace with yourself, but also that you are engaged in soul-searching, withdrawing into the garden of your soul or its abode.

Castle

The castle is usually assimilated with the fortress. It is a fortified, enclosed place, protected by high and supposedly impregnable walls, often situated on unassailable heights overlooking a valley or an entire region. Symbolically, it is important to distinguish between the castle of obscure desires – pride, greed, the desire for absolute power – and the castle of enlightened consciousness, the seat of the soul, pure love and the divine spirit.

When a castle seems to occupy a dominant place in a dream, always try to remember the atmosphere that pervades and surrounds it, whether you are actually inside the castle or whether you only caught a glimpse of it. Its shape, colour and appearance will tell you which type of castle it is and therefore which sentiments it represents.

Catastrophe

Originally, the word 'catastrophe' (from the Latin *catastropha*, from the Greek *katastrephein*, 'to overturn') implied some kind of revolution, overturning or return to the point of departure. It was subsequently used in the sense of a 'denouement' or 'end', especially in connection with a play and a classical tragedy in particular. By extension, it came to mean a decisive event or disastrous conclusion.

Today, it is generally used to describe a dramatic and devastating event linked to some unpredictable and uncontrollable natural phenomenon or disaster. In a dream, however, a catastrophe should rarely be interpreted as a dramatic event and should certainly not be taken at face value. It usually predicts or indicates that a salutary upheaval is likely to disrupt your way of life, your behaviour, your way of thinking or your mental outlook, or that there is a need for such an upheaval.

Caterpillar

Symbolically, the caterpillar is associated with the larva and the butterfly, and a caterpillar in a dream always implies the emergence of a butterfly. As such, it often predicts an essential or decisive transformation, or an inevitable and radical change that must take place in your situation

or behaviour, or a vital realization that must occur if your circumstances or state of mind at a particular point in your life are not to remain in the larval stage.

Dreaming about a caterpillar can quite simply predict a birth or some form of creation, as well as the imminent conception of a child. Finally, it can also help you to understand that you should be less attached to your body (the caterpillar), which is mortal (metamorphosis), and be much more preoccupied with your soul (the butterfly).

Cauldron

A cauldron is a fairly deep, circular or cylindrical container with a rounded bottom and a handle for hanging it on the chimney-hook above the fire and for moving it from one place to another. It is made from cast iron, bronze or copper and is one of the oldest utensils used to cook food and make jams and preserves.

The symbolic significance of the cauldron lay in its power to provide nourishment for human beings by transforming the fruits of the earth by bringing them into contact with fire, in an almost invisible and therefore magical way. The contents of a cauldron were always mysterious.

The cauldron was therefore associated in a number of mythologies with the powers of both good and evil. It was the attribute of the gods preparing a divine meal – the symbol of wealth, prosperity and abundance – and in this context was comparable to the famous 'horn of plenty'. But it was also the cooking pot of the Devil and, of course, the famous witches' cauldron of so many tales and legends, in which they prepared their wicked spells and magic potions.

These beliefs may well be rooted in Celtic mythology, according to which a druid had three types of cauldron, each with its own particular function. The first, the cauldron of plenty, had the gift or virtue of being able to satisfy the hunger of mortals. But its nourishment was celestial and spiritual as well as earthly and those who were hungry for knowledge could also satisfy their hunger from this cauldron. Dead bodies were thrown into the second cauldron, the cauldron of resurrection, so that they would be revived and resuscitated by being transformed in the same way as the fruits of the earth, under the effects of the heat released by the fire. The third cauldron was that of the sacrifice of those who renounced worldly and earthly wealth, and even life itself, in order to achieve inner transformation and become free entities. Abundance, resurrection and eternal life, the ultimate, liberating sacrifice – the three symbols associated with the three druidic cauldrons or attributes of Celtic mythology – are not so very different from the symbols of Christianity.

The cauldron also occupies a prominent place in Chinese symbolism. Hexagram 50 of the I Ching (Book of Changes) is the cauldron (*ting*): 'The whole hexagram [...] is the image of a *ting*, from the legs below to the handle-rings at the top. [...] the

symbol of the *ting* carries also the idea of the preparation of food. The *ting* is a ceremonial vessel reserved for use in sacrifices and banquets.' (*I Ching or Book of Changes*, the Richard Wilhelm translation rendered into English by Cary F. Baynes, Routledge & Kegan Paul, 1968.) Here, the image of the cauldron symbolizes human destiny, with fire and the preparation of food representing the inner transformation. 'Fire over wood [is the image not of the *ting* itself but of its use]. Fire burns continuously when wood is under it. Life also must be kept alight, in order to remain so conditioned that the sources of life are perpetually renewed. [...] relationships and positions must be so regulated that the resulting order has duration.' This second extract from the I Ching shows how the ancient Chinese invested an everyday utensil with a symbolic significance that furthered their inner and spiritual development. It demonstrates how symbols, the tools of reflection, were a part of their everyday lives. In this way, human beings, who originally read and interpreted all kinds of signs and messages in the natural world, learned to apply this language to their day-to-day lives, to the tools and utensils that they themselves had created.

A dream about a cauldron can sometimes simply be interpreted in the sense of 'keeping the pot boiling', which means working, producing, earning your living and acting in a way that will maintain or improve your material situation. However, if the cauldron is full, you can regard it as a symbol of your bubbling mental energy and activity. It is also often a sign of future plenty, wealth and prosperity at home or in the workplace. On the other hand, if the cauldron is empty, it indicates that your vital and material resources run the risk of being deficient. But it can also refer to an empty period in your life, a period of reassessment, during which you are preparing to embark on a new undertaking or creation without knowing exactly what that undertaking or creation is. This interpretation is even more likely if you see yourself cleaning out a cauldron, pan, saucepan or indeed any other kind of cooking pot.

Cave

Caves are associated with the womb, the mysterious depths of the earth and primordial telluric powers. The ancient Egyptians believed that the source of the

Nile sprang from a fissure in a rock while, in ancient Greece, caves were often sacred places dedicated to the divinities of the earth. In this sense, the cave was regarded as a doorway leading to the Hereafter, to another, unknown world, the subterranean world that lay at the centre of the earth, but also to the Underworld. In the early history of the human race, caves were certainly used as dwellings and places of refuge, but they were also temples, mystical and hallowed places where human beings came into direct contact with the primordial energies and forces of the earth.

Dreaming that you are in a cave is usually less important than what you are doing there. The cave itself represents an archaic, ancient place and, as such, is symbolic of our distant past. It is a place where something new, unprecedented and unexpected can or must happen. Particularly in our dreams, the cave is often associated with the womb, gestation and everything that precedes birth.

Cedar tree

The cedar is a tree whose roots plunge deep into the earliest and most ancient myths. The fact that it still grows on the mountains of modern Lebanon and the slopes of the Taurus Mountains in Turkey attests to its longevity. The architects of King Solomon used the wood of the cedar, which grew in abundance around the ancient cities of Byblos (Lebanon), Ebla (Syria) and Jerusalem, to build the magnificent framework of the Temple of Jerusalem.

The ancient Egyptians used cedar wood to build boats and statues. According to Egyptian legend, the rustling of the leaves when the wind blew through the cedar forests was in fact the moaning of Osiris, whose body was enclosed in a cedar-wood coffin (the word for 'cedar' also meant 'to moan'). The tree therefore came to symbolize immortality and incorruptibility, reflecting the immortality of the soul of Osiris, and Egyptian carpenters used cedar wood to make coffins since its strong, resinous aroma was reputed to temper the smell of decay and drive away insects.

The cedar had so many qualities in the eyes of our forebears that the compilers of the Bible came to regard it as the symbol of the tree that stood in the Garden of Eden, one branch of which became Moses's rod and another Aaron's, while its wood was used to make the cross of Christ. The Bible also echoes the ancient Egyptian image of the tree's incorruptibility and immortality:

> 'The righteous shall flourish
> like the palm tree:
> He shall grow like a cedar in
> Lebanon.'
>
> (Psalm 92: 12).

Centaur

In spite of the fact that the centaur is nowadays often regarded purely as a symbol of the libido, dreaming about a centaur often represents an emotional drive, an affective energy that is trying to assert itself or is emerging from the depths of your being and threatening to submerge you. Determining whether this energy will have positive or devastating effects depends on the context in which the centaur appears in your dream, what it is doing and how you relate to it. Because the centaur is the symbol of Sagittarius, the ninth sign of the zodiac, its presence in a dream can also indicate that an important and usually propitious event will occur in your life during the period covered by the sign (22 November to 21 December), or that the number 9 and its associated symbols will play an important role in the near future (see *Nine*, page 388).

Centaur
Centre
Cerberus (the
capture of)
Ceryneian
hind (or stag)
Chaffinch

The symbolic significance of this mythical creature – part-man, part-animal – is dealt with more fully in the articles on *Sagittarius* (page 575) and *The mares of Diomedes* (page 244).

Centre

See Circle, wheel, page 100

Cerberus
(the capture of)

See Hercules, page 244

Ceryneian hind
(or stag)

See Hercules, page 233

Chaffinch

The chaffinch (*Fringilla coelebs*) is an attractive little migratory bird with beige plumage and brown and white markings. One of the unusual features of this species of bird, which is common throughout Europe and from northern Africa to central Asia, is that only the female migrates every spring and autumn, while the male is non-migrant. As a result, early naturalists who studied its behaviour and habits dubbed it *coelebs*, from the Latin word for bachelor. The chaffinch is also unusual in the particular care it takes when building its nest, which is so cunningly woven and concealed that it blends into its surroundings and cannot be seen by possible predators. The female lays four to six eggs that she incubates alone, while the male provides the seeds and small insects that form this bird's staple diet.

The chaffinch is a genuine musician with an apparently innate talent for singing that it hones by listening attentively to its father's example when young. Because it sings from morning to night, it is regarded as a symbol of gaiety and good humour. However, paradoxically, its sustained song was not seen as a good omen by our forebears, who interpreted it as a sign of rain or bad luck.

Chain

The chain is self-evidently a symbol of attachment, dependency and slavery. But although it often signified submission and servility, it could also represent the strong bond that existed between two things, elements or living beings. Furthermore, it was the symbol of the fatal or inevitable sequence of circumstances and events, the famous law of cause and effect or chain reaction, according to which every thought brought about an action that in turn caused a contrary or complementary action. Certain areas of modern scientific research have shed new light on what is known as the 'butterfly effect', based on the premise that a butterfly beating its wings in one part of the world can directly affect the climate in another part of the world. If this theory could one day be scientifically proven, it would be the physical representation of a principle accepted long ago by our ancestors, the principle of chain reaction.

Rather than signifying a possible dependency, bond or attachment, a dream about a chain is much more likely to be the expression of situations and circumstances in which we have become embroiled and which we have actually created unwittingly by our past thoughts, initiatives, choices and actions.

Chair

Did you know that the chair you sit on every day was once an attribute of the gods? In the past, a person seated on a chair (or throne) was invested with a divine right, a superior power, and was the equal of the gods or possibly even a god themselves. Remember this if you see yourself in a dream, sitting on an ordinary chair, and are tempted to dismiss it as ordinary or banal. In fact, regardless of whatever else is happening in your dream, sitting on a chair means that you are enthroned, in the true sense of the term, and that you have been raised and elevated to the rank of king or queen – symbolically, of course.

Chameleon

The chameleon, a type of lizard found in Africa, Asia and on the island of Madagascar, is renowned for its remarkable ability to change the colour of its body and blend in with its surroundings. Its name derives from the Greek *khamaileōn*, from *khamai* ('on the ground') and *leōn* ('lion'). It was therefore associated in the minds of our forebears with the lion, a symbol of strength, power and domination, but also with a word whose origins have been lost in the mists of time, which is roughly translated by 'ground' but which in fact emphasizes the creature's telluric, tectonic and volcanic nature.

The chameleon is therefore an animal associated with the primordial principles of earth and fire, and, as such, it has magical and sacred connotations. This is why it was regarded by certain African and Asian peoples as a chthonic (underworld) divinity that originated in the centre of the earth but had the power to remain close to the gods by perching in the treetops.

The mythical and symbolic qualities attributed to the chameleon by the cultures and civilizations of Africa and Asia are also found in Europe where it was for a long time regarded as a strange and fantastical creature that had emerged from the depths of the ages. This is not so far from the truth when you consider that zoologists estimate that the chameleon has existed on earth for 170 million years. These qualities – wisdom, patience, perseverance, knowl-

edge, the beginning and end of all things here on earth – are obviously related to its naturally slow movements, its aura of placidity, its ability to remain immobile for hours on end, to the point of blending perfectly with its surroundings. To achieve this, it appears to be able to inflate, deflate and change the colour of its body at will. It also has protruding and extremely mobile eyes which allow it to see forwards, backwards and sideways continuously, if not simultaneously. Its eyes are also the key to its colour changes since, depending on the colour of the light that touches the retina, an immediate reaction causes the pituitary gland to increase or decrease the secretion of the hormones that change the colour of its skin. In this way, the chameleon can adopt the colour of a branch or the leaves of a tree and camouflage itself when hunting. In addition to this ability to adapt and change colour –

'chameleon-like' being used to describe someone perfidious, deceitful, untruthful, a base flatterer, fickle and hypocritical – the chameleon is also renowned for the quickness and agility of its extremely long, prehensile tongue which enables it to catch insects from some distance away.

With its wisdom and exemplary deftness, on the one hand, and its weakness and duplicity, on the other, the chameleon symbolizes the duality of human nature. In actual fact, it is only behaving like any other species by developing its inherent qualities and abilities in order to survive in the environment in which it lives.

Long before Walt Disney attributed typically human characteristics and behaviour to animals, humans had recognized symbolic, idealized or caricatured representations of their attitudes and feelings in the animal kingdom. And since human nature is intrinsically double-sided, having a lighter and darker side, the animals of myth and legend were automatically subjected to this human interpretation of their world, their life and their reality. This is why a dream about a chameleon can be interpreted in one of two ways. In a positive sense, it represents adaptability, flexibility, understanding, attentiveness and patience, the ability to see all sides of a problem and carefully consider every aspect of a situation. However, in a negative sense, it indicates hypocrisy, deceitfulness, underhandedness, double-dealing and treachery.

So how do you know whether the appearance of a chameleon in your dreams is a positive or negative sign? It very much depends on the context and circumstances in which the creature appears but, because of its ancient origins, it always relates to the deepest and most subconscious layers of your mind. It could even be seen as a message for you from the depths of your being that has risen to the surface.

Deep within each and every one of us, in areas that we either do not understand or of which we are, more often than not, simply unaware, lie innate abilities that we do not know how to use. These abilities impinge upon our consciousness symbolically, in the form of strange and fantastical creatures likely to make an impression or fire our imagination so that we remember them when we are awake. By deciphering the symbolism of the messages they bear, we are able to discover more about ourselves.

Chaos

It was from chaos that life on Earth originated. According to the *Enuma Elish*, the great Babylonian creation myth, in the beginning there was neither heaven nor earth, nothing but the sweet waters underground (*Apsu*, or 'rest') that merged with those of the sea (*Tiamat* or 'inertia'). It was from the mingling of these primordial waters that the first gods – the representations of energy and activity – emerged.

The ancient Egyptians subscribed to a similar belief. According to their creation myth, the primeval waters of chaos were a shapeless mass personified by the god Nun. It was from this formless ocean that the universe was created. The Yahwist priestly code, the earliest source on which the Pentateuch is based, describes primordial chaos in a similar way: 'In the beginning God created the heaven and the earth. And the earth was without form, and void; and darkness was upon the face of the deep. And the Spirit of God moved upon the face of the waters.' (Genesis 1: 1–2.)

As can be seen from the examples above, the image of chaos is often associated with water. This is why the ocean is sometimes described as tangible chaos. According to a theory of physics, all elements associated with chaos – marine currents, swirls of smoke, the movements of clouds – are thought to have a certain coherence within disorder, so to speak.

Be that as it may, dreaming about chaos should not be taken as an indication of catastrophe (see page 83). If you are in a chaotic situation in a dream, it often means that something new is going to happen in your life. This type of dream is never the sign of a catastrophe, it is more likely to be a sign of a birth.

Chapel

The term 'chapel' derives from the Old French *capele* – from the Latin *capella*, a diminutive of *capa* ('cloak') – and was originally used in the 7th century to designate the sanctuary at the court of the Frankish kings where the cloak of St Martin of Tours was kept as a relic. It gradually came to refer to a building adjoining a church or a royal estate, dedicated to God and used to house the saints' relics that were so highly valued by believers from the 8th century onwards. The Latin *capa* and its derivative *capellus* ('hood') also gave rise to the Old French *chapel* ('hat') –

modern French *chapeau* – which in turn gave rise to *chapelet* ('garland of roses') and the English 'chaplet'. Originally used to refer to the crown of roses worn by the Virgin Mary, 'chaplet' became more generally used for an ornamental wreath of flowers or beads worn on the head. By extension, it came to refer to a string of beads and, in the Roman Catholic Church, to the string of prayer beads that forms one third of the rosary, or the prayers counted on these beads. The practice of counting the prayers gave rise to the expression 'bidding' or 'telling one's beads'.

Dreaming of a chapel or a chaplet can therefore imply a reference to the past (relics, bygone days, reliving things in your mind, quibbling, even obsession). This is why origins and etymology are so important since a number of different meanings often stem from one root and understanding the etymology of a word or words is therefore vital to understanding the symbolism of the images that appear in dreams.

Chariot

The chariot was a two-wheeled, horse-drawn vehicle used by the ancient civilizations of Egypt, Greece and Rome. The term

derives from the Old French *char*, which shares the same Latin root – *carrus* (a four-wheeled wooden wagon) – as the French *charpente* meaning 'framework' or 'roof timbers'. In etymological terms, the chariot could therefore be deemed to be a framework on two wheels, while *charpente* in the sense of 'roof timbers' reinforced the chariot's mythical link with the sky. This link was based on the idea that, since the roof of a house rests on the roof timbers (*charpente*), these timbers became a symbol for the sky, the roof of the world. For the ancients, the chariot was a popular symbolic representation of the sun or solar wheel as it pursued its daily course across the sky, from morning to evening, above and within the roof of the world. The chariot was also regarded as the attribute of Apollo, the Greek god of light. As the vehicle of the gods, the chariot, sun or solar wheel was also the vehicle of the soul and, by extension, a symbol of the body. The chariot may now have disappeared from our everyday lives, but it has been replaced by the automobile, which has the same symbolic significance in relation to the body (see *Automobile*, page 45).

Cherry

In Japan, the cherry is regarded as a fruit of great symbolic beauty since it represents the vocation of the warrior or the hero. The cherry tree, which flowers so beautifully in the Land of the Rising Sun, is a symbol of the ephemeral purity, prosperity and happiness experienced on earth, which prefigure those eternal qualities that will be experienced by human beings after their death. In Japan, springtime 'cherry-blossom viewing' is a seasonal event that in many areas occurs around Golden Week (April to early May).

The cherry tree was imported to Rome from Asia Minor by Lucullus in 74 BC, and was subsequently introduced into Britain and other regions of Europe. It was highly prized for its delicious fruit but its symbolism was very different, possibly due to its distant origins. While the flowers and fruit of the cherry tree are symbols of happi-

ness for the Japanese, in Europe they are associated with demons and blood.

In European terms, therefore, dreaming about cherries has often been regarded as the prediction of a death. However, as has already been pointed out, this is not a physical but a symbolic death – for example, the end of a situation, a relationship or a period in your life. Most of us, while gathering or eating cherries, have at one time or another hung two cherries joined by a stalk over our ears. But how many of us know that, in so doing, we are invoking love in its purest form? Wearing cherries on your ears is a symbol of physical union, but also, and above all, of a spiritual vocation.

Chestnut, Sweet/Horse

As well as being renowned for its longevity, the sweet chestnut (*Castanea sativa*) is also the symbol of foresight, since its highly calorific, nutritious and delicious fruits (chestnuts) fall from the tree in autumn and provide for the coming winter. In a book on natural remedies, Daniel Maurin describes sweet chestnuts as a useful cure for all human ailments. He recommends eating them often, before and after meals, since they develop and nourish the mind. They also fortify the nerves and cure headaches (*Les Remèdes*, éditions Mame, 1992). Their virtues were also extolled in the 12th century by the Christian mystic Hildegard von Bingen, but they have been eaten grilled, boiled, as a soup or a purée since early antiquity. A tree producing such beneficial fruits as the sweet chestnut could not but be honoured by our forebears who were acquainted with its reputation for longevity. They used its branches to make staffs and handles so that,

whenever they touched them, they drew strength from the wood and were reinvigorated.

The sweet chestnut should not be confused with the horse chestnut (*Aesculus hippocastanum*), which, although its common name derives from its having been used to treat broken wind and respiratory diseases in horses, is not edible – at least not by humans.

The fact that horse chestnuts, known informally as 'conkers', could sometimes fall on people's heads and hurt them may have given rise to the 19th-century term 'to conk' meaning to strike a blow, especially on the head or nose. This parallels the 17th-century French usage of *châtaigne* ('sweet chestnut') meaning a 'clout' or 'biff' and which gave rise to the verb *châtaigner* still in use today. The English term 'conker' also gave its name to the game ('conkers') in which each of the two players, armed with a chestnut threaded onto a string, tries to break their opponent's 'conker'.

China
(cosmogonies in)

See Cosmogonies in China, page 111

Christmas

The birth of Jesus is celebrated on Christmas Day in the West, prompting the question: is there any historical basis for this birth-date or any link between this Christian festival and the winter solstice? Noel, another word for Christmas, means 'day of birth' and is derived from the Latin [*dies*] *natalis*. It could be said, therefore, that astrologers take everyone's *dies natalis* into consideration when calculating and interpreting their birth chart. However, Christmas and Noël refer specifically to the Christian festival of the Nativity, even though, as myth, legend, symbols and history have merged in people's minds, it has gradually become less of a religious event and more of a folk ritual, a meaningless custom lacking in devotional significance. This is not the place for an account of the Nativity, however; we are more interested in the development of the festival, religious for some, social for others, celebrated on the night of 24/25 December and characterized by the exchange of gifts.

The winter solstice. A look at the calendar shows that Christmas Eve always falls two or three days after the northern hemisphere's winter solstice, the

Why do we give presents on Christmas Day?

This custom dates back to the Roman Saturnalia, held every year between 17 and 24 December, at the time of the winter solstice.

During these festivals, held in honour of Saturn, all social roles were overturned: slaves were served by their masters and it was a time of debauchery and excess when all taboos were lifted.

Those taking part in the Saturnalia gave each other gifts on 25 December in celebration of the first day of the year, New Year's Day. The Feast of Fools – still a source of inspiration for contemporary carnivals – took place between Christmas Day and Epiphany throughout medieval Europe until the 15th century and was probably an adaptation of the Roman Saturnalia.

longest night of the year, when the hemisphere is leaning farthest away from the sun. This is the first day of winter, when the sun enters Capricorn in the zodiac, symbolically heralding the day's rebirth, the resurrection of the sun, since from then on the days grow longer and the nights shorter, until the spring equinox when light triumphs over darkness and day is longer than night.

Celebrating the winter solstice. Many ancient civilizations throughout the world accorded great importance to sun worship and celebrated the day of the winter solstice. However, there is no truth in the belief that the Celts celebrated the solstices and the equinoxes. Although the winter and summer

> ### What is the origin of the yule log and the Christmas tree?
>
> The Celts and Gauls called the night of 21/22 December or the winter solstice 'the night of the silver fir', and the Celts used to burn an enormous fir log to mark the occasion. As a result, although the Christmas tree is often associated with the myths of the tree of life, the axis of the world, the tree of knowledge and the tree of the cross, this goes some way towards explaining why the fir was chosen to symbolize it.

solstices and the spring and autumn equinoxes were featured in the Celtic tree calendar and were marked by four significant trees – beech (winter solstice), oak (spring equinox), birch

Right: after a sculpture in the
Ostiense Museum, Ostia.

Christmas

(summer solstice) and olive (autumn equinox) – the year was divided into two seasons, 'the cold season (Gallic *giamon*) starting on 1 November and the warm season (Gallic *samon*), starting on 1 May. According to M.-L. Sjoestedt, author of *Gods and Heroes of the Celts*, the Celtic calendar was governed not by the solar year, by the solstices and equinoxes, but by the agrarian and pastoral year, by the start and finish of the labour involved in stock-breeding and farming. As a result, the mythical world of the Celts was dominated by the goddesses of the earth, whereas solar deities were nowhere to be found. However, if we direct our attention towards the East, the sun was honoured as a god in his own right in Babylon and Egypt. Pharaoh Amenhotep IV, better known as Akhenaten, worshipped the god Aten (literal meaning, the sun disc) in the 14th century BC, making this the first known monotheistic religion.

Whatever the case, it seems virtually certain that it was the Roman emperor Aurelian who, in the third century AD, established 25 December as the day of the sun's festival (*Natalis Solis Invicti*, or 'the birth of the invincible sun'), to celebrate the cult of Mithra, very popular with the Roman legions. This god appears to have originated in Persia at least six centuries before the birth of Christ, although there is no proof that he was exclusively a solar god.

There are obvious similarities, however, between the Persians' Mithra and the Hindus' Mitra, a sun god who, together with Varuna, lord of the night, were the guardians of heaven and earth, according to the Vedas (texts containing the sacred doctrine of the Hindus, dating back to 1500 BC). Furthermore, the Romans celebrated the Saturnalia from 17 to 24 December and 25 December corresponded exactly to the day of the winter solstice in the Roman calendar. This is probably why the day of the 'birth of the invincible sun' became the day of the 'birth of

---

Do we know the exact date of the birth of Jesus?

This is a highly controversial subject and opinions differ. However, historians think that he must have been born before the death of Herod the Great in 4 or 749 BC by the Roman calendar. On the other hand, the crucifixion is thought to have probably taken place on 7 April in AD 30 or 33, during the reign of Pontius Pilate, the Roman prefect of Judaea.

Christ' for Romans who had converted to Christianity. It is also a historical fact that it was at the instigation of Constantine, the Roman emperor who founded Constantinople – known as the 'New Rome' – that the pagan festivals of the Western Empire became Christian religious festivals. Because the pagan festivals of the winter solstice coincided with the day of Jesus' birth according to the Christians, who originally celebrated the Baptism and the Epiphany – the adoration of the Christ Child by the three Magi (who were astrologers, seers and sorcerers) – on the same day, this was the date chosen to celebrate Christmas.

Circle, wheel

The circle is a square. This may seem a strange way to begin an article on the circle but it is impossible to write about this universal symbol without making reference to the quadrature of the circle, i.e. the process of determining a square having an area equal to that of a given circle, figure or surface. It goes without saying that this process involves a series of mathematical calculations and has given rise to the popular expression 'it's like trying to square the circle',

meaning 'it's attempting the impossible', when faced with an insoluble problem.

For many ancient civilizations, heaven was a feminine principle represented by a circle and earth was a masculine principle represented by a square. For our ancestors, it seemed logical that the square of the earth was contained within the celestial circle or sphere and not vice versa. They imagined the land in which they lived as part of a flat world, suspended in a sort of globe, with sky above and sky below. In their eyes, day and night, punctuated by the movement of the planets, followed a circular, rotational movement. The symbol of the circle was

Circle, wheel

therefore invested with a special significance that related to the completeness of the world.

Furthermore, they used the lines formed by the successive points on the horizon where the sun rose and set day after day, throughout the year, to establish the exact boundaries of their own land and their own world. From then on, their world was delineated by straight lines and angles, beyond which was only the void, nothingness, the end of the world.

It is easy to see how and why the circle soon came to play a protective, magical and sacred role. Being inside the circle meant being inside life, being part of this world. Outside the square of the earth and beyond the circle of heaven lay the unknown. These boundaries were all the more frightening since, beyond them, you ran the risk of falling into the sky below where it was generally thought the kingdom of the dead was located.

This is admittedly a somewhat simplified explanation but it illustrates the point that, for many ancient civilizations and cultures, the definition of the circle always related to the feminine principle of heaven, while the square was attributed to the masculine principle of earth.

Because the square of the earth was located in the middle of the circle of heaven, they both had a common centre, since the concept of the circle always implies the concept of centre or a central point, which is also circular.

In order to understand the symbolic significance of the centre, it might help to try and follow the reasoning of our ancestors by considering the inescapable principle of physics involving the axis and the wheel. How could they even conceive of circular movement without focusing on a fixed point around which they saw certain external elements revolve, or around which they themselves turned or revolved? In this way they undoubtedly came to the gradual understanding that the centre was the point towards or around which all elements converged or revolved. It was for this reason that the dwelling of the clan or tribal chieftain had, very early on in history, been placed at the centre of the community.

By extension, the world could only be placed at the centre of the universe, since heaven was a circle. As human beings pursued their speculations over the ages, they developed the concept of the world as the centre of the universe, the primordial and ultimate point of convergence of all natural elements and phenomena.

And so the centre, more so than the circle, became a symbol of perfection, of the absolute and of unity – but this was unity rediscovered. In the words of Origen (c. 185–254), the most important theologian and biblical scholar of the early Greek church: 'Marvel not that we say these are within you. Understand that you are another world in miniature and that there is within you the sun, moon and the stars [...] Do you doubt that the sun and the moon are within you to whom it is said that you are "the light of the world"?' (Homily V, 2 in *Homilies on Leviticus 1–16*. Origen translated by Gary Wayne Barkley. (The Catholic University of America Press, 1990.)

It is tempting to think that it was by following this line of reasoning that human beings made the discovery that would revolutionize their social life and customs, namely the wheel. But was it really a discovery? In reality, it is far more likely to have been the skilful, practical and useful application of the living symbol of the circle in which the centre became an axis that enabled the circle to revolve. It was therefore no longer a question of everything revolving around the centre, but of the centre or axis of the world making the sun, moon, planets and stars revolve around the earth. The celestial wheel was therefore not a wheel turning uncontrollably and haphazardly in the void, but a wheel with an axis, i.e. the world.

But where did the celestial wheel come from and who or what made it turn on its axis? In the same way that it took the intelligence and hands of human beings to make the wheel, the celestial wheel also had to be driven. It needed some form of impetus, movement or traction to make it turn, but this could only be done by a supreme intelligence and a divine hand.

In the Buddhist religion, for example, the wheel is the symbol of Vairocana (the 'illuminator'), the central *cakravartin* buddha of the Five Celestial

Buddhas – one for the centre of the universe and the others for the four cardinal directions. Similarly, the wheel of the sun was believed to be turned by the hand of an all-powerful god. In this way, day and night followed one another as the sun pursued its course around the circle of the heavens, a rhythm paralleled by the succession of life and death as it followed its course around the square of the earth. Such is the great principle of the wheel of life, the magic wheel, the divinatory wheel of the ancient Egyptians, the wheel of rebirth or the Buddhist wheel of the law (*dhammacakka*).

Living, dying and being reborn – if not on earth, at least in another world – is the great principle of the wheel of fortune, the wheel of destiny or chance whose spokes are like the sun's rays.

Cloud

A cloud is first of all something that conceals or obscures the daylight, darkening day and making night seem blacker. It blots out the sun and moon – called the two lamps, because they light up the sky – and plunges the earth into darkness. Heavy black clouds were associated with bad omens, threatening danger or the anger of the gods, divine wrath being seen in storms, lightning and torrential rain falling from menacing clouds. However, swollen rain clouds were seen in a more beneficial light in times of drought, when shamans invoked the gods of rain and summoned clouds full of heaven's water, a symbol of fecundity, regeneration and life.

According to Egyptian legend, Thoth, the lunar god represented by an ibis-headed man, creator of time division and the calendar, played the role of the great divine scribe recording all the deeds of gods and mortals. He was also their messenger, bearing close similarities therefore to Hermes-Mercury (see *Mercury*, page 330). During a terrifying storm, Thoth obligingly moved the clouds, which represented the god Re's locks of hair and were obscuring the god's eye, and gently wiped away the tears blurring his vision. Accordingly, clouds represent both thunderbolts from heaven and its fertile, beneficial waters.

A dream in which dark clouds conceal the heavens can therefore be interpreted both in the light of an impending crisis or an imminent disruption that is about to change your life, and also as a sign of rebirth, creation or a long-awaited or promised birth. Last but not least, clouds can sometimes simply relate to something light, ethereal or unreal, as in the popular expressions: 'to have one's head in the clouds' or 'to be on cloud nine'. The first indicates a lack of attention or concentration, a tendency to daydream; the second refers to intense happiness or joy that leads to detachment from reality: both are valid interpretations of clouds appearing in a dream.

Clown

See Jester, page 289

Cockerel

The cockerel (or cock) is the male of the many different species of domestic fowl. Like the hen, it feeds on cereal grain such as wheat, corn, buckwheat and oats. Male chicks can be distinguished from female chicks by the spur – a horny projection just above the claws – that first appears as a sort of scale, becoming a slight protuberance at around five months and then growing as a spur from seven months onwards. However, male chicks are also covered in a very fine, yellowish down with small feathers appearing on their wings about ten days after hatching.

For the ancient Chinese, the cockerel was a solar animal and they chose it to represent the tenth sign of their zodiac. According to Chinese mythology, it was the crow of the celestial cockerel that punctuated the rising, zenith and setting of the sun, which was itself represented by a fiery cockerel.

The cockerel as the symbol of pride or arrogance, courage or cowardice, determination or presumption, is found throughout the ancient world. Because it crows at sunrise, the cockerel was also often regarded as a herald of the birth or rebirth of daylight and, symbolically, as the guardian of eternal life who told mortals of the other life to come.

Coffin

Although a coffin is not a particularly uplifting object to discuss, it is invested with major symbolic significance. It often appears in our dreams because it is one of the images associated with physical death, and is sufficiently impressive and disturbing for us to remember when we wake up. The more powerful the representation of certain symbols, the more vivid they are and the more likely to remain imprinted on our minds and etched on our memories, thus making it easier to interpret their meaning.

But it should always be remembered that we dream in the language of symbols and the presence of a coffin in a dream often represents something in our lives that should be buried, symbolically of course, and forgotten once and for all. It can equally well symbolize something we saw fit to conceal, that we thought was dead and buried, eliminated from our lives, when

in fact it wasn't. Since our dreams should rarely be taken at face value, dreaming about an empty coffin doesn't mean that you or someone close to you is about to die. It is more likely to predict the 'death' of a situation, a period in your life that is coming to an end and from which, for whatever reason, you find it difficult to extricate yourself.

Column

Originally, the column was probably a post made of wood or stone. During the Stone Age, human beings erected megaliths – stone columns arranged in such a way that their groupings are thought to have had an astronomical and sacred purpose. The most famous group of megaliths known to date is undoubtedly that of Stonehenge, located on Salisbury Plain, in Wiltshire, England. However, an identical structure thought to be around seven thousand years old has recently been found

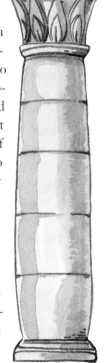

in Egypt, some 100 km (60 miles) from the famous site of Abu Simbel. It consists, primarily, of a circle of stone blocks arranged so as to indicate clearly two axes (north-south and east-west) that correspond exactly to the rising, zenith and setting of the sun on the day of the summer solstice. It therefore appears that the column has always been regarded as a form of link between heaven and earth, as well as a means of measuring time.

Furthermore, since the roofs of the earliest dwellings and the first temples were supported by wood and stone columns, by analogy the roof of the world (or heaven) must also be supported by one or more columns. The symbolism of the column is therefore not only related to that of the mountain (see *Mountain*, page 348), but also to that of the tree of life (see *Tree of life*, page 498).

Thus, when a column features prominently in a dream, it is important to take account of its association with the axis, the link between heaven and earth (i.e. the relationship between the energies that are constantly moving upwards and downwards within us), its role as a support and prop and, of course, its association with the tree as a symbolic representation of man

(see *Tree of life*, page 498) and also with the spinal column. A column can refer to or represent all these things. If a column collapses in a dream, it is obviously not a particularly good sign. On the other hand, if you are looking at or erecting a column, it is often the precursor of a remarkable personal success.

Compass

The compass is to the circle what the set-square is to the square. In other words, you use a compass to draw a circle and a set-square to draw a square.

For many ancient cultures, the circle represented heaven, a feminine principle associated with the spirit, while the square represented earth, a masculine principle associated with matter. The compass, which forms a circle, can therefore be regarded as a symbol of the spirit, while the set-square, which forms a square, can be regarded as a symbol of matter.

In ancient Egypt, where heaven was represented by the sky-goddess Nut and earth by the earth-god Geb, the compass and the set-square played a key role. They were used as instruments of measurement by the architects who built the pyramids,

Compass

but were also associated with the divine laws and principles governing the universe.

Without these instruments, Imhotep (*fl. c.* 2975 BC), the architect of the 3rd-Dynasty pharaoh Djoser (*c.* 2668–2649 BC), would not have been able to design and build the famous 'step pyramid' at Saqqara. The structure was an innovation for its time and an architectural feat in its own right. Not only did it use stone rather than mud-brick, but it was also the first step pyramid and, as such, the prototype for the distinctive pyramidal shape that evoked the ascension of the soul of the dead pharaoh and its union with the celestial and divine powers.

The compass is also one of the symbols of the Masonic brotherhoods, which evolved from the mediaeval guilds of stonemasons and cathedral builders. Although the first of these guilds was not established until AD 643, they appear to have been inspired by architects of the Temple of Solomon in Jerusalem, built in 957 BC. The men and materials for its construction were supplied by Hiram of Tyre, but it could not have been built without the plans drawn up by the architects who, like Imhotep, must have used a compass and a set-square. Thus the historical origins of the Masonic brotherhoods and their admiration for these early architects is presumably why they adopted one of the tools of their trade as a symbol. While it is not our intention to trace the history of freemasonry, it seems appropriate to refer to it within the context of the symbolism of the compass.

This is borne out by the fact that, in a dream, a compass not only refers to ideas of measure, rule, rectitude, exactitude, precise and well-defined limits, and boundaries to be delineated, prescribed and never overstepped, but it also represents a group of individuals, a body of people who will play or have already played a role in the dreamer's life.

Finally, the appearance of a compass in a dream implies a call to intellect rather than other resources to resolve any potential problems. It also symbolizes a long-term project that will need to be patiently worked out and realized.

Cosmogonies: ancient and modern

From the big bang theory of the origins of life, via the creation of the stars, modern man scans the universe in search of a beginning before the beginning of time. Why do human beings have this propensity for wanting to find out about their origins, for wanting everything to have a beginning? Is it simply because they are born and die that they need at all costs to tell a story that begins and ends with them? From the dawn of reason, humans appear to have been preoccupied with beginnings and origins. This inevitably raises the question as to when they began to think and reflect. When did they realize that they were different from other species, that they had a memory and the ability and means to transfer this memory, that the memory of every individual could be transmitted to the memory of others? In this way, mankind is able to defy time and death because we continue to live in the memory of our fellow human beings after death.

Universal gravitation and the big bang theory. It is not our intention to list the many discoveries and theories made and advanced by modern scientists, especially astrophysicists, worldwide. Suffice it to say that these discoveries and theories relate to the universe, its beginning, the creation of the solar system, the appearance of the earth and the origins of life on our planet which, incidentally, we are rather too inclined to treat like a vast rubbish dump by burying our nuclear waste, using the sea to swill out the holds of the monstrous oil tankers that sail back and forth across the oceans delivering the precious fuel with which we are gradually polluting the air we breathe with increasing difficulty.

For the past hundred years or so, each decade has seen a new theory on the origins and structure of the universe. However, one of these theories, advanced in 1920, proved more enduring and is now widely accepted. It certainly seems to appeal to the collective consciousness of the men and women who populate the planet and constitute contemporary civilizations. This is the famous big bang theory, based on another theory that is now accepted as a certainty – Sir Isaac Newton's law of universal gravitation, which states that every particle of matter in the universe attracts every other particle with a force that is proportional to the product of their masses and inversely proportional to the square of the distance between their centres.

According to the big bang theory, an initial and original explosion, caused by a 'primordial atom' containing an extremely high concentration of energy, led to the appearance and subsequent development of the universe. A number of radio-astronomical observations appear to confirm this theory, while other scientists and researchers have advanced theories that either coincide with or oppose it. One thing is certain, however – and this is a phenomenon that can be observed from Earth – depending on the angle and direction from which you observe it, the universe does not always have the same appearance. In scientific terms, the universe is not isotropic. However, the main point of this introduction is to stress that the big bang theory – certain radio astronomers claim to have 'heard' and recorded this 'big bang' somewhere on the outer edges of the cosmos, using highly sensitive equipment – echoes the creation myths and cosmogonies of ancient civilizations. These cosmogonies, which were in their time undoubtedly transpositions or adaptations of

much earlier beliefs and visions of the world, prove that, from very early on in their history, human beings have been preoccupied with their origins.

After the initial explosion or 'big bang', a sort of cosmic 'ball' seems to have appeared and gradually cracked open, giving rise to the first galaxies. Subsequently, and still in accordance with the principle of universal gravitation, vast nebulae – clouds of particles and gases – appeared, were fragmented and concentrated to their highest intensity, and gave rise to the first stars in the entire universe. In short, according to the big bang theory,

The universe according to Hildegard von Bingen.

matter (the universe) was born of energy (the 'primordial atom') some 10 or 20 billion years ago – the figure is vague since, at this stage of the Earth's history, time is immeasurable.

From the myth of the creation to the first second of the universe. In the past, the story of creation was purely a matter of faith, or, to be more precise, the story of the progressive or simultaneous creation of the world, life and man, according to beliefs that appear to date from the dawn of time, was handed down from generation to generation. Nowadays, the same story is explained in terms of theories but, on closer examination, nothing much has really changed. For example, the big bang theory – although couched in different terms, using different points of reference and technical measures that our ancestors wouldn't have understood or even regarded as

useful or necessary (can we be sure that they are?) – is incredibly similar to the myth of the cosmic egg found, in different forms, in the cosmogonies, myths and legends of many ancient peoples. Similarly, the primordial chaos described in the Greek, Chinese, Egyptian and Indian cosmogonies in particular, the great ancestor of the Chinese and the autogenous (self-engendering) demiurge of the Egyptians, are all reminiscent of the cosmic 'ball' that cracked open to form the galaxies and the famous 'primordial atom' that produced the big bang (see *Cosmogonies in China, in Egypt, in Greece* and *in India*, pages 111–122).

In spite of a nostalgia for their past that seems to haunt them, human beings are inclined to regard their contemporary beliefs as the definitive and enduring truth. Our modern times and civilizations are no exception to this tendency. Nowadays, we don't talk about cosmogony but about cosmology. In the eyes of today's men and women, especially scientists, a cosmogony is a theory that attempts to explain the creation of the universe while cosmology is a science in its own right, whose aim is to seek and, if possible, to find and explain the general laws that govern and structure the universe.

The universe according to NASA.

Cosmogonies in China

Chinese myths and legends about the creation of the world and the beginning of time echo those of other cosmogonies (see pages 108–110 and 114–131). On closer examination, it becomes apparent that these myths of initial chaos, of the creation of heaven and earth long before human beings existed, of the creation of the first humans from clay, of the primordial couple, of the great flood and a hero who has a number of points in common with Noah and the 'super-sage' (see *Noah's Ark*, page 359 and *Flood*, page 188) are found in the Chinese cosmogony. The Chinese myths may be in an original and unique form, different from that of the stories passed on by word of mouth or inscribed on tablets, but they are basically the same, thereby proving that, in ancient times and even earlier, Middle- and Far-Eastern cultures had a more or less similar view, give or take a few details, of the creation of the world and of life on earth. From this it can be deduced that, even if the peoples of the world do not share common roots and origins, their paths have certainly crossed and given them the opportunity to exchange ideas, beliefs, visions and fears of the world and life, long before the development of the communications equipment and technology that now enables us to connect and make contact with each other from anywhere in the world.

The mother-creator of humanity. According to a popular Chinese legend, of which a written form can be traced to the second millennium BC but which probably dates from much earlier, heaven and earth were created long before human beings existed. However, the great mother-creator, Nu Kua, existed, so how was she born, where did she come from and who was she? The legend gives none of these details. It seems it is enough for us to know what she did and the role she played in the creation of the world by fashioning mortals from yellow earth, the earth of China. However, the legend goes on to say that earth alone was not the ideal material or the one best suited to this purpose so, after fashioning a few mortals from yellow earth, she created the rest out of clay. This explains why there are two sorts of mortals on earth – the 'nobles' made from yellow earth and the 'lowly' made from clay.

The demiurge born of chaos. Another legend, earlier than or contemporary with the legend of Nu Kua, tells of the appearance of an extraordinary, supernatural being who was not divine in the sense understood by Western religions and mystical traditions, but was rather an inconceivable and intangible demiurge, able to adopt the traits and appearance of a typically human hero. He was part-god,

has a number of points in common with the divine Egyptian trilogy formed by Shu (the air) and his offspring Nut (the sky) and Geb (the earth) (see *Cosmogonies in Egypt*, page 114), with the noticeable difference that for the ancient Egyptians, the sky was female and the earth male. In Chinese mythology, it was the appearance

part-demon, part-man and, like so many Chinese heroes, was invested with every kind of power. This mythical hero, P'an Ku, was born out of a chaos that resembled an egg in which he had lived for eighteen thousand years, and was therefore the first living being to emerge from chaos. His birth, as described in this ancient legend,

of the sky (or heaven), born of the pure male elements (*yang*), and the earth, produced by the pure female elements (*yin*), that resulted in the birth of P'an Ku. Initially, he was sometimes identified with the *yang* elements of the sky, and sometimes with the primordial *yin* principles of the earth, but he was always located somewhere between the two, continuously imbued with their qualities and gradually transformed until he finally became himself. In other words, P'an Ku, the first human being, emerged from chaos and was born at the same time as the sky (heaven) and the earth. As he was transformed and finally revealed as a living being, the sky gradually rose higher and higher above the earth, until they were separated and in the position they occupy today, with the sky, according to the legend, perceived as infinitely high and the earth as infinitely deep.

The creation myth of P'an Ku. The creation myth of P'an Ku is of comparatively late origin. It is thought to date from the 4th century AD and to have been brought from Siam by emissaries returning to China in the 6th century. It was not incorporated into the *Wai chi* by Liu Shu until the 11th century. (*A Dictionary of Chinese Mythology*, E.T.C. Werner, Kelly & Walsh Ltd, 1932.) The myth of P'an Ku follows on from the legend outlined above and provides additional information reminiscent of the creation myth of the Bible (see *Cosmogonies in Israel*, page 123). According to this account, in the beginning, there was P'an Ku, the Chinese equivalent of Yahweh. P'an Ku is in fact the 'great ancestor' of the 'ten thousand beings' who populate the universe. Although P'an Ku was the creator of all life, he had to sacrifice himself and die in order to create the world since it was from his body that the world was created. His head became the sacred T'ai Shan mountain, his eyes the sun and the moon, his blood the rivers and seas, and the hair on his head and body the trees and plants of the earth. The wind was born of his breath, thunder of his voice and lightning of his eyes.

However, there is every reason to believe that the myth of P'an Ku may be based on an earlier myth, since a text of obscure origin, dating from the 3rd century AD, appears to identify Lao Tzu – the Chinese philosopher, accredited author of the *Tao Te Ching* and contemporary of Confucius (*fl.* 6th century BC) – with P'an Ku. According to this text, 'Lao Tzu deified' created heaven and earth before being transformed … his left eye became the sun, his right eye the moon, his head the K'un Lun mountains, his hair the stars, his bones dragons, his flesh quadrupeds, his intestines serpents, his belly the seas, his fingers the five sacred peaks, his body hair plants and his heart Hua Kai mountain – *Lao-tzu Hua-hu ching* ('Lao Tzu's conversion of the barbarians').

Cosmogonies in Egypt

According to the ancient Egyptians, Atum, Khnum, Khepri, Amun and Sobek were all representations of the same demiurge and creator of the world. Why does the human mind require everything to have a beginning and an end? It may quite simply be that human beings are not particularly objective and can only see and experience the world and what they have made it partially and subjectively. In other words, the human mind can only apprehend the universe and the concept of creation in terms of its own reference points.

Because human beings are born on a particular day, they therefore consider it logical that 'their' world was also created at a given point in time. To our early ancestors, it seemed reasonable that, if human beings had a mother, the world should have one too, a great mother from whose womb the world in which they lived suddenly emerged from the void, from chaos, from nothingness. And if there was a mother who gave birth to the world, there must also be a father to beget it.

For a long time, human speculation did not venture beyond the mythical mother and father. For although the cleverness and resourcefulness of the human mind is a constant source of amazement – for instance, facilitating the reproduction or imitation, sometimes in an extremely complex manner and sometimes very simply, of the phenomena and wonders of the natural world – it often remains limited when confronted with creative ideas and abstract perceptions. There is a barrier that its thought processes, sophisticated as they may be, simply cannot surmount. To prevent ourselves from becoming totally disorientated – i.e. so as not to become the victims of a sort of existential angst that would 'destructure' our minds or conscious selves and endanger our powers of reasoning, analysis and synthesis – we have opted for an acceptable interpretation of the world, governed by a fairly consistent order and logic of life, and laws and rules that are relatively unchanging and coherent. But in order to place ourselves within this well-organized system, it must have a beginning and an end and must therefore have been created at a particular point in time.

The demiurge and creator of the world in the mythology of ancient Egypt. In Egypt, this famous beginning was represented by a great autogenous (self-engendering) demiurge. If you are tempted to say or even think it is absurd to believe that a being, anterior and superior to everything that exists, could have engendered itself, created itself from nothing, and then created the universe in all its glory and complexity, just pause and reflect for a moment. For not only is it not absurd but, to coin a phrase, it took some thinking about, especially when no one had yet conceived of it. How old is this belief in the probable existence of a demiurge? It is impossible to say, but it certainly dates from before the birth of the Egyptian civilization since there is no doubt that its founders were inspired by earlier beliefs. However, what is interesting about the concept of the primary demiurge – which appeared towards the

end of the fourth millennium BC, during the first pharaonic dynasty (3100–2890 BC) – is that it seems to provide the inspiration for the concept of the one and only god, invisible but omnipresent, on which all monotheistic religions are based, not least of these being the worship of Yahweh, which, thanks to Moses or Moshe – who, as everyone knows was as much a Hebrew as an Egyptian – would become the most representative.

The different representations of the great demiurge. Although the concept of the demiurge remained constant over the centuries, through changing beliefs and shifting centres of power, in fact throughout the long history of a civilization that lasted for some three thousand years, he assumed various forms in the eyes of the ancient Egyptians. However, it was Re, the supreme god, represented by the sun, who won the day, since all demiurges were sooner or later assimilated with him.

Then there was Atum – 'he who came into being of himself' – who begat the first divine couple, Shu and Tefnut. Shu was the personification of air, the primordial atmosphere, the space between heaven and earth, without which mortals could not breathe or live, while Tefnut was the personification of moisture, the water without which mortals could not live here on earth. On reflection, it is quite extraordinary that long before science would prove that life on earth would have been impossible without air or water, our great and distant ancestors already accepted the fact as a foregone conclusion. It was therefore Shu (air) and Tefnut (moisture) who formed the primordial couple and in turn begat Nut (the sky), the roof of the world, and Geb (the earth), the floor of the world.

According to the myths of Heliopolis, Shu and Tefnut were born of the seminal fluid ejaculated by Atum-Re as he copulated with himself,

or of his spittle or his tears – his sperm, spittle and tears being none other than the sun's rays.

Then there was Khnum, the procreator god, the origin of all life on earth – often depicted as a man with a ram's head – who fashioned with his hands a child, the first man, and then made all men on his potter's wheel.

Then there was Khepri, the sacred scarab or dung beetle, also know as 'he who came into being of himself', probably since, in early times, he was regarded as a manifestation of Atum. Khepri – the Egyptian *kheperer* meant 'insect' and *kheper* 'creation' or 'renaissance' – was the creator of the universe. He engendered the world, life, the gods and mortals by undergoing a permanent transformation of his own substance and existence. He therefore became the symbol of eternal resurrection, metamorphosis and immortality.

Then there was Amun, the great Theban god, the most human of the Egyptian demiurges since he was depicted as a man with a blue body, representing the celestial vault, accompanied by his wife and son. His wife Mut, the mother-goddess of Egypt, was usually represented with a vulture skin on her head. This was because she was assimilated with Nekhbet, the great vulture-goddess, a bird of prey with undeniable maternal qualities (see *Moon*, page 342, and *Vulture*, page 523). Their son Khons was a moon god and for this reason was known as the 'traveller', a reference to the moon's course across the sky. According to this myth, the moon, a masculine divinity, was born of the union of Amun-Re (the sun) and Mut (the earth).

Finally, there was Sobek, the crocodile god and creator of the world. But he was a fearful, voracious and fierce god, equally capable of creating or devouring his progeny, of both giving and taking life.

Cosmogonies in Greece

Since the Renaissance, the thinking, philosophy and ideology that formed the foundations of Greek civilization have had a significant impact on western scientific and political thought. Greek literature, sculpture and architecture have also fired the European imagination, in spite of the interdictions imposed by the Church, which did its utmost to ensure that Greek art and learning were obscured, censored, pushed aside and forgotten. The Romans – and later the nations of Europe, and even the world – were greatly inspired by the Greek model, to the point of adopting its democratic system, parliamentary assemblies and senate.

However, for some time historians have been looking at Greek civilization rather more critically, and this has led them to examine its origins a little more closely.

It was primarily by studying and analysing the tales and legends of Greek mythology and tracing them to their source that it became apparent that Greek thinkers and artists drew much of their inspiration from the myths and beliefs of Mesopotamia, Egypt and possibly even certain primitive peoples and tribes of Africa.

The origins of Greek mythology. Greek mythology has exerted such a strong influence on Western cultures, notably influencing the thinking of philosophers, theologians, scientists and politicians, that it was for a long time believed to be the definitive mythological source. It is well known that myths and symbols, and their associated legends, form a constant in the history of the human race. They are found throughout the world, through the ages, albeit in different forms, but always telling more or less the same stories, recounting the same episodes, events and amazing happenings. However, the supremacy enjoyed by Greek mythology over the centuries must surely be due to the fact that it presents a well-constructed history of gods and mortals, with a strict divine hierarchy, using fantastical and spectacular tales that remain etched on our consciousness but, above all, echo human customs, weaknesses and emotions. The emotions and actions of the gods of Olympus are remarkably similar to those of ordinary mortals.

Freud and other psychoanalysts were not mistaken when they saw in Greek myths, if not the archetypes for all human behavioural reflexes and intellectual, moral and emotional habits, at least the moulds in which they were cast. In other words, the events that feature the great gods of Olympus are a sort of sublimation or exaggeration, depending on the case in point, of the more banal but no less dramatic or comical situations and circumstances encountered by ordinary mortals.

But to understand how the Greeks imagined the creation of the world, or more precisely their world, it should be remembered that theirs was a civilization that existed in an almost permanent state of war, and that the Greek people were on the whole racist, segregationist, elitist and barbarous. This may explain why their art was so rich, so highly developed and sophisticated, and why it aspired to perfection. In fact, this aspiration to beauty and aesthetic purity, and the idealism that underlies all Greek thought, might never have prevailed without the bloody and tormented history of the great Greek city-states.

The *Theogony* or Greek cosmogony according to Hesiod. The many similarities between the Sumerian, Akkadian, Egyptian and Hebrew creation myths (see *Cosmogonies in Mesopotamia*, page 126, *in Egypt*, page 114 and *in Israel*, page 125) and the Greek version of the creation of the world suggest that the Greek cosmogony drew its inspiration from these earlier myths and legends.

According to this version, in the beginning, there was not chaos, but Chaos, a personification of the absolute primordial void. Chaos begat the demon-god Erebus (darkness) and his sister-goddess Nyx (night) who in turn begat two offspring of their own

– the god Æther, the bright upper air, and the goddess Hemera (day). This is the Greek version of the creation myth according to the poet Hesiod (*fl. c.* 70 BC), who wrote the *Theogony*, a long poem describing the cosmogony or creation of the world in accordance with the beliefs of his time. (Recommended reading: *Theogony* and *Works and Days* in *Hesiod – Homeric Hymns – Epic Cycle – Homerica*, translated by Hugh G. Evelyn-White, Loeb Classical Library, Harvard University Press, 1998.) At this point in the creation of the world, earth and heaven did not exist. However, Nyx later begat – this time without the help of her brother Erebus – strange entities that would play a key role in the history of the gods of Olympus and, later, in the life of mortals. These entities included Eris (strife), the Hesperides ('daughters of evening'), Hypnos (sleep), the Keres (female death-spirits or warlike demons who accompanied heroes into battle), the Moerae or Fates (divine beings who determined the destiny of mortals), Momos (sarcasm), Moros (doom), Nemesis (divine retribution) and Philotes (tenderness).

It was after this that Uranus (heaven) and Gaia (earth) first made their appearance and subsequently begat countless offspring, the best known and most important being the six Titans and six Titanesses. One of the sisters, Rhea – who was the oldest divinity on earth and mother of the gods according to the Greeks – married her own brother Cronus (time) and gave birth to Zeus, who became the chief god of Olympus.

Cosmogonies in India

In Hindu mythology, there are several versions of the creation myth centred around Brahman and Maya. Brahman was a term that referred to the power (the 'absolute') behind all creation, personified by Brahma, the creator of the universe. Maya ('miraculous power') referred to the power that creates the illusion of the 'reality' we perceive, an illusion that is dispelled when we understand the universal reality of Brahman or the 'absolute'. The earliest scholarly texts in India were the four Vedas, the holy scriptures of ancient India, which, like the Bible, are a collection of historical, legendary, mythical and religious accounts. According to modern historical sources, they are thought to have been written towards the middle of the second millennium BC, which means that the first texts of the Vedas appeared at about the same time or just before the Code of Hammurabi, a collection of 282 administrative, political and religious case laws put together towards the end of the reign of Hammurabi (1792–1750 BC), the sixth Amorite king of Babylonia. The laws were inscribed on a stele that was placed in the temple of Marduk, the national god who was central to the code and one of the early examples of monotheism. The code also has links with the Bible in that it is now widely believed to have provided the inspiration for the Decalogue (Ten Commandments) of Moses, written at least five hundred years later. A glance at any map suggests that the possibility of common influences and sources is less than remote since the distances between Babylonia, Israel and India were not prohibitive. Furthermore, given the trading and commercial exchanges that existed in ancient times, it seems highly likely that there was an interchange of cultural influences between these three civilizations that would explain the similarities and parallels between the Code of Hammurabi and the Ten Commandments, and the accounts of the Vedas and the Bible.

The creation according to the Rig Veda. Taken as a whole, the texts that constitute the Vedas are roughly equivalent to six times the length of the texts contained in the Bible. They were collected together in four huge volumes that are simply known as the four Vedas. The Rig Veda ('Veda of verse') – so called because all the accounts contained in it are written in verse – is the most recent of the four Vedas and contains the following Creation Hymn (Nāsadīya):

> 'There was neither non-existence
> nor existence then;
> there was neither the realm
> of space
> nor the sky which is beyond.
> What stirred?
> Where?
> In whose protection?
> Was there water, bottomlessly deep?
> There was neither death
> nor immortality then.
> There was no distinguishing sign
> of night nor of day.
> That one breathed, windless,
> by its own impulse.
> Other than that there was
> nothing beyond.'
>
> The Rig Veda, An Anthology,
> 108 hymns translated by
> Wendy Doniger O'Flaherty,
> Penguin Books, 1981, p.25.

Reading this hymn, it is impossible not to compare it with the Mesopotamian *Enuma Elish* (see *Cosmogonies in Mesopotamia*, page 126), on the one hand, and with the Yahwist account in Genesis (see *Cosmogonies in Israel*, page 123), on the other. Another hymn from the Rig Veda relating to the creation of the world – 'The Hymn of Man' or *Purusa-Sūkta* – is reminiscent of the Chinese creation myth of P'an Ku, the great ancestor of the 'ten thousand beings' who populate the universe (see *Cosmogonies in China*, page 111):

> 'The Man has a thousand heads,
> a thousand eyes, a thousand feet.
> He pervaded the earth on all sides
> and extended beyond it as far as
> ten fingers.
>
> It is the Man who is all this,
> whatever has been and whatever
> is to be.
> He is the ruler of immortality,
> when he grows beyond every-
> thing through food.'
>
> The Rig Veda, An Anthology,
> 108 hymns translated by
> Wendy Doniger O'Flaherty,
> Penguin Books, 1981, p.30.

As can be seen from the above hymn, there was also a Great Ancestor in India. This was Purusha, primordial or 'cosmic man', original, eternal and supreme, whom the Hindus perceived as the beginning and the end of everything – the 'absolute'.

Brahman and Maya or supreme reality and absolute illusion. Rather than becoming submerged in the myriad hymns and accounts of the creation of the world that abound in the four Vedas, we will 'cut a long story short' and focus on two myths of paramount importance in a religious culture with such a vast pantheon. These myths involve Maya and Brahman – not to be confused with Brahma, the creator god, the superior divinity of the Trimurti or Hindu trinity (roughly the equivalent of the Christian trinity), composed of Brahma, Vishnu (the 'pervader' or 'sustainer') and Shiva (the 'auspicious one'). According to the Hindu concept of the construction of the world, Brahman and Maya are the personifications of being and non-being. They have no equivalent in the cosmogonies, beliefs and religions of other peoples and civilizations of the ancient world, apart from the later concepts of the Jewish cabbalistic tradition. Like *aleph*, the first letter-number of the Hebrew alphabet that forms the cabbalistic code, Brahman is a principle that cannot be formulated or fixed by thought, or defined in any way. It is therefore an inconceivable concept that exists without existing, but which has to be explained nonetheless. Thus Brahman is the beginning and end of all things but also exists before the beginning and has no end. It is unchanging and impermanent, as absolute being, supreme conscience and total reality beyond which nothing exists. According to the Hindus, it is through the concept of Brahman that Maya has been fabricated– the illusion of the world or the world of the illusions created by our imagination – to give the world body, substance and multiplicity of form. Maya is the world of illusions and appearances, the

illusion that causes Brahman to appear in the form of the universe or, from a subjective point of view, the illusion that causes us to see Brahman in the form of the world. Thus, Brahman and Maya are continuously created at each moment or, to be more precise, are in a state of permanent creation, since one is the supreme reality of non-being (i.e. of that which does not exist) and the other the absolute illusion of being (i.e. of all that exists).

Cosmogonies in Israel

It is impossible to discuss the creation myth according to Israel without referring to Genesis, the first book of the Bible. It is now generally accepted that the compilers of the Bible fused two accounts of the creation of the world in Genesis, which opens the Old Testament. But the biblical account of creation is much more than a myth, it is a religious conviction deeply rooted in the minds of Jews and Christians worldwide, since both faiths refer to the teachings of the Old Testament.

The Bible therefore combines two accounts of creation. The older Yahwist account is believed to date from the 10th century BC, and is so-called as it refers to Yahweh, the personal name given to God by the Israelites, while the more recent Elohist account, believed to date from the 8th century BC, uses the general name for God, El or Elohim. Elohim was referred to by the Hebrews as 'man on high' as opposed to Adam who was 'man below'.

The first day of the creation of the world according to Jewish legend. Before embarking upon an analysis of the Yahwist and Elohist accounts of the creation and identifying what they have in common and where they differ, it is worth looking at another account whose distant origins may have been contemporary with but are more likely to have been earlier than the Yahwist and Elohist texts. The account of the first day of the creation of the world according to Jewish legend opens with the following lines: 'On the first day of creation, God produced ten things: the heavens and the earth, Tohu and Bohu, light and darkness, wind and water, the duration of the day and the duration of the night.' (*The Legends of* *the Jews*, Vol. 5, 'From the Creation to Exodus', Louis Ginzberg, translated from the German by Henrietta Szold, The Jewish Publication Society of America, 1937.)

These 'ten things' that 'God produced' according to this legend are extremely interesting since, as they are listed here, it becomes apparent that the heavens and the earth, the celestial vault and the terrestrial earth, were created simultaneously, as were light and darkness, wind and water, the duration of the day and the duration of the night, i.e. time. In other words, heaven, earth, the four elements – fire, earth, air and water – and time were all created on the same day, in this instance on the first day of creation. Tohu and Bohu, also created on the first day, were the terms used by the Hebrews to designate the original chaos from which the creation emerged, according to the Elohist account of the creation, which was chosen as the opening text of the Bible, even though it was written after the Yahwist text.

The Yahwist account of the creation. Rather than follow the order in which they appear in the Bible, we will consider the Yahwist and Elohist accounts of the creation in the order in which they were written. On reading the earlier Yahwist text, it is immediately obvious that the opening lines have a number of points in common with the first lines of the *Enuma*

Elish, the great Babylonian creation myth (see *Cosmogonies in Mesopotamia*, page 126). This is hardly surprising when you bear in mind that, historically, the culture of Israel was greatly influenced by those of Sumer, Akkad, Babylonia and Chaldea.

The Yahwist account states that '… the Lord God made the earth and the heavens, and every plant of the field before it was in the earth, and every herb of the field before it grew: for the Lord God had not caused it to rain upon the earth, and there was not a man to till the ground' (Genesis 2: 4–5), so the world was virgin earth or desert.

The Elohist account of the creation. The opening phrase of the Elohist account is also the opening phrase of the Bible. It echoes the text referred to above but also provides additional information: 'In the beginning Elohim [God] created the heaven and the earth. And the earth was without form, and void; and darkness was upon the face of the deep. And the Spirit of Elohim [God] moved upon the face of the waters…' (Genesis 1: 1–3).

With regard to this famous 'In the beginning …', it should be noted that, according to the cabbalistic interpretation, it is a rendering of *Bereshith*, the first Hebrew word of the Torah, an untranslatable term which for the cabbalists sums up the entire tradition of the Torah. It is, however, possible to read *Bereshith* as *Brit-Esh* ('covenant of fire'), a symbolic and archetypical representation of life, the source and origin of all life. But, here again, the meaning is lost in translation and cannot be perceived and interpreted in terms of its original significance.

However, it is interesting to note that, while the earlier, Yahwist account of the creation seems to have derived from the more poetic and legendary oral tradition, the Elohist account, which opens the Bible, is more in the style of a formal document. It is therefore not unreasonable to assume that it was written at the time of transition from the oral to the written tradition, a major turning point in the history of humanity. It was also a time when religious scholars and writers felt the need to protect the hidden and initiatory meaning of the words, method and tradition preserved by the cabbalists over the centuries and millennia. Furthermore, in the first paragraph of the Yahwist account, there is an immediate reference to man, albeit to say that he did not exist, while in the Elohist account, there is no mention of man until the tenth paragraph, when he appears in the person of Adam.

Cosmogonies in Mesopotamia

In the great and ancient civilization of Mesopotamia – which was almost certainly the cradle of Western civilization and whose culture, attitudes and beliefs are still echoed by the Western way of life and thought – the cosmogonies or creation myths, common to all structured societies and civilizations, were initially noticeable by their absence.

It appears that the inhabitants of Mesopotamia, '(the land) between rivers', from the Greek *mesopotamia*, the Sumerians and, later, the Akkadians, who formed the famous independent city-states, were not particularly concerned about when and how the world was created. It was only with the arrival of the Babylonians, during the second half of the second millennium BC, that a very elaborate creation myth appeared, in the form of the famous *Enuma Elish*, which tells how the universe was created by the primordial couple engendered by Tiamat (the primeval salt water) and Apsu (the primeval sweet water).

The Sumerian creation myth. This emerging civilization, with its extensive pantheon, dates from the fifth millennium BC. The Sumerians, of obscure origin, and the indigenous Semites (the Akkadians) lived in a state of alternate harmony and opposition. The population was probably too bound up in the present, in the organization of their increasingly large, structured and autonomous primitive villages, to try and conceive of the world, their world, before its creation. It is also quite likely that, as people acquired the means to control nature, they felt the need to justify their actions. It was as if, by acting in this way, they had unleashed disorder in a world that had previously seemed perfectly harmonious and coherent.

Thus, according to the Sumerians, the creation of the world was the result of a rupture and a separation. An (the sky) and Ki (the earth), originally united, were torn apart and An pulled upwards and Ki downwards. This separation was caused by the disruptive and untimely intervention of Enlil ('lord of the wind') who represented the power of nature. Although Enlil was born of An and Ki, he was also regarded as an extraneous factor, an intruder.

Thus, the wind or atmosphere created the order of the world as we know it today with the sky above and the earth beneath, and the wind or atmosphere, a divisive factor, between the two. But Enlil was not alone. He had a companion named Enki ('lord of the earth'), lord of Apsu and 'master of destiny', who provided the earth with the water it required for life. For this reason, Enki became the primordial and principal god of Sumer, since he was regarded as the organizer of the world, pragmatic and tangible and in no way mystical, with attitudes and behaviour similar to those of a man going about his daily business. Through his words, gestures, thoughts and actions, Enki was the origin of all that was created, of mortals and of civilization.

The Akkadian and Babylonian creation myth. The most beautiful and most explicit creation myth in the Akkadian cosmogony, which succeeded the Sumerian cosmogony, is found in the famous text that Assyriologists have agreed to call 'the epic of the creation', but which was originally known by the first words of the account: *'Enuma Elish ...'* ('When on high ...') (see page 128).

It appears that this early text was inscribed, in cuneiform writing, on seven tablets of 150 lines each. In the early 19th century, a great many dispersed fragments were found that made it possible to reconstruct the complete poem. These various fragments dated from the 9th to

2nd centuries BC, but it is widely believed that the *Enuma Elish* was written at the beginning of the second millennium BC. This means that it predates the Sumerian version of the beginning of time outlined above.

After an introduction that gives an account of the creation of the world, the poem primarily centres around the epic combat between Marduk and Tiamat. Marduk – who probably provided the inspiration for the Greek god Zeus and the Roman god Jupiter (see *Jupiter*, page 293) – was not only the elected champion of all the gods, but also a god himself and saviour of the world. Tiamat was a great primeval divinity surrounded by a cohort of terrifying monsters and demons. As a result of their magnificent and titanic combat, the order of the world, embodied by Marduk, emerged from original chaos, represented by Tiamat.

According to the *Enuma Elish*, Marduk killed Tiamat by piercing her stomach with a deadly arrow. He then cut her body – in the form of a huge fish that covered heaven and earth – in two halves; one half became the celestial vault and the star-studded sky, while the other became the earth. Thus Marduk enabled the world to emerge from its original chaos and estab-

> ## The opening lines of the Enuma Elish
>
> The First Tablet
>
> *'When in the height heaven was not named,*
>
> *And the earth beneath did not yet bear a name,*
>
> *And the primeval Apsu, who begat them,*
>
> *And chaos, Tiamat, the mother of them both*
>
> *Their waters were mingled together,*
>
> *And no field was formed, no marsh was to be seen ...'*
>
> Enuma Elish, The Epic of Creation, translated by L.W. King (from The Seven Tablets of Creation, London 1902).

lish order, rules and unchanging, universal laws. Then, like the Sumerian god Enki ('lord of the earth'), he gave Anu, the first mortal, the tablets of destiny, the Anutu, or the talisman of supreme power. According to this account, therefore, as the universe emerged from chaos – due to the benign and magnificent intervention of a saviour god – and man was created, the latter received the keys of his destiny from the hands of Marduk, the supreme god, and became master of that destiny.

Cosmogonies in Tibet

Why devote this last article on cosmogonies to Tibet rather than a European people such as the Celts, who had their own vision of the beginning of time and the creation of the world? Quite simply, because Tibet – whose culture and traditions are, as everyone knows, currently being subsumed by China – is a world apart. Known as the 'roof of the world', Tibet forms a natural frontier between China and India, two very different civilizations in terms of habits and customs. But, historically speaking, it also lies at the crossroads between the East, the Far East and Europe and, as well as being influenced by China and India, was also affected by the cultures of central Asia, Iran and central Europe.

The Tibetan account of the origins of the magic and mystery of the world. In spite of the influences of the Indian and Chinese Buddhistic traditions, the Tibetans were able to preserve and subscribe to a very particular form of Buddhism, a singular cosmic and cosmogonic vision of the world in which the belief in reincarnation played an important role. According to the ancient Tibetans, the visible and invisible worlds were closely linked and formed three super-imposed levels. In the centre were human beings who lived in close contact with the mythical beings known as gNyan, spirits who inhabited trees and stones, and bTsan, demons who lived in the air. These supernatural beings are similar to the concept of genies in Eastern cultures and angels in the West. However, these Tibetan spirits were definitely not benign. Above them, in the sky, lived the gods of light, or 'white gods', the Lha, and below them, in the underworld, lived the Klu, demons in the form of bluish-black serpents.

This appears to have been the original structure of the world as perceived by the ancient Tibetans, before Buddhism appeared in the region in the mid-7th century, when the Tibetan king Srong-brtsan-sgam-po (*c.* 627–650) converted to the faith on the advice of his two queens – the Chinese and Nepalese princesses Wen-Cheng and Tri-Tsun – who were early patrons of the religion. Thus Buddhism replaced the indigenous Bon religion of Tibet, whose shamanistic rites and beliefs were based on a desire for ecstatic communion with the great forces of nature, the elements and the visible and invisible worlds.

The esoteric tradition that preceded Buddhism in Tibet is recorded in the *Bon-po* (the 'pure book of the 100,000 serpents'), the first version of which is thought to date from around the 8th century AD, shortly after Buddhism appeared in Tibet. It was as if there was a need on the part of certain religious scholars and writers to record and preserve the beliefs and traditions that were about to disappear as they were supplanted by the Buddhist faith. According to the texts of the *Bon-po*: 'In the beginning, creation was not created. And this creation was called "existence"; it was so called, and yet there was no intermediate space [between heaven and earth]. There was nothing tangible. There was neither reality nor symbol. Since [this world] had neither the nature of existence, nor the nature of non-existence, it was called "the potential world" and all that exists, all that is visible came from [this world].' (Translation of extracts from the *Bon-po*, cited by Ariane Macdonald, in *La création du monde au Tibet*, éditions du Seuil, 1949.)

The great ancestor. The text goes on to describe a mythical figure who has several obvious points in common with the Hebrew God Yahweh and the Chinese demiurge P'an Ku (see *Cosmogonies in Israel*, page 123 and *in China*, page 111): 'A man with a prodigious capacity for metamorphosis was created [first]. He gave himself a name. He took the name "master of the potential world, pure conqueror". Then, since the master of the potential world had power over all that existed, he experienced great joy.' (Translation of extracts from the *Bon-po*, cited by Ariane Macdonald, *op. cit.*) This mythical figure of the great ancestor continued to exist after Buddhism had made its appearance in Tibet. However, whereas the 'master of the potential world, pure conqueror' of the *Bon-po* had emerged from chaos, from the subterranean forces and the lower level of the world, according to the ancient Tibetan cosmogony, the great ancestor who subsequently intervened was the 'son of heaven'. He had therefore been chosen by the celestial gods to come down to earth among mortals and become their king. He did this by sliding down the magic rope linking heaven and earth and landing on the 'mountain of the gods'.

The myth of the appearance of the first man on earth according to the Tibetan cosmogony led certain writers, especially during the first half of the 20th century, to believe they had discovered accounts of the intervention of extraterrestrials who were responsible for the appearance of the first human beings on earth. There is no great leap of imagination required to identify the great ancestor or 'son of heaven' – who descended from the sky on the rope of the dMu (supernatural beings who lived in heaven) and landed on the 'mountain of the gods' – as an extraterrestrial.

However, it is worth pointing out that belief in extra-terrestrial visitations appeared and grew in the minds of modern men and women the more they rejected the ancient myths and the close links with the great forces of the nature established by their ancestors. In other words, having lost all real and physical contact with the won-drous and the fantastic, and unable to feel the emotions that had elevated their forebears to the level of the gods and enabled them to experience the sacred, the exceptional and primordial, modern men and women invented other supernatural beliefs. They now interpret ancient myths, whose meaning they no longer understand, from the point of view of their present beliefs. The belief in extraterres-trials is therefore a modern myth (see page 171).

Crane

Since the transformation of many European marshes into fields, the crane has tended to abandon Western Europe to spend the summer in Scandinavia and Russia, migrating to Africa, India and China for the winter. The crane is a large, long-necked 'wader' of the family *Gruidae* (order *Gruiformes*), whose long legs enable it to wade through shallow pools and marshes. It is a monogamous bird (it mates for life) and is renowned for its spectacular mating displays. Couples build a nest of rushes and reeds, usually in the centre of the marshes. In May, the female lays two eggs and she and the male take it in turns to sit on the nest until the eggs hatch about a month later. The best-known species is the common crane (*Grus grus*) with its characteristic long feathers. Cranes feed on plants and seeds, as well as insects and worms. Their piercing and somewhat sad cry evokes the sound of a trumpet. Apart from the fact that it was often associated with a rather slow-witted, gawky or socially inept person – simply because it often stands motionless on one leg, which makes it look slightly ridiculous – the crane was above all a symbol of conjugal fidelity for our ancestors who were aware of its monogamous habits. It was its mating display, rather than its flight, that fired their imagination, especially in China, where they saw it not only as a dance of love, but also a sacred dance symbolizing the purity, prosperity and power of life and regeneration. As such, the crane was regarded as a symbol of the immortality of the soul.

Crete
(the bull of)

See Hercules, page 243

Crocodile

Like the toad (see page 494), the crocodile is an amphibian but, unlike the toad, it is a reptile. It is quite possible that, with its long, tapering snout and thick covering of bony plates or 'scales', it inspired those who had never seen it before to identify it as a dragon. The crocodile and toad

are both primeval animals but the crocodile possibly more so, since not only is it a reptile but it is fierce, voracious and unpredictable. It was not by chance that the ancient Egyptians regarded it as an attribute of Seth, the god of chaos, confusion and war, who was usually depicted with a human body and the head of a strange animal and was, for this reason, later identified with the Greek monster Typhon. The god's terrible rages were greatly feared as the harbingers of plagues, catastrophes and destruction. But for the Egyptians, the crocodile was above all the symbolic representation of Sobek, the creator god, a belief reinforced by the fact that it had not emerged from the primeval mud or the primordial waters. However, Sobek's role as creator of the world did not preclude his ferocity and he was equally capable of creating and devouring his progeny, of giving and taking life.

If you dream about a crocodile, the presence of this reptile that has emerged from the depths of the ages should above all be associated with the principles and symbols relating to the dragon (see *Unicorn and dragon*, page 508). It often means that dark and obscure forces are in the process of emerging from the depths of our subconscious. In this sense, the crocodile represents emotions and inhibited or suppressed urges that threaten to engulf us and provoke primary or primitive reactions.

It is worth noting that our fascination for those distant ancestors of the crocodile, the dinosaurs – of which it appears to be a direct descendant – reveals the extent of the obscure and primitive forces that lie dormant within us. There is an ever-present fear (represented by the crocodile) that they will awaken, overwhelm and destroy us, just as those great saurians were once destroyed in a manner that has never been conclusively explained, in spite of extensive scientific speculation and research on the subject. According to the Egyptians, the crocodile god Sobek, creator of the world, could equally well be the destroyer of the world.

Cross

The cross symbolizes the union of heaven and earth, the tree of life, the sacred place where space and time merge. It is one of the most beautiful and ancient symbols. Before becoming the insignia and then the symbol of Christianity, the cross was undoubtedly one of the first universal magical and mystical symbols used by mankind to represent a spatial orientation, as well as the connection or link between two sets of two points, two worlds, or two opposite and opposing forces – above and below, heaven and hell, right and left, good and bad. This crossing of the celestial and terrestrial, visible and invisible, divine and human elements forms the basis of a union or an accomplishment that can occur within man if he identifies with and becomes part of the cross. If he does so, he finds himself at the point of convergence of the vertical and horizontal energies. By linking north and south, this universal symbol is a representation of the vertical axis of the world, the cosmic tree or tree of life (see page 498). By linking east and west, it symbolizes the horizon above and below which the stars and planets rise and set, and mortals are born and die. Since the

vertical axis of the world is situated in the centre of the axis of the horizon, their point of intersection creates the divisions into four seasons, that is, into four elements and four periods of the year. By placing this cross – which is also a representation of the square – inside a circle, human beings became aware of the implications of the circle and created or 'invented' the wheel. In one respect, the cross, the centre, the circle and the square form an indivisible whole and, in this way, the cross can be used to represent or symbolize the centre, circle or square since the cross is all of these simultaneously. The circle contains the cross and the square, just as the square also contains the cross and the circle, but the cross automatically implies a circle and a square. In each case, the centre – which for mankind is represented by the heart, the 'sun' of the body and the source of life (see *Circle*, page 100) – appears as the common and inescapable symbol of the circle, the square and the cross. The cross is also a crossing of paths, a point of convergence, a crossroads and, in this sense, a symbol of human destiny. A crossroads is where four paths or roads meet and, as such, it is a magical place, a centre, a crossing place, a doorway and a threshold. It is easy to see why people commonly speak about being at a crossroads in their life. This idea is reinforced by the fact that, until the 10th century, Hecate – the Greek magician-goddess endowed with the power of granting the wishes and satisfying the desires of those who believed in her – was worshipped at crossroads, which were once regarded as sacred places dedicated to magic. Mothers often went there to implore the goddess to bestow her blessings on their children. The Roman Catholic Church regarded Hecate as the queen of witches and forbade her worship.

Ancient crosses and Christian crosses. *Ankh, the ansate or Egyptian cross:* this is a T-shaped cross surmounted by a loop that could be used as a handle, which is why it is known as the ansate cross (*crux ansata*), i.e. 'having a handle' (from the Latin *ansatus*, from *ansa* meaning 'handle'). This loop was the emblem of the sun, the source of life, but also of the eternal and divine life after death, while the cross proper represented temporal life. The Egyptians also called it the key of life or the key of the Nile, the great dispenser of life that fertilized the earth.

The swastika or lucky-charm cross: this very ancient cross, whose name derives from the Sanskrit *svasti*, was unfortunately used by the Nazis with the result that it now has sinister connotations. In the ancient language of India and the language of the Vedas, *svasti* means 'happiness' and 'prosperity' and is associated with the belief that prosperity brings good luck. Its four inward-curving branches, each in the form of the Greek capital gamma (hence *crux gammata*), create the illusion of continuous circular movement and evoke both a wheel and a spiral (see *Circle*, page 100, and *Spiral*, page 467). As such, it was used to represent the labyrinth (see *Labyrinth*, page 306), especially in ancient Egypt, in the third millennium BC. The swastika is in fact a universal symbol found in China, Egypt, Greece and other parts of Europe. In Greece, it represents the quadruplication of the letter gamma, while in Norse mythology it is the emblem of the hammer of Thor, the god of thunder and defender of the gods and mortals who, paradoxically, during pagan times, opposed the Christian cross. For Buddhists, it is the symbol of the 'wheel of the law' (*dhammacakka*), the seal on the heart or spirit of the Buddha. In China, it relates to the number 10,000 that represents infinity. Finally, in Tibet, it appears on talismans and is often represented in mandalas, the mystical drawings used as an aid to meditation.

The St Andrew's cross is a diagonal cross with equal arms, like the cross on which Christ's first apostle was crucified. According to Byzantine tradition, St Andrew, the brother of St Peter, was known as *protokletos*

('first called') in the area around the Black Sea where he was a missionary. The cross of the Orthodox Church, of which St Andrew is the patron saint, has three horizontal bars, the third and lowest of which slants slightly downwards to the right, like one of the diagonal arms of the St Andrew's cross. However, the St Andrew's cross dates from much earlier – it has been found carved on prehistoric bones and, in many primitive societies, appeared on the instruments used to ward off ill fortune and disease.

The St Peter's Cross is an inverted cross, with the horizontal bar at the bottom. It is attributed to St Peter, who was crucified upside down, in Rome, during the reign of Nero, in AD 64. The fact that the Father of the Apostolic Church was crucified in the inverse position to that of Christ is not without symbolic significance. For example, in the Hebrew *Sefer ha-zohar* ('book of splendour') and the Hindu *Upanishads* (speculative texts that elaborate on the Vedas), the universe is perceived as an inverted tree whose roots are planted in the sky and whose leaves and branches cover the earth (see *Tree of life*, page 498).

Crossroads

A crossroads is associated with the square, the circle and the centre, but above all with the cross of which it is one of the symbolic representations (see *Cross*, page 134). In the Middle Ages, the association of crossroads with the centre (i.e. as the convergence of four different points or several distinct directions), and therefore with the cross, led to their being used as places for the worship of pagan divinities, spirits of the natural world, protective forces, sprites, fairies and angels. Crossroads were therefore often dedicated to a particular pagan divinity or saint and even today, in many European countries, you will still come across the stone statue of a saint or the Virgin Mary watching over a crossing of paths or minor country roads.

To dream of finding yourself at a junction or a crossroads always implies that you have an important choice to make or a particular direction to take. This type of dream can herald a period that will mark a major turning point in your life. You have reached a point where you can make a choice, take control of your destiny and follow a particular direction in your life rather than another.

Crow

There are two main types of crow. The more common carrion crow (*Corvus corone*), although gregarious and sometimes roosting in large numbers, nests in individual pairs in dense woodland and forest, while the rook (*Corvus frugilegus*) nests in large colonies or 'rookeries' in wooded countryside. Although the rook is similar to the carrion crow in size – 45cm (18in) – and colour, the crow has a pure black bill, black eyes, a round head and a face completely covered in feathers, while the adult rook usually has shaggy thigh feathers and bare whitish skin showing at the base of its sharp bill. The crow flies at

heights of up to 500m (1,640ft) and tends to be sedentary. It is a very sociable bird and is easily tamed – some pet crows have been known to 'talk', count and recognize symbols.

However, the crow has not always had a reputation for intelligence. For example, in Aesop's 'The Fox and the Crow', the crow – De la Fontaine's 'maître corbeau' – is tricked by the fox's flattery into dropping a piece of cheese it is holding in its beak (see *Animal*, page 31).

Just as the raven was once regarded as the bird of Apollo (see *Raven*, page 428) and was believed to share the god's prophetic powers, the crow was associated with the Greek god Cronus (the Roman Saturn) and was also invested with oracular powers. According to one Greek myth, the crow was the companion of Athena, goddess of war, an association echoed in Celtic and druidic mythology, where the crow represented a fearful, warlike goddess, whose very battle song was terrifying and even fatal. For the ancient Egyptians and Greeks, the crow symbolized longevity, while in the Middle Ages, it was widely regarded as the symbol of conjugal fidelity, owing to its habit of living in pairs. However, the bird's association with war continued to survive in Europe where it was believed that large numbers of crows portended war or some form of imminent destruction.

Crown

See Hat, page 218 and Horns and crowns, page 262

Cuckoo

Like the crow and raven (see pages 137 and 428), the cuckoo is a passerine bird, i.e. it belongs to the *Passeriformes*, an order of birds – including larks, finches, thrushes and sparrows – characterized by a habit of perching. However, although we all like to hear the cuckoo's song, from which its onomatopoeic name is derived, it also has a reputation for being both lazy and parasitic. The female lays her single egg in the nest of another, usually passerine, bird and the chick is hatched and fed by the foster parents. As it grows, the young cuckoo pushes the eggs or chicks of its adoptive parents out of the nest, a trait that has understandably earned it a rather bad reputation.

However, in spite of its rather unusual habits – which are undoubtedly justified by basic needs that have nothing to with human moral values – the cuckoo is regarded as the harbinger of spring throughout Europe (where it is considered lucky to hear the first cuckoo call of the year) and Asia. This is particularly true in India and Tibet where, as well as heralding the arrival of spring and eternal renewal (the 'good news' of Christianity), the bird and its song also announce the spiritual happiness achieved by spontaneous renunciation. In the Far East, the fact that the female cuckoo lays her eggs in the nests of other birds is regarded as a symbol of the renunciation of the world and a sign of great spiritual elevation that coincides with the arrival of spring and therefore the renewal of life.

Cybele

See Athena, Cybele and Hecate, page 40

Cypress tree

In the past, the cypress tree, with its strange properties, magical powers and living strength, was regarded as the tree of life. According to some, you only had to rub your heels with its resin and you would be able to walk on water. Others held that, by watching the flames of a cypress-wood fire, you could consult the oracles and discover gold or something even more precious.

If it could speak, this tree would be able to tell a great many tales, legends and stories – from the fantastic to the historical – since it was one of the first trees to appear on earth, hundreds of millions of years ago, long before the broad-leaved trees.

The cypress is known as the 'tree of resurrection', probably as its appearance remains unchanged throughout the year, regardless of the season. It was also a funerary tree dedicated to Hades (the Roman god Pluto), the Greek god of the underworld. Cypress trees are often found planted in cemeteries

around Europe, giving rise to a French proverb: 'Cyprès au cimetière éloigne de l'enfer' ('cypress in the cemetery will keep you out of hell').

However, according to the Roman poet Ovid (43 BC–AD 17), the cypress is in fact Cyparissus, a young boy loved by Apollo who inadvertently killed a beautiful pet stag, dedicated to the nymphs, with a javelin. Filled with grief and remorse, he asked Apollo to let him mourn forever and the god finally changed him into a cypress tree as the symbol of eternal grief (*Metamorphoses*, 10, 106–142).

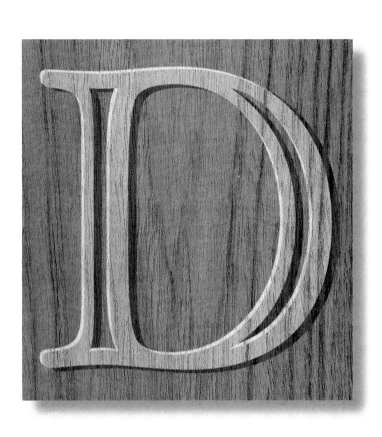

Dance

With its body movements, graceful gestures, figures, rules and rhythms, dance is a language in its own right that preceded the spoken and, of course, the written languages. Initially men and women danced to imitate the great phenomena of the natural world, to represent heaven and earth, the stars, mountains, valleys, rivers, oceans, trees, flowers and animals, by invoking their forms and imitating their movements. They went on dancing to recount their history, but also, and above all, to convey the stories of their myths and legends, and the adventures and misadventures of their gods. Dance was quite naturally ritual and sacred since it was religious in the pure sense of the word, that is to say it enabled the men and women of a particular tribe or people to come together in a religious spirit, to share the communal feelings that united them. Throughout the world, countless ritual dances, whose traditions dated from the dawn of time, drew their inspiration from the creation myths of the great cosmogonies of the world. Some of them have survived, although nowadays they tend to be labelled with the outdated and fusty term 'folklore'.

For the Hindus, Nataraja ('Lord of Dance') is the god Shiva ('Auspicious One') in his form as the cosmic dancer. His dance derives from a universal cosmic principle that contains the five great manifestations or expressions of life – creation, conservation, destruction, incarnation and liberation. In some Indian and African tribes, medicine men still perform rain dances and dances during fertility rituals to obtain the favour of the gods and the great forces of nature.

But the whirling of the dance also leads to ecstasy, and in this way imitates the movement of the stars, of the atoms and particles, the great swirling of universal life. According to the Sufi mystic and poet Djalal ad-Din ar-Rumi (1207–73), whose disciples became known as the order of the Whirling Dervishes: 'Those who know dance live in God' – *Fihi ma fihi* ('There is in it what is in it').

Throughout the world, dance is also regarded as a supreme act of erotic love, the union of man and woman symbolizing the union of heaven and earth, the great cosmic union. For all these reasons, and for many others that we simply do not have the time or space to consider here, a dream in which you are dancing means that you experience a vital need to express or reveal your primordial and instinctive nature. It also highlights your desire to achieve a more perfect union with your environment, your need for love in the broadest sense, i.e. for communion and complete integration with others. In fact, dancing is a means of achieving harmony with the rhythms of life, with the whirling of the stars and the atoms, enabling you to immerse yourself in your original environment.

If you dream that you are dancing with someone else, this quite simply represents the desire for union with the other, your opposite, which eradicates and effaces tensions and antagonism. In other words, it symbolizes a desire for both harmony and perfection.

Dawn, daybreak

Unfortunately, the English words 'dawn' and 'daybreak' do not have the associations and distinctions of the French *aube* and *aurore* (both meaning 'dawn') derived from the Latin *auba* and *aurora* respectively. English does, on the other hand, have the terms 'aubade', a song or poem greeting the dawn, and 'aurora', a poetical term for dawn, derived from the same roots. 'Aurora' also refers to the well-known atmospheric phenomenon – bands or curtains of red, green or yellow light moving across the sky – common to polar regions, especially in the 'aurora borealis' or northern lights.

The Latin and French *auba* and *aube* derive from the Latin *albus* ('white') and are therefore associated with whiteness and purity, while *aurora* and *aurore* are closely associated with the Latin *auratus* meaning 'golden' or 'relating to gold'. These different associations give rise to two very different images of dawn that are reinforced by the symbols corresponding to white and gold (see *White*, page 536, and *Gold*, page 209).

The whiteness of dawn, which is not a colour but a synthesis of all colours or, if you prefer, an absolute colour that has absorbed all the others, symbolizes virginal purity, birth, all that is naked, natural, innocent and true. In this sense, dawn (*auba*) is associated with the moon. By contrast, the golden dawn represents supreme royalty, divine light, perfection and great richness and, in this sense, dawn (*aurora*) is associated with the sun. From this it can be deduced that, on the one hand, dawn as the birth of day underlies the disappearance or death of night. On the other, dawn is the full and complete, superior and absolute manifestation of the power of light.

If dawn features prominently in your dreams, a white dawn won't have the same significance as a golden dawn. A white dawn often symbolizes a need for purification, which may be physical or mental and can therefore equally well refer to your physi-

cal health as your psychological or moral well-being. But this purification or cleansing involves or will involve a sacrifice, a symbolic period of mourning announced by the white dawn. A golden dawn, on the other hand, is always a sign of clarification, a truth that explodes into the daylight, a complete success, great joy or perfect happiness.

Day

Day actually and symbolically contrasts with night. In this sense, day represents light and night represents darkness. However, the day is also a period of time stretching from dawn to dusk and, metaphorically, it symbolizes the span of a human life on earth. In other words, man is born at dawn, is a child in the morning, is an adult at midday, an old person in the evening and dies at dusk. In the same way, astrologically, the degree indicated by the cusp of the First House, or ascendant, takes 24 hours to circle the zodiac, wherever you are in the world. The astrologer-priests of Babylon perfected a forecasting system based on the following observation and principle: one day = one month. Thus they believed that a day in the life of a newborn child corresponded to a month in its life, that 48 days were the equivalent of 48 months or 4 years, that the 240th day could provide valuable information about the 20th year, and so on.

As a result, if you dream of days passing by very quickly or if a specific day appears in a calendar, this will always teach you a great deal about the future. It is therefore important to remember the number of days that went by or the exact day indicated or shown on a calendar in order to interpret the dream.

.

Decans

See Zodiac (the 12 signs of the), page 553

Deer

This animal of myth and legend was particularly revered in ancient times, but also in the Middle Ages, when it was a real adventure to enter the dark world of the forest and encounter or hunt a deer.

Nowadays, although you are still just as unlikely to come across a deer in a forest or to hear it bell, the reasons for this are, unfortunately, entirely different. However, it is still regarded as a mythical solar animal associated

with the tree of life, as the companion of the gods and the initiator of human beings.

As a symbol of power, spiritual strength and material wealth, a deer appears in a dream as a guide and harbinger of good news, a messenger announcing a birth, a revelation or a realization, or as an indication of the sudden appearance of an exceptional person or event in your life.

Demeter

See Earth, page 160

Desert

The desert symbolizes the absolute void, a wilderness, desolation, the absence of life, sterility, abandonment, solitude, a horizon stretching as far as the eye can see and leading nowhere, thirst, hunger and wandering. It is also a well-known fact that the desert is a place of mirages, hallucinations and the occasional oasis (a word that is probably of Egyptian origin). According to mystical tradition, it is an ideal place to encounter God and attain a state of supreme compassion. Isaac of Nineveh (or Isaac the Syrian), a 7th-century monk, bishop and theologian who retired to a solitary monastic life in the desert, described this state as one where the heart is filled with loving kindness for all God's creatures – for human beings, birds, beasts and even

demons – indeed for all living things. Anyone who has such a heart cannot see or think about these creatures without their eyes brimming with tears because of the vast compassion that fills their heart. It was in the vast emptiness of the desert that certain hermits discovered this vast and all-enveloping compassion. In this context, the desert becomes a symbol of material deprivation and spiritual purifi-

cation, and the oasis a magical and supernatural place with a source and well at which to quench our absolute thirst (see *Source*, page 461 and *Well*, page 533).

If you dream that you are walking in the desert, you may be quite simply 'spending time in the wilderness'. In this sense, the dream is announcing a difficult and painful period, during which you will have to rely on yourself, your own strength and resources and, of course, use them sparingly. But it can also be a dream with a much richer and deeper significance, indicating that you aspire to material deprivation and want to get rid of everything that clutters up your life and distracts you from your inner self. In this sense, you feel the need to create a void around yourself and perhaps even, and above all, within yourself, in order to find your own truth. Sometimes seeing a desert in a dream simply reflects an impression of emotional emptiness, an absence of feelings and emotions. Alternatively, it may confirm what we already know intuitively but do not want to admit to ourselves because of the anguish it causes us, namely that, in spite of the whirlwind of relationships into which we are drawn in our social and family lives, we are ultimately alone.

Devil

Whether we are believers or non-believers, most of us find the image of the Devil disturbing, upsetting or distressing. But do we know why? On closer examination, the Devil, as we generally refer to him, is not what we think. Once again, etymological origins provide a clue as to the exact meaning of the term and reveal that our interpretation and the images we create are incorrect.

The origins of the Devil. The English term 'devil' derives from the Greek *diabolos* ('enemy', 'accuser' or 'slanderer'), from *diaballein*, meaning 'to throw across', 'disunite', 'separate', 'set at odds' and, by extension, 'to slander'. It was *diabolos* that the Greek translators of the Bible

used to translate the Hebrew word *satan* meaning 'plotter' or 'accuser' since, in the Judaic tradition, one of the roles of the Evil One was to accuse the righteous before the tribunal of God. For the Greeks, therefore, *diabolos* was an accuser, a calumniator, in short a generally unpleasant person. It was not until the 9th century that the Latin *diabolus*, which gave *diaule* and *deable* in Old French, acquired the meaning of demon. Thus the ancient concept of the devil as a public accuser – a function fulfilled nowadays by a public prosecutor in a court of law – was superseded by the mediaeval and then the modern concept of a demon. But it is the image of the demon that remains etched on our collective memories and to which we still refer, without knowing what the term really means, apart from the significance with which we have invested it as the representation or incarnation of Evil.

However, if we refer to its original meaning, the demon *per se* has nothing wicked, negative or evil about it. It was not until the early 14th century that the term *daemon* or demon acquired the meaning of an infernal spirit, bad angel, fallen angel or devil. Before that, the Greek *daimon* ('spirit', 'deity' or 'fate') was a

divine and beneficent power that attributed and shared out, thereby incorporating the meaning of 'to throw across' referred to above. The *daimon* was originally a protective genie or spirit attached to each human being or natural element. In other words, it had the same attributes and functions as the famous spirits of the natural world that provided the inspiration for the celestial hierarchy of angels developed by Dionysius the Areopagite (*fl.* 1st century AD), the first bishop of Athens (often identified with St Denis, patron of France).

'Giving or sharing out' and 'throwing across' relates to an essential principle represented by the *daimon* – the principle of destiny, whether good or bad, fortunate or unfortunate. The *daimon* was therefore the dispenser of destiny, but also a protective spirit, a good angel or what we would nowadays refer to as conscience. Those who remained in contact with their *daimon* heard and followed the voice of their conscience. It was

therefore a good and just entity, the giver of intuitions and inspirations, talents and innate gifts.

So how did this beneficent component of the human being acquire such a negative, dark and evil connotation that ultimately became the only meaning associated with the demon or the Devil? Paradoxically, the explanation lies in a Greek word of Indo-European origin – *daiesthai* – meaning 'to share out', or 'divide', from which the Greek *demos* ('people', or 'population') derives. The same root is found in 'demagogue ('leading the people')' and 'democracy', 'epidemic' and 'demiurge' ('working for the people'). The Greek word *epidemia* ('among the people') was used to refer to the installation of a person among the people or an illness contaminating the people. However, the real reason is to be found in the parallel between the demagogue or demiurge – who leads or works for the people – and the

DR

protective spirit that guides human beings. History has taught us that those who lead or work for the people have not always acted in their best interests and it is therefore logical to assume that the *daimon* who presided over human destiny and was supposed to play a protective and benign role could also betray its original nature and sometimes exert an evil influence. It was in this way that the demon gradually became assimilated with forces that were more specifically evil and destructive, since it was the tragedies, persecutions, wars and violence generated by individuals with a strong personality, an excessive desire for power and division (the better to rule), and an overweening ambition, that remained etched on the collective memory. This same principle still applies today. For example, we may be a long way from the mediaeval imagery of the witches' sabbath or the black mass, during which the Devil – the incarnation of the spirit of evil, as opposed to God, the spirit of good – was supposedly worshipped, but the image we have of these practices is completely exaggerated. They were usually pagan rituals based on pre-Christian beliefs, most of which were founded on the powers attributed to the gods, genies and protective spirits of the natural world. However, they were not intrinsically evil and the diabolic character, in the pejorative sense of the term, attributed to these beliefs, cults and rituals has distorted their original and deep-rooted significance. For historical reasons that it would take too long to explain here, these rituals disrupted the established order of those troubled times and disturbed their leaders, with the result that demagogues, or 'those who led the people', in the etymological and literal sense of the term, invented the Devil and demons. It was a time when anything that threatened to upset the status quo was automatically attributed to evil, to demons and to the Devil. Since then, the Devil and demons have had a very bad reputation and have been represented by images that have little to do with their true identity.

Diana

*See Athena, Cybele and
Hecate, page 40*

Diomedes
(the mares of)

See Hercules, page 244

Dog

'*I am a lean dog, a keen dog, a
wild dog, and alone.*'

Irene Rutherford Macleod

It is generally believed that the
dog is the direct descendant of
the wolf. However, it appears
that 'man's best friend' – thought
to have been domesticated in the
Middle East in the 11th millennium BC and known to have been
domesticated in Europe in the
7th millennium BC – is a type of
canine resulting from a strange
cross between the wolf, jackal
and coyote, all members of the
family *Canidae*. This is why
myths associated with dogs often
involve references to these three
wild animals, depending on the
origin of the myths in question.
But, whatever the myth or type
of canine, it appears that the dog
was the first wild animal to have
been domesticated by human
beings.

There is one question that
has so far remained unanswered.
Was it in fact humans who tamed
and domesticated the dog or was
it this naturally opportunistic
creature that, over the ages and
for readily understandable reasons, instinctively drew closer to
human tribes and communities?
The evidence tends to support
the second theory.

The dog is frequently associated with nocturnal myths and symbols, dark and obscure worlds, the underworld and even death. The ancients regarded the dog as the guardian or god of the dead, as in ancient Egypt, for example, where Anubis was the canine or jackal-headed god of the dead. It was as if the dog – this wild, carnivorous, hybrid (wolf-jackal-coyote) that usually hunted by night and was also associated with the moon – had emerged from the unfathomable and terrifying depths of the earth to negotiate with our ancestors and take advantage of them, enjoy the bounty of their hunting and the warmth of their fires. Our ancestors, who saw signs in all natural phenomena, could not fail to recognize the significance of the fact that this wild animal, possibly the first with which they had experienced this type of relationship, not only accepted their authority but also demonstrated a typically human characteristic, greatly exaggerated in the dog – fear.

For these reasons, although the appearance of a dog in a dream often represents the darkest, wildest, most impure, untameable and amoral side of our nature, it can also symbolize the most loyal, affectionate and submissive side. From this, it is self-evident that the dog has been endowed with many, often contradictory, characteristics. The dog also represents excessive heat and all-consuming, devastating passions – an image that gave rise to such expressions as 'dog days', used to refer to the hot period of summer and calculated by the ancients from the heliacal rising of Sirius (the dog-star). In astrological terms, 'cynic' or 'cynical' (from the Greek *kuon*, meaning 'dog') means 'relating to Sirius or the dog-star'. Figuratively, it means 'believing the worst of others' and obviously derives from the negative side of the dog's nature. The dog is therefore a symbol of the beneficent instinct that protects and the maleficent instinct that endangers. A dog prowling around you in a dream signifies that a new and unexpected event, which can be either positive or negative, is about to occur in your life. Being bitten by a dog is a warning against a potential enemy.

Dolphin

In ancient times, the dolphin (*Delphinus delphis*) was regarded as a sort of 'sea horse' and was closely associated with Greece, a civilization with origins that were deeply rooted in the

Mediterranean. According to Greek mythology, the city of Delphi was founded by Apollo, whose epithet Delphinius meant 'he of the dolphin'. Although Apollo had a shrine there, the city was in fact named after Delphus, the king of Crete and son of Melantho by Poseidon (the Roman god Neptune) who had seduced her in the form of a dolphin. Thus, Delphus ('the dolphin') became king of Delphi, the city of the dolphins. Another legend tells how Arion, a Greek poet and bard, was about to be killed for his wealth by the crew of a ship on which he was sailing. However, they allowed him to sing one last song and he sang a hymn to Apollo that attracted a school of dolphins, Apollo's creatures. Arion jumped overboard and was carried to safety by one of the dolphins.

Other legends depict Poseidon, god of the sea, surrounded by dolphins, or transformed into a dolphin or a horse. In Greek mythology, Poseidon is in fact credited with the creation of the horse.

If you dream about a dolphin, it can usually be interpreted in terms of the symbols associated with the horse. As we shall see (*Horse*, page 264), the horse is associated with psychic, instinctive and subconscious forces and urges, which, although destructive, can also be creative and regenerative. With regard to the dolphin, this association is even more obvious, since the natural element of this marine mammal is the primeval waters, the waters of the womb, into and from whose depths it is able to plunge and resurface with ease, thereby symbolizing its ability to frequent the darkest and most luminous areas of being. Many accounts tell how dolphins have saved shipwrecked sailors from drowning which, in symbolic terms, means that we can be saved by something that has the power to plumb the darkest depths of being. There is a general tendency to believe that it is better to ignore, repress, reject or eradicate the areas of our personality that we do not like or of which we are ashamed. A dolphin

Door

in a dream signifies that we should never try to eradicate any of the components of our personality. For, who knows, one of these components, which we may wrongly perceive as the basest or most dangerous part of ourselves, could one day save us.

Door

Generally speaking, a door is regarded as open or closed. We find ourselves either before or behind the door, inside or outside the house. When a door plays a key role in a dream, it is important to note where you are in relation to it. To dream that you are inside a house, on the point of opening a door, but are unsure whether to turn the handle, reveals excitement or fear of the unknown. In other words, this door is symbolically closed against an alien, unknown, mysterious world that either attracts or repels, depending on the situation – sometimes both at the same time. This type of dream often occurs when someone is keen to leave behind their customary life, their humdrum routine, to go in search of adventure, become independent, escape from themselves. It is therefore a dream of escape, hope and freedom. On the other hand,

dreaming that you are outside a house, in front of a closed door, symbolizes the quest for sanctuary, the need for comfort or protection, or even a conscious or subconscious desire to revisit the past.

As a result, the symbolic meaning of the door bears many similarities to that of the bridge, since they are both crossing points between two worlds or two interpretations of the world and reality (see *Bridge*, page 73). For example, the transition from waking to sleeping or from consciousness to unconsciousness can be represented by a door.

The door of a temple, and the altar inside, are probably the two most important areas of this sacred place. In fact, by crossing the threshold of the temple door, man leaves a profane world to enter a kingdom consecrated to the divine. There are also doors or gateways leading to death, heaven and paradise, among others. The winter and summer solstices have often been compared to doors, the first opening on the light and the second closing on it. Likewise, astrologers often compared the two axes of the nodes of the moon to doors: the ascending or north node being like an opening door, representing the strong points an individual can exploit to surmount obstacles, progress, grow and develop, while the descending or south node is like a closing door, symbolizing the handicaps, weaknesses and failings that hold people back and cause them to stagnate or go into decline.

Lastly, birth and death are the two doors that man passes through when entering and departing this world. However, between the two, in Christianity and many other beliefs, there is a 'strait' or narrow door, a difficult, tricky passageway that leads to the light, to revelation, to deliverance, in the mystical sense of these terms. This is an entirely different approach to the world's reality that can only be experienced in a state of complete devotion.

Dove

The dove is a member of the pigeon family (*Columbidae*) renowned for it distinctive, pure white plumage. It is easily tamed and feeds almost exclusively on grain and seeds. Its broad wings enable it to fly rapidly and cover relatively long distances without resting. In view of this, it is hardly surprising that it was the dove that Noah sent forth from the ark to see if the floodwaters had subsided. The bird returned with an olive leaf in its beak.

The story of Noah's Ark is one of the most beautiful legends in which a dove appears: 'And he [Noah] stayed yet other seven days; and again he sent forth the dove out of the ark; and the dove came in to him in the evening; and, lo, in her mouth was an olive leaf pluckt off: so Noah knew that the waters were abated from off the earth. And he stayed yet other seven days; and sent forth the dove; which returned not again unto him any more.' (Genesis 8: 10–12.)

Today, the 'dove of peace' – a dove holding an olive branch in its beak – is the universal symbol of peace. But for the writers and compilers of the Old and New Testaments, it also represented the purity and simplicity of the soul and love, the

Holy Spirit or the Spirit of God. In Greek mythology, it was the symbol of Aphrodite (the Roman Venus), goddess of love. Last but not least, in ancient and mediaeval times, it symbolized the immortal and eternal soul.

The turtle dove (*Streptopelia turtur*) has always primarily been a symbol of purity, fidelity and virginity, renowned above all for its fidelity. The male coos much of the time, but always to the same female and, if one of the pair dies, the survivor never mates again. In the hieroglyphic writing of ancient Egypt, the dove was used as the biliteral phonogram (or ideogram) signifying a dancer, musician or art lover.

The best-known species of dove in Europe is the collared dove (*Streptopelia decaocto*) with its white and light grey plumage. This bird, although native to southern and eastern Asia, left its area of origin in the 1930s and has since become extremely common throughout Europe. A non-migratory bird, it frequents urban parks and gardens. The rather s h o w y courtship display of the male bird, which is accompanied by

continuous cooing, lasts throughout the winter. In the spring, the mating pair build their nest with anything they can find in a treetop, on an electricity pylon, on a rooftop, sometimes even on a windowsill. The female lays two eggs up to five times between March and May, which she incubates with the male. Doves eat mainly seeds, although they also feed on refuse.

Dragon

See Unicorn and dragon, page 508

Duck

Everyone knows this aquatic, migratory bird – with its broad, blunt bill and webbed feet – that became an international movie star in the 'person' of Walt Disney's Donald Duck. It is a greedy feeder that adapts easily to all climatic conditions but prefers to live in wet regions, on the edge of ponds and lakes. The female, also known as the duck (as opposed to the male drake), is extremely prolific and can lay up to 80 eggs per year! There are a great many breeds of duck worldwide, some of which are bred for food and others as game birds.

It seems that, from time immemorial, the distinctive 'quacking' – the harsh guttural sound made by the duck – has been an object of ridicule for human beings. Even so, it has found its way into modern terms of endearment ('ducks', 'ducky' or 'me duck') and has also provided the imagery for such popular expressions as 'to take to something like a duck to water', meaning to like something or become adept at something very quickly, and 'like water off a duck's back', used to describe an action that has little or no effect on someone. 'Ducks and drakes' is a game in which a flat stone is skimmed across the surface of the water, and 'to play ducks and drakes' with something means to waste, squander or use it recklessly.

The duck is also regarded as the symbol of conjugal fidelity owing to the fact that pairs tend to swim together on pools and lakes. This image of the duck is particularly strong in China where, since ancient times, a pair of ducks has been given to newly married couples as a good-luck charm. Generally speaking, this garrulous but faithful bird has always been regarded sympathetically by our ancestors.

Dwarf

Although the tendency is to play down the symbolic significance of fairy tales and the initiatory messages they conceal, these stories frequently feature characters resembling dwarfs in looks or stature. Versions written over the last two centuries have often presented these small characters as children, since fairy tales were regarded merely as folklore and their fanciful content was thought better suited to children. However, these diminutive characters were generally employed to emphasize the quick-wittedness, intelligence, cunning, cleverness and subtlety of the hero. The fairy tale actually became an initiatory journey: the dwarf symbolized the burgeoning intelligence of the hero who sharpened his wits by triumphing over a host of exacting situations. Although the generally anonymous authors of these stories made it clear that the dwarf in question – like Tom

Dwarf

Thumb, who was originally a dwarf, not a child – had various physical deformities, thereby suggesting he had been branded by nature and thus barred from social acceptance from birth, this was merely to draw our attention to one of the key morals of these tales: physical appearance is never a handicap. Size does not matter: keen intelligence and a noble spirit are all that count.

In many ancient mythologies, dwarfs often appear with gods or deities. This was the case with the five Idaean Dactyls, who owed their name, meaning 'fingers', to their manual dexterity. These sorcerers, demons and blacksmiths, who were sons of Rhea and Cronus, were called Hercules (not the hero who performed the famous 12 Labours), Epimedes, Idas, Paeonaeos and Iassius. According to Greek legend, these five small brothers organized the first Olympic Games, now a major international festival devoted to physical supremacy, in order to entertain Zeus.

Mention should also be made of the house of the seven dwarfs, hidden in the depths of the forest, where Snow White took refuge and where she did the housework before taking a bite from the poisoned apple and falling into a death-like sleep.

This fairy tale could plausibly be interpreted as a dream in which the seven dwarfs, who each possess one prominent characteristic, represent the seven personality traits that Snow White must learn to control or accept if she is to find out who she really is and learn to express herself fully. To do this, she must put her own house in order and ensure that every aspect of her personality is properly developed.

As can be seen, therefore, the appearance of one or several dwarfs in a dream often highlights a specific aspect of the dreamer's personality that must be reckoned with or accepted. In addition, the fact that manual dexterity is traditionally attributed to dwarfs highlights the symbolic analogy drawn between these figures and intelligence, shrewdness, careful deliberation and an understanding of the ways of the world.

Eagle

The Latin name (*aquila*) of this huge, diurnal bird of prey is closely associated with the word *aquilus*, an adjective meaning 'dark coloured' (a reference to its plumage) or a noun meaning 'north wind' (also *aquilo*), whose strength and velocity are both characteristic of the eagle's flight. *Aquila* also gave rise to the English term 'aquiline', which describes a hook-nose reminiscent of an eagle's beak.

The eagle is a carnivorous bird with an impressive wingspan and hooked talons that it uses to snatch up the snakes and field mice on which it feeds. Eagles mate for life and use the same nest (eyrie) each year to rear a small clutch of eggs. Since time immemorial the eagle has inspired admiration and fear in human beings. Today, hunters and pesticides have pushed it to the very brink of extinction and it is now an endangered species.

In ancient times, the eagle was considered the equal of the sun and, as such, was associated with that most beautiful of planets. The Greeks, Hindus and Persians regarded it as a solar being, a bird-god and the symbol of royal and imperial power. According to their traditions and beliefs, its acute vision made it clairvoyant and it was the only bird, animal or indeed living creature that could look directly at the sun.

As the symbol of power, victory, triumph over the elements, and invincible strength, it is hardly surprising that the eagle became the representative or messenger of the gods. It was therefore identified with Zeus in Greece and Christ in Western Europe, but it was also seen as the embodiment of the good and bad angels. Finally, because one of its main prey is the snake, it was also regarded as the conqueror of evil, since it could annihilate the snake – and therefore evil – by devouring it with impunity.

Earth

Whether cultivated or wild, the nourishing earth is a living element that gives and takes away. Everything comes from the earth and returns to it. The Earth, with a capital E, is the name of the planet on which we live, as opposed to the fundamental element on which we walk and which provides our sustenance. After all, Mother Earth grows everything we need to stay alive – long before it was cultivated the fertile garden of Earth provided abundant food to eat.

However, our forebears knew better than we do that it is essential to give the earth as much as it gives us and that it is impossible to distinguish the physical earth from the planet Earth. In their minds, therefore, physical matter and the planet merged into the image of a single deity, a mother-goddess who, although she assumed many guises according to different beliefs, cultures and civilizations, was always more or less identical.

The great feminine principle. The earth, the primordial matter that generates all forms of life, that gives life and takes it away, can be wild, untameable and malevolent or cultivated, domesticated and beneficial. It is the great feminine principle, set against the sky, the great masculine principle. In the zodiac, therefore, the axis formed by the signs of Taurus and Scorpio corresponds to the great feminine principle and the great opposite masculine principle that complements it. The sign of Taurus is identified with the appearance of plant life on this planet, while Scorpio is associated with the birth of animal life. This axis represents the positive and negative aspects of the earth: on the one hand, it is productive and fertile – it generates a wide variety of plants and fruit, and nothing is ever lost or wasted as everything is transformed. The seeds from all the plants and fruit return to the earth, inseminating it, so that it can produce new plants and new fruit. On the other hand, the fact that everything returns to the earth suggests the supremacy of the vital yet fatal principle that makes life on earth possible and this is its negative, dark, malevolent side. Just like the seed produced by the plant or fruit, man also returns to the earth. 'Naked came I out of my mother's womb, and naked shall I return thither…' said Job (1: 21). Our forebears therefore thought it

logical that the kingdom of the dead was situated beneath the earth, underground, in the subterranean worlds that are the home of the dark forces, the shadows, often associated with decomposition and putrefaction. However, as fertilization and germination also take place underground, there was always the hope of a rebirth, a resurrection. This underlies the persistent belief that throwing a handful of earth was enough to banish harmful forces and avert death: this ritual gesture is still performed today in the West when burying the dead.

Gaia and Demeter, the great earth goddesses. According to Greek mythology, Gaia, the great mother-goddess, was the second deity to appear, just after Chaos had generated night and day. She gave birth to Uranus (heaven), the mountains and the ocean. With Heaven, her own son, she conceived Cronus (time), which meant that she was Zeus's grandmother. It may be thought surprising that the earth is missing from the celestial hierarchy of the zodiac, which bears close similarities to the pantheon of the Olympian gods, themselves modelled

on older entities. In actual fact, the earth is omnipresent in the zodiac, although astrologers never specifically allude to it. This is because it is its centre and is therefore extremely receptive to all the influences for which it originally served as the receptacle, since it was the Earth that generated them, as can be seen in the myth of Gaia and the birth of the Greek gods. Gaia, often depicted as a curvaceous, voluptuous woman, was therefore the mother of the gods, the universal mother, an inexhaustible wellspring of fertility. She also knew the secrets of the Fates and ruled over human fate. Demeter/Ceres, a great mother-goddess of Greek mythology, was the daughter of Cronus and Rhea, another earth deity, both offspring of Gaia. However, she differed from her grandmother insofar as she was a mythical representation of the cultivated earth, a grain goddess. She therefore bears similarities to the sign of Virgo, which is often represented by a young girl sitting on the ground and holding ears of wheat. The story of Demeter's daughter, Persephone, whom she conceived with Zeus, can be identified with the sign of Libra (see page 569). When Persephone was kidnapped and imprisoned in the underworld by Hades, Demeter/Ceres turned the earth barren, causing drought and famine as a token of her anger and dissension. This legend illustrates the power over life and death that the earth has always been thought to wield, since drought and famine are scourges against which man, even today, must struggle.

Earth goddesses and gods throughout the world. In the pantheon of Egyptian gods – according to the Memphite creation myths or cosmogony – Ptah, the great creator-god of Memphis, was both a male and female deity; one of the Memphite texts says: 'He is the father of the gods and also the mother. And his nickname is "The Woman". He is the womb into which pours the seed from what has emerged. He made man from barley and woman from wheat'. Later, Geb or Seb was an earth-god, representing clay, peat, primordial matter, and the fertile, cultivable and nourishing earth. In China, the creation of the earth was the work of P'an-ku, the primordial Chinese giant who was born as a dwarf from the cosmic egg. The upper part of the egg formed the heaven (yang) and the lower part formed the earth (yin). According to the *Chu Yi Ki*, a text dating from the 6th century AD: 'Living beings began with P'an-ku, who is the ancestor of the 10,000 beings in the universe. When P'an-ku died, his head became a sacred peak, his eyes became the sun and the moon, his fat, the rivers and seas, his hair and bristles, the trees and the plants.' In India, the earth is sometimes Lakshmi, the goddess of fertility and wealth, whose symbol is gold, sometimes Kali, the black, bloody goddess of sacrifice, and it can also be Bhumi, the maternal aspect of the earth. For the Mayans, the earth was Itzam Cab, Iguana Earth, and for the Aztecs, it was a monster with gaping jaws, Tlaltecuhtli, Lord of the Earth, these two figures having more in common with the myth of the dragon than that of the mother-goddess.

Easter

It is no coincidence that the magical, solar festival celebrating the perpetual rebirth of light and life follows hard on the heels of the spring equinox. It is an unfortunate fact that people are now so disillusioned and so materialistic, living in a world dictated by profit and survival, where everything appears to have been planned and organized in advance, that many have lost any appreciation of the true and original meaning of the festivals in our calendar.

These festivals not only had a meaning, they had great symbolic significance. They provided a link between mankind and the great principles of nature at a time when people had a genuine love for its mysteries and rhythms. Rites and rhythms merged. By using ritual to reproduce the important events in nature's annual cycle, people showed they were in harmony with the natural world, moving in step with it, using its language, communing with it. No one really knows what suddenly caused people to see nature as an enemy, but the spell was broken. Nature came to be regarded as a guinea-pig, a vast field of exploration that people strove less to understand than to dominate, subdue and exploit, when they were not attempting to eradicate what they believed were imperfections. However, it is wrong to believe that by eliminating certain genetic diseases and artificially reproducing various key principles of nature, we will finally master life. In our ignorance of the great laws, rhythms and cycles of nature, so important to our forebears, we disregard the fact that, in nature, everything is handed down, reproduced, reborn, regenerated and modified *ad infinitum*: nothing ever disappears for good. As a result, no sooner have we arduously eliminated a natural phenomenon that was supposed to be injurious than another phenomenon, possibly similar to, yet different from the one we have wiped out, may appear, perhaps to even more devastating effect.

Shamanic rites. The answer is not to lay down arms,

refuse to fight evil, suffering, pain and the forces of destruction that are an intrinsic part of nature. If we are to remedy these things, however, it is of paramount importance to know their underlying, hidden causes, many of which can be found within man himself, in his thoughts and acts rather than in his genes. This is what the shaman, the sorcerer, the seer and the healer strove to do with the help of such techniques as ecstatic experiences and exorcism: '[The soul of the shaman] can leave his body with impunity and travel very long distances; it can enter the Underworld and ascend to Heaven. His own ecstatic experience has taught him the paths through these extraterrestrial regions. He can descend to the Underworld and ascend to Heaven, because he has already been there. There is always a great risk of becoming lost in these forbidden regions, but sanctified by initiation and armed with his guardian spirits, the shaman is the only human being

Where does the festival of Easter come from?

Between 20 May and 25 July 325, in the reign of Pope Sylvester, the Roman emperor Constantine the Great convoked 250 bishops and presided over the first ecumenical council in ancient Nicaea, now Iznik, Turkey. This council decreed that Easter would be celebrated on the first Sunday following the full moon after the spring equinox.

This period of the year was chosen to celebrate Easter because the Celts, whose sacred tree was the oak, used to celebrate the Night of the Gorse Bush on 21 March. During this ceremony, they honoured a female deity who bore similarities to Aphrodite, the Greek goddess of love, whose attribute was the hare, symbol of fertility and the perpetual rebirth of life. This is why the hare and rabbit have remained living symbols of Christian Easter celebrations.

Why do we give Easter eggs?

The egg is the symbol of perpetual rebirth, therefore a symbolic image of resurrection. However, the fact that it has been assimilated into the festival of Easter may also stem from a tradition according to which, during the Lenten fast – the 40 weekdays before Easter – the early Christians had to abstain from eating eggs. As a result, at the end of these 40 days, the hen-house was overflowing with eggs, so they were decorated and handed out on Easter Sunday. This custom has survived to this day.

who can run this risk and venture into a mystical geographic region.' (Mircea Eliade, *Shamanism: Archaic Techniques of Ecstasy*, Routledge & Kegan Paul, 1972.) The role of the shaman was to perform sacrifices, ascend to heaven, discover the causes of diseases and find suitable remedies and treatments for them, accompany the soul of the deceased into the underworld and purify the house. These magical rites may seem absurd and irrational today, particularly when practised by certain money-grubbing or ill-advised individuals who know nothing of the language of nature, who have not undergone any initiatory rite, but who do have a highly developed sense of theatre.

The spring equinox or the triumph of light. The very idea of the ultimate sacrifice that liberates us from the forces of evil, or of the destructive forces that promote the regeneration and rebirth of nature and life on earth, comes into play when the forces of good and light triumph over the forces of evil and darkness. This happens on 21 March in Western calendars, in other words, the spring equinox, when day and night are of equal length. For six months from this date, days are longer than the nights. The equinox therefore marks a transition from night to day, a type of dawn that returns every year on a set date, heralding the triumph of light.

Passover, the Jewish festival commemorating the flight from Egypt, is derived from the Hebrew *pesach*, meaning 'passing over'. For the Jews, this festival symbolizes mankind's escape from a trap. People do not realize that all myths and symbols live within us at all times. Therefore, symbolically, the Egyptians who drowned in the Red Sea after the Jewish people passed through represent the death of the old within us so that the new can be born. Such is the meaning of the Jewish Passover: the ultimate form of self-sacrifice so that a new person may be born within.

The Christian festival of Easter, when Jesus died on the cross and was resurrected, also refers to the same ultimate sacrifice, once performed by the shaman. St Paul seems to have fully understood the meaning of this sacrifice: 'Now that he has ascended, what is it but that he also descended first into the lower parts of the earth? He that descended is the same also that ascended up far above all heavens, that he might fill all things.' (Ephesians 4: 9–10.) This might lead us to deduce that Easter is a solar, shamanist festival, although it is not regarded as such today. However, whether we realize it or not, we are celebrating the sun, light, good and life, the sun that sinks below the horizon, then rises above it to 'fill all things'.

Eclipse

An eclipse or occultation of the sun was always a negative sign in the minds of our ancestors since they regarded it as a voluntary interruption of divine light. It was therefore an ominous sign or bad omen that, even nowadays, is associated with disastrous consequences.

A dream about an eclipse of the sun often predicts a loss, a disappointment, a frustration or a period in your life dominated by misfortune, chaos, disorder and confusion. It can also be a sign that the dreamer is becoming submerged by dark, negative thoughts and, as such, is a sign of depression. An eclipse of the moon indicates a lack of receptiveness on the part of the dreamer.

Eel

The European freshwater eel (*Anguilla anguilla*) is an amphibious fish, with a long snakelike body (Latin *anguis*, meaning snake), slimy skin and reduced tiny fins. The word 'eel' derives from the Old English *ael* (cp. Old Frisian *el*, Old Norse *all* and Old High German *al*). It symbolizes secrecy, mystery and dissimulation, but also something that 'slips through your fingers', that you can't hold on to or understand. In this respect, it lives up to its Latin name – *anguilla* means 'eel' or 'slippery customer'. However, because it lives in clear water, it generally has a much better reputation than the snake.

For the ancient Egyptians, the serpent or snake – and by association the eel – was a creature of the underworld. It was also closely linked with the process of creation and was the divine symbol of primeval life emerging from the waters of chaos. The ancients, while lacking the advantages of modern methodology and scientific proof, were convinced that life on earth had originated in the ocean.

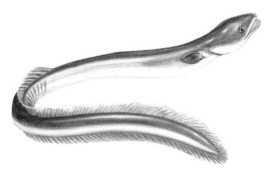

In dreams and predictions, an eel may therefore signify that there is something you haven't quite grasped, that you are about to discover something that has been hidden from you, or that you have been hiding something from yourself that will soon be revealed. A live eel swimming near the surface of the water is a sign that a secret will soon be revealed to you or that someone is about to confide in you. Finding an eel under a rock means that you will understand or discover something you hadn't quite grasped or been aware of even though it existed, albeit unbeknown to you. A dead eel means you will discover something relating to a past circumstance or event that you didn't grasp at the time because it was either hidden from you or you were deliberately deceived.

Egg

According to a picturesque Greek myth, Eros, the god of love, was born at the same time as earth and heaven. Night, seduced by the wind, laid what the Greeks regarded as the primordial egg. This egg cracked open to give birth to Eros, splitting into two halves that formed the roof of heaven and the earth. According to this legend, therefore, the primordial egg, spawned by the unimaginable primeval chaos that prevailed before all manifestations of life, even the appearance of heaven and earth, represented absolute, perfect unity. In giving birth to Eros, night simultaneously created heaven and earth and therefore the duality of this world. This implies that it is through love or for love that one becomes three and three creates two: one being the primordial egg, three being Eros, heaven and earth, having emerged from the primordial egg, and two being heaven and earth.

The strange mathematical byway to which this myth led us is also the one followed by the ancient Chinese to create the two numbers forming the basis of the 8 trigrams and 64 hexagrams of the I Ching. This is yet another illustration of the fact that ideas and concepts develop in the same way throughout the world,

Egg
Egypt
(cosmo-
gonies in)
Eight
Elements
Elephant

despite the very different attitudes, cultures or civilizations involved.

It also illustrates the underlying significance of the primordial egg, which means that, originally, everything came from the same mould, the same beginning, and that the countless different forms of life today share a common ancestry which, on close examination, can be seen from the many similarities and analogies that exist between them. The egg therefore encapsulates the concept that all things are rooted in unity, that they long for this state and return to it sooner or later.

As a result, although dreaming of an egg often indicates birth, creation, a new occurrence in your life, something new and unprecedented, as well as something pure that has never been sullied by the outside world, you should never ignore the possibility that it may also suggest a disruption, a break or a parting. This is because to obtain the two, or the pair of opposites – heaven and earth – that make the world what it is, the one (the primordial egg) must be broken to give birth to Eros to enable heaven and earth to appear. Although this obviously creates a disruption, it can be seen from this Greek myth that it is

through love or for love that heaven and earth exist.

See also *Easter*, page 163.

Egypt (cosmogonies in)

See Cosmogonies in Egypt, page 114

Eight

See Numbers, page 384

Elements

See Air, page 19, Earth, page 160, Fire, page 186, Water, page 528, and Five, page 374

Elephant

In India, the elephant plays a dominant role in the celestial and divine hierarchy of the Hindu religion, where it is first and foremost the mount of Indra, the regent of the heavens and god of rain. Indra is also a warlike divinity and chief of the Vedic gods whose attributes – thunder, lightning and the thunderbolt – are the same as those of his Greek

counterpart Zeus (see *Lightning*, page 317). Indra signifies divine omnipotence manifested on earth, peace, prosperity, the physical strength of achievement, temporal and timeless power. In the Hindu pantheon, the elephant is also a divinity in its own right as the elephant-headed god Ganesha, also known as Ganapati, the patron of learning and wisdom and the 'remover of obstacles'. As such, he is a protector god, a benevolent guide, the equivalent of a good spirit or guardian angel. There are far too many myths and symbols associated with the elephant to consider them all here, but it is worth mentioning in passing that, as may be imagined, there are a great many African myths and legends about elephants. Nor is there sufficient space to devote to the erotic and sexual symbolism related to the animal and its trunk, although we cannot ignore this completely since, far from being unimportant, it can have great significance in a dream. It is, however, worth stressing the obvious analogy between the symbols associated with the horse and those attributed to the elephant. Like the horse, the elephant often represents instinctive, primary, animal forces and urges that can sometimes be destructive when unleashed. But these urges can also be extremely useful to an individual's personal development and self-realization when he or she masters them, brings them under control and uses them wisely (see *Horse*, page 264).

If you dream about a herd of elephants, be warned. It is a sign that instinctive and irrepressible forces and urges that may have been suppressed for too long are about to be unleashed.

Elm tree

The elm tree was thought to be magical, prophetic and dedicated to the Devil. It was a particular bugbear of the Grand Inquisitors, who took great pleasure in having it burned or chopped down in the belief that they were

Elm tree
Erymanthian
boar
Eve
Extra-
terrestrials

uprooting evil and vanquishing demons. In fact, pagans or unbelievers, as they were dubbed by the clergy, dispensed justice beneath the elm tree as well as the oak. This was not divine, Christian or Catholic justice, but earthly justice, that of men and nature, fairies and elves.

When two people had a difference of opinion, it was the custom for them to stand under the elm, one on the right of its trunk, the other on the left, until a leaf dropped on the person who, according to this judgement, was in the right or had been telling the truth. Medieval villagers regarded the elm as a father, a wise old man whom they could consult at their leisure and who would dispense justice impartially.

However, in ancient times, the elm had the more sinister reputation of being a funerary

tree or a tree that could cause sterility, simply because it bore no fruit.

Erymanthian boar (the)

See Hercules, page 235

Eve

See Isha, Eve and Lilith, page 278 and Paradise, page 410

Extra-terrestrials

Nowadays, certain writers, researchers and even scientists readily assert that beings from another world are already among us, surreptitiously influencing the development of our attitudes, our behaviour, our interpretation of the world and life, and, of course, our technological progress, with a view to elevating us to their level, so to speak. One thing that seems to be generally accepted, however, is that life as we know it on earth, or more precisely all the ingredients that make it up, exists throughout the universe. However, this universe is so vast that its dimensions are beyond human imagination and comprehension. It is therefore not impossible that – in another place, at another time and in another way – the same ingredients that make up the vast concoction of life on earth could have been put together to create a form of cellular life identical or very similar to our own in form and essential principles.

But there is a gap between extraterrestrial life and intelligence. Without realizing it, by envisaging the possibility of an extraterrestrial intelligence that has absolutely nothing to do with life as we know and experience it on a day-to-day basis, we touch upon an issue of great theological and metaphysical importance. If intelligence or forms of intelligence, different from those with which we are familiar, can exist without being based on the foundations of life as we know it, then intelligence precedes life and not

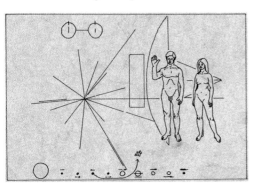

vice versa. This in turn means that the basic principles of modern science, which demonstrate that intelligence derives from life rather than the other way round, are obsolete. But surely the desire – which has become a reality for some – to see, recognize and read signs of life and, above all, signs of extraterrestrial intelligence in the sky, can be compared to the visions of men lost or alone in the desert who eventually see what they want to see? In other words, we may well be looking in the sky, the universe and the cosmos for the signs, links, origins and gods that we have lost here on earth. It is worth considering what history has to say on the subject.

The 20th century was by no means the only century when human beings saw visions in the sky, encountered visitors from other planets or distant galaxies, and recognized the presence of a life or an intelligence that was different from their own. Certain myths and legends could be easily interpreted in terms of creatures from another planet. Certain phenomena that occurred on earth in the past and were invested with a divine nature, especially in antiquity and during the Middle Ages, could also be perceived as manifestations of a superior intelligence.

Furthermore, while it is true that the human race has more or less succeeded in providing a logical and tangible explanation for the evolution of life on earth and the existence of the human race, at least from a biological point of view, the same cannot be said when it comes to explaining the soul and the intelligence. Why and how did human beings distinguish themselves from other species? Why did their brain develop? Why do they have a conscience? Is the world in which they live the world as they see it or a world made in their own image? Is it possible that there are forms of life on earth – vegetable and animal, cellular and microscopic – that have completely eluded human perception, that we encounter in our everyday lives without seeing or even suspecting they exist? If we have nearly always known that nature abhors a vacuum, we now know that the infinitely small is a fully charged and laden universe in its own right, in which the laws of life are the same as those that apply everywhere else in nature.

Therefore, there is nothing to prevent us thinking or believing that, if we are living at the same time and alongside terrestrial forms of life about which we know nothing, nor they about us, but with which we are, nevertheless, associated and involved, we may equally well be living and existing simultaneously and alongside extraterrestrial forms of life that we know nothing about nor they about us.

Be that as it may, the appearance of extraterrestrials in a dream is very often related to the manifestation, in our life or consciousness, of a different reality or truth, which has been there, staring us in the face, for a long time, without our being aware of it. A dream of this nature bears an important message that should encourage us to integrate all the components and levels of our inner consciousness. Although this is usually a spiritual dream, on a more mundane level, seeing or encountering extraterrestrials can represent a feeling of being surrounded by people whom we perceive as 'strangers' or regard as very different from ourselves.

Fairies or
fairy people

From a modern standpoint, it is often hard to appreciate that the magical power of fairies was a reality for our Celtic ancestors. However, our own lives would still be invested with some of this magic if we had not depleted most of these tales of their meaning, of the subtle echoes they stir within us, and of the role they played in awakening dormant or dulled consciences at a time when wisdom, knowledge and experience of life were passed on by word of mouth rather than in writing. Today we tend to dismiss them as old wives' tales, with a mixture of affection, nostalgia and derision that proves they are no longer taken seriously in this lucid and realistic day and age.

So what do we know about these tales of fairies, heroes, heroines and mythical and legendary figures? Are they purely the product of the imagination of men and women who belong to a past so distant that we have lost track of the origins and reasons for these creations that stemmed from our collective dreams? Or were they invented by early poets already skilled in the art of transforming an often harsh and brutal reality into more palatable daydreams?

We will probably never know the answer, but it is reasonable to assume that, as always in the history of mankind, each tale, legend or myth is part truth and experience, part sublimation, speculation and pure poetry. All this should be borne in mind as we embark upon a quest that may well reveal that the elves, fauns, gnomes, sprites, imps and goblins – indeed all the fairies of the forest – did in fact exist and may still exist today.

So what exactly are fairies? Whatever you do, don't say the word out loud and don't think about it too often either. Pronouncing it is one way of invoking those it represents and it is impossible to predict the intentions, actions or reactions of the 'little people' or people of the 'middle kingdom' as they are known in Celtic mythology. They are capable of doing their worst or their best since their behaviour is not exactly consistent and their thoughts, attitudes, deeds and actions are totally unpredictable.

According to the legends associated with fairies, their origins are angelic, divine or necromantic. They are therefore either fallen angels that God, in his infinite mercy, has saved from destruction and allowed to live on earth, divinities who have come down to earth and live both in this and the 'other' world, or spirits of the dead, lost souls with one foot in the tomb and the hereafter and the other on earth and in the visible world.

Fairies also have a great deal in common with the spirits of the natural world that provided the inspiration for the celestial hierarchy of angels (angels, it should be remembered, are associated with the 'astral body'). This is why fairies are often encountered in woods and clearings, near ancient trees, on the edge of springs and pools, in the depths of impenetrable forests, concealed by tall ferns and bushes, or shrouded in mist. It also explains why they are the masters – or mistresses – of a particular place and are able to exercise certain powers associated with the great forces of nature and the elements.

However, the fairies of the forest – as well as the elves, sprites, gnomes, fauns, imps and goblins that are also regarded as fairies (see box, page 178) – have other characteristics which they do not share with the spirits of nature or angels; they have human qualities that are often extreme or caricatured.

In this respect, American developmental psychologist Bruno Bettelheim and German psychoanalyst Marie-Louise von Franz – a leading disciple of C.G. Jung and an expert on the significance of fairy tales – considered that characters in fairy tales were a reflection of the characteristics inherent in subconscious human behaviour (see Bruno Bettelheim, *The uses of enchantment: the meaning and importance of fairy tales*, Thames & Hudson, 1976 and

The etymological origins of the word 'fairies'

A fairy is a supernatural being usually represented in reduced human form and generally depicted as playful, clever and invested with magical powers. The term 'fairy', like the associated word 'fay' (meaning 'fairy' or 'sprite') and the French fée, derives from the Latin fatum ('destiny' or 'fate'), personified in the form of the Fata ('the Fates'). Fatum is also the past participle of the verb fari ('to speak' or 'say') from which the word 'fable' derives via the Latin fabula. A fable is a fictitious account, a story or tale about supernatural characters, a myth or a legend. The Latin fata also gave rise to the Provençal word fada – meaning 'barmy' or 'cracked' but in a pleasant sort of way – from which the French fadets ('imps') and farfadets ('goblins') derive. Finally, the Old French term faerie – used to refer to the magical power of the fairies and magical powers in general – had an equivalent in the archaic English 'faerie' or 'faery', meaning 'land of the fairies' or 'enchantment'.

Marie-Louise von Franz, *The Interpretation of Fairy Tales*, Kendra Crossen, 1996).

From fairy to witch. Fairies already existed long before the dark and troubled period of the Inquisition. However, it appears that from the 14th century onwards, the beliefs, wisdom, myths and symbols of our ancestors were systematically plundered. The nostalgia we feel for these myths and beliefs is due to the fact that without them, we lose our sense of direction and no longer know where we come from, who we are or where we are going. Can fairies help us find our bearings?

This nostalgia probably also explains our renewed interest in what makes us dream and takes us – temporarily at least – away from this materially comfortable, but morally and spiritually uncomfortable and increasingly disenchanted world. Originally, fairies had the same attributes, the same powers and, one could say, the same duties and responsibilities as those now attributed to guardian angels. They were associated with the good spirits of the natural world – the spirits of the woods, forests, valleys, hilltops, mountains, springs, rivers, rocks and caves. When the Romans invaded Gaul and Europe, they called these Celtic spirits – often worshipped by the druids in female form – the *Fata* ('the Fates'), i.e. goddesses of destiny, a term derived from the Latin *fatum* ('destiny' or 'fate') that gave rise to the term 'fairy' (see box above).

From the spinner of fates, the fairy who spins the threads of the destiny of the child in its mother's womb, it was only a short step to the witch who casts evil spells. This step was made by narrow-minded people, avid for power and wealth, who 'proved they were right' by committing the most terrible atrocities. They felt further justified by the fact that the female spirit or fairy had a reputation for being able to transform herself into a vixen, a weasel, a hind or a unicorn, and was invested with such supernatural powers as being able to grant fortune and love, provide miraculous cures for the sick and wounded, seduce men and give birth to magicians as a result of the union, or invest them with strength, courage, bravery and victory in combat. These were all regarded as suspect virtues.

Dame (or Frau) Holle is the perfect example of this type of female spirit. She was a sort of water nymph and the good fairy of Christmas – or sometimes the

guide of St Nicholas (Father Christmas) – who presided over the New Year and travelled the length and breadth of Northern Europe between Christmas and Twelfth Night. When it snowed on earth, it was because Dame Holle was shaking her feather bed. She granted health and fertility to the women who sought her out and their newborn babies came from her pool. She punished lazy spinners by soiling their distaffs, tangling their threads and setting fire to their cloth. Conversely, she sent spindles to girls who spun industriously, and continued or completed their work during the night. She invited children into her pool and granted good fortune to those who were good and hard-working and misfortune to those who were bad and lazy.

These female spirits of the flora and fauna of Celtic Europe were the good spirits of our ancestors. They were particularly honoured by the womenfolk who passed on, by word of mouth and from generation to generation, the rites, rituals and wisdom acquired over the centuries, particularly in the realm of medicinal plants or 'simples' – nowadays back in favour as herbal medicine and herbal remedies. These benign spirits first became equated with evil spirits when, in 1199,

Pope Innocent III declared that heresy was 'treason against God' in his papal bull *Vergentis in senium*, and from the 15th century onwards they were regarded as a scourge throughout Europe. And that was how fairies became witches. (See also *Witches and Sorcerers*, page 542.)

Two of the best-known fairies who were 'demonized' in this fashion are the Celtic fairy Morgan le Fay, the sister of King Arthur who was taught magic by Merlin, and the French fairy Esterelle, who gave her name to the forest and massif (Estérel) in her native Provence and was well known in medieval France for her magic potions that made barren women fertile.

The origins of Halloween. Nowadays, only the Bretons, Scots, Welsh and Irish have preserved the traditions and beliefs of Celtic culture. The Celts worshipped the forces and spirits of the natural world and paid homage to the key elements of nature – forests, mountains, hills, springs, rivers, lakes, pools, plants, herbs and animals. One of these ceremonies took place on the eve of Samhain ('Summer's-End'), celebrated on 1 November, New Year's day in the Celtic lunar calendar.

Traditionally, it was on this night that the fairies – heirs to the gods in that they were past masters in the art of magic and were sometimes evil and malicious and sometimes benign and generous towards human beings – left the visible world to return to their 'other world', the mythical kingdom of the Sidhe. They were therefore particularly active and ubiquitous in the forests on the eve of Samhain, and the Celts went in search of them so that they could dance, sing and get drunk with them, often naked, to celebrate their New Year and the passage of the fairies from one world to the next. This was the famous night of Halloween that was celebrated throughout Celtic Europe.

Falcon

Although the term 'falcon' is applied to many species of hawks belonging to the family *Falconidae* (order *Falconiformes*), true falcons belong to the genus *Falco*. These diurnal birds of prey, with their strong, tapering wings and rapid flight, are found throughout the world. The merlin (*Falco columbarius*) – also known as the pigeon hawk, from the Latin *columba* ('pigeon') – is an aggressive hunter used in falconry. Its English name, derived from the Old French *esmerillon*, from *esmer* ('to calculate', or 'judge'), reflects the bird's ability to swoop down on its prey (birds or insects) with great accuracy when in full flight. The peregrine falcon lives up to its Latin name *Falco peregrinus* ('foreigner' or 'stranger') in the sense that it is found throughout the world and tends to be migratory rather than sedentary. The hobby falcon (*Falco subbuteo*) is midway between the merlin and peregrine falcons in terms of size and strength. It feeds on small birds and insects and also has a tendency to appropriate other birds' nests rather than build its own.

In ancient Egypt, the falcon or hawk was both a sacred animal and a major celestial and divine principle. It was first and foremost the sacred bird of the falcon-headed god Horus, the son of Isis and Osiris, whose Egyptian name Har means 'the one on high', or 'the distant one'. The falcon, hovering high above the earth, also represented the sun, which became the right eye of Horus and then the 'solar eye'

or 'eye of Re', the supreme god and solar deity of Egypt. The falcon or hawk (Egyptian *hik*) was also sacred to the god Sokar, a mortuary god worshipped near the necropolis of Memphis, who was represented as the divine falcon. The hawk-god Soped (or Sopdu) was depicted as a crouching falcon or as a man wearing a headdress of two falcon feathers, while the 'Pyramid Texts' describe him as a star born of the dog-star (the goddess) Sopdet. As such he was associated with the dog-star Sirius (Sothis) on whose annual astronomical position the Egyptians based their calendar and zodiac.

Feather

See Scales to feathers (from), page 443

Feet, legs and knees

Using the symbols evoked by the letters-numbers of the cabbala, it is possible to paint a portrait of a human being showing the body as a tree of life. If man can be compared to a tree – or if he is one – are the roots at the head or the feet? In terms of the tree, it is tempting to say that the roots are represented by the feet, or that they form invisible ties linking mankind to subterranean areas. After all, roots exist, even if they cannot be seen.

However, if we consider the symbolic representation inherent in the XIIth card of the Major Arcana of the Tarot, the Hanged Man, man is viewed as an upside-down tree, an overturned tree that resumes its first and last position in the guise of the Hanged Man. In this case, his head represents the roots, while his feet represent branches.

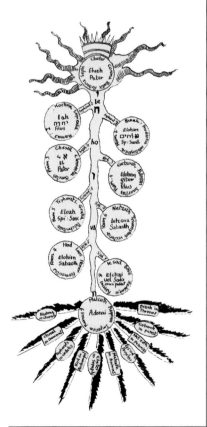

However, the meaning of this roots/branches or head/feet inversion could be interpreted as follows: that each of us, like the upside-down man, must overturn our inner values, energies and consciousness, making an immense, regenerative gesture that is symbolized in the sign of Aquarius, the water-carrier, since the function of the water-bearer is to overturn his pitcher to pour out the water it contains, thus circulating its energy. This is known as the 'reversal of light'.

Feet. If our feet are our branches, then the solid ground on which we stand is our heaven, which is a beautiful poetic image.

Conversely, according to this principle, it can also be said that heaven is our earth, since our roots are not in heaven but in the sky, from which we draw all our energy.

In this respect, we can see that the baby developing in the womb adopts a half-moon or C-shaped position. As a result, its feet, hands and head come together; this curled-up position is known as the foetal position. Now, when the moon forms a C in the sky, it is actually on the wane, from which one might deduce that the biological growth of a human being coincides with or implies a necessary decline in consciousness. After

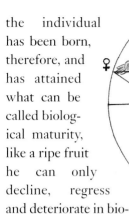

the individual has been born, therefore, and has attained what can be called biological maturity, like a ripe fruit he can only decline, regress and deteriorate in biological terms, since his cells degenerate with the ageing process. To break out of this vicious circle, one can adopt the yoga pose known as the bow, or the inverted foetal position, gripping the ankles with the hands to bring head and feet close together by stretching out the arms and legs behind. Like the waxing moon, the body forms a D. In this way, all the seeds of the primordial energies found beneath and within the feet are linked to the head, brought back to themselves, turned in on themselves in foetal life, open to the world, to everything, to life, to themselves, in this acrobatic pose which represents ultimate self-fulfilment.

The feet therefore contain the beginning and the end. So, when the bottom that is the top (the feet) joins the top that is the bottom (the head), when earth/ heaven and heaven/earth merge and become one, man attains complete self-fulfilment. See also *Foot*, page 195.

Legs. As we shall see, humans have another pair of feet, although they do not realize it because they cannot see them on a daily basis. These are the kidneys, which are shaped roughly like feet and perform a similar function, in the sense that they encourage forward movement. In fact, most of the individual's urges and impulses are produced by the kidneys or revealed by them. They are also a source of balance, strength and inner resources.

The kidneys influence the legs, which they encourage to move in order to go somewhere, reach something or satisfy a desire. Legs may run of their own volition, through fear or other strong emotion, sometimes despite or against the will of the individual, but they can also obey his thoughts, his mind, his will. Legs are like wild animals with simple but unbridled instincts that must be controlled, mastered and tamed.

Knees. We have seen how one can bring head and feet together behind the back to join and regenerate energy from top to bottom, by overturning the usual process, bringing about a 'reversal of light'. However, before attaining this supreme state of self-fulfilment, it is necessary to resist the temptations of pride, vanity and arrogance, feelings that man discovers when he becomes capable of mastering his instincts and making his legs advance or stay motionless at will. He must therefore experience humility, symbolized by kneeling.

Thus, one who kneels, who leans forward and places his head between his knees is in a state of *baraka*, an Arab word meaning 'benediction' or 'heaven-sent grace'. *Baroukh*, in Hebrew, means 'the blessed', while *berekh* means 'knee': it is almost the same word. This similarity can also be found in the etymology of 'knee', which comes from Old English *cneow*, which in turn derives from *g(e)neu*, an Indo-European root shared by the Latin *genu* as in genuflect and genuine, later associated with *genus*, thus gene, gener-ate, genesis, generous, genie, etc. The person who is blessed by heaven, the humblest of them all, is therefore the one who kneels.

Fig tree

The fruit of this prolific tree is said to grant wisdom to those destined to be wise without knowing it, and madness to those who think they are wise but are not. Adam and Eve used the leaves of the fig tree to hide their nakedness after they had tasted the fruit of the tree of the knowledge of good and evil: 'And the eyes of them both were opened, and they knew that they were naked; and they sewed fig leaves together, and made themselves aprons.' (Genesis 3: 7.)

Similarly, it is possible that the fruit of the forbidden tree was not the apple but the fig, and the tree in the Garden of Eden from which Adam and Eve ate the forbidden fruit may have been a fig tree. But how did this regenerating power of life, this fertilizing strength of intelligence, become attributed to the fig tree and its fruit from time immemorial?

According to the *Upanishads* – sacred texts that represent the final stage in the tradition of the Vedas (the most ancient texts in Hindu literature) and constitute the essential elements of the teaching known as the *Vedanta* ('Conclusion of the Veda') – the fig tree is the world tree that links earth and heaven. Furthermore, the fig tree was found throughout the world of our ancestors. In India, it was the tree of Vishnu, in Greece, the tree of Dionysus, in Egypt, the tree of initiation and wisdom, in China, the tree of Buddha and, in Rome, the tree under which Romulus and Remus were born.

The men and women of antiquity ate figs – dried, crystallized or marinated in olive oil – with barley bread and goat's cheese. As well as being familiar with the fruit's delicious flavour, they were also aware of its nutritional value; in fact, the fig contains iron, manganese, calcium and Vitamins A, B1, B2 and C.

Figs are full of goodness and recommended for children, anyone recovering from illness, old people, athletes and pregnant women.

Finally, an article on the fig would not be complete without a reference to the fact that, for our ancestors, the fig symbolized the female vulva and the male scrotum. In Greek, the verb 'to gather figs' also had a more obscene meaning.

Fingers

See Hand (and fingers),
page 214

Fir tree

To the Celts this tree was just as important as the beech tree (see page 56), which they burned in the hearth on 21 December, the night of the winter solstice, as a symbolic act to ensure protection from divine wrath. However, this night was called 'the night of the silver fir', which is why they also often burned an enormous fir log or even a whole fir tree. Anyone who has watched a fir tree burn will know that it is difficult to light because of the

The gods and attributes of fire

Gibil was the Sumerian god of light and fire, while Moloch was the fire-god of the Canaanites in old Palestine. In Mazdean Persia, Atar was both the spirit of fire and the fire-god who had the power to see into the hearts of men and whose temple was known as the 'Kaaba of Zoroaster'. According to the Hindu tradition, Agni is the fire-god but also the fire of the sun, of lightning and of the hearth, Surya is the sun and the sun-god, Indra the chief Vedic god whose weapons were lightning and the thunderbolt, while Brahma, the supreme god, is likened to fire. In Greek and Roman mythology, Hestia and Vesta were the respective goddesses of the hearth and their priestesses – in Rome the Vestal Virgins – were the guardians of fire.

Pyromancy is the art of divination – reading omens and predictions – in fire or flames.

The salamander was a mythical reptile that supposedly lived in fire. It was the guardian of flames and a representation of the dragon, the symbol of primordial energy, the spark of life, the divine fire.

In Rome and the countries of Northern Europe, and especially Europe during the Inquisition, trial by fire was used to test the guilt or innocence of those accused of a crime. The accused was forced to hold a red-hot iron rod; if it burned their hands, this 'proved' their guilt and they were sentenced accordingly.

The Midsummer's (or St John's) Eve bonfires lit on 24 June are thought to be pagan in origin and to derive from the fires of fertilization and purification lit on the day of the summer solstice (21 June), before the harvest to honour the gods and thank them for their bounty, or afterwards to purify the earth.

needles and resin, but how impressive it is when it does catch fire.

As well as being associated with the concepts of immortality and eternity, therefore, these two trees became emblematic of Christmas: the beech being symbolically represented in the guise of a Yule log and the fir serving as the Christmas tree.

Fire

Whether it is heavenly or terrestrial fire, sacred or domestic, or the fire of paradise or hell, fire is a primordial element, expressing both good and evil. Fire symbolizes creation, birth, the beginning, original light, joy, the divine element or the element deified by man. Having traversed the mysteries of the night, man rejoices when his eyes open upon the light of day and are lit by the fire of the sun.

But fire is also destructive since it burns and consumes everything. This ambivalence was perceived at an early stage by our ancestors who made fire a symbol of good and evil.

The fire of the gods. Primitive and ancient man did not

need scientific instruments to measure and understand the advantages and dangers associated with fire. Their survival depended on daylight and the fiery planet (or solar wheel) that was its cause and effect, and on the light and warmth produced by fire. But they had also learnt to be wary of the fire that sometimes fell from the sky in the form of lightning, since they believed that when the gods wanted to punish mortals, they expressed their displeasure, disapproval and anger by means of these celestial fires. The earth also spewed forth fire from its mountains, and it was with a finger of fire, in the crater of a volcano, that God wrote the Ten Commandments on the tablets of the Law, before giving them to Moses. Fire is therefore the principle of life, revelation, illumination and purification, but also of passion and destruction. Fire shines in paradise but burns in hell. It gives life but also takes it and transforms it into ashes.

Hephaestus, Prometheus and the fire of mythology. In Greek mythology, Hephaestus, the counterpart of the Roman Vulcan, was the son of Zeus (Jupiter) and Hera (Juno). He was also the god of fire and metalworking who ruled over the fires of volcanoes. In his capacity as blacksmith to the gods he forged weapons, in particular for Achilles, and he also fashioned out of earth the first woman, Pandora, as the gods' punishment of man for obtaining fire, which, unbeknown to Hephaestus, Prometheus, the son of a Titan, had stolen from the forge of the gods and given to mortals. As a result, Prometheus was regarded as the benefactor of mankind since he had stolen the celestial fire, hitherto the privilege of the gods, with the sole aim of improving the lot of the human race. But the gods were less impressed and, as a punishment, Zeus chained Prometheus to the side of a mountain, with chains forged by Hephaestus, and condemned him to have his liver (which was continuously regenerated) eternally torn out by an eagle.

In the punishment of Prometheus, there are two symbols related to fire. The first is the eagle, the solar bird also associated with the thunderbolt, the

messenger of the gods that carried the celestial fire. The second is the liver, regarded as the seat of the soul or, to be more precise, the organ linking the soul that generates the spark of life and the body to which it imparts life. The liver is therefore the seat of the fire of the soul's passions. The Hebrew word *caved* ('liver') also means 'heaviness' and 'weight' as well as 'wealth' and 'power', in the sense of divine power.

The origins of the term fire. The Latin *ignis* ('fire') was used by the translators of the Bible and by physicians to translate the Greek equivalent *pur*. Both words have given rise to words in modern English associated with fire. For example, words such as 'ignite', 'ignition' and 'igneous' derive from the Latin *ignis*, while *pur* gave rise to such terms as 'pyrotechnics' and 'pyromania', in fact most words with the prefix 'pyro-'. The English word 'fire' also derives from the Greek *pur*, via Old High German *fuir*, Old Norse *fûrr*, Old Saxon *fiur* and Old English *fyr*. The image of fire ranges from the welcoming warmth of the fire in the hearth, an essentially good and beneficent fire, to the idea of conflagration or catching fire expressed by the Latin *ignis*, which was also used for the fire of the funeral pyre (i.e.

purification through destruction, good achieved through evil). Interestingly and confusingly enough, however, the Latin word for hearth (*focus*) was also used for an altar-fire or funeral pyre.

Five

See Numbers, page 374

Flood

Although myths of the flood are found, in different forms, throughout the world, their symbolic significance is always the same. The Bible is certainly the oldest known compilation of texts but the accounts it contains were not written at a given time by a single author, and certainly not in the chronological order in which they are presented. Furthermore, the themes of some of these accounts were borrowed from or inspired by myths and legends that already existed before the first biblical accounts were written, probably in the 9th century BC. Since archaeological excavations were first undertaken in Iraq some 150 years ago, thousands of clay tablets have been discovered, bearing historical, religious, mythical, poetic and literary accounts inscribed in

cuneiform writing with the *cala-mus*, a sharpened reed or burin used by the Sumerians, Babylonians and Assyrians. The oldest of these accounts date from at least 3000 BC – which means they were inscribed in clay some five thousand years ago! – and include the earliest account of the flood, written *c.* 1700 BC.

This flood myth begins at a time when the earth was inhabited by the gods and when mortals had not yet been created. The earth and underworld were inhabited by deities known as the Anunnake, while the sky was inhabited by an inferior class of gods called the Igigi. These gods were given the task of digging out the beds of the Tigris and Euphrates, supervised by the god Enlil, the supreme god of the Anunnake, who represented the power of nature. However, the Igigi became tired and exhausted and decided to rebel. Enlil did not know what to do and therefore consulted Ea (Enki), the god of fresh water and wisdom.

Ea advised him to create a new, inferior race that could replace the Igigi and assume the tasks previously performed by these gods. It was no sooner said than done, and mortals were created to be the slaves of the gods.

The human race was created from the clay found widely

The flood narrative from the Mesopotamian Epic of Gilgamesh

'With the first glow of dawn,
A black cloud rose up from the horizon.
Inside it Adad[1] thunders,
While Shallat and Hanish[2] go in front,
Moving as heralds over hill and plain.
Erragal[3] tears out the posts[4];
Forth comes Ninurta[5] and causes the dikes to follow.
The Anunnaki lift up the torches,
Setting the land ablaze with their glare.
Consternation over Adad reaches to the heavens,
Turning to blackness all that had been light.
The wide land was shattered like a pot!
For one day the south-storm blew,
Gathering speed as it blew, submerging mountains,
Overtaking the people like a battle.

(1) god of storm and rain; (2) heralds of Adad;
(3) god of the nether world; (4) i.e. of the world dam;
(5) god of war also associated with the irrigation of
the land. (Translation by E.A. Speiser, in Ancient
Near Eastern Texts, (Princeton, 1950)

From **Le Ciel, ordre et désordre** *('Heaven, order and disorder'),*
Collection Découvertes Gallimard.

in the region and, so that mortals would be related to the gods they were replacing, the clay was moistened with the blood of one of the Igigi who was sacrificed for that purpose.

The new slaves performed their task so well that they prospered and multiplied, but made such a din that they disturbed Enlil and the Anunnake. Furious, Enlil decided to annihilate this noisy race of inferior beings by sending a plague upon the earth. But Ea had played a key role in their creation and he warned one of them, Atrahasis, so that he could save the human race by telling them to keep quiet. However, soon everything had returned to normal and mankind was making as much noise as before. Beside himself with anger, Enlil decided to send a drought to starve the noisy humans to death. Again Ea intervened and warned Atrahasis who again saved humanity from the new threat. But, just as before, life went back to normal and the noise grew even louder. This time, Enlil lost all patience and determined upon the radical solution of sending a great flood. But Ea, ever on the alert, warned Atrahasis in time. He told him to build a strong, sturdy boat with two decks, solidly rigged and well caulked, and to load the boat with provisions, possessions, his wife and family, craftsmen, and domestic and wild animals. Then all he had to do was board the boat himself and batten down the hatches.

The symbolism of the flood. Whether the writers of the Bible were inspired by earlier accounts, whether they interpreted and transposed events in their own way, whether the main characters were Ea or Yahweh, Atrahasis or Noah (whose Hebrew name is linked to the verbs to lead, console and repent), the symbolic content of

Flower

the flood myth is the same. The flood heralds and represents a necessary regeneration, a renewal that can only emerge from chaos. This chaos can occur on earth in the form of a natural disaster – a flood, tempest or tidal wave – or within each and every one of us when we suffer an illness or when our desires, emotions and passions engulf and submerge us. The Mesopotamian and Hebrew accounts were not the only versions of the flood myth and similar accounts are found in other civilizations.

In Indian mythology, the Hindu god Vishnu, protector and preserver of the world, assumes the form of a fish to save Manu – the first man and precursor of mankind whose name is related to the Indo-European 'man' – from the flood by carrying him to the Himalayas, where he will be safe from the waters.

In Greek mythology, Zeus decided that early man was a lost cause and determined to destroy the human race by causing a great flood. Only Deucalion, the son of Prometheus, and his wife Pyrrha, the daughter of Pandora – who was the first Greek woman – were spared by the god. He told them to build a boat or an ark and, as the flood raged, Deucalion and Pyrrha were saved. When the waters had sub-sided, Zeus told them to make a wish. They were lonely and longed for the company of other mortals, so Zeus told them to throw stones over their shoulders – Deucalion's stones became men and Pyrrha's women.

Whatever the version of the myth, the flood always brings hope, renewal and rebirth. It may be a catastrophe or a cataclysm, but it is neither the end of the world nor the end of time. It is the 'overflowing' or 'rush of water' associated with its synonym 'deluge', which is derived from the Latin *diluvium* ('washing away'), in turn derived from *diluere*, meaning to 'wash away' or 'drench', and from *lavere*, meaning 'to wash' or 'to cleanse'.

See also *Noah's Ark*, page 389.

Flower

Generally speaking, the flower is a symbol of the soul, but a happy, fulfilled soul, detached from material possessions and free from the passions that can disturb and distort it. However, each flower has its own particular symbolism and there is also an actual language of flowers that deserves to be considered at great length and in depth since, not only is it is incredibly rich, but it is also plays a key role in our customs, memories and every-day lives (see *Anemone*, page 30, *Hawthorn*, page 219, and *Lotus*, page 319). We still give flowers as a sign of affection, gratitude, remembrance, joy and happiness. 'Flower' is used in the sense of 'prime' or 'peak' and 'the best or choicest part', as in the expres-sions 'in the flower of one's youth' and 'the flowers of the forest', while 'flower' and 'petal' are also used as terms of endearment.

Flute

It was Pan ('he who feeds'), the Arcadian god of shep-herds and flocks, who used reeds to make the first flute – from the Old French *flahute* or *flaute* – whose etymo-logical root simply means 'to blow'. Pan is an extremely ambiguous, as well as incredibly agile, mythical figure who frequented streams and woods and was particularly attracted to nymphs and beauti-ful young men. The sound of his flute had the same hypnotic effect as the song of the sirens and bewitched those who heard it. Flutes and reed pipes are universal instruments found throughout the world. Their forerunner, the decoy pipe, made from animal bones pierced with holes, seems to have appeared during the middle palaeolithic, a period extending from *c.* 200,000–35,000 BC. The flute and the lyre, which were often symbolically opposed, as in Apollo's contest with Pan, are in fact entirely complementary since, while the flute evokes the breath of the spirit and the lyre is related to inspiration, both are dependent on divine grace. However, because the flute is the attribute of the pastoral divinities Pan and Dionysus, the Greek god of wine, fruitfulness and vegetation, it also has significant licentious, amorous, erotic and even orgias-tic connotations.

Hearing a flute or a pipe in a dream can simply have an erotic meaning as the song of love that attracts or calls us. However, given Pan's ambiguous nature and the flute's ability to bewitch the listener, seeing or hearing a flute player in a dream should lead us to question the sincerity of what that person says or what his or her presence in our dream signifies.

Finally, it should be borne in mind that flute players appear in many tales and legends and, like the god Pan, whose ambiguity does not prevent him from being a good spirit, they generally spread joy and happiness and restore order and peace by playing their instrument.

Flying

Day or night, waking or sleeping, flying appears to have been a recurring dream since the dawn of time. It might be thought that this dream has now become a reality, since airplanes cross the sky daily and many other machines have been designed to fly over land and sea and travel through space. Nevertheless, no one has ever succeeded in flying with his own wings, as the birds in the sky have done since time immemorial. This is why, symbolically, flying is both a sign of freedom and of ambition. Freedom, firstly, because birds seem free to travel from one place to another, ignoring gravity and skilfully riding the air currents. Then ambition, but also presumption, because man has believed that having wings would place him on a par with the gods and that he could soar skywards, as high as the moon

and sun, or even fly to the stars. This arrogant ambition, that incites man to aim always higher, is illustrated by the famous Greek myth of Icarus, whose name seems to indicate that he was dedicated to the moon goddess, Car. Icarus, the son of Daedalus, was imprisoned with his father in the Labyrinth by King Minos (see *Labyrinth*, page 306). However, Daedalus, who would never acknowledge defeat, had the idea of making wings for himself and his son, which he attached to their shoulders with wax. He had thereby found a way to escape from the Labyrinth unbeknown to Minos. Before taking flight, Daedalus advised his son not to fly too close to the ground and not to climb too high in the sky. However, Icarus was a rash young man who ignored his father's sensible advice. He gave in to the temptation to climb ever higher in the sky and flew so close to the sun that the heat melted the wax attaching the wings to his shoulders. The arrogant young man plummeted into the Aegean sea and drowned (this stretch of water was called the Icarian Sea for many years). The moral of this myth is that pride, ambition, presumptuousness and recklessness bring about man's fall. Nevertheless, with regard to both freedom and ambition, it can be seen that the ability to soar unaided has always been associated with intelligence. The human mind and spirit can free the individual from all bonds, but can also lead to their fall, depending on how they are put to use.

This ambivalence always comes into play when men and women, whatever their origins and culture, dream of flying through the air like birds. How many of us have not had this dream at least once? A dream of flying, therefore, indicates that you are either freeing yourself from certain restrictions and winning back your independence and freedom in a certain area of your life, or that you may have fallen victim to an inflated ego,

an overestimation of your own abilities . 'People who have unrealistic ideas,' wrote the Swiss psychologist C.G. Jung, 'or too high an opinion of themselves, or who make grandiose plans out of proportion to their real capacities, have dreams of flying or falling.' (C.G. Jung, *Man and his Symbols*, Aldus Books Ltd, London, 1964.)

Fog

Fog is rather like a low-level cloud. It is caused by droplets of condensed water vapour suspended in the air and reduces visibility considerably. Mist is a similar phenomenon but, because it is less dense than fog, it does

not reduce visibility to the same extent. The origins of the term 'fog' are unclear, whereas 'mist' derives from the Middle Dutch and Swedish *mist* and, ironically, the Greek *omikhle* ('fog').

Symbolically, fog represents everything that is undifferentiated, undefined, indistinct and indeterminate. It can also apply to a state of mental obscurity, confusion (in such phrases as 'fogging the issue') and uncertainty. Dreaming about fog can be a sign of inner confusion, a period of turmoil, discord and conflict with those around you. Mist has similar connotations of haziness and lack of clarity – for example in the expressions 'misty eyed' or the 'misty past' – but the symbolism is much less intense.

Finally, fog can be compared to the chaos and lack of order that preceded creation. In the Bible, fog often preceded a great revelation. In this sense, it can be seen as the harbinger of an important event, a creation, a birth, something new that is about to occur in your life.

Foot

Although feet symbolize walking and, by analogy, human behaviour – the way people act, their impulses, their progress or haste,

their decline or stagnation – they are also associated with taking possession of a property, a piece of land.

Thus, when someone set foot on virgin soil, this was generally a sign of ownership of the land in question. In this respect, the foot is linked to the footprint and is regarded as a type of signature, since every foot – despite being reproduced in pairs by nature to the same unchanging design over thousands of years – is unique in terms of shape and size.

In the Rig Veda, the oldest sacred collection of Vedic hymns that formed the basis for the Hindu mythology, cosmogony and religious philosophy, written between 1500 and 800 BC, the sun is called the 'Soliped', and the supplicant begs the sun to place its foot on his face, to mark him with its footprint, to inhabit his soul. Feet firmly placed on the ground are a symbol of stability, steadfastness and balance, as indicated by the word 'foothold', which means a secure position or advantage. We will briefly mention the link established by Freudian psychoanalysts between the foot, which is a phallic symbol, and the earth on which it rests, which is a female symbol. Earlier cultures all over the world regarded the arch of the foot as a type of map, an open book of the human body. In other words, there are reflex points on our feet that are directly linked to the organs and nerve centres of our body.

The Chinese are past masters in this science called reflexology, a somewhat off-putting term to describe a variety of therapeutic foot massages. The *Nei Ching*, dating from 2700 BC and signed by Huang Ti, the Yellow Emperor, is a treatise on Chinese medicine that devotes a chapter to the numerous meridians beneath the arch of the feet, which can be stimulated by certain massages. This explains why portrayals of the Buddha and of Vishnu displayed numerous symbols on the arches of their feet: these were representations and 'signatures' of the universe, suggesting that man incarnate on earth has the world at his feet. It should be remembered here that, in the zodiac, the feet are symbolically and analogically linked to the sign of Pisces, the fish.

The fish plays an important role in Christian symbolism, since the first Christians adopted *Ikhtus*, the Greek word for fish, as a distinctive sign, its letters forming an acronym for *Iesus Khristos Theou Uios Soter,* or Jesus Christ, Son of God, Saviour. The fish is a symbol of the primeval, maternal life-giving waters, representing the seeds that spawned the human race. Thus the man-fish is the fully developed being. This perfect state of development is achieved when you fuse all the energies in your body, whose reflex points are beneath your feet, with those in your mind, whose reflex points are on your skull. In yoga, this position is called the *dhanurasana* or bow pose and consists in gripping the ankles – while lying flat on the stomach, arms at the sides – raising the torso and thighs by

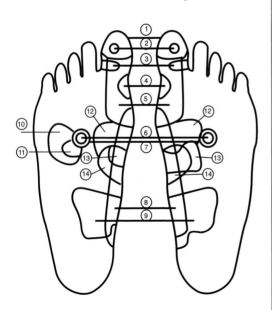

1 *Head*	8 *Spine*
2 *Pituitary gland*	9 *Small intestine*
3 *Nape of the neck*	10 *Liver*
4 *Parathyroid gland*	11 *Gall-bladder*
5 *Thyroid*	12 *Stomach*
6 *Plexus*	13 *Duodenum*
7 *Suprarenals*	14 *Pancreas*

pulling on the ankles so that feet and head almost meet. This posture was clearly depicted in the 12th century by the sculptors of the central portal of the cathedral at Vézelay, where 'cosmic man' is shown in this position.

See also *Feet, legs and knees,* page 181.

Four

See Numbers, page 371

Fox

Almost everywhere in the world, the fox is popularly associated with cunning. It is seen as a creature at once creative and destructive, bold but cautious, defensive yet at ease in its environment. It is therefore full of contradictions and, in this respect, displays typical human qualities. However, according to these popular beliefs, the fox, particularly the vixen, was also the favourite disguise of sorceresses who lurked in forests,

sometimes assuming the appearance of a beautiful, irresistible woman who changed into a vixen as soon as she had achieved her purpose or cast her evil spell. This was not only the case in Asia, but also in Europe. The Hasidic Jewish tradition in particular held that the fox or vixen was possessed by a *dybbuk*, an evil spirit whose sole aim was to torment mankind.

Cunning, seduction and bewitchment are the chosen weapons of the spirit that appears in the guise of a fox, and this is usually how you should interpret the presence of a fox in a dream. However, it should be remembered that the Celts regarded the fox as a guide rather than a sly creature. This was probably because the cunning fox knew the forest inside out, and if our European forebears lost their way they could find the path again by following its tracks.

Frog

Since ancient times, the fact that the frog is particularly prolific and develops from the larval stage (frog spawn), via the tadpole, into a four-legged amphibian, has meant that it is not only a symbol of fertility, but also of regeneration, metamorphosis and transformation. It is therefore as much a product of the nourishing earth as of the original, primordial waters (the waters of the womb) and, as such, is associated with the female principle. However, the primitive life form that it represents was perceived negatively by the writers of the Bible, who made it the instrument of the second of the ten plagues that Yahweh inflicted upon Egypt through the voice of Moses and the hand and rod of Aaron: 'And the Lord spake unto Moses, Say unto Aaron, Stretch forth thine hand with thy rod over the streams, over the rivers, and over the ponds, and cause frogs to come up upon the land of Egypt. And Aaron stretched out his hand over the waters of Egypt; and the frogs came up, and covered the land of Egypt. And the magicians did so with their enchantments, and brought up frogs upon the land of Egypt.' (Exodus 8: 5-7.)

In respect of this biblical account, it should be pointed out that, in the Egyptian pantheon, the frog-goddess Heket was associated with childbirth. Therefore, if the account is interpreted in symbolic terms, there is every reason to believe that the plague of frogs that emerged from the streams, rivers and ponds of Egypt and that eventually 'died out of the houses, out of the villages, and out of the fields' and were 'gathered [...] together upon heaps' so that 'the land stank' (Exodus 8: 13-14), was in fact an epidemic that decimated the new-born babies of Egypt. In this context, the prolific frog has an obvious negative connotation that is often found in connection with Mother Nature or the primordial waters, which can equally well give life and take it, submerge, destroy and annihilate it.

A dream about a frog often puts us in touch with the most primitive and uncharted depths of our being, from which a new and fertile life can arise, but from which may also surge a proliferation or plague of subconscious ideas, thoughts and feelings that are likely to submerge and overwhelm us because we are unable to control them. Thus, although the presence of a frog or frogs in our dreams often indicates a birth or some kind of transformation in our life, it is important to determine what sort of birth or transformation this is, whether it will prove useful, positive and regenerating or destructive and degenerating.

Gaia
or the myth of Mother Earth

Although there is a singular lack of factual evidence and historical proofs of its age and origins, the myth of the great goddess in the form of Mother Earth – the nourishing earth, the great feminine principle and the source of all creation and all life – is extremely ancient. It probably appeared in the collective consciousness of the human race at a time when people began to infringe certain laws and rise up against each other, and therefore the need, if not the necessity, was felt for superior laws and some form of established order.

Gaia, the great goddess of cosmic and social order. The ancient Greeks knew what they were doing when they made Gaia – whom they originally regarded as the mother of the gods and therefore the mother of humanity – the goddess of creation and the goddess of cosmic order. It is generally considered that this example of cosmic order formed the basis for the Greek social and political order that continues to remain a model for all modern world democracies. However, there is a strong possibility that the reverse was true, that Greek mythologists and philosophers, inspired by much earlier myths, developed a mythology that was so well orchestrated, organized and classified that it became exemplary. But in so doing, they created a sublimated representation of an ideal human and social order by unreservedly stressing its imperfections, dangers, outrages, deviations, excesses and, sometimes, its abominations and aberrations. The psychoanalysts also knew what they were doing when they identified the Greek myths and associated legends as a vehicle for the presentation of human feelings and emotions.

A shared image of the world. Today, experts on the origins of mankind agree that symbolic figures drawn and then painted on rock first appeared around 50,000 BC. It seems that, for at least forty thousand years, all the peoples of the earth represented and therefore perceived the world in much the same way. However, since there is no evidence to suggest that the peoples living in China or Australia were remotely aware of the existence of the peoples of Africa, they could not have encountered or known one another and passed on their

Gaia

beliefs and images of the world in which they lived. Although there is any number of modern theories and speculations on the subject, nobody knows why these early humans felt the need to represent the world at a certain point in time. For example, images of landscapes did not appear until around 10,000 BC at the earliest. Prior to this, our early ancestors apparently did not feel the need to represent their everyday environment. Was it because they were so much a part of it that they did not feel the need to question its existence? To understand how such a projection of the world became necessary, it might be useful to compare it to what every new-born child must surely feel, and possibly realize, when it becomes aware that it is no longer part of its mother, no longer part of her body, but a distinct and independent being in its own right. Does this mean that, at a given moment, the instinctive and innate relationship between mother and child has changed, either degenerating or developing, depending on your point of view?

Mother Earth, a pure and harsh goddess. We might well be tempted to think of Mother Earth as a pure and harsh goddess when considering the myth of Gaia. According to this myth, Gaia is a representation of Mother Earth, born of primordial chaos, who imprisoned this chaos within her own body. Then, according to the account of creation given in the *Theogony* of the poet Hesiod (*fl. c.* 70 BC): 'And Earth [Gaia] first bare starry Heaven [Uranus], equal to herself, to cover her on every side, and to be an ever-sure abiding-place for the blessed gods. And she brought forth long Hills, graceful haunts of the goddess-Nymphs who dwell amongst the glens of the hills. She bare also the fruitless deep with his raging swell, Pontus, without sweet union of love.' (*Theogony in Hesiod – Homeric Hymns – Epic Cycle – Homerica*, translated by Hugh G. Evelyn-White, Loeb Classical Library, Harvard University Press, 1998, pp. 87–89.) According to this account, Gaia is the mother of the Uranus (the sky), Ourea (the mountains) and Pontus (the sea). In other words, she is Mother Earth or Mother Nature who, by imprisoning primordial chaos within her body, created order in the world. But the account goes on to describe how she lay with Uranus, the Sky, who naturally 'cover[ed] her on every side'. As a result of this union, Gaia bore the Titans, Titanesses, the Cyclopes and a number of other monsters, but was so horrified by her own progeny that she asked one of her sons, Cronus, to kill his father, whom she held responsible for this disaster. We all know what happened next – Cronus castrated his father Uranus but was later killed by his own son Zeus.

After this, Mount Olympus, the home of the gods, became the scene of interminable tragedies and settlings of scores that we can reasonably suppose reflected the fratricidal conflicts fought by the Greeks throughout their history. Nevertheless, Gaia remained pure and innocent in the minds of both gods and mortals from the beginning to the end of this account, in spite of her original error. For, after all, it was she who had created order in the world, who had given birth to the monsters and gods who were constantly quarrelling and killing one another, and alternately tormenting and protecting mortals who appeared to be their playthings and victims of their whims. It was as if Gaia, the great Greek goddess, the representation of Mother Earth, had,

naturally and in all innocence, created the order of the world, the perfect and ideal order, the only order that existed, the only possible order, one that would inspire gods and mortals to create a divine and social order. However, it was an order based on the constant renewal and permanent regeneration that is the great principle of nature and Mother Earth. As long as gods and mortals refuse to accept and abide by this principle, they appear to be doomed to destroy one another.

See also *Earth*, page 160.

Games and playing

Playing is synonymous with winning or, at least, this is how most of us regard games today. Never before have games, particularly lotteries or so-called games of chance, aroused so much interest, even though they are games in name only. This is because we do not actually play, we just pay our money in the hope of winning and the smaller the sum we spend, the more spectacular the winnings appear to us. All we are actually doing is submitting blindly to sophisticated probability theories, which are formulated by the companies who run the lotteries and whose obvious aim is to ensure that they have a minimum number of winners in the so-called games they are offering.

If you are a 'player' and you apply these theories to yourself, you will know your real 'chances' of winning and what your likely profits will be if you regularly gamble the same sum of money for a certain period of time, preferably using more or less the same combinations of numbers. This knowledge, of course, does not stop people dreaming and wanting to believe that one day, perhaps, as if by magic, they will become rich overnight. For most of us, being rich means being able to give up work, buying whatever we want, never wanting for anything again, living like kings and queens. As a result, game-playing is no longer a matter of life and death, as it once was, but a way of enabling us to gain enough time to do nothing or to waste time, without having to answer to anyone. Playing can now be interpreted metaphorically as a means of losing the life we know rather than literally losing one's life.

Games once had an initiatory nature in primitive societies and ancient civilizations. Pressure of space makes it impossible to explore the chronological, religious and social history of games. It should simply be stressed that games-playing was originally a matter of life and death, in other words, it was a way of winning the right to hold on to life, to be in control of it, to wrest it from the gods. Winning a game was like a second birth.

If a player won, if he passed all the tests set for him during an initiation, he saved his soul, became master of his own fate. This is because the game comprised a series of trials or a supreme trial that the player had to overcome to become equal to a god. By taking part in the game, he met the challenge issued by the gods or he challenged them. So a game, like life, was often an adventure or a deadly experience, while the gods, the masters of the game, never died. The man who emerged as the winner, naturally became the gods' equal and immortal in his turn.

As people became more socialized, as they curbed or tamed their instincts and as they created concepts or ideas, these initiatory experiences became ritualized. From a spiritual point of view, therefore, games became social, recreational or educational, a leisure activity whose sole aims were relaxation or profit, when

Garden

the lure of easy money or the vision of winning the jackpot were brought into play. However, although people are greedy for possessions and gain, they also enjoy having fun: there is a ludic aspect to games-playing. Discovery, understanding and knowledge are also underlying motives.

In modern societies that are swamped by information whose true worth is hard to determine and that provide virtually everything we need within easy reach, we are becoming less and less inclined to search, discover and exercise our natural curiosity, which is essential for stimulating and developing our intelligence and our mental powers. This is why dreams about games and playing are very frequent, and why we generally do not win in them. They are in some way a call to order. Over the millennia, people have always extricated themselves from dangerous or difficult situations by using their intellect. Playing boosts the intellect. This does not apply to games like the lottery, of course, but to the type of game that involves imagination, inspiration, careful thought and determination. It should also be noted that most myths or folktales portray characters taking part in a game: the game of life.

The garden is a place of creation and regeneration, a heartland, a paradise and a place of rest. Everyone has an inner garden that they can visit to find their true self, recharge their batteries and grow. The garden outside – the natural world – is a source of nourishment, fulfilment and wonder. The commonly held view, therefore, is that the garden is a magical, sacred place, a heaven on earth, whether seen from within or without. However, the Bible does not actually make any mention of a paradise when referring to the first garden that, according to Genesis, was like a heaven on earth: 'And the Lord God planted a garden eastward in Eden; and there he put the man whom he had formed.' (Genesis 2: 8.) According to the cabbalists, the Garden of Eden – symbolically represented as a garden filled with delights and consequently as a paradise, a unique place of unbroken peace and tranquillity – actually referred to an inner state, a stage that mankind, in the person of Adam, had to pass through in order to mature and grow. 'Man lost paradise through impatience and through laziness he does not return,' wrote Franz Kafka. However, people long for the natural world and the garden. At one time or other, particularly when they are battered by the din and chaos of big cities, people feel the need to recharge their batteries surrounded by grass, plants, trees and flowers, since nature provides both physical and spiritual sustenance. According to the cabbalists, though, Eden was actually the symbolic representation of a place that was perilous for the soul, not a place of refuge. As such, they believed it was to be avoided at all costs, the implication being that Adam had every reason to eat the forbidden fruit in order to be expelled from Paradise. In some respects, this is the case. In calling Eden dangerous, the cabbalists meant that it represented the comfortable, stable condition into which mankind, by nature, tends to settle and which causes them to stagnate, preventing or destroying any potential for self-development. The history of mankind contains many examples to support this theory: each time a tribe, nation or civilization has become accustomed to a certain degree of comfort or conformism, gradually rejecting any creativity, anything new or strange that might have an impact on its customs or mindset, it appears to have signed its own death warrant.

As a result, the magnificent gardens grown all over the world, from East to West, by all races, reflecting their particular style, their world vision, may be nothing more than a snare, a delusion. Mankind is continually searching for a place of rest, a refuge, a way of getting back to basics, to all that they were forced to renounce a long time ago for their own good. In this respect, it could be said that the need for a garden is regressive. This is certainly arguable, judging from the current success of disaster movies that can be seen as the expression of a repressed desire or hope in our collective consciousness for the destruction of the garden of the world so that we can create a new garden, a new world.

For this reason, however beautiful and enchanting the garden that appears in your dream, always remember that it may be a trap set by yourself, because it is human nature to

prioritize safety and comfort over self-development and personal growth.

Gemini (sign of)

See Zodiac, page 558

Genie

Originally, a genie – derived from the French *génie* and Arabic *jinni* ('demon'), influenced by the Latin *genius* ('attendant spirit') – was the spiritual and divine being within each and every one of us, a representation of the soul or the spirit. In general terms, the word now usually conjures up the image of the genie from Aladdin's lamp, the servant who appeared by magic and was ready to grant Aladdin's wishes. However, the two concepts are not mutually exclusive since the genie imprisoned in the lamp symbolizes the soul or spirit imprisoned within the body. In its bid for freedom, the genie has

to grant three wishes to whoever opens – or, in Aladdin's case, rubs – the lamp, since the genie (or spirit) represents light, inner clarity, perfect vision and the gift of clairvoyance. If the wishes expressed by its liberator are futile, incoherent and exclusively centred on the material, temporal and transitory aspect of life, then this person has wasted their opportunity, their wishes and their life, and loses their genie and therefore their soul. At least, this is the moral of the tale of Aladdin and his magic lamp, since that was how the genie was perceived in the Middle East.

In ancient Egypt, the genie was not always such a benign symbolic and mythical figure, while in Arabic mythology, a genie or genius was a demon or jinn (*jinni*). This automatically leads us to consider good and bad genies associated with the spirits of the dead, whose intentions were not always generous and altruistic. By contrast, to the Romans, a *genius* was a guardian spirit who attended a person from birth to death and the word also meant the guardian of a place. The concept of familiar spirits associated with places, and especially nature, was echoed in medieval Europe, where they were found in woods, near springs and pools, or in caves, and where a person's spirit or genius might be represented by an animal, a tree or any other natural element. It was this principle that formed the basis of the celestial hierarchy of angels (see *Devil*, page 147), a type of structured organization of the good spirits and genies of nature, which, it should be remembered, also have a darker side.

The appearance of a genie in a dream often coincides with the hope of realizing a wish. However, since the genie also represents 'light, inner clarity, perfect vision and the gift of clairvoyance', a dream about a genie sometimes puts us in touch with our more enlightened side.

Genitalia

See Thighs, pelvis, lower back and genitalia, page 489

Geryon
(the cattle of)

See Hercules, page 249

Giant

Palaeontology is a relatively new science and one which, like natural history, demands a great deal

of patience and expertise, a sense of 'touch' and a certain fascination for reconstructing the jigsaw puzzles created by nature over the millennia. But it was long before the sciences of natural history and palaeontology were developed that our ancestors first discovered bones dating from the Triassic, Jurassic or Cretaceous eras, the three periods during which dinosaurs walked the earth. It was probably the discovery of these bones that gave rise to the image and belief in the existence of a giant man – in popular myths and legends about giants, the latter are always men and never women – or a dragon. We may therefore assume that, from early on in their history, our forebears may have been haunted not only by the image of a great

dragon or sea serpent, but also by that of a primitive, original being, an extraordinary and rather monstrous Adam, who ruled the earth or possibly belonged to a superior race. If we accept that giants and dragons have been part of our collective imagination from time immemorial, it is easier to understand our fascination with dinosaurs. This fascination is heightened by the fact that these huge creatures met a tragic, not to say cataclysmic, end that inspires our sympathy, regardless of whether they were in some way responsible for or merely innocent victims of their fate. Modern man is fascinated by gigantism in the form of excessive growth, large-scale expansion and massive over-production while taking few, if any, precautions and at the risk of destroying the environment and the ecological balance of the planet, without which, as everyone knows, all this growth and production would have been impossible. There is therefore something primitive and primary about the myth of the giant that is associated with the generosity and prodigality of Mother Nature, whose elements are nevertheless sometimes fearfully and uncontrollably violent. The myth of the giant can also be related to what psychoanalysts refer to as an inflated sense of self, which is sometimes reflected in feelings such as pride, presumption, self-importance or a superiority complex.

It is often when suffering from such a complex that we dream about a giant or see ourselves as a giant. To identify the area of our life in which we are experiencing this inflated sense of self, all we have to do is observe the behaviour, actions and gestures of the giant in our dream. This is a primitive, crude and unsubtle expression of one aspect of our personality, but it has become such a dominant part of us that it now controls our behaviour and actions. The giant is trying to make us aware of this fact.

Girdle (Hippolyte's)

See Hercules, page 247

Goat

During the early Stone Age, some thirty-five thousand years ago, the goat appears to have been hunted mainly for its meat and hide. It does not seem to have been domesticated until *c.* 6000 BC when it was reared for its milk and cheese.

The goat is reputedly an irascible and capricious animal. Interestingly, 'capricious' shares the same etymology as 'caprine', meaning 'goat-like', since both are derived from the Latin *caper* ('goat') and *caprinus* ('goat-like'). However, the symbolism was readily associated with a nurturing earth-goddess – probably because of its milk – who suckled humans at her breast or udder, as at the udder of a cow. The goat therefore tends to be associated with benign symbols, except in the myth of the Chimera (Greek *chimaira*, meaning goat), which is depicted as a fantastical creature with a lion's head, a goat's body and a dragon's tail. The goat usually represents the abundance of the earth's nourishment and, by analogy, spiritual nourishment.

But it also symbolizes agility, light-footedness and gracefulness owing to its ability to run and jump from rock to rock, often on steep mountain slopes.

When a goat appears in a dream, it is the animal's capricious nature that is being emphasized since its unpredictability is in tune with the laws of the nature. Both are governed by a logic that is not the logic of intellect or reason, but of instinct. This is why a goat may appear in your dream if you are tending to prioritize reason to the detriment of instinct, represented by the goat. It usually means that an unforeseen event is likely to occur in your life or that you will or should react instinctively and against all reason.

Gold

Gold, which over the centuries has been regarded as a supremely precious metal by every civilization in the world, is still associated with anything beautiful, rare and valuable. The picturesque saying that someone has a heart of gold, for example, means that a person is kind and generous, while the Golden Age has always been regarded as an idyllic time experienced once by mankind and

which, according to numerous myths, still awaits him, like a promised land. Gold conjures up thoughts of riches, treasure and wealth both in your waking life and in your dreams. However, gold in a dream usually represents inner riches, the finest human qualities that someone can possess, sometimes without even suspecting it.

However, it should never be forgotten that since gold is a precious metal, it is also an object of greed and desire and thus the cause of many rivalries, conflicts and wars. This is perhaps why that mythical Golden Age appears to be a time when, paradoxically, gold has ceased to exist and mankind is free from ambition and greed.

Goose

The domesticated, battery-reared goose, whose fatted liver is used to make pâté de foie gras, is descended from the so-called snow goose, which is still found in North America and Greenland. However, there are many other species, including the Egyptian goose with its russet, grey, black and white plumage and green, brown, black and white wings, and the greylag goose, whose long grey wings are edged with white. The greylag goose is known for its loyalty to its mate and the male and female pair for life, which is rare for birds. The female goose lays on average from four to eight eggs every year. She nests and lives close to lakes, ponds, rivers and streams and feeds on grasses, seeds and sometimes small aquatic animals.

In ancient Egypt, Amun, the tutelary god of Thebes, who was associated with Re, the supreme god of the Egyptian divine pantheon, had two sacred animals: the ram and the goose. In fact, although the pharaoh was

identified with Amun-Re, and therefore with the sun, his soul was symbolized by a goose. For this reason, the goose was seen as a type of angel, a messenger between heaven and earth, gods and mortals. In the Roman Empire, the goose was a representation of Juno, the sister-wife of Jupiter, a couple also identified with Hera and Zeus. Thus, in Rome, Juno Moneta ('she who warns') was an oracular goddess, a prophetess who was frequently consulted and who handed out abundant advice, predictions and warnings. Juno possessed some sacred geese whose cackling warned the Roman soldiers of an invasion by the Gauls in 390 BC, an episode better known as the Legend of the Capitoline Geese.

Greece (cosmogonies in)

See Cosmogonies in Greece, page 117

Green

Green is the colour of pastureland, grass, the countryside and nature. And yet, since the distant past, this colour has been associated with water, particularly the sea and the ocean, which are only blue when they reflect the cloudless sky. So green is both the colour of the earth and of water: the regenerated earth covered with grass, lush with rainwater in the spring, and the sea, with its algae and coral. Like grass, which is reborn in spring, green is a symbol of hope, youth and renewal, and, like the surface of the sea, it is a sign of strength, power and longevity. Green is a cool, bracing colour. Numerous popular expressions illustrate the characteristics and properties of green. For example, a 'greenhorn' is a novice at anything – someone who is young and inexperienced – while a jealous person is said to be 'green with envy', since a greenish complexion was once thought to denote this base emotion. A 'green old age' is one in which the faculties are not impaired and the spirits are still youthful, since green can also mean young and vigorous. These aspects all have a bearing on the interpretation of a dream that features this colour prominently.

Gull

The best known of these coastal birds – the seagull – is found on the coasts of the Atlantic, the North Sea and North America but also further south, especially in Spain.

Unsurprisingly, as well as using grass and twigs to build their nests, these gulls also use seaweed. They have an impressive wingspan and are noted for their beautiful, wheeling flight as they negotiate the air currents above the sea. They feed mainly on fish, but also attack other birds and sometimes even their eggs and chicks. With their predominately white plumage and large yellow beaks, gulls are impressive birds, magnificent in flight, but also rather disturbing when seen tearing at carrion or picking through the rubbish that all too often pollutes our shores.

This darker side of their nature was superbly represented in Alfred Hitchcock's classic film *The Birds* (1963).

The gull's ability to navigate sometimes extremely turbulent air currents and fly above stormy seas led sailors to believe that their presence in the open sea was because they were the embodiment of souls of dead mariners following the vessels on which they had lived and sailed. According to an ancient legend, the seagull represents the soul of a mariner who died or was lost at sea, a legend so deeply rooted in the minds of seamen that, even today, they consider it disastrous or sacrilegious to kill a gull.

Hair

According to popular myth and legend, a man's hair is seen as symbol of his strength and virility – the legend of Sampson and Delilah is the obvious example of this. A woman's hair, on the other hand, represents pure and perfect femininity, a pledge of immortality, wisdom, absolute love and union with God. This is illustrated by the Christian legend of Mary Magdalen, who, according to French legend, was found dead in a cave in Provence, where she had lived as a hermit for many years. She was buried in the shroud of her hair that had grown to her ankles.

If you see yourself in a dream with beautiful long hair, it is often a sign of happiness, prosperity and love. If you dream that someone is cutting your hair, it is a sign of physical or moral weakness, while short hair and baldness symbolize vulnerability or a lack of energy.

Halloween

*See Fairies or
fairy people, page 176*

Hand
(and fingers)

When someone illustrates the point they are making with gestures, they are said to be 'talking with their hands'. Deaf-mutes use sign language based on an alphabet in which each letter corresponds to a sign made with the hand. Perhaps the most beautiful and most compelling representation of the hand, however, is the symbolic meaning contained in the Hebrew verb *yada*, 'to know', formed from the root *yad*, 'hand', plus the letter *Aeïn*, meaning 'eye'. In Hebrew, *yada*, 'to know' also carries the sense of 'to love'. Thus one can say that, in the religious Jewish and cabbalistic sense, knowing and loving are

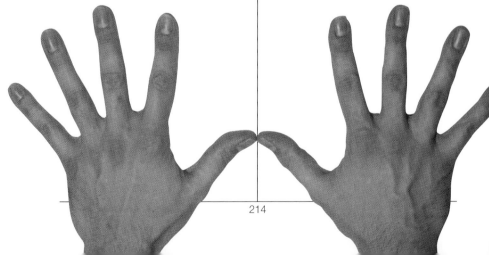

identical and are both embodied in the hand. This helps to explain why Adam was said to have 'known' Eve and how knowledge is indistinguishable from love.

A similar interpretation can be found by examining the French words derived from the root of the verb *prendre* ('to take'): *apprendre* ('to learn'), *comprendre* ('to understand'), *s'éprendre* ('to fall in love'). This also sheds light on the symbolic meaning of the laying on of hands. Although more is now made of the link between hand and brain and the vital role this plays in the early development of intelligence, the relationship between hand and heart, deemed important in the past, should also be taken into account.

The brain is now considered the ultimate vital principle. Clinical death is measured by the complete loss of brain activity rather than cardiac arrest. Is it a coincidence that manual skills are on the decline and that more and more inventions are doing away with what would once have been manual work. The downside of this trend is that the satisfaction that comes from a job well done is rarely experienced in modern societies that prioritize profitability and care little for craftsmanship. The result is that traditional crafts are gradually disappearing.

In ancient times the hand was believed to be linked just as much to the brain or head as to the heart, in particular by the five fingers. The thumb, corresponding astrologically to Venus, was connected to the head and brain. It is interesting to note in passing that the head and brain were linked to the finger associated with Venus, i.e. with love and human emotion, not with the one linked to Mercury, the planet governing intelligence, as might have been expected in the light of modern concepts about the relationships between the brain, mental agility, intellect, reason, reflection, learning, knowledge, etc. It was the little finger, the smallest on the hand, that was, in fact, linked to Mercury and thought to relate to the heart. For this reason, our forebears believed that intellect came from the heart, while love had its seat in the brain. It is worth re-examining this interpretation of human phenomena closely, since it completely challenges contemporary postulates.

Between the thumb and the little finger are the index finger, linked to Jupiter – again in accordance with the astrological correspondences established by the Chaldeans, among others – the middle finger, associated with Saturn, and the ring finger, linked to the Sun. Accordingly, each finger has a specific meaning and this is extremely important when one plays a dominating role or draws our attention in a dream. The dream should be interpreted according to the indications associated with the relevant finger.

In Hinduism, there is a type of finger yoga called Mudra yoga, commonly used in sacred dances, in which each position of the fingers, each movement or gesture of the hands has a particular meaning and forms a language in its own right. Elsewhere, the right hand and the left hand do not always mean the same thing. In China, for example, the right hand is often regarded as the hand linked to action, the will and determination, while the left hand is thought to be the one that lets go. Simply put, it could be said that the right hand is active and the left hand is passive.

By focusing on the relationships and analogies between the hand(s) and the heart and brain, you will be able to understand the meanings that may be attributed to hands that are dirty, tied, paralysed, injured or severed in a dream. In such cases, it is often the dreamer's ideas, thoughts and emotions that are being challenged or brought to the fore. Also, when you see yourself or another person using an object, a utensil or a tool in a dream, take note of the object in question, because its symbolic meaning will often help you to understand what is (figuratively) being manipulated.

Hands

See Senses, page 448

Hare

Hares or ferrets run like the wind and multiply in our dreams as in our nursery rhymes. The hare is known to be swift and agile. Our ancestors regarded it as a lunar animal simply because it goes to ground during the day, but it loves capering through the woods, fields and meadows at nightfall. The Chinese, who chose this animal as the fourth sign of their zodiac, believe that the moon is inhabited by a jade hare grinding ingredients in a bowl to prepare an elixir of immortality. Also in China, the hare is said to possess the qualities of clear-headedness

and perceptiveness, because this animal, which has long ears and longer, better-developed legs than the rabbit, is born with open eyes. With the unrivalled reputation of being particularly fertile, the hare was a symbol of abundance, wealth and prosperity, and also of waste; it often stood for a rather unsavoury individual with dissolute morals and uncontrollable urges. There is, however, another subtle difference that should be stressed: our forebears generally associated the shorter-eared rabbit with lust, while the hare was linked with racing, speed and swiftness.

It is important to make this distinction between the hare and the rabbit in a dream, which can be interpreted quite differently depending on whether it features a rabbit – generally many small rabbits – or a hare. When a rabbit(s) appear in a dream this reveals an overactive sex-drive, or libido. The rabbit always heralds some sort of increase: fantasies, ideas, emotions, anxieties, etc. The hare, on the other hand, is associated with dynamism, agility, fast mental reflexes and the type of instinctive intelligence that knows exactly what needs to be done and when.

Harp

It is important to distinguish between the harp and the lyre and cithara (zither), which are often incorrectly regarded as ancient forms of harp. Originally the harp – which was probably invented before the lyre – was quite possibly a simple wooden bow with strings and a 'soundboard' hollowed out of the bow. It was widely used by the ancient Egyptians, the Celts and throughout medieval Europe.

The harp's symbolic feminine attribute was not only associated with the ladder, due to the arrangement of its strings, but also with the journey into the hereafter and the quest for perfect happiness suggested by the elegance and subtlety of its softly resonant notes. A dream about a harp often represents this quest (or desire) for well-being, happiness and harmony and, since it is a very ancient instrument, it has a nostalgic quality that evokes paradise lost. The harp also has a negative aspect, since the word evokes the winged monsters of Greek mythology known as the Harpies that, as their name suggests (Greek *harpazein*, 'to seize'), were the 'snatchers' of children and souls.

Hat

It almost goes without saying that it is our ancestors who hold the key to the origins and symbolic significance of the hat. Etymologically, 'hat' and 'hood' share the same Latin root *cassis*, meaning 'helmet' – 'hat' via the Old English *hæt* and Old Norse *höttr* ('cap'), and 'hood' via Old English *hod*, Old High German *huot* and Middle Dutch *hoet*.

There are a great many popular expressions involving the hat that are based on its historical use and symbolism, for example 'cap in hand' (humbly), 'at the drop of a hat' (immediately), to 'keep something under your hat' (keep a secret), 'out of a hat' (as if by magic), 'to talk through one's hat' (to talk foolishly), 'to throw your hat into the ring' (to enter a competition, especially political), 'to pass the hat round' (to collect money, especially for a good cause).

Historically, the hat was a piece of headgear that served to protect men and women from the rain and cold, and women in particular from the sun. It was also worn as an accessory or as a symbol of office, power or authority. In this last respect, it has associations with the Latin root *caput* ('head') and *capitalis* ('concerning the head, chief') from which the adjective 'capital' – meaning primary, chief, principal or first-rate – is derived. By extension, the hat in the form of the crown was the attribute of kings and queens, of those invested with divine power. One obvious example comes from the hat-like crowns of pharaonic Egypt, the best known being the white crown (*hedjet*) of Upper Egypt, the red crown (*deshret*) of Lower Egypt, the double crown (*pschent*) of Upper and Lower Egypt, the 'blue crown' or 'war crown' (*khepresh*) and the famous *nemes* or headcloth represented on the gold mask of Tutankhamun. All these are symbols of the power, sovereignty and authority invested in the royal wearer. In more primitive, warlike cultures, tribal chieftains appear to have worn a helmet or crown surmounted by two horns, possibly the bull or buffalo horns that formed one of the earliest symbols and were subsequently rotated to form the letter *a* (see page 18).

In the past, the hat appeared to be associated with some form of superiority, a major or primary role played by a particular individual, and this is how its appearance in a dream should be interpreted. Constraints of space make it impossible to describe the individual significance of each type of hat, which often indicates function, professional position or social status. For example the cap, top hat, military cap, boater, wide-brimmed hat, beret and bishop's mitre all have their own particular meaning.

However, it should be remembered that to interpret a dream about a hat correctly, it is not enough to focus on its shape. You also have to take account of its etymology and historical associations, as outlined above. To dream that you are wearing a hat on your head can be interpreted in the figurative sense of 'being in charge', but you should bear in mind that this type of dream is always more subtle and complex than it appears and that, at the very least, it will force you to think.

Hawthorn

Hawthorn was widely used by the Gauls to calm palpitations and combat insomnia. In ancient Greece, its purity and whiteness made it a symbol of the pure love and fidelity of newlyweds who were given branches, sprigs and bunches of hawthorn. Later, the Romans consecrated the birth of a baby by decorating its crib with hawthorn. Finally, the Christians saw the shrub as a symbol of the

purity they attributed to Christ and the Virgin Mary. Hawthorn has always enjoyed a good reputation due to its beneficial and protective properties.

Dreaming about hawthorn or seeing it unexpectedly is therefore a sign of providential protection, beneficial action, relief, a birth or a happy marriage.

Hazel tree

The hazel tree is prominently mentioned in the poetic and mythological legends of the Germanic *Edda*. The hazel staff was one of the attributes of Thor, son of Odin, along with the hammer he used to strike the anvil, a symbolic act representing his formidable strength and terrible wrath. However, Thor escaped drowning in the sparkling river Vimur and defeated the giants with the help of the hazel staff given to him by the giantess Gridr, whose name means 'greedy one' or 'violent one'. The name

of this staff was Gridarvorl (Gridr's rod) from Gridr, the giantess, and *vorl* or *volva*, the word for the divinatory, magic wands used by seers.

Later, in the Middle Ages, probably inspired by this legend from Germanic mythology, the hazel rod became the magic wand of fairies, just as the sorcerer's baton was said to be made of hornbeam.

Hazel was also the wood used for the magic staff given by Zeus to Hermes-Mercury, which was called a caduceus and was often carried by heralds or messengers (see *Caduceus*, page 78).

Heart

The symbolism of the heart is similar to that of the centre (see *Circle*, page 100) since it is often associated with the concept of 'centre'. The ancient Egyptians regarded the heart as the fundamental vital function, a belief which has been so widely accepted that, even though modern medicine considers clinical death to occur with the complete arrest of brain activity, as registered by an encephalogram, the popular conception of death is when the heart stops beating. Opinion is divided on the subject since one school of thought believes that the brain controls all vital functions, while the other asserts that it is the heart that is the driving force or 'motor' of life. The heart is symbolically the seat of the emotions, a word that shares the same etymology and therefore the same origins as 'movement' and 'motor'. Although movement is not the origin of life, it is certainly one of its most obvious manifestations.

In ancient times, it was believed that the relative weight of the virtues and vices of the dead person could be estimated by weighing his or her heart. The example that springs to mind is the Egyptian 'Weighing of the Heart' ceremony during which the heart of the deceased was placed on the scales of justice and weighed against the feather of Maat (the symbol of truth), in the Hall of Judgement. This aspect should be taken into account when interpreting a dream in which the heart plays a predominant role.

Hecate

See Athena, Cybele and Hecate, page 40

Hedgehog

The hedgehog was a symbol of wealth in the Far East and of domestic fire among the Mongol peoples of eastern Siberia, that is, of fire controlled by humans and used to their advantage. However, in spite of its peaceable nature and usefulness – it feeds almost entirely on insects and earthworms – this little mammal has never enjoyed a particularly good reputation. This is probably because, as everyone knows, it is covered in spines and its timid nature often causes it to roll up into a ball that pricks anyone or anything that tries to harm it.

This is why a dream about a hedgehog often represents a defensive attitude, 'prickly' behaviour and a tendency to lose your temper and fly off the handle. These characteristics can equally well apply to you, to someone close to you, a friend or family member, or to someone you meet in your everyday life and who, in spite of an apparently friendly nature, has a tendency to be 'prickly'. A dream of this nature can sometimes also be warning to tread carefully, both literally and figuratively. While stepping on a hedgehog can be a painful experience, this little animal also has a reputation for being the enemy of snakes. So, a dream about a hedgehog may also involve a few snakes.

Hell

As well as being related to the idea of sin, the concept of hell is often closely associated with that of heaven or paradise (see *Paradise*, page 410). In other words, if we act and behave well, if we respect the established order and 'do our duty', not only will we avoid going to hell but we can be sure of going to heaven. However, if we contravene the laws of nature and life, or the rules and conventions imposed upon us by society, we can expect to go to hell. These are – admittedly in a simplistic and very condensed form – the principles of heaven and hell that underpin our dormant consciences, principles that are nowadays often regarded as old-fashioned and outdated.

In ancient times, hell was a quite different concept. According to ancient Greek mythology, for example, hell, traversed by the river Styx, was the domain of Hades (Greek, *Aïdes*, 'the unseen'), who ruled as absolute master over the 'kingdom of the dead'. However, he was not simply the god of hell, he was the god of the underworld, a vast kingdom with many subdivisions, filled with great riches. As if to prove that his underworld kingdom was 'blessed' with infinite treasures and eternally replenished wealth, Hades (aka Pluto, 'the rich') was often depicted holding a horn of plenty (see *Horns and Crowns*, page 262). Some people see in this symbol a sort of black humour, as if Greek mythologists were being ironical about the infinite riches of death.

On the other hand, there is a very obvious analogy, found widely in the symbolism of civilizations all over the world, between death and riches, between the unseen, subterranean life and fertility, and therefore the potential riches buried in the earth and – why not? – in the universe of the invisible world. Do we not sometimes draw on mental resources, of which we are often unaware and that are obviously an entirely invisible phenomenon, in order to regenerate ourselves, to achieve remarkable feats or exploits and to excel ourselves? This leads us to conclude that the underworld of Greek mythology was not a kingdom in which shades and souls were condemned to be imprisoned 'for death', so to speak, but a place of necessary or compulsory exile that enabled them to be regenerated and transformed. In fact, whatever the culture, civilization or belief, it appears that hell was perceived as an obligatory rite of passage in order that souls could be reborn, a place that they could only leave renewed. The fact that this mythical kingdom of hell or the underworld was imagined to be deep in the bowels of the earth, in subterranean depths ravaged by the most voracious fire or the most unbearable cold, confirms that it was perceived as a return to the womb, as a regression, but not as a drastic and definitive sentence. Although Christianity has placed great emphasis on eternal damnation, it appears to be the only religion in the world to have this concept of a terrible and irreversible punishment, a concept that is relatively recent. Although the principles of

Helmet

sin, misdeeds and transgression exist in all other cultures and religions, they do not share the belief that sinners have no right of appeal, no hope of salvation. The concept of hope was emphasized in all the original religions of the world, including Christianity, but over the centuries this has been lost through intolerance.

Even so, the images of hell were so numerous that they have been totally integrated into our culture and, in spite of what we may rationally think and believe, are etched on our collective memory. Thus, we may very well dream that we are in hell, although a dream of this type does not mean we are doomed to lose our soul. It is more likely to mean that, by taking a wrong turning in our life, losing our way or acting against our better nature at the time of having the dream, we are becoming disorientated and ultimately destroying ourselves through our own actions. In other words, we are turning our life into a living hell and the dream is telling us to do something about it. A dream in which we see ourselves going down into hell can also make us aware of our situation. We are in fact seeing the inner demons that embody our negative thoughts and behaviour and this can prove to be an extremely salutary experience.

Helmet

The helmet was believed to have magical qualities by the first warriors to wear this piece of protective headgear since, like the shield (see page 454), it made them feel relatively invulnerable. As one of the attributes of Hades (aka Pluto), the Greek god of the underworld, the helmet made the wearer invisible. Furthermore, because it was worn on the head, the helmet was also considered to protect or conceal the wearer's thoughts. It therefore represents carefully guarded, impenetrable secrets or hypocrisy, depending on the circumstances. If you dream about a person wearing a helmet, you should always ask yourself whether that person is concealing something from you. If you are wearing the helmet, it is because you are trying to keep a secret, or are hiding or concealing something.

The helmet can also be a symbol of your own moral strength, of which you do not realize the full extent, or of the providential protection you are enjoying.

Hercules
(The twelve labours of)

Everyone knows the legendary Greek hero Hercules, the demi-god endowed with superhuman strength. However, less widely known is that the cycle of the twelve labours of Hercules, one of the best-known legends in Greek mythology, is associated with the twelve signs of the zodiac.

Like Tarzan and Zorro, Hercules was one of the 'pantheon' of heroes featured in B-movie epics that delighted the younger generation of the 1950s, 1960s and 1970s. It goes without saying that the directors of these movies had few scruples about interpreting the legends of Greek mythology loosely, not to say casually, and this was particularly true of the twelve labours performed by the Greek hero Hercules. For example, *Hercules in New York* (aka *Hercules Goes Bananas*, 1970) – now available on video and DVD starring Arnold Schwarzenegger – tells how Hercules is thrown out of Mount Olympus into New York city, where he becomes entangled with wrestling promoters and the mob, among others.

Although the Greek name of this legendary figure is in fact Heracles – Hercules was the name given to him, much later, by the Romans – we have opted for the Roman rather than the Greek name since it is more widely used in the English-speaking world and is familiar to most readers.

Furthermore, we have decided to focus on the cycle of Hercules' twelve labours as they are the symbolic representation of the twelve stages encountered by man as he makes his way along the path of freedom, knowledge and truth. They can also be interpreted on a spiritual and mystical level as the twelve obstacles surmounted by the soul to liberate itself from the body, cast off its earthly frame and free itself from desires, passions, good, evil and the endless and eternal cycle of rebirth and regeneration.

Mythology and mythologies. Long before they were adopted by modern psychoanalysts and psychologists as the projections of the human psyche, the gods of myth and legend and their incredible adventures were regarded by our ancestors as the mythical representations of the virtues and weaknesses of ordinary men and women, their joys and sorrows, pleasures and sufferings, and the good and evil of which they are capable.

The twelve labours of Hercules
and the twelve signs of the zodiac

First labour
The Nemean lion: associated with the sign of Leo
(see page 564).

Second labour
The Hydra of Lerna: associated with the sign of Libra
(see page 569).

Third labour
The Ceryneian hind: associated with the sign of Cancer
(see page 561).

Fourth labour
The Erymanthian boar: associated with the sign of Capricorn
(see page 578).

Fifth labour
The stables of Augeas: associated with the sign of Virgo
(see page 556).

Sixth labour
The Stymphalian birds: associated with the sign of Aquarius
(see page 581).

Seventh labour
The Cretan bull: associated with the sign of Taurus
(see page 556).

Eighth labour
The mares of Diomedes: associated with the sign of Sagittarius
(see page 575).

Ninth labour
Hippolyte's girdle: associated with the sign of Pisces
(see page 583).

Tenth labour
The cattle of Geryon: associated with the sign of Aries
(see page 554).

Eleventh labour
The apples of the Hesperides: associated with the sign of Gemini
(see page 558).

Twelfth labour
The capture of Cerberus: associated with the sign of Scorpio
(see page 572).

Although, historically speaking, the concept of the zodiac predates that of Mount Olympus, both are products of the same mythical representation of the world and, while astrology has retained the Roman names of the gods to designate the ruling planets of the zodiac, these names are in fact derived from or closely associated with the Greek. For example, the sun in Greek was Helius but its characteristics, as envisaged within the zodiac, are much more closely linked to the myth of Apollo than to that of the sun-god Helius (see *Sun*, page 478). Apollo was a solar deity who shared a number of characteristics with the Akkadian solar deity Shamash and his Sumerian counterpart Utu, while Helius was more closely associated with Re, the Egyptian sun god. For reasons that would take too long to explain here, the Greeks drew their inspiration from both the Mesopotamian and Egyptian pantheons to create their own mythical universe and a mythology that so faithfully represented the components of human nature and behaviour that, for a long time, mythology and ancient Greece were closely identified in our minds. People referred to Greek mythology as if there were no other mythologies and only a handful of scholars and acade-mics knew that the Greeks did not have the monopoly on mythology, that it was a phenom-enon inherent in all civilizations, all cultures and all periods in the history of mankind.

Who was Hercules? Born of a divine father and a mortal mother, Hercules was a demigod, i.e. part-man, part-god. According to legend, his father Zeus, the chief god of Olympus, assumed the appearance of Amphitryon in order to lie with the latter's wife, Alcmene, for a single night that he contrived to make last for thirty-six hours.

To this end, he abused his power over Helius (the sun), whom he ordered not to reappear before the appointed time, and Hypnos (sleep), whom he com-manded to extend the sleep of mortals and gods alike. He also ordered the moon to slow its course and so delay the reappear-ance of the sun. Thus Hercules, one of the many natural sons of Zeus (the Roman Jupiter), was conceived with the complicity of the sun, the moon and sleep.

The birth of Hercules. Nine months later, Zeus boasted to the other gods of Olympus that a son was about to be born to him and that he had already decided to call him Heracles (his Greek name), which means 'glory of Hera'. Hera was the sister-wife of

Zeus and a lunar goddess whom the Romans identified with Juno. In astrological terms, Hercules can therefore be regarded as a lunar being placed under the influence of the moon – personified by the goddess Hera whose name he bears – and the planet Jupiter (Zeus), his divine father. This fact is of major importance since, as already stated, this interpretation of the legend of Hercules focuses on the twelve labours and their association with the twelve signs of the zodiac.

An apparently insignificant and little-known fact should also be borne in mind when considering the birth of this legendary hero. Hercules had a twin half-brother Iphicles ('famous might') who was the son of Amphitryon ('harassing on either side'). Iphicles was born at the same time as Hercules, who was originally named Alcaeus ('mighty one') in honour of Amphitryon's father. The first myth associated with the birth of Hercules is therefore that of the twins, of dual nature and dual personality, reinforced by the fact that he was born of a divine father and a mortal mother, and therefore of the union of heaven and earth (see *Androgyne*, page 26).

According to the legend of Hercules, the Greek hero led a far from restful life. In a fit of mad-

ness brought on by the unrelenting hostility of Hera, Hercules killed his own children and possibly his wife. To atone for his crime, he had to perform voluntarily the labours prescribed by his brother Eurystheus who, at Hera's instigation, had usurped his title as King of Mycenae. Not only did Hercules have twelve labours to accomplish but his journey was punctuated by endless obstacles and combats. Even so, the extremely difficult destiny allotted to him at birth enabled him to achieve glory and self-fulfilment. Eurystheus, on the other hand, was a lowly individual, crushed by the weight of a divine destiny that was beyond his capabilities; he felt unworthy of the role he had to play and did everything in his power to distance himself from the brother he feared so much.

Interpretation of the first labour and its association with the sign of Leo

An interpretation of the first labour involves identifying the principal symbols contained in the account, considering their significance and establishing the lessons to be learnt, in particular by those born under the sign of Leo (the lion) or with a birth chart dominated by Leo.

Who was Typhon? Typhon was a mythological monster, born of Hera's anger – it should be remembered that Hercules' Greek name, Heracles, means 'glory of Hera' (see the birth of Hercules, page 226). It had the appearance of a man, but its fingers were dragons' heads and the lower part of its body, from waist to ankles, was wreathed in serpents. This winged creature, with eyes of flame and a body so huge that it covered half the earth, symbolized instinctive, irrepressible and destructive urges and the emotional violence that destroys everything in its path.

As the son of Typhon, the Nemean lion was engendered by uncontrolled instinctive strength, comparable to the cataclysmic forces of nature that nothing and no one seems able to prevent. The sign of Leo is ruled by the sun, which represents the instinctive will of the individual in his or her birth chart. The sign of Leo is therefore the place or point at which the will (i.e. the free will of the individual) can take on the unpredictable and uncontrolled instinctive strength that corresponds to the vital elements of life, to the laws of Mother Nature – who continuously creates and destroys, gives and takes away, generates and regenerates – and the laws of destiny.

The lion preyed upon the people of Nemea in punishment for an unfulfilled sacrifice. Symbolically, this omission – the cause of the events recounted in the legend – indicates that we should not forget to acknowledge the instinctive and emotional impulses within each and every one of us. If we do, we risk seeing them, sooner or later, turn against us, but in a much stronger and more violent form, since we cannot live without them – they are vital to our existence.

Hercules could not find anyone to tell him where the lion was hiding. If we reject or inhibit these instinctive impulses, we not only become their victims but we are also duped by them. We no longer know where they are hiding and they can surprise us, devour us and destroy us at any moment. This certainly applies to the feelings of pride and the tyrannical attitudes to which those born under the sign of Leo can be inclined.

Hercules finally tracked down the lion, but was unable to kill it with his bow, sword or club and finally had to strangle it with his bare hands. In symbolic terms, weapons, which are obviously the attributes of warriors, have always been perceived as the instruments of the mind and intellect, probably because man created them using his intelligence. The hero's bow and arrows therefore represent ideas, the sword represents choices, decisions and justice, while the club symbolizes the power of knowledge. This means that man cannot overcome the uncontrollable violence of the instinctive forces within him by using the weapons of the intellect. It is by getting to grips with them in hand-to-hand combat, by fighting them with their own weapons, that he will overcome them, just as Hercules finally overcame the Nemean lion by seizing it bodily, grasping it, and using his own dominance and physical strength against it. The symbolism of the first labour is the same as that of the XIth card in the Major Arcana of the Tarot – 'strength' or 'fortitude', the ultimate quality that can be attained by those born under the sign of Leo or that must be learnt from their sign. In other words, only creative moral strength (or fortitude) can overcome destructive physical strength.

Divine inspiration told Hercules to use the lion's own claws to flay it, so that he could wear its pelt as armour and the head as a helmet, and thereby assume its invulnerability. Once the forces and impulses of instinct have been conquered, their own weapons can be used against them to strip them of their invulnerability. The helmet made from the lion's head was not only a symbol of invulnerability but also of invisibility (see Helmet, page 223). At this point, man has not only become master of his own instincts and impulses, but also of his destiny. He can exercise his free will – his instinctive will – without being afraid of being assailed, attacked, submerged, blinded, devoured or destroyed by the powers of the great earth goddess, Mother Nature, since he has donned her 'pelt' and resembles her while at the same time remaining true to himself.

First labour: The Nemean lion

The first labour that Hercules had to accomplish was to kill and flay the Nemean lion: 'an enormous beast with a pelt proof against iron, bronze, and stone. Although some call this lion the offspring of Typhon [a monster born from two eggs given to Gaea by Cronus so that she could avenge her sons, the Titans, defeated by Zeus], or of the Chimaera [a fantastical and terrifying creature with a lion's head, a goat's body and a dragon's tail, the daughter of Typhon] and the Dog Orthrus [the son of Typhon and, according to certain myths, the father of the Sphinx of Thebes], others say that Selene [or the moon, the daughter of Helius, the sun] bore it with a fearful shudder and dropped it to earth on Mount Tretus near Nemea, beside a two-mouthed cave; and that in punishment for an unfulfilled sacrifice, she set it to prey upon her own people. [...] Heracles reached Nemea at midday, but since the lion had depopulated the neighbourhood, he found no one to direct him; nor were any tracks to be seen. [...] Heracles visited Mount Tretus, and presently descried the lion coming back to its lair, bespattered with blood from the day's slaughter. He shot a flight of arrows at it, but they rebounded harmlessly from the thick pelt, and the lion licked its chops, yawning. Next, he used his sword, which bent as though made of lead; finally he heaved up his club and dealt the lion such a blow on the muzzle that it entered its double-mouthed cave, shaking its head – not for pain, however, but because of the singing in its ears. Heracles, with a rueful glance at his shattered club, then netted one entrance of the cave, and went in by the other. Aware now that the monster was proof against all weapons, he began to wrestle with it. The lion bit off one of his fingers; but holding its head in chancery, Heracles squeezed hard until it choked to death. [...] For a while, Heracles was at a loss how to flay the lion, until by divine inspiration, he thought of employing its own razor-sharp claws, and soon could

wear the invulnerable pelt as armour, and the head as a helmet.' (Robert Graves, *Greek Myths*, Cassell, London, 1961, pp. 465–467. NB: comments in square brackets added.)

Second labour: The Hydra of Lerna

The second labour that Hercules had to perform was to kill the Hydra of Lerna, a monstrous creature with a dog's body and five, six, seven, eight or nine serpent's heads, depending on the version of the myth. Its mother, Echidna ('she-viper'), was a monster that was part-woman, part-serpent, and its father, Typhon, was a demon born from two eggs given to Gaia by Cronus so that she could avenge her sons, the Titans, defeated by Zeus (see *Nemean lion*, page 229). Typhon was also part-man, part-monster, a winged creature with eyes of flame that had been raised by Python, a monstrous serpent or dragon.

Thus the Hydra of Lerna, Echidna, Typhon and Python take us into the world of the serpent and its associated symbolism (see *Snake*, page 459). However, the Hydra was raised by Hera, the sister and wife of Zeus – after

Interpretation of the second labour
and its association with the sign of Libra

Initially, it may seem strange to associate the Titanesque combat between Hercules and this monstrous creature with serpents' heads and a dog's body with the symbolism of the sign of Libra (the scales). However, it should be remembered that the twelve labours of Hercules represent the ordeals confronted by the human soul as it strives to attain peace, harmony and deliverance from all the passions and demons that torment it. Thus Hercules' journey as he accomplishes his twelve labours is paralleled by an initiatory journey – a sort of 'pilgrim's progress' – through the zodiac.

But how does killing the Hydra relate to the sign of Libra? Librans aspire to achieve balance, harmony, serenity and justice. They also have an innate sense of beauty, harmony, form and colour, as well as being elegant, charming, fair and straightforward. But this is only the tip of the iceberg, since it is the outward appearance affected by those born under the sign of Libra, at least until they have assimilated or attained the qualities of their sign. Librans take great care of their appearance and are very attached to

norms and principles but, in so doing, they deny, reject or suppress the basic and spontaneous aspects of their personality.

Because they respect rules and regulations at all costs, they never want to make a stand, stand out or upset the balance. They ultimately live in a state of indecision and allow themselves to be swayed by circumstances and influenced by other people. By over-developing their feminine qualities of charm, sophistication and compromise, they inhibit their masculine quality of – potentially despotic – authority since the associations between their sign and the symbols of justice often lead Librans to want to establish their own law and impose it on others, despite their show of understanding, sensitivity and tolerance. The Libran personality is in fact dominated by feelings of power, despotism and intransigence, although these are well concealed and often suppressed. However, they continue to proliferate, in spite of the efforts made to stifle them, just as the Hydra's heads with their deadly venom multiplied each time Hercules tried to destroy them. Negative thoughts and emotions tend to proliferate if we try to eliminate them superficially and externally.

For them to cease to have any effect, we have to cut them out, sever the vital head and bury it forever, just as Hercules did in order to defeat the Hydra at last.

He was then able to make use of its venom, not to kill and destroy indiscriminately, but justly and in full knowledge of the facts.

whom the hero was named – who was one of the most powerful goddesses of Olympus.

The Hydra terrorized the region of Lerna, renowned for the mysteries celebrated in honour of Dionysus, the Greek god of wine, fruitfulness and vegetation. It was here that, according to legend, Dionysus had entered the underworld via the bottomless Alcyonian Lake to rescue his mother, Semele, from the hands of Hades, god of the underworld.

It was here, too, that the mysteries of Demeter, goddess of the earth, were celebrated since it was via this same lake that Hades had seized Persephone, Demeter's daughter, and carried her off to the underworld. When the Hydra made its lair in this sacred region, the terrified inhabitants stopped celebrating the mysteries.

With the help of Athena, the Greek goddess of war (the

Roman Minerva), Hercules soon found the lair of the Hydra, whose venom was reputed to be so powerful that merely inhaling its breath would prove fatal. On the advice of Athena, his 'guardian angel', Hercules flushed the monster into the open with burning arrows. With the Hydra choking on the smoke, Hercules had nothing to fear from its breath and was able to seize hold of the monstrous creature. However, as in his first labour (see *Nemean lion*, page 229), he found his club powerless against it. Worse still, each time he crushed one of the serpent's heads, two more immediately grew in its place. Depending on the version of the legend, the Hydra grew as many as a hundred, a thousand and even ten thousand heads! At this point Hercules' nephew Iolaus, who accompanied his uncle on all twelve labours, built a huge fire and, using burning brands to cauterize the wounds of the heads crushed by Hercules, prevented more growing in their place. In this way, Hercules was eventually able to cut off the vital and immortal head of the Hydra – the one that gave life to all the other heads – and bury it alive. Finally, he dipped his arrowheads in the monster's gall and in the venom of its lifeless mouths and thereby rendered them poisonous.

Third labour: The Ceryneian hind

Having acquired moral strength and fortitude during his first labour and justice during his second (see *Nemean lion*, page 229, and *Hydra of Lerna*, page 230), Hercules spent a year tracking down a third and equally important virtue. This third virtue was symbolized by the Ceryneian hind, or female deer, whose golden horns were radiant with sunlight and its body so large and powerful that some took it for a stag.

According to the original legend this bronze-hoofed hind was one of a group of five but fled when its four companions were captured and harnessed to the chariot of Artemis, the goddess of wild animals, who pursued it to the Ceryneian Hill where it had taken refuge.

Although she renounced the idea of harnessing it to her chariot, Artemis (who would later become Diana, the Roman goddess of hunting) refused to renounce the deer, which eventually became her sacred animal.

This greatly angered Hera, who had instigated the twelve labours of Hercules, and she demanded that he capture the Ceryneian hind, but without

using force. He therefore pursued the animal for an entire year and, in so doing, broke a taboo, since this was a sacred animal dedicated to a goddess.

According to a legend that predates the account of Hercules' third labour, the hind of Artemis was once Taygete, one of the seven daughters of Atlas – the giant who supported the sky on his shoulders – who subsequently became the seven stars in the constellation known as the Pleiades. To save Taygete from the attentions of Zeus, who had fallen in love with her and succeeded in lying with her once, Artemis temporarily transformed her into a

Interpretation of the third labour and its association with the sign of Cancer

At first glance, the myths and symbols of the third labour seem to have little in common with those associated with the sign of Cancer (the crab).

However, on closer examination, there is one obvious analogy. The third labour describes how Hercules captured the sacred hind without wounding or killing it, or even shedding a single drop of blood, by shooting an arrow that passed between tendon and bone, pinning its forelegs together. It should be borne in mind that Cancer derives from the Greek karkinos, meaning 'crab' or 'canker' but also 'pincers' or 'compass', and that a compass is an instrument with two straight legs pivoted to each other at the top with a hinge or bow-shaped spring. In this sense, the arrow that pierced the hind's forelegs evokes the hinge or spring joining the legs of the compass.

The two protagonists of the third labour of Hercules were Taygete, embodied in the hind of Arcadia, and Artemis, to whom the animal was dedicated. Who exactly was Artemis? She was the beautiful virgin goddess of wild animals, hunting, chastity and childbirth, whose name means 'high source of water'. She was often depicted carrying a bow and spent much of her time hunting (and protecting) deer and mortals. Homer described her as: ' the virgin […] the far-shooting goddess who delights in arrows'. ('To Artemis' in the Homeric Hymns, in Hesiod – Homeric Hymns – Epic Cycle – Homerica, translated by Hugh G. Evelyn-White, Loeb Classical Library, Harvard University Press, 1998, page 435.) Wild and quick-tempered, Artemis was also assimilated with the moon, just as her brother Apollo was a personification of the sun.

This brings us to the second analogy between the Ceryneian hind and the sign of Cancer – Artemis, the goddess to whom the hind was dedicated, was a representation of the moon, the ruling planet of Cancer. With regard to Taygete ('long-checked'), it should be remembered that Zeus only lay with her once, when she had fainted, and that it was Artemis who changed her into a hind so that she could escape his renewed attentions. However, as a result of her union with Zeus, she bore a son, Lacedaemon, the 'lake demon'.

So why was the hind so precious and why did Hercules pursue it for a year in order to capture it without harming it? Because it was undoubtedly the most beautiful mythical and symbolic representation of Wisdom. The hind of Arcadia was dedicated to Artemis and therefore to the moon, its golden horns were radiant with sunlight, thereby stressing its inner strength, while its bronze hoofs linked it to the earth, material possessions and earthly desires. Like all Cancerians, the hind also had a certain innocence, since Zeus succeeded in lying with Taygete against her will. And yet she bore a demon, her son Lacedaemon, the 'lake demon'. In fleeing towards the legendary land of the Hyperboreans, Taygete, like those born under the sign of Cancer, was turning towards original purity and wisdom.

Thus, after gaining moral strength and justice in the first two labours, Hercules acquired wisdom in the third by capturing the Ceryneian hind.

hind. Having escaped Zeus's amorous pursuit and regained her original form as a nymph, Taygete dedicated the hind to Artemis as a token of her gratitude. This episode is crucial when it comes to understanding the symbolic significance of the third labour performed by Hercules.

As you may imagine, the hind was extremely fleet of foot and this is why it took Hercules a year to catch up with it. He finally managed to take it by surprise in Arcadia (it is sometimes referred to as the hind of Arcadia) as it was about to cross the river Ladon into the legendary land of the Hyperboreans, renowned for their great wisdom. Hercules drew his bow and shot an arrow that pierced the hind's forelegs between bone and tendon, pinning them together and thereby

immobilizing it. He did this without shedding a single drop of blood since Hera had expressly ordered that he must neither kill nor wound the hind. He then lifted the animal on to his broad shoulders and carried it back to Mycenae.

Fourth labour: The Erymanthian boar

It is well-known that Hercules was endowed with superhuman strength, to the point that, even today, we sometimes refer to an extremely strong person as 'a real Hercules' or as having 'Herculean strength'. However, this physical strength counts for very little without the much more vital and essential strength that animates and controls it, the spiritual strength that confers real

Interpretation of the fourth labour
and its association with the sign of Capricorn

To understand the symbolic significance of the myth of the fourth labour of Hercules and its association with the sign of Capricorn (the goat), it is important to point out that, according to traditional astrology and within the context of the coherent whole formed by the zodiac, Capricorn is perceived as the initiator, the sign that initiates the world into knowledge and wisdom.

As already stated, the region of Erymanthus terrorized by the boar was named after a son of Apollo, whose name literally means 'divining by lots'. What is 'divining by lots' ('lot' is synonymous with 'fate') if not a divinatory art, a form of necromancy used by the Greeks and, later, by the Romans to choose the person to be entrusted with a mission, invested with an honour or assigned to a particular role? By drawing lots, they were consulting fate and addressing the gods who indicated the person to be chosen.

The boar therefore terrorized the region of the choice made or the prophecy revealed by 'divining by lots'. However, it should not be forgotten that, according to the legend associated with the mountain and river of Erymanthus, the boar was originally Apollo ('destroyer'), who had assumed this form to avenge his son and kill Aphrodite's lover Adonis. In ancient Greece, the boar symbolized courage and pure strength as well as fertilizing or destructive forces, depending on the circumstances. Thus it was the attribute of Demeter, mother goddess of the earth and daughter of Cronus, the Roman Saturn, the ruling planet of Capricorn. Furthermore, the boar's crescent-shaped tusks made it sacred to the moon.

This explains the association between the fourth labour and the moon–Saturn axis of the zodiac, the axis of the sign of Cancer, ruled by the moon, opposite the sign of Capricorn, ruled by Saturn. As well as being renowned for the damage it can do to crops, the boar, a lunar animal, is also a solitary creature. As such, it not only represents lunar destructive madness but also solitude, isolation, the Saturnine figures of the ascetic and hermit of the forest that are associated with the sign of Capricorn.

From this it can be deduced that lunar madness can be controlled and transformed into pure wisdom, perfect knowledge and – in accordance with the perception of Capricorn as the 'initiator' of the zodiac – spiritual authority. This spiritual strength is so impressive that, when Eurystheus, the usurper of temporal authority, sees it alive on the shoulders of Hercules in the form of the Erymanthian boar, he hides in a storage jar. In so doing, he is symbolically returning to his mother's womb.

power. It was this inner strength that Hercules sought in his fourth labour, a myth that explores, symbolically of course, the most obscure but also the most luminous aspects of the sign of Capricorn with which it is associated.

Before undertaking his fourth labour – the capture of the wild boar of Erymanthus, a mountain that nowadays forms part of the Erymanthos Mountains in the Peloponnese – Hercules killed a bandit named Saurus and then confronted and even killed some of the Centaurs in order to save his own life. At last he was able to set off in search of the wild boar, a monstrous creature that terrorized the snow-covered slopes of Mount Erymanthus and the neighbouring valley through which the river Erymanthus flowed. According to legend, the mountain and river were named after a son of Apollo, whom Aphrodite, the goddess of love, had blinded because he had seen her bathing. In revenge, Apollo had transformed himself into a boar and killed the goddess's lover Adonis.

It was no mean feat to capture this enormous boar, let alone take it alive and without harming it. To do this, Hercules used ingenuity rather than strength.

He uttered animal cries that lured the creature into a snow-drift so that it was unable to move as he sat astride it, overcame it with his bare hands and trussed it up. He then carried it back in triumph to Mycenae on his shoulders, while Eurystheus, terrified by the sight of this monstrous creature, hid in a large storage jar.

Fifth labour: The stables of Augeas

Although this is not one of Hercules' more spectacular labours, it is significant in that it highlights human behaviour and attitudes towards the fruits and riches of the earth. It stresses the need to avoid wasting nature's abundant resources and to introduce order by putting an end to abuse and excess. This may not be so extraordinary, but it is certainly of primordial importance. These themes and preoccupations are particularly relevant in an age when pollution caused by the over-exploitation of the earth's natural resources is devastating our planet and seriously threatening its ecosystem.

Augeas ('bright ray') was king of Elis, in the Peloponnese, the mountainous peninsula in

Interpretation of the fifth labour
and its association with the sign of Virgo

People born under the sign of Virgo (the virgin) are said to be obsessive about order and detail. It is less well known that they are obsessive precisely because they are naturally lacking in any form of order. Their preoccupation with detail is therefore a compensatory reflex that gives them a sense of direction and prevents them losing their bearings and, above all, the precious identity to which they are so attached and so desperate to preserve, but which they are just as likely to question.

As a result, Virgoans are inclined to calculate, accumulate and hoard rather more than the rest of us. But, as you have probably guessed, they are fundamentally negligent and disorganized since they focus on detail, which they certainly see better than anyone else, but are unable to stand back and look at the wider picture. They become fixed in the present, at the point they have reached in their lives, and only envisage the future in terms of security. They can see the tree, but cannot see the forest. This is exactly what Augeas does when he fails to realize that his herd is destroying the Peloponnesian valley and stinking out the entire region.

This is surely what the human race is doing today, as we constantly strive to increase production in order to maximize profits and achieve more security or satisfaction, without giving a thought to conserving our natural environment. In so doing, are we not, like Augeas, making the land sterile and polluting the atmosphere?

Hercules's feat of building two dams and diverting two rivers in a single day contains an important symbolic message – if we continue to take without giving, everything will eventually become sterile. Similarly, if we allow the earth's riches and resources to proliferate, without controlling them, they will eventually suffocate us. The concept of control and lack of control also falls within the province of the Virgoan obsession with detail. The isolation of natural principles that form natural links in an equally natural chain – of which they are an integral part and outside which they cannot exist – engenders a monstrous system.

This may be a fine legend, but try to imagine a valley covered in a layer of dung several metres thick, filled with cattle that are constantly reproducing. The only way to put an end to this unnatural situation is to create a natural disaster, which is exactly what Hercules did by provoking a 'flood'. It is also what Mother Nature does when we abuse and take advantage of her, and the catastrophes we are witnessing today, whether they are termed natural or ecological, are often the earth's way of calling us to order and re-establishing the status quo.

southern Greece. He was generally regarded as the son of Helius (the sun) and Hyrmina ('murmur of the beehives').

As the son of the sun and the bees, Augeas could not but be blessed by the gods and had in fact inherited the largest cattle herds on earth from his father. What is more, these cattle, which never contracted any form of disease, were so fertile that they continuously reproduced and gave birth almost exclusively to heifers. Augeas also owned 300 black bulls and 200 breeding bulls as well as keeping 12 white bulls dedicated to his father, Helius. The latter also served to guard his immense herds against the wild beasts that abounded in the surrounding hills.

However, since he had owned these herds, which continued to increase in number, Augeas had never cleared away the dung, which was piling up dangerously inside the stables, and the valley pastures of Elis were covered with such a thick layer of excrement that it was impossible to till or plant grain. Not only did this beautiful valley stink, it had also become sterile as a result of Augeas's negligence.

Eurystheus sent Hercules to the kingdom of Augeas to rid it of the stench and render the land fertile once again. Hercules appeared before the king and undertook to clean the stables in a single day. In exchange, it was agreed that once he had accomplished this, Augeas would give him one tenth of his herds. However, Augeas did not believe for an instant that Hercules would succeed in cleaning the stables in a single day. For him, it was a fool's bargain.

Of course, he did not know Hercules who, to win the wager and achieve his goal, used his intelligence and ingenuity as much as his strength. First of all, he opened two large breaches in the walls of the stables and, building two huge dams with the tree and stones from the hills, he diverted two rivers that flowed nearby. Their waters surged into the stables and along the valley, carrying away all the dung that had accumulated over the years.

Sixth labour: The Stymphalian birds

The sixth labour imposed on Hercules by Eurystheus was to destroy the birds that were devastating the shores and region of Lake Stymphalus, in Arcadia. As they are described in the legend, these birds, dedicated to Ares (the Roman Mars), god of war, would do justice to a work of science fiction. They were about the size of a crane or a heron, but looked more like an ibis, the mythical bird of ancient Egypt, and their straight beaks, feet, wings and feathers were made of bronze. They killed and ate all animals and humans living in or passing through the region, while their droppings rendered the land over which they flew stinking and infertile. In their constant search for food, they also

devastated the fruit trees, orchards and crops of the surrounding area.

These birds, which had taken refuge in the dark forests around Lake Stymphalus, had become a scourge throughout the region. The inhabitants were reluctant to join against them and, since no one hunted them and no one was prepared to confront them, they reproduced unchecked and their numbers were constantly increasing. When he arrived at the Arcadian lake, Hercules was, above all, struck by their vast numbers.

There are several obvious similarities between the scenario of this legend and that of the fifth labour (see the *Stables of Augeas*, page 237). Both describe a sort of ecological disaster caused by the negligence of King Augeas in the first instance, and, in the second, by the resignation of a people lacking determination and solidarity in the face of the forces of destruction.

To destroy these birds, Hercules had to solve two major problems. Firstly, to reach the dense forests in which the birds roosted, he would have to cross the Stymphalian marshes. These marshes were like quicksand, so he could obviously not walk there. Secondly, the birds, through unchecked reproduction,

Interpretation of the sixth labour
and its association with the sign of Aquarius

At first glance, the symbols encountered in this legend appear to be more closely related to the sign of Aries (the ram) than Aquarius (the water carrier). The birds of the Stymphalian marshes are in fact dedicated to Ares, the god of war, whom the Romans identified with Mars, the ruling planet of the first sign of the zodiac. The birds' bronze beaks, feet, wings and feathers are reminiscent of the armour worn by warriors. Finally, it was Athena, goddess of war, who gave Hercules the castanets that enabled him to drive away the birds. These symbols are a far cry from those attributed to Saturn and Uranus (the Greek gods Cronus and Uranus), the first and second planets ruling the sign of Aquarius.

Even so, the legend does in fact refer to the eleventh sign of the zodiac, for the reasons outlined below. Firstly, the vast numbers of birds evoke an army of darkness, spreading terror, destruction and death, while the bronze of their beaks, feet, wings and feathers is a metal associated with invulnerable military power rather than the strength of a solitary warrior. Secondly, the birds seem to form one body, a single and united entity that the inhabitants of the region are powerless to fight and drive out due to their lack of solidarity. Finally, the situation that reigns in the vicinity of Lake Stymphalus and the behaviour of the birds that have invaded and devastated the region are totally anarchical.

The combination of planets governing the sign of Aquarius – Saturn and Uranus – is awesome since it represents a sort of extreme impulsive determination, which nothing and no one seems able to oppose.

It is the Greek gods Cronus (Roman Saturn) – the god of time and the embodiment of destiny and fatality – and Uranus – the god of the sky and the representation of the freedom of infinite spaces, of all possibilities and therefore of free will – who are united.

It is therefore possible to say that Aquarians can choose between resigning themselves to their destiny or exercising free will. This is precisely what can make them so versatile, and sometimes so unstable, since they can take a long time to decide between the two alternatives. They are confused, like Hercules when confronted with the two problems he had to solve in order to destroy the birds. However, Aquarians with a greater sense of opportunity are often helped by circumstances and therefore by destiny, which thus offers them the chance to exercise their free will. This is what happened when Athena came to Hercules' aid and gave him the castanets that enabled him to flush out the birds or, symbolically, to exercise his free will. Etymologically, the term 'castanets' derives from the Spanish castañeta, the diminutive of castaña, meaning 'sweet chestnut', the fruit of the sweet chestnut tree, the symbol of foresight (see Chestnut, page 95).

Aquarians can often foresee and anticipate, act and react before anyone else as they know what is going to happen. This is the great potential quality of anyone born under the sign of Aquarius and, if they acquire it, they are able to control their own destiny and fully exercise their

Interpretation of the seventh labour
and its association with the sign of Taurus

The association with the sign of Taurus (the bull) is obvious since, to accomplish his seventh labour, Hercules had to confront and capture the mythical animal that symbolizes the second sign of the zodiac. However, the sign of Taurus is usually invested with the qualities of placid strength, sensuality, the aspiration to live in harmony with nature and lead a peaceful, healthy, quiet and simple life. Astrologers acknowledge that the anger of those born under the sign of Taurus can indeed be terrifying, but theirs is an anger based on resentment rather than violence.

Furthermore, the Taureans' need for security and material comfort inclines them towards preservation rather than destruction. It should also be remembered that, in terms of the natural cycle, the period of the year during which the sun passes through the sign of Taurus is a period of reproduction and procreation.

Given all the factors outlined above, the description of this vengeful and destructive fire-breathing bull in fact incorporates characteristics more usually associated with Scorpio (the Scorpion), the sign that lies directly opposite Taurus in the zodiac. For, although the seventh labour accomplished by Hercules is very evidently linked to the sign of Taurus, it also alludes to the destructive forces of unbridled instinct, the vital impulses characteristic of the bull, which are also the deadly impulses attributed to the scorpion.

In any consideration of the meaning of the seventh labour of Hercules it is important to realize that the impulses of life and death are one and the same thing, and form a complete whole that creates and sustains life. This is best illustrated by the beating of the human heart, which contracts and lives, relaxes and dies approximately seventy times per minute. In this way and without realizing it, each of us passes continually between life and death around seventy times every minute. This rhythm of systole (contraction of the heart and arteries) and diastole (dilation of the heart and arteries) that regulates the beating of our heart pumps the blood around our body and regenerates it. This wonderful organic mechanism is associated with the instinct of life and death and, consequently, with the Taurus–Scorpio axis of the zodiac. So what exactly does the legend of the seventh labour of Hercules tell us? It tells how Minos kept the bull given to him by Poseidon, which he had promised to sacrifice to the god. The king was so dazzled by the creature's beauty and power that he broke his promise and

decided to deceive Poseidon by keeping this magnificent animal – which, like Aphrodite ('foam-born'), emerged from the primordial waters – for himself. In so doing, Minos was succumbing to the instinct of preservation, to the weaknesses attributed to the sign of Taurus – possessiveness, egotism and opposition to change. However, paradoxical as it may seem, life cannot exist, endure or pursue its normal course if it does not die, if it is not interrupted at a given moment in order to be regenerated and reborn. This is why sacred bulls were sacrificed in antiquity, as depicted in the rituals dedicated to Dionysus – the Greek god of wine, fruitfulness and vegetation – and associated with blood. The biblical legend of Jesus was often compared with that of Dionysus since, in both cases, an ultimate sacrifice was required, life and death merged, and wine symbolized blood or life, which dies and is resurrected. However, death obtained by sacrifice is not fixed or final – it is a necessary stage, a vital necessity. Nor is it death in the accepted sense of the end of a human existence. By contrast, life diverted from its normal course and fixed, preserved, immobilized and possessed egotistically ultimately dies, precisely because it no longer has the potential for regeneration. This was how Minos offended, in selfishly attempting to keep for himself the bull born of the mythical universe of Poseidon, the sea, the primordial waters from which all life emerged. It was the offence which Hercules rectified by fighting and overcoming the Cretan bull with his bare hands.

had become so numerous that he would never be able to kill them all with his bow and arrows.

Perplexed, Hercules was wondering what to do when Athena, the goddess of war, appeared and gave him a pair of castanets forged by Hephaestus ('he who shines by day'), the god of fire and metalworking. They were made of bronze, like the birds' beaks, feet and wings, and Hercules made such a deafening racket with them that it echoed throughout the region and flushed out the frightened birds. As they took off in a flurry of feathers, flying overhead in serried ranks, Hercules killed as many as he could with his arrows. In this way he accomplished his sixth labour and restored peace, charm and prosperity to Lake Stymphalus and the surrounding region.

Seventh labour: The Cretan bull

Minos, the king of the mountainous island of Crete, was said by some to be the son of Zeus and Europa and therefore a demigod. Minos had promised Poseidon, the god of the sea, that he would sacrifice whatever appeared on the waters in the god's name. Taking him at his word, Poseidon caused a magnificent bull to emerge from the waters of the Mediterranean. The bull was so beautiful and so strong that Minos was filled with wonder and, breaking his promise to Poseidon, captured the bull and hid it among his own herds. But the god of the sea, realizing what Minos had done, made the bull he had created so wild that it ravaged the island, breathing fire through its nostrils as it burnt and destroyed the crops in the fields and the trees and fruits in the orchards. According to another version of the legend, the bull was not created by Poseidon, but was the form assumed by Zeus when he carried off and seduced Europa, the mother of King Minos. A third version suggests that it was the famous Minotaur, a monster with a man's body and a bull's head, the guardian of the Labyrinth and the son of Minos' wife Pasiphae (see *Labyrinth*, page 306).

Although mythologists may prefer the first version of the legend, it is easy to understand why the other two exist, since both bulls are associated with Minos through his mother and his wife.

In all three versions, Hercules' seventh labour was to capture this wild, ravaging, fire-breathing bull, whose wildness was only equalled by its indomitable strength, and take it back alive to Greece. Having overcome it with his bare hands during a legendary and Titanesque combat, in which he used sheer strength to immobilize it by its horns, Hercules carried the Cretan bull back to Greece on his shoulders.

Eighth labour: The mares of Diomedes

Were the so-called mares of Diomedes in fact mares or stallions? This is a question that arises in connection with the eighth labour of Hercules and its association with the sign of Sagittarius (the Archer). According to mythologists' interpretations of the two versions of this exploit, one describes them as mares and the other as stallions. Be they mares or stallions, legends and mythologists agree that they

Interpretation of the eighth labour
and its association with the sign of Sagittarius

The link between the four savage mares and the sign of Sagittarius (the archer), which is represented by a centaur – a creature with the upper torso, arms and head of a man and the body and legs of a horse – is obvious. One might comment on the fact that there is a conspicuous absence of centaurs in the legend. However, one of the characteristics of centaurs is that they eat human flesh. From this, it can be deduced that the mares (or stallions) of Diomedes were centaurs in disguise.

Were they four mares or four stallions? According to the qualities inherent in the sign of Sagittarius, they were both mares and stallions, and the most savage imaginable. The sign of Sagittarius, as indicated by the dual – human and animal – nature of the mythical centaur by which it is represented, is simultaneously related to the deepest, most primeval and primitive layers of the natural, terrestrial world and the most elevated, superior and spiritual levels of the celestial world. However, if man's extremely strong primeval and spiritual energies are not controlled, channelled and directed towards a particular end or in a precise direction – represented by the arrow aimed by the Archer – they either sink into excessive sensuality, debauchery and physical death, or become immersed in excessive mental activity, intellectualism and sterile learning. 'Learning', which often has an element of pompousness about it, is not the generous, open-minded and beneficent knowledge that leads to wisdom.

The proof lies in the fact that the sign of Sagittarius is often associated with expansionism and colonialism, as well as the type of good will described in the proverb: 'the road to hell is paved with good intentions'. This explains why the eighth labour of Hercules is set in Thrace, a region colonized by the Greeks who coveted it for its natural wealth. Sagittarians, like the centaurs, are intent on unifying head and body, mind and flesh, their masculine and cerebral component, on the one hand, and their feminine and instinctive component, on the other. However, they often fall prey either to a mental agitation that makes them wild and untameable and encourages them to play at life rather than live it, or to a sensual and instinctive frenzy that not only makes them wild and untameable but also unable to control or contain themselves. This is why there is an element of doubt as to the sex of the four horses of Diomedes, which are in fact both the mares of unbridled instinct and the stallions of intellectual madness, but which can also be the horses of unified mind and body. (See Sagittarius, page 575, Horse, page 264, and Centaur, page 88.)

her as a huntress-nymph, who wrestled and overcame a lion with her bare hands, was seduced by Apollo and bore another son, Aristaeus, before becoming queen of Libya. This merely reinforces the fact that, over the centuries, myths and legends have overlapped and merged.

But to return to Diomedes, king of Thrace, and the mares that terrorized the region, these four mares (or stallions), which were tethered to their bronze mangers by iron chains, had the peculiarity of being carnivorous since Diomedes fed them on human flesh. Hercules' task was to capture these flesh-eating mares, which he did with characteristic courage, strength and skill. He arrived in Thrace and appeared before Diomedes whom he killed with his legendary club. He dragged the king's lifeless body to the edge of a huge artificial lake he had created by cutting a channel between the sea and the low-lying plain, and fed it to the four mares that he had already driven onto a mound in the centre of the lake. Having eaten the flesh of their master, the voracious mares were pacified and Hercules was able to capture the now docile creatures and successfully accomplish his eighth labour.

were four extremely savage horses whose names were Podargus ('bright foot'), Lampon ('beaming'), Xanthus ('yellow') and Deinus ('terrible'). They belonged to the Thracian king Diomedes ('god-like cunning') who ruled over the warlike tribe known as the Bistones. The region of Thrace lay between the River Danube, the Black Sea and the Aegean Sea and was settled from the second millennium BC by peoples of Indo-European origin. The fact that it was rich in wood, gold and silver explains why the Greeks invaded and colonized this beautiful region in the 7th century BC, a fact whose importance will become clear when interpreting the setting of this myth.

Diomedes was the son of the Greek god of war Ares (the Roman Mars) and the Thessalian nymph Cyrene, known as 'mistress of the bridle' and 'sovereign queen'. Another legend describes

Ninth labour: Hippolyte's girdle

Hercules would have accomplished his ninth labour – to bring back Hippolyte's girdle – without spilling a drop of blood, had he not been betrayed by Hera, the goddess after whom he was named (see box *The Twelve Labours of Hercules*, page 225).

To please his daughter Admete ('untamed'), Eurystheus had given Hercules the task of going to the kingdom of the Amazons, a tribe of legendary female warriors, and bringing back the girdle of their queen, Hippolyte, whose name literally means 'of the stampeding horses' (Greek *hippos*, meaning horse). Hercules chartered nine ships and set sail with an army of courageous volunteers on what amounted to a full-scale expedition to the land of the Amazons, or 'moon-women'. It involved a long and perilous voyage that few had attempted, but this did not deter Hercules, dedicated to the glory of Hera ('protectress').

The Amazons were said to be the daughters of the incestuous union between the Greek god of war Ares – the Roman Mars – and the nymph Harmonia ('concord'), the daughter of Ares ('male warrior') and Aphrodite ('foam-born'). They lived in a land that mythologists have identified historically and geographically as being either in the Caucasus Mountains, or in Thrace, to the north-east of Greece, or in Scythia, on the plains of the River Danube. Wherever it was, the Amazons were a completely autonomous tribe of redoubtable and much-feared women. Theirs was an exclusively female community that didn't tolerate any form of male presence and had a reputation for mutilating boy children at birth by breaking their arms and legs and putting out their eyes. They only lay with men, whom they killed immediately afterwards, as an act of physical procreation to enable them to give birth to girl children. As these future Amazons grew to womanhood, one of their breasts was seared off so that it did not

Interpretation of the ninth labour
and its association with the sign of Pisces

A comparison of the account of the ninth labour of Hercules and the characteristics attributed to the sign of Pisces does not immediately reveal the association between Hippolyte's girdle and the last sign of the zodiac. The link lies essentially in the emotion of pure love that can engender and achieve everything, and the uncontrolled emotions that can destroy everything in their path.

What the legend doesn't tell us is that Admete, daughter of Eurystheus, was a priestess of Hera, the wife and female counterpart of Zeus, and, as such, the tutelary goddess of wives. Devoting yourself to the goddess of wives was rather like devoting yourself to a marriage deemed by the gods to be the wisest and most normal of institutions. Nowadays, such a marriage would be regarded as a social arrangement or a marriage of convenience, one that people embark upon because everyone else does, to fulfil a social role, have children and toe the line. This doesn't necessarily exclude feelings but it may well involve feelings without emotion.

The Amazons embody and represent the very opposite of the security afforded by the social system. They were free, immodest, fierce, cruel and warlike women who used men for their own ends without loving or needing to be loved by them. In many respects, they were the caricatures of the men they excluded from their lives, precisely because they, too, had destroyed their emotions. Thus, being a priestess of Hera or an Amazon amounted to the same thing since, in both cases, the emotions suffered or were denied.

What scandalized and revolted Hera, to the point that she betrayed Hercules and caused the ensuing carnage when he could have accomplished his ninth labour without violence or bloodshed, was that Hippolyte, the wild and untamed Amazon, was capable of love. Even though the legend glosses over this important detail, the fact remains that, by giving Hercules her girdle as a token of her love, Hippolyte united herself with him in the purest, deepest and truest sense of the term. Her gesture represents the ultimate physical and spiritual union between man – in this instance Hercules, who embodies controlled moral strength – and woman – Hippolyte, who represents the fertilizing power of restrained emotion. It is the ultimate union of the solar and lunar principles, since the Amazons, as already stated, were also known as 'moon-women'.

By contrast, the headlong gallop of the avenging Amazons represents the unfurling of the waves or the unleashing of primitive emotions that destroy everything in their path and of which Pisceans can often be the victims.

Anyone born under this sign aspires to achieve the union of physical and spiritual love. They are immersed in emotion and receptiveness, and their many contradictory feelings and emotions can sometimes be overwhelming and inhibiting, sometimes clear-sighted and productive. In absolute terms, they want to bring together, unite and unify all the emotions and forces of this world, a union symbolized by the girdle of Hippolyte.

interfere with their handling of a bow, sword or javelin – the name Amazon was usually interpreted by the Greeks as 'breastless'. These fierce female warriors and horsewomen each carried a bow and a crescent-shaped shield – from which the name 'moon-women' derives – and wore a helmet and a belt or girdle of animal skin. Their queen Hippolyte drew her strength and power from her girdle.

When Hercules led his expedition to gain possession of Hippolyte's girdle, the Amazons were living on the banks of the Thermodon River, on the southern shores of the Black Sea. The Greeks dropped anchor in the port of Themiscyra, at the mouth of the river. According to legend, Hippolyte went to meet Hercules and, attracted by his great strength, muscular body and charisma, gave him her girdle as a love token. And it would have ended there if Hera, disguised as an Amazon, had not spread a rumour among the tribe that their queen had betrayed them. Mad with rage, the Amazons mounted their horses and joined battle with Hercules and his companions. With the onslaught of this deadly combat, Hercules in turn thought he had been betrayed and killed Hippolyte, whose belt he took back to Mycenae.

Tenth labour: The cattle of Geryon

Hercules accomplished his tenth labour with the help of Helius (the sun) and Oceanus (the ocean), both of whom he had to confront before they became his allies. Geryon, a monstrous giant with three heads and three bodies joined together at the waist, was the king of Tartessus, an ancient city situated in what is now the Spanish region of Andalusia and destroyed by the Phoenicians in 500 BC. Geryon, whose name means 'crow', was the child of Chrysaor, son of Poseidon, and of Callirrhoë ('fair-flowing'), who herself was the daughter of Oceanus. He was reputedly the strongest man alive and owned a herd of cattle that were much coveted for their beauty. For his tenth labour, Eurystheus sent Hercules to bring back the cattle of Geryon.

Interpretation of the tenth labour
and its association with the sign of Aries

The tenth labour is unusual in that, even before he attempts to capture the cattle of Geryon, Hercules has to overcome the sun and the ocean, the symbolic representations of two primordial elements – fire and water. It is also interesting that, although the legend involves a herd of cattle rather than sheep, which might have been expected since it is associated with the sign of Aries (the ram), it does include a 'shepherd' and his dog.

Most of us know that Aries, the first sign of the zodiac, is preceded by Pisces, a water sign (see Water, page 528). In terms of the natural and seasonal cycle, Pisces corresponds to the period when the waters are unleashed, springs and rivers swell and sometimes overflow. It is the period of the year that precedes the spring equinox, the 'celestial moment' that marks our entry into spring and into the sign of Aries, but it is above all the period when the days will be longer than the nights, when fire will be dominant.

As Hercules journeys to the island of Erytheia, he is in fact passing through these two stages or signs of the zodiac. Helius (the sun or fire) gives him the golden cup that will enable him to overcome Oceanus (the ocean or water). Symbolically, this means that to overcome the emotional swirls and eddies that threaten to engulf and paralyse us, plunge us into total confusion and drown us – Oceanus stirs up his waves to overturn the golden cup in the shape of a water-lily in which Hercules is sailing – we must use our mind, our active energies, our fervour

and inner fire, in fact all the qualities attributed to Aries.

As the grandson of Poseidon, the god of the sea, and of Oceanus, the ocean, Geryon is born of a family dominated by water. If Hercules steals Geryon's herd of magnificent cattle, it is because the giant – whose three heads and three bodies (i.e. a body, mind and soul divided and not united) signify that he is submerged by his hereditary emotions – is unable to appreciate it or allow it to develop.

In this respect, there is not a great deal of difference between cattle and sheep, in that both are weak and submissive and easily led or driven. However, it's another matter to turn a cow or a sheep into a ram (the symbol of Aries), that is, to give it the opportunity to become its own herdsman or shepherd, its own guide, and to assert itself as a separate individual.

In the same way, the plant that emerges from the earth and the bud that opens at the beginning of spring, when the sun moves into the sign of Aries, are breaking free of their past. By stealing the cattle of Geryon, Hercules is doing the same – he is asserting his individuality.

To guard his magnificent herd, Geryon had a herdsman called Eurytion and a two-headed hound, Orthus, the brother of Cerberus, the three-headed watchdog of Hades.

To carry out this labour, Hercules had to cross the sea. In other words, he had to overcome the god Oceanus – the son of Uranus (the sky) and Gaia (the earth) – who, according to Greek mythology, represented the primordial waters, the great universal river with no beginning and no end that encircled the earth (see *River*, page 431). The only way to get the better of Oceanus was to acquire the golden cup of Helius (the sun). Helius, however, was not so keen on the idea and shone his rays mercilessly on Hercules as he crossed the Libyan desert in the unbearable heat.

Furious, Hercules stopped in the middle of the desert, drew his bow and shot several arrows at Helius, who enjoined him to stop, which he did and immediately apologized. To show that he did not bear any grudges and to seal their pact, Helius gave him the golden cup that he needed to overcome Oceanus.

The cup was in the shape of a water-lily and floated on water. Hercules was therefore able to use it to sail to the island of Erytheia ('red island'), the home of Geryon. But Oceanus stirred up his waves so that the golden cup was in danger of capsizing and Hercules almost drowned. Furious, he again drew his bow and shot arrows into the body of the Titan of the seas, who was alarmed and calmed the waves. Thus Hercules was able to reach his destination safe and sound but no sooner had he set foot on the island than he was attacked by the two-headed hound Orthus, which he immediately killed with his club.

Geryon's herdsman Eurytion flew to his dog's rescue and suffered the same fate. Hercules was preparing to make off with the herd of cattle and take it back to Greece when Geryon, who had got wind of his presence on the island and his plan to steal the cattle, challenged him to single combat. As might be expected, Hercules defeated the giant by piercing his three bodies simultaneously with one of his deadly arrows.

Eleventh labour: The apples of the Hesperides

The garden of the Hesperides, the symbol of fertility, was the garden of Hera, the sister-wife of Zeus and 'stepmother' of

Hercules. In it she had placed or planted the golden apple tree given to her by Gaia (the earth) as a wedding gift. The garden and especially the golden apples were guarded by the three goddesses known as the Hesperides ('daughters of evening' or 'nymphs of the West'), the daughters of Nyx (night). The first was called Aegle ('dazzling light'), the second Erytheis ('crimson') and the third Hespera ('evening'). They were also the daughters of Atlas ('he who suffers'), the Titan condemned by Zeus to support the sky on his shoulders (in works of art this was often represented as the celestial globe) for having rebelled against the gods of Olympus. In Greek mythology, Atlas, who was instrumental in the accomplishment of Hercules' eleventh labour, was also the king of the legendary kingdom of Atlantis (see *Atlantis*, page 43) and, according to Herodotus, a wise astronomer who taught mankind the laws of the heavens.

One day, Hera noticed that the three 'daughters of evening', the nymphs whose duty it was to guard the golden apples that grew on the apple tree given to her by Gaia, were themselves stealing her apples. To protect the magic tree and prevent them from touching its rare and precious fruit, she sent the serpent Ladon to coil around the trunk. This monster, part-serpent and part-dragon, 'had one hundred heads, and spoke with divers tongues' (Robert Graves, *op. cit.*, p. 507).

Hercules' eleventh labour – to steal and bring back the apples of fertility – involved a very long voyage. En route, he delivered Prometheus from the punishment inflicted on him by Zeus for having stolen the sparks of fire from the wheel of Helius (the sun), by using one of his poisoned arrows to shoot the eagle that eternally devoured his liver. Prometheus ('forethought') repaid him by advising Hercules not to pick the golden apples himself

Interpretation of the eleventh labour and its association with the sign of Gemini

One of the most obvious associations between this myth and the sign of Gemini (the twins) is the symbol of fertility and primordial energy, represented by the serpent-dragon that coiled itself around the tree. The serpent (or snake) is a representation of the famous caduceus, the attribute of the Greek god Hermes and his Roman counterpart Mercury, the uncontested master and ruling planet of Gemini. There is also an obvious association with the garden of Eden where a similar tree was guarded by a serpent. However, in the biblical legend, Eve, who could just as easily have been one of the Hesperides, allowed herself to be tempted by the serpent to pick the fruit, whereas, in the legend of Hercules, it was the serpent Ladon who, on the instructions of Hera, coiled itself round the tree to prevent the 'daughters of evening' from stealing the apples.

Everything indicates that both the Greek and the biblical legends drew their inspiration from the same source and, although the interpretations may be different, their meaning is essentially the same.

Both legends involve a symbolic representation of the mind and the intellect linked to primordial instinct. Thus the tree symbolizes man and his vertebral column and the snake or serpent-dragon the primordial energy (kundalini) that circulates within him. The golden apples represent the fruits of the knowledge he has always possessed – since these fruits are on the tree before the serpent-dragon coils itself round the trunk – but of which he is unaware until he has experienced revelation.

Hercules became the instrument of this revelation by accomplishing his eleventh labour. In so doing, he killed Ladon, the serpent-dragon that 'had one hundred heads, and spoke with divers tongues' (idem). Like the mind, the serpent can learn, comprehend, understand and know everything, but once it has taught or told us what we wanted to know, we no longer need it. Hercules could therefore kill the serpent-dragon of the mind or intellect since, if it takes control, it will swallow its tail, rather like the ouroboros or circular snake. In other words, domination by the intellect means that ideas turn endlessly on themselves and the mind will become sterile.

In this labour, Hercules went in search of the fruits of knowledge and, if he used ingenuity to enlist the help of Atlas to achieve this, it is because knowledge and truth are more readily granted to those whose intentions are innocent, candid and pure, than to those who are motivated by acquisitiveness, 'learning' and power.

but to send Atlas instead. At the gates of the garden of the Hesperides, Hercules therefore offered to relieve Atlas of his burden and support the sky on his head if, in return, Atlas would go and pick the apples for him. But the Titan was afraid of the serpent and dared not approach the tree.

Hercules therefore pierced the serpent's one hundred heads with a single arrow and the monster died instantly. Hera later placed the mortal remains of this monstrous creature in the heavens and they became the constellation known as the Dragon. With Ladon dead and Hercules supporting the sky for him, Atlas went into Hera's garden and bade his daughters, the Hesperides, pick three golden apples. He then suggested that, since Hercules had been kind enough to relieve him of his burden, he should take the apples back to Eurystheus himself. However, Hercules, who had been warned by Prometheus not to be tempted by Atlas and to use ingenuity to achieve his ends, asked the Titan to support the sky for a moment while he put a pad on his head. He then picked up the apples that Atlas had placed on the ground as he naively took back the sky, believing what Hercules had said.

Twelfth labour: The capture of Cerberus

This was undoubtedly the most dangerous of Hercules' labours and the most remarkable of his exploits. For his twelfth labour, Eurystheus sent him down into the kingdom of Hades (the underworld) to capture Cerberus, the three-headed hound that guarded the gates of hell. However, no mortal, not even a demigod like Hercules, might enter the kingdom of the dead with impunity and he therefore had to be initiated into the Eleusinian Mysteries. According to legend, only Athenians could aspire to these mysteries, which enabled initiates to enter the other world and live to tell the tale. They took place in Eleusis, a Greek port to the northwest of Athens, and involved the initiate re-enacting the life and death of Dionysus, the Greek god of wine, fruitfulness and vegetation. Dionysus, whose name means 'lame god' but who was also known as 'twice born', was regarded as the liberator from death and hell. According to legend, he had rescued his mother Semele from Hades when she was killed by a thunderbolt sent by her lover, Hercules' father Zeus, whom she

Interpretation of the twelfth labour
and its association with the sign of Scorpio

The allusions to the kingdom of the dead and the sting in Cerberus' tail are very evidently symbols associated with the sign of Scorpio (the scorpion). This eighth sign of the zodiac is either little-known, misinterpreted or, at best, seen in a dark and sombre light, if not perceived as evil or wicked. However, although the setting for the twelfth labour of Hercules is rather disturbing, not to say harrowing, the legend of this labour, on the other hand, is full of life and hope. It is not by chance that the twelfth and final labour of the Greek demigod is the labour that enables him to achieve his greatest victory – victory over death. At least, over death as we imagine it and as it is represented, or rather as we refuse to imagine it, since we prefer to believe that death is some-thing that only happens to other people and has nothing to do with us. Thus all the phantasmagoria surrounding death, the rituals we go through when we have to confront it, in fact leave us totally ignorant of it. Can anyone honestly say they are not afraid of death? The French journalist, author and playwright Jacques Audiberti (1899–1965) once wrote that he wasn't afraid of death but of what separated him from it. In the legend of the twelfth labour of Hercules, all that separated the kingdom of the dead from the world of the living was Cerberus, the guardian of hell. What does Greek mythology tell us about Cerberus? His name, which means 'demon of the pit', is probably of eastern origin. Etymologically, this is rather an overstatement since, for the Greeks, 'pit' or 'abyss' meant 'bottomless depths'. So, are we meant to infer from this overstatement or

exaggeration that Cerberus, the 'demon of the pit', was the guardian of something that didn't exist, something absurd because it had no bottom, no end and therefore no meaning? But if something has no end, it is because it continues.

This is tantamount to saying that Hades' kingdom of the dead was pure illusion, a fantasy, and that it was enough to be initiated – into the Eleusinian Mysteries in Hercules' case – to be able to return unharmed from the kingdom from which no one usually returned.

Thus, just as Medusa was a shade and an illusion – as Hermes pointed out to Hercules – the kingdom of the dead exists only in our imagination. Death itself is only the idea or image we create of it.

The kingdom of the dead, where the dead are said to be condemned to live – or rather cease to live – eternally, is in fact a mental construct. The passage from the land of the living to the kingdom of the dead, and the return to the land of the living, is a metaphor for the great principle of regeneration attributed to the sign of Scorpio. The driving force of the Scorpion is as much that of life as of death, of life and death simultaneously, representing that unthinkable moment when life and death are one, precisely in order to engender new life. So, if death is part of life, and if we love life, why should we be afraid of death?

Hercules came to understand this by accomplishing his twelfth and final labour, and was at last able to live life a free man.

had challenged to demonstrate his power. Before being initiated, Hercules had to be purified since no one was allowed to participate with blood on their hands. Once initiated into the Eleusinian mysteries, Hercules, like Dionysus, could enter the underworld without fearing for his life. This was in itself, if not an exploit, certainly an amazing achievement.

So, accompanied by Athena – who was always there to comfort him when he was exhausted by his labours – and Hermes, the guide of travellers, Hercules embarked upon his final labour. He crossed the Styx, the river that flowed through the underworld, and entered the kingdom of Hades (Greek *Aïdes*, 'the u nseen'). The dead were terrified by the sight of Hercules and fled, apart from two who stood their ground.

One was the Gorgon

Medusa, a fearful monster that froze the blood of those who beheld her, a snake-haired creature with boar's tusks, hands of bronze, wings of gold and eyes whose gaze was so piercing that whoever looked into them was turned to stone. Hercules was about to run Medusa through with his sword when Hermes advised him against it, telling him that she was only a shade, an illusion, a phantom.

The other was Meleager and Hercules drew his bow, ready to shoot one of his arrows. But this Greek hero merely told the story of his life and the tragic circumstances of his death. Hercules was so moved that he promised to marry Meleager's sister, who was still alive, when he returned to the land of the living.

Hercules had many other encounters and adventures in the kingdom of the dead before he eventually came before Hades and told him he had come to capture Cerberus. Hades agreed to his demand on condition that he subdued the hound with his bare hands, clad only in his breastplate and the lion's pelt he wore as armour. Hercules seized the guardian of hell by the neck – for although it had three heads, it had only one neck – and held it fast. There ensued a fierce and terrifying combat during which the hero was stung several times by the scorpion's sting at the end of the hound's tail. Needless to say, Hercules emerged victorious.

Heron
Hesperides
(the apples
of the)
Hind (the
Ceryneian)

Heron

There a four main types of heron – the night heron, found throughout the world, the squacco heron, a native of southern Europe and North Africa, the common heron, found throughout Europe, and the purple heron (*Ardea purpurea*), which lives mainly in south-eastern Europe but which can also be found in south-western France and Portugal. The common and purple herons are the most well-known breeds in Europe. They are slightly larger than the stork and live mostly in marshes and on the shores of lakes. The female lays three or four eggs each year, between March and May, and she and the male take it in turns to hatch them for around 28 days. Herons feed on fish, frogs, small reptiles, molluscs and insects. They spend the winter in Africa, flying south in early October and returning in March of the following year.

In Greek mythology, the heron is associated with the legend of Scylla, the daughter of Nisus, who betrayed her father out of love for Minos, the king of Crete. Minos had invaded Megara, the kingdom over which Nisus ruled, and it was Scylla's betrayal that enabled him to conquer Nisus and gain possession of his kingdom. However, he broke his promise to marry Scylla and, horrified by her treachery, chained her to the prow of his warship. The gods of Olympus took pity on her and saved her from drowning by transforming her into a heron that flew free up into the sky. According to this legend, the heron symbolizes blind passion, treachery and redemption. Our ancestors also regarded it as the living symbol of curiosity and indiscretion because of its habit of probing the marshes with its long beak as it searched for food.

Hesperides
(the apples of the)

See Hercules, page 251

Hind
(the Ceryneian)

See Hercules, page 233

257

Hippolyte's girdle

See Hercules, page 247

Hippopotamus

This impressive animal – whose Greek name *hippopotamos* means 'river horse' (*hippos*, 'horse' + *potamos*, 'river') – weighs more than 4 tonnes and can reach lengths of up to 4m (13ft). In ancient Egypt, it was the form taken by Taweret, 'the great goddess' and protectress of women in childbirth. It was probably the association of the destructive male hippopotamus with Seth, god of chaos and confusion – whose voice, according to the Egyptians, was the rolling of thunder – that led the Greek biographer and author Plutarch (*c.* AD 46–119) to describe Taweret as the 'concubine' of Seth. Thus, although the ancient Egyptians worshipped the hippopotamus in the form of a divinity presiding over childbirth, they also recognized the animal's great strength and potentially destructive nature. They were therefore not averse to hunting it in the Delta marshes where they tracked it down and speared it among the papyrus thickets, before cutting it up with great ceremony. One of the demons most feared by the ancient Egyptians was the 'eater of hearts', depicted in the *Book of the Dead* as a creature that was part-crocodile, part-lion and part-hippopotamus, crouching beside the scales in the 'Weighing of the Heart' ceremony in the 'Hall of the Two Truths'.

But the Egyptian word for hippopotamus was *p-ehe-mau*, assimilated to the Hebrew *b'hemah* (beast), i.e. behemoth, to which Yahweh refers when speaking to Job:

Behold now behemoth,
which I made with thee;
He eateth grass as an ox.
Lo now, his strength is in his
*   loins,*
And his force is in the navel of
*   his belly.*
He moveth his tail like a cedar:
The sinews of his stones are
*   wrapped together.*
His bones are as strong as pieces
*   of brass;*
His bones are like bars of iron.

(Job 40: 15–18.)

So who or what was this behemoth, whose original Hebrew name was not singular and masculine, but plural and feminine? Behemoth is the representation of the superior strength and intelligence that deliver man from death. This is why, when speaking of behemoth, Yahweh adds: 'He is the chief of the ways of God' (Job 40: 19), that is, a masterpiece created by God. Behemoth is therefore a representation of man and not a demon as has often been wrongly assumed. In spite of the physical strength depicted so vividly in the text of Job – in this image of a heavy, immutable mass, of the power and weight to which the hippopotamus certainly alludes – man, God's masterpiece, possesses a strength and an intelligence that give him the potential to attain pure weightlessness, to free himself from the weight of physical death. Behemoth, the hippopotamus, is therefore one of those paradoxical images that are so common in the language of myths and symbols which, it should be remembered, is the language of our dreams.

A dream about a hippopotamus is therefore often a crude representation of the dreamer, who may be inclined to confuse physical and inner strength.

Hole

Human skeletons at least a million years old have been discovered with a hole in their skulls, particularly around the occipital bone, at the point where the brain meets the spinal column, but also at the top of the skull.

Palaeontologists have deduced from this that our early ancestors not only worshipped their own ancestors, but that they also knew that intelligence, the mind and all that comprises human identity were concentrated in the brain. It seems, therefore, that they made this hole in the skulls of their dead to remove their brains, although it is not known why. Was it to symbolize the fact that death is a plunge into the unknown, since this is what is generally represented by a hole? Or was it because the sex act performed by a man and a woman also seemed like a submersion in an unknown world, because the hole was identified with the female sex organs or because orgasm was often regarded as a 'petite mort' ('little death')?

Although these are all possibilities, it is more likely that the hole represented the birth canal: numerous beliefs from various different cultures all over the world associate the hole with fertility and the door to life. The hole also represents a trap into which someone might fall, although this would, generally, be an initiatory trap. The most explicit story in this respect is the account in the Bible of the incident that befell Joseph, Jacob's favourite son: 'And it came to pass, when Joseph was come unto his brethren, that they stript Joseph out of his coat, his coat of many colours that was on him; And they took him, and cast him into a pit: and the pit was empty, there was no water in it.' (Genesis 38: 23–24.) The fact that Joseph was betrayed by his brothers and thrown in the pit sealed his fate. In making him a victim, they turned him into one of the chosen. What is more, if we continue reading the story of Joseph, it can be seen that he again fell into a trap or hole: the prison of the pharaoh Potiphar, from which he was eventually released owing to his talents as an oneirologist or interpreter of dreams. Pharaoh then made him his equal: 'And Pharaoh said unto Joseph: "See, I have set thee over all the land of Egypt".' (Genesis

41: 41.) However, someone who dreams of falling into a hole need not be too concerned. Although it is true that, in one way or another, they have fallen into a trap, whether virtual or real, this may only be temporary. In fact, if we examine the above-mentioned symbolic meanings, the hole is a type of transit point through which you must pass if you are to develop or make a transition. That being the case, there is no doubt that dreaming about a hole often heralds a radical change that will eventually prove beneficial for the dreamer.

Honey

Although honey is often associated with sweetness, subtlety, the fruits of the earth, all that nature provides, it should be remembered that it is the product of a great deal of collective hard work and the result of a subtle transformation through the labour and alchemy of bees,

As a result, when this pure, natural product appears in one of our dreams, it can be a sign of sweetness, a state of grace and easy wealth, but it can also imply that these things can only be obtained at the cost of a great deal of blood, sweat and tears. Similarly, if you see someone bearing a spoonful of honey to their lips or if their lips are coated in honey, this can either herald sweet words or honeyed words that are inherently hypocritical. You must also never ignore the erotic connotations of honey or its regenerative properties, well known to the Celts who concocted a honey-based elixir of immortality: mead.

Hoopoe

This migratory bird (*Upupa epops*) is found in southern and eastern Europe, Russia and North Africa between April and the end of August, when it flies south for the winter to central and southern Africa and India. It has a distinctive long beak and an erectile crest of feathers, which

the male turns to good account during mating displays when he presents the female with one of the tasty morsels that form part of their staple diet. The hoopoe likes to nest in stone walls and sometimes even inside buildings. The female lays six or seven eggs in late spring or early summer and sits on them for two weeks while the male feeds her with worms, spiders and small lizards.

In the 13th century, the Persian mystical poet Farid od-Din 'Attar (*c.* 1142–1220) immortalized the hoopoe by making it the heroine of his famous allegorical poem *Manteq ot-teyr* (*The Conference of the Birds*) in which 30 birds (symbolizing Sufis) set out in search of the mythical Simorgh, or Phoenix, which they want to make their king (i.e. God). One of the birds, a hoopoe, acts as their guide. The poem tells how, when they reach the end of their journey and find the object of their quest, they realize that they and the Simorgh are one and the same thing. Throughout the account, the hoopoe fulfils the role of messenger, intermediary between the visible and invisible world,

and the embodiment of truth and wisdom. Tales and legends ante-dating this poem associated the hoopoe with King Solomon since it was regarded as his attribute and companion.

Hornbeam tree

There was once a tree with smooth, grey bark and hard white wood that was quite enchanting. So enchanting in fact that, through the ages, those who sat or lay beneath it, or dreamed at the foot of its trunk, claimed they had fallen under its spell. From time immemorial the hornbeam has been associated with the spells of wise men, shamans and sorcerers who made magic wands from its branches. They used these wands when reciting the rectifying magic formulae and incantations that broke the evil spells cast by

malevolent beings. For this reason these formulae or beneficial spells, which were often carved on the wands, became closely associated with the tree.

The tree was highly valued by the Celts for its protective properties and they used it to build defences against potential enemies. For this reason, they invested it with the quality of loyalty because they never had cause to doubt the effectiveness and solidity of the hornbeam pickets, placed in serried ranks around their fortified villages. The name hornbeam ('horn + beam') is a reference to its tough wood, a quality that also earned it the name 'ironwood'.

Horns and crowns

Very early on in human history, hunters and warriors regarded horns as a symbol of power, victory, glory and, in the hunters' case, triumph over the animal they had killed. By killing an animal in an evenly matched combat in which he identified with it, the hunter assimilated the power and primordial instinct that, as our ancestors knew better than we, linked the animal closely to the great forces of nature. Traditionally, these early hunters had great respect for the animals they hunted for their meat, hides or pelts, whose horns, claws and teeth they took as trophies. So great was this respect that, after killing them, they said prayers or recited incantations in praise of their bravery, strength and beauty, and to thank them for providing food and warmth. In so doing, they invested themselves with a sort of divine protection against the spirit of the animal they had killed. Like the natives of North America or the tribesmen of Africa, our ancestors were in no doubt as to the existence and power of the animal's spirit or its capacity for revenge, in this life or the next, if its human hunters did not pay homage or humble themselves and respect its laws.

Thus the horns of such animals as the aurochs, bull, buffalo, bison, ram, deer, stag and goat formed the first crowns. This is illustrated in the article on the letter A, which was originally symbolized by the horned head of a buffalo or an ox and, later, by the crowned head of a king (see page 18). Subsequently, and probably because of their shape, the horns of these animals became the attributes of the moon and sun, the two great rulers of night and day. For example, the sacred animal of the Egyptian god Amun, identified with the sun-god as Amun-Re, was a ram with curved horns. In early times, the Egyptian goddess Hathor was regarded as the sky-goddess (before she was replaced by Isis) and mother of the sun-god, and the concept of the sky as a cow led to her being depicted wearing the sun-disc flanked by a cow's horns. In Christian mythology, the Devil was also depicted with horns as a symbol of his power. But his was an illegitimate, usurped power, while the crown of a king was the attribute of a legitimately conferred, superior power that was originally divine as well as temporal.

However, while a pair of horns can be regarded as the forerunner of the crown and a symbol of the power conferred on an individual by the gods or obtained by great merit or deeds, the single horn has a more subtle and ambiguous symbolic significance. As well as being associated with the moon, by analogy with its crescent, it is also a powerful phallic symbol. This ambiguity is represented by the unicorn, the mythical creature with a single horn that is both male and female (see *Unicorn*, page 508). In this sense, the horn represents the androgyne, the primordial being whose origins date from the dawn of time (see *Androgyne*, page 26).

The horn is also the horn of plenty, one of the attributes of Fortuna, the Roman goddess of chance. Fortuna was also associated with prosperity, abundance, fertility and fruitfulness and is often represented holding a cornucopia (horn of plenty) as the giver of abundance. In Greek mythology, the origin of the horn of plenty stems from the infancy of Zeus, the chief god of Olympus. According to the myth, the infant Zeus was playing with his nurse Amaltheia – sometimes represented as the goat that suckled him and sometimes as a nymph who fed him goat's milk – when he broke off one of the goat's horns. To ask forgiveness, he gave the horn to Amaltheia promising that it would be eternally replenished with the fruits of the earth. Thus the horn of Amaltheia became the horn of plenty.

Last but not least, the horn was undoubtedly the earliest form of wind instrument, although it was probably more often used to convey a warning or transmit information from village to village than to play music.

The interpretation of a dream depends on whether the horn or horns appear singly or as a pair. As already stated, a single horn has a sexual significance that can be masculine or feminine – for example, the horn of a unicorn is usually a phallic symbol, whereas the horns of a deer have feminine connotations (see *Unicorn*, page 508). A pair of horns, on the other hand, represents power in a particular domain or personal power, often symbolized by the animal whose horns they are. Finally, a crown is a symbol of victory and success achieved through merit and effort. It predicts the recognition of your qualities or, quite simply, of you as an individual.

Horse

The earliest proof of the domestication of the 'wild ass' – inscriptions on slate tablets dating from the second half of the third millennium BC – was found in the ancient kingdom of Mesopotamia and Elam ('the Land of the God'), present-day Iraq and Iran.

However, since the horse did not originate in these distant regions, it must have been imported from the steppes of central Asia and, in particular, the northern Caucasus; there were well-established trading relations between Sumer (later Babylonia) and Maikop, the Caucasian settlement, now capital of the Adygeya Republic. There is also every reason to believe that it was on the plains of the Caucasus that the horse first became what the French naturalist Buffon (1707–88) described as 'man's most noble conquest', in the middle of the third millennium BC. Before that, it was unknown in Mesopotamia and Egypt while, elsewhere, especially in Europe, it was a wild animal that was primarily hunted for food.

Since the horse was originally of European stock, it will come as no surprise that the Celts were highly skilled horsemen. They also gave the horse an important place in their pantheon, since they made it the attribute of their goddess Epona whose name means 'divine horse' or 'horse goddess'. She was represented by a superb mare or a woman seated between two horses, and finally appeared – especially in Rome where she became a Gallo-Roman divinity – as a horsewoman bearing a horn of plenty, the symbol of fertility and the inexhaustible riches of Mother Earth.

Unfortunately, it appears that mankind domesticated the horse in order to use it for war. This probably explains the dark and destructive imagery associated with this undeniably beautiful and amazingly powerful animal that became a creature of myth and legend, the mount of the gods and, for this very reason, assumed a somewhat diabolic character.

As the symbol of darkness invested with mysterious and dangerous powers, the horse, with its wild, primeval and apparently indomitable strength, is associated with death and destruction. So much so that death and the forces of destruction were sometimes represented by horsemen, most obviously in the case of the Four Horsemen of the Apocalypse who, according to the Bible, first appeared in visions to Ezekiel and Zechariah.

However, as is often the case with strong symbols and recurrent myths found – in different forms but with essentially the same significance – in various parts of the ancient world, the horse is an ambivalent animal. It sometimes represents death in its most violent form, and sometimes the elevation and greatness of the soul, the sun's course across the heavens, the regenerating power of water and the purifying power of fire, instincts controlled, desire dominated, the body as the vehicle of the soul or, more precisely, the mount that the soul must tame and use in order to attain the divine. In certain myths and legends, the winged horse has the power to carry the person who can ride it from night into day, from the visible to the invisible world, from death into life. No door remains closed, no frontiers are insurmountable, once the rider is at one with the horse.

Dreaming about a horse is therefore often associated with psychic, instinctive and subconscious forces and urges. They may be destructive but, as such, they are also creative and regenerative. It should also be remembered that the horse, because of its fiery and generous nature, was associated with the goddesses of the earth, the symbols of fertility. Dreams about a horse can be interpreted in so many different ways that it would be possible to devote an entire book to the subject, so diverse are the symbols and myths associated with this beautiful animal.

For example, the horse can be associated with each of the four elements – fire, earth, air and water. As a representation of thunder, lightning, conflagration and fire it symbolizes a sudden, unexpected, unforeseen, unavoidable and devastating event that has occurred or is about to occur in the life or mind of the dreamer. It can also represent the tremors of an earthquake, telluric shock waves and, as such, predicts an upheaval in the dreamer's situation or life. It can symbolize a storm, a tornado or cyclone that sweeps away everything in its path, implying that many things should or will be eliminated from the dreamer's life. Finally, as the embodiment of the unfurling tidal wave, it is the symbol of an emotional crisis.

Horseman

The horseman of myth and legend, created by 12th-century bards and storytellers, is a legendary hero clad in armour, sometimes carrying a sword and magic shield, who defies tyrants and monsters. Above all, he is a symbolic figure who still fires the modern imagination.

As has already been pointed out, the tales and legends peddled from village to village, usually by word of mouth, were often embellished, exaggerated, simplified and distorted by those with a gift or liking for telling such tales – professional storytellers or people in positions of responsibility. However, they were more often than not inspired by real events that had been mythicized. The storytellers, who travelled from place to place recounting their tales, were certainly not without talent or a certain sense of spectacle and were skilled in the art of impressing their audiences using the early equivalent of what we now call special effects. Today, as we close the doors of our houses and apartments at the end of a busy day, it is hard to imagine people gathering around a fire at nightfall to listen spellbound to these stories and legends. But, in the past, when a bard, storyteller, troubadour, trouvère, juggler or even a priest came to a village to tell their tales of fantasy based on actual happenings, it was regarded as a major event.

The same method was used by Christians to spread the

word in the most distant corners of Europe where they found that firing the imagination and appealing to the emotions was far more effective than using military force or fear.

Like it or not, human beings have always had a vital need to dream, believe and imagine, to be transported into another world or a mythical universe. Our modern age is no exception, as clearly evidenced by our movie and TV industries. It is within this context that the myth of the horseman came into being, at a time when our forebears did not have the technological tools to transmit long-distance images that awaken echoes in minds and imaginations avid for dreams and enchantment.

Originally, the mythical horseman was probably just an ordinary man whose experience had taught him the skill of handling weapons, a skill that was usually the privilege of certain people of rank. To do this, he was of course divinely inspired or chosen by the gods or by God himself. He had probably performed a remarkable or spectacular deed that had faded from memory – rebelling against a tyrant, for example, or meting out justice, naturally by force of arms. The tale of his deed grew in the telling and what would

today probably be regarded as a minor news item or trivial event became a major exploit.

Gradually, the myth of the legendary hero-horseman became part of the tradition and culture of the harsh and troubled times of medieval feudal Europe. He was given a mystical quest, the quest for the Holy Grail, the sacred vessel that could only be found after accomplishing such superhuman feats as slaying a dragon.

In this way, over the ages, the quest of the horseman became the symbolic representation of Everyman's search for God or, more simply, the search for self, for contentment, happiness, peace of mind and inner harmony.

This is the most usual interpretation of a dream about a horseman, who is often a messenger of peace, reconciliation and inner harmony. He shows you the path to follow, the fight to be fought in order to make peace with yourself and, in so doing, with others.

House

The house is primarily a dwelling place, a home, residence, abode or domicile. Originally, though, the place where people sheltered

House

with their family, clan or tribe was part of the natural landscape. When people lived by hunting and gathering and there was no natural shelter available, they had to make a shelter with their bare hands to protect themselves from the cold and rain, perhaps from wild animals or even from the demons of the night. To retain the good grace and protection of the nature spirits and surrounding deities, as yet unnamed, when they settled in one place – drawn, no doubt, by abundant food and game – they had to be doubly cautious. These primitive peoples regarded nature as sacred and believed that the way they dealt with the natural world was crucial. If, therefore, they were permitted to build a house with their own hands, from the natural elements and materials found in their surroundings, they felt that nature was granting them a great favour. They were therefore duty-bound to demonstrate their respect and gratitude to the gods concerned.

As a result, dwellings were always regarded as sanctuaries or temples and each individual house or, later on, each group of houses, was associated with a tutelary deity. Originally, the name of the house, like that of the place, had magical and protective

powers. This may now seem rather outdated but in the past the naming of places and things sanctified them. If a house had a name, it was believed that it had a spirit, a soul, an existence in its own right. Similar beliefs persist to this day: some places are thought to be charged with positive or negative energies that cause them to feel welcoming or hostile to their inhabitants. Because the house is inhabited by people, as the body is inhabited by the soul, houses soon came to be linked with men and women, the body and soul. They also came to be associated with the symbolism of the mother, as being places where people can gather, enjoy intimacy and seek refuge, shelter or protection.

All these factors must be considered when a house appears in a dream. A dream like this is open to countless interpretations: it all depends on whether the dreamer is inside or outside the house, on the house's shape, structure or location, or on what room of the house the dreamer is in and on what he or she is doing. Unfortunately, pressure of space precludes listing all the possible interpretations of a dream relating to a house, but the idea of a temple, the concept of body and soul, and maternal symbolism may all be relevant.

Hunchback

It is not known exactly at what point in history touching a hunchback's hump with the palm of your hand, or simply meeting or passing a hunchback, became an omen of good fortune. It may have been by association with the French perception of the hump as an unopened bud that contained the beauty of the flower it would become – the French *bosse* ('hump') shares a common root with *bouton* ('bud'). What is known is that this protuberance – possibly by analogy with the flower bud – was regarded as a special gift that contained great future riches for the hunchback who could bring only happiness and good fortune to those he encountered. Protuberances on the head were also perceived as manifestations of certain gifts and became associated with the expression 'having a (good) head for', again possibly via the French – 'avoir la bosse des maths' ('having a head for maths'), 'avoir la bosse du commerce' ('having a head for business').

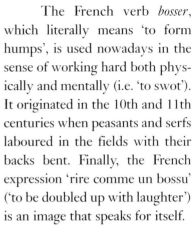

The French verb *bosser*, which literally means 'to form humps', is used nowadays in the sense of working hard both physically and mentally (i.e. 'to swot'). It originated in the 10th and 11th centuries when peasants and serfs laboured in the fields with their backs bent. Finally, the French expression 'rire comme un bossu' ('to be doubled up with laughter') is an image that speaks for itself.

From the above, it is obvious that dreaming about a hunchback is a sign of good fortune, but it is also a sign of joy, good humour, an unexpected present, or a gift that we will receive or discover within ourselves. But it can also be a warning of hard work ahead, a task to be undertaken or completed in order to achieve a modest material result but which will bring spiritual satisfaction. Finally, a hunchback can quite simply be the symbol of a situation which is developing or in the making and that, when it occurs in our lives, will bring a number of surprises.

Hunting

Hunting can be interpreted on two levels. At one level, it can be perceived as one of the most ancient and vital of human activities, since it seems that human beings originally hunted for food. In this respect, they imitated the carnivores of the animal kingdom by assuming the role of predator. At another level, hunting is a quest, the ultimate combat, glorified and sublimated, between human beings and animals, in which the former must show their superiority over the latter. Human beings therefore hunt either for food or to prove their superiority. But either way, there is a predator and a prey, an executioner and a victim, even if their chances appear to be equal.

To interpret a dream about hunting, it is therefore very important to determine whether you are in the role of predator or prey since the significance will obviously not be the same. If you are hunting, it either means that you need to satisfy uncontrolled or repressed primary instincts or urges, or that you are trying to track down and capture something for which you have a very vital need. There is every reason to suppose that you have to rely on your instincts to achieve this. If you are being hunted, on the other hand, this dream is often similar to the dreams of pursuit in which the dreamer feels he or she is being hunted down and is

panic-stricken at the thought of being caught and possibly killed. This type of dream often occurs when we are gripped by an obsessive idea from which we cannot free ourselves. However, it can also be the expression of a suppressed desire to attract attention to ourselves at all costs, to the point of feeling hunted and trapped.

Hydra of Lerna (the)

See Hercules, page 230

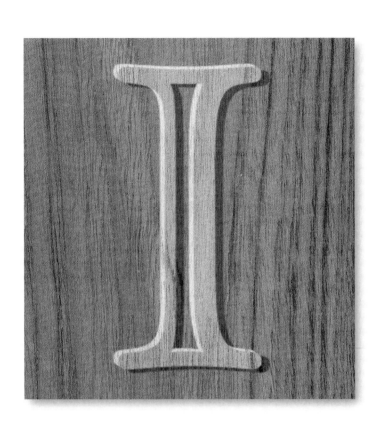

Ibis

Ibises tend to live in colonies of several hundred couples, alongside ravens, cormorants and herons, on the banks of slow-flowing rivers, in deltas, on the shores of lakes and the edge of marshes, which are its preferred nesting sites. In April, each couple builds a nest of reeds and branches in which the female lays four or five dark blue-green eggs in May. She and the male take it in turns to sit on the eggs for just over two weeks, but it is the male who goes 'fishing' and returns to feed his brood with crustaceans, worms and molluscs. The ibis has long, straight legs and a very distinctive long, curved beak. Its superb gliding flight is extremely impressive.

In ancient Egypt, the ibis (*Threskiornis aethiopicus*) was the bird sacred to the god Thoth who was often depicted with a man's body and the head of an ibis. Thoth was the god of writing and knowledge, and the protector of scribes. His role as guardian of the dead in the netherworld probably led the Greeks to regard him as the Egyptian representation of the god Hermes, who equated to the Roman god Mercury.

Inanna, Ishtar, Astarte, Aphrodite and Venus

It appears that for most ancient Near- and Middle-Eastern civilizations, the concept of love was embodied by a woman whose physical beauty was certainly equal to the canons of beauty prescribed for the female form and portrayed in the publicity images that inundate our modern societies. But these ancient goddesses were at the same time wild and domesticated, and associated myths and legends describe them as uninhibited, untamed and entirely governed by their instincts. However, because of love, or more precisely because of the new feelings generated in spite of themselves and as a result of having been the victims of

Ibis
Inanna,
Ishtar,
Astarte,
Aphrodite
and Venus

their own instincts, they gradually became more sociable, more subdued and more civilized.

On closer examination, the mythical development of these goddesses of love appears to reflect the progressive domestication of woman – some will say by man. However, it is quite likely that woman herself made a significant, or at least an equal, contribution to the process as new relationships and relations of strength between men and women were gradually developed and established, as human societies became increasingly settled.

Furthermore, it appears that, with the advent of farming, more than 60 per cent of the work of land cultivation was carried out by women. It is even possible that agriculture, which was obviously a turning point in the history of humanity, was invented by women. This would

explain the sacred nature of agriculture and cultivation, and the fear and guilt it engendered, characteristics that were synthesized in images of mother-goddess figures, of which the Jewish and Christian Eve is a perfect representation (see *Isha*, page 278).

Inanna, the first Eve. The legend of Inanna, the great Sumerian goddess, most probably dates from the beginning of the third millennium BC, at least two thousand years before the story of Eve was written. However, the mythical and initiatory journey of Inanna has a number of points in common with that of Adam's companion as recounted in Genesis. For example, the Sumerian myth tells how Inanna, daughter of An, the god of the sky who reigned over the heavens, was leaning against an apple tree marvelling at the beauty of her vulva, when she decided to

go in search of Enki, 'lord of the earth' and lord of Apsu (the fresh waters beneath the earth), who was delighted by her visit. Overwhelmed by sensual feelings, she used her physical charms to seduce Dumuzi, the son of Enki, and was united with him. Their union is depicted in terms of a carnal agrarian ritual, with Dumuzi compared to a ploughman and Inanna to the rich, moist, fertile soil being sown with seed. For the Sumerians, this divine union, described in a long cycle of poems engraved on tablets in cuneiform writing, was of an exceptional and sacred nature. It was as if they were trying to justify the union of man and woman, while at the same time placing the responsibility for the initiative with woman. Furthermore, this carnal union proved as fatal for Dumuzi as it would for Adam, who was later cursed by Yahweh.

Ishtar, Ashtart, Astarte: the many faces of the goddess of love. The myth of Inanna undoubtedly inspired the much richer, more complex, myth of Ishtar, the Babylonian, Assyrian and Phoenician goddess of love and war (see *Athena*, page 40).

However, some of the goddess's divine attributes – for example, the lioness, the bow and arrows, and the girdle of stars –

were also the attributes of the Egyptian goddesses Neith (bow and arrows), Sekhmet (the lioness), Nut and Isis (the girdle). The fact that Ishtar was worshipped equally and successively by the civilizations that dominated the Near East for more than two thousand years proves that the qualities, strengths and virtues attributed to the goddess were based on relatively unchanging foundations and beliefs shared by these cultures.

The legend of Ishtar initially coincides with that of Inanna and then gradually diverges and become distinct, especially in the famous poem known as the Epic of Gilgamesh. Unlike Dumuzi, the hero Gilgamesh rejects the advances of Ishtar and, in so doing, angers the goddess. She takes her revenge by creating an enormous celestial bull and sending it down to earth to crush or gore Gilgamesh. However, the latter is saved by his friend Enkidu who subsequently dies as a result of Ishtar's magic. Inconsolable after the loss of his friend, Gilgamesh swears he will never die and embarks upon a quest for immortality. But the beauty of this tragic myth should not distract us from the fact that the poem shows woman as an abusive, tyrannical and destructive divinity, and man as an innocent victim seeking immortality – that is, to conquer death, embodied in the vengeful goddess Ishtar.

From the girdle of Ishtar to the girdle of Aphrodite: from carnal to spiritual love. In spite of the image of Ishtar portrayed in the Epic of Gilgamesh , it should be remembered that she was first and foremost the goddess of love, magic and divination, whose girdle was made from the stars. In the middle of the fourth millennium BC, the zodiac was in fact known as the 'girdle of Ishtar'. Ishtar was sometimes referred to as 'the eastern one', worshipped under the aspect of a war goddess as the morning star (Dilbah) and goddess of love as the evening star (Zib), in much the same way that the Greek goddess Aphrodite, who became the Roman goddess Venus, was later identified with the evening star, the planet Venus, associated with the goddess of love (see *Shepherd*, page 452). Aphrodite, the goddess and inspirer of love whose name means 'foam-born', was born of a sea impregnated with the sperm from the severed genitals of the god Uranus (the sky), castrated by his son Cronus (the Roman Saturn). She was the wife of Hephaestus, the lame god of fire, but was renowned for her infidelity and was the sometimes passionate, sometimes tearful lover of Ares (Mars) and Adonis, among others, and mother of Eros. As already stated, Aphrodite, the spiritual daughter of the Babylonian goddess Ishtar, became the Roman goddess Venus who gradually became identified with the planet in the zodiac to which were ascribed her virtues and weaknesses. By the beginning of the first millennium AD, Venus had become the evening star that guided the three Magi to the magical and sacred place where, according to Christian belief, an exceptional being – the incarnation of pure love, free of the passions of the flesh – was born.

Thus, the carnal and fatal love of Inanna – based on

agrarian rites and the principle of procreation that ensures the survival of the human race – and the spiritual and eternal love towards which Venus, the evening star, guided the three Magi, represent the beginning and end of a myth. It is a myth that moves from relationships based on dependency and submission towards a certain political, economic and – inevitably, at that time in history – religious concept that men and women had of love, before they were given the opportunity to free themselves from it – a process that is a long way from being completed some 2,000 years later!

See also *Venus*, page 515.

India (cosmogonies in)

See Cosmogonies in India, page 120

Isha, Eve and Lilith

Was there an original sin? Was one woman, the representative of all women, responsible 'in the beginning' for the human condition with all its imperfections, trials and tribulations, weaknesses and torments?

Why was it a woman rather than a man? The answers to these questions go far beyond the demythologization of the biblical legend of Genesis to

which the apparently distinct but fundamentally similar Jewish and Christians beliefs refer. For this is a legend that is, as the saying goes, as old as the hills. It is the story of man and woman, their relationship, their love, their individual *raisons d'être*, and all the taboos engendered, for economic, social and political reasons, since the first human communities were established.

Although we may try to convince ourselves otherwise, these taboos are so firmly rooted in our customs and behavioural reflexes that simply passing or voting in new laws is not enough to change the relationship between men and women, to create a new balance or to establish equality between the sexes, since women should no more be expected to integrate or take control in a social system created and decreed by men – i.e. dominated by rational and intellectual values that are both tyrannical and paternalistic – than men should be expected to acquiesce in a microcosm in which only material, tangible and conservative values have force of law.

Once again, the myth of the great goddess in her many different guises may help us to understand the origins of certain thought patterns and attitudes that we regard as normal. It may help to explain why these attitudes are so firmly rooted in our minds and why they make the tree of humanity – which draws its vital substance from the depths of the earth, to the point of exhaustion – so solid and strong, so vast and powerful. According to this myth, it was woman (the earth) who committed an original sin and thereby engendered a monster (modern man) whose vocation, not to say mission, appears to be to destroy her in order to punish her for that sin.

Lilith, Isha and Hava: three faces of a goddess. Were Lilith, Isha and Hava (Eve) scatterbrained women solely concerned with satisfying their

instincts, or were they three symbolic figures, three feminine representations of the human psyche, three components of the personality – which contains both masculine and feminine – of every human being? If we step back in time and look at the world through the eyes of our early ancestors, it becomes apparent that the heroes of the creation myths and cosmogonies would not have been able to fulfil that role without the women who were the source of creation. By contrast, in the myth of Adam and Eve, woman was made from the rib of the first man.

However, it appears that the writers of Genesis were inspired by a much earlier Mesopotamian myth. According to this myth, the Sumerian god Enki, 'lord of the earth' and lord of Apsu (the fresh waters beneath the earth), was made ill and cured by his consort Ninhursag – a mother-goddess figure known as the 'mother of the gods' and 'mother of all children' – who placed him in her womb so that he could be reborn. Ninhursag, also know as Nintu, 'lady of the living earth' and 'lady of birth', was the tutelary goddess of the Sumerian rulers who called themselves the 'children of Ninhursag'.

By deliberately overshadowing any earlier cosmogonies, the biblical account made man the first creation of Yahweh and, in so doing, gave rise to a major misunderstanding, for reasons that must surely have been ideological and political on the part of the writers of the myth of Genesis. Consequently, Yahweh appears as the only supreme god, a masculine figure and a father (God the Father) rather than a feminine figure and a mother.

According to certain other Hebrew sources, another representation of Inanna or Ishtar – the great-goddess figure who exerted a dominant influence in the Near East for at least three thousand years (see page 275) – was incorporated into the Scriptures in the person of Lilith. It appears that Lilith was created at the same time as Adam, that they formed an androgynous couple but that,

once separated from Adam's body, Lilith refused to obey him. Lilith symbolizes the instinct that refuses to submit to any law other than the law of nature. According to an associated myth, Lilith knew the secret name of Yahweh, just as the Egyptian goddess Isis discovered the secret name of Re, the supreme god of ancient Egypt, and became known as 'mistress of the gods who knows Re by his own name'. Her discovery of this secret enabled Lilith to acquire wings and fly from the garden of Eden, thereby gaining her freedom.

It may well be Lilith who appears in Genesis as Isha. Whereas, according to the Bible, Hava or Eve is the mother of the human race, Isha, Adam's first companion and wife, refused to be tempted by the serpent, which symbolizes the primordial energies that are the source of all life.

By giving way to temptation, Hava or Eve releases her primordial energies in the form of emotions, passions, ambitions, anger, conquests, possessions and contradictory feelings. Isha, on the other hand, keeps them within her and is therefore able to escape the controlling influence of the external world, just as Lilith was able to fly out of the garden of Eden. If we refer more readily to Hava or Eve than to

Isha or Lilith, it is obviously because the world we have chosen is much closer to Hava's than to Isha's. But these two worlds coexist in all human beings, whether male or female. The concept of original sin is therefore merely an illusory projection by a humanity that has been diverted from its sense of being and living, and become fixed in space and time. This is exactly what happened to our hunter-gatherer ancestors when, in order to satisfy their ambition, they became farmers and herders. In so doing, they abandoned their Eden and their Paradise, the great garden of the natural world with which they were so attuned, in favour of a world that they began to carve and mould in their own image. This gradually took them further and further away from what they were, alienating them from their inner being, to the point that, today more than ever before, we are totally divorced from a state of perfect harmony with nature, at a time when our nature and the natural world were very possibly one and the same thing.

Ishtar

See Inanna, Ishtar, Astarte, Aphrodite and Venus, page 276

Isis and Kali

Isis and Kali are both representations of the mother goddess who, over the ages and depending on the culture, has assumed various different guises. Intrinsically, however, the goddess has always remained an archetype of what Swiss psychologist and psychiatrist C.G. Jung referred to as the collective subconscious, a great feminine principle, i.e. a sublimated, idealized, transcendent representation of this principle.

The separation of the sexes. To understand how this great feminine principle, this vision-cum-apparition of a mother goddess, her aspect, the need to create her, and her cult – which have varied throughout history and according to the civilization – was first conceived by the human mind, we have to take a speculative leap into the past, since there is no historical certainty on this subject. In so doing, we are admittedly cutting a few corners.

Certain anthropologists and historians of pre-history now believe or speculate that our ancestors, the hominoids who first populated the earth – although the exact moment of this beginning is unclear – shared identical beliefs and even, according to some, a common religion. To support their theories in this respect, they envisage either extensive and continuous geographical migrations leading to interchanges that would have enabled primitive tribes to share beliefs and customs, or a shared vision and interpretation – which could be described as subconscious – of life and the world, of their idea of themselves (microcosm) and of everything around them (macrocosm).

Frankly, there is no evidence to support either theory. Envisaging a shared primitive and original religion requires a great effort of imagination to see the world through the eyes of our ancestors, since their natural environment and their relationship with it were far removed from, if not entirely alien to, our current preoccupations and lifestyle. However, one thing has been increasingly confirmed by discoveries made by archaeologists, palaeontologists and anthropologists throughout the world. The development of agriculture in human commu-

nities and the gradual transition from the nomadic to the settled lifestyle brought about a radical change in the collective consciousness, which was probably not fully understood by these early humans who, for thousands of years, had lived in harmony with their natural environment, content to find and take what it offered by hunting and gathering.

In view of this, the cultivation of the land appeared as an attempt to control their natural environment, as a violation of nature, and this transformation was mainly experienced as a break, a rupture, a dramatic event. This explains why the creation myths and cosmogonies nearly always refer to an original catalyst, a cataclysmic separation of the primordial waters for example, in which the sky above, the seat of the mind, the masculine principle or the light-god – of which the jealous, dominating, authoritarian and exclusive Hebrew god, Yahweh, is probably the best example – is separated from the sky below, the seat of the soul, the feminine principle or the dark goddess. When, according to certain myths, the great masculine principle of the mind and the great feminine principle of the soul are united, the former illuminates, elevates, transcends and renders the latter fertile, while the latter tarnishes, obscures and annihilates the former and, even worse, renders it sterile.

Thus the myth of the great goddess probably appeared during a period that lasted for thousands of years, as human communities gradually became herders and farmers, and finally adopted a sedentary lifestyle. Although their form and appearance changed, the mother-goddess figures all derived from the same belief and the same principle, based on a certain feeling of guilt that may well be a mental construct, but which woman ultimately bore and continues to bear alone.

Isis 'great in magic' and Kali, the black goddess. The great goddess can therefore be associated with whiteness, transparency and ethereality, in which case she is protective and reassuring, or she can be associated with blackness, darkness and obscurity, in which case she is destructive and terrifying. This concept helps to explain the origins of the myths and legends about fairies and witches that were so prolific in mediaeval times. The Egyptian goddess Isis 'great in magic', whose name literally means 'seat' or 'throne', is a major representation of the great white goddess. She was the daughter of Nut (the sky) and Geb (the earth) and was therefore of divine parentage and, to a certain extent, embodied these two primordial principles. Although the body of Nut represented the starry celestial vault, Isis was regarded as the mistress of the stars and, as such, was associated with the dog-star Sothis (Sirius) whose rising marked the beginning of the new year for the ancient Egyptians. Furthermore, although Geb was the salt of the earth, Isis was the source of the annual Nile floods that inundated the land of Egypt and made it fertile. In other words, she held destiny – associated with the sky and life, and linked to the earth – in her hands. Isis was a healer, a magician, a musician and an enchantress. Not only did she give life, by giving birth like all women, but she recreated it and rendered it eternal. This was symbolized in the Egyptian accounts of the Osiris legend by the fact that she reassembled the dismembered body of her brother-husband Osiris and subsequently conceived the child Horus.

By contrast, Kali is a fierce and terrifying great 'black' goddess, as her epithets Bhairava ('terrible one') and Chandi ('fierce one') suggest, while her own Sanskrit name means 'the black one'. She represents primitive and primordial energy, she is fearful and violent but also dynamic and life-giving. She is usually depicted as a black goddess, with blood-red eyes, a fiery tongue lolling out of her mouth, a headdress of intertwined serpents, a necklace of human skulls, a girdle of severed heads or hands around her waist, and four arms – one holding the severed head of a giant, one brandishing a sword, a third making a gesture designed to inspire fear, and the last raised in blessing. Kali's terrifying aspect does not prevent her being regarded as the mother goddess who blesses and delivers those whose aspirations are noble and elevated but mercilessly destroys those who live in ignorance. She is also the goddess of the end of time, the embodiment of the beginning and end of all things, who conceals, protects and preserves in her womb a seed that is capable of generating eternal life.

Island

The island is invested with the same symbolism as the centre, the mountain and the tree of life (see pages 100, 348 and 98). Those of you who have lived, or still live, on an island will be familiar with the atmosphere of calm that pervades it, combined with the strange feeling that you are at the centre of the world, or on another planet, and that something unexpected may appear at any moment, anywhere around you, on the horizon encircling the island. The island in question is, of course, not very big.

Try to put yourself in the place of our ancestors and imagine what they must have felt and thought as they set out across the sea for the first time, defying the limits of the horizon and therefore the boundaries of their world. Imagine what it must have been like to sail in uncharted waters without knowing what you are going to discover, and finally to come across an island or a group of islands. It must have been a truly amazing experience. This is why, for peoples all over the world, regardless of their culture and beliefs, the island represents a place of refuge and protection, a gift from the gods to the wanderer who has finally found a place to rest. But because an island can arise suddenly from the depths of the ocean, during some form of marine cataclysm, and can disappear in the same way, engulfed by the waves, it is also symbolically associated with the life that is given to and taken from mankind.

The island as the centre of the world, the island as a place of refuge and protection, the island of birth and death are all images evoked by the appearance of an island in a dream. Finally, the island also represents the enchanted and wonderful place that we long for, dream about and discover. It is therefore the symbolic representation of the place within each and every one of us where we can find peace and harmony.

Israel
(cosmogonies in)

*See Cosmogonies in
Israel, page 123*

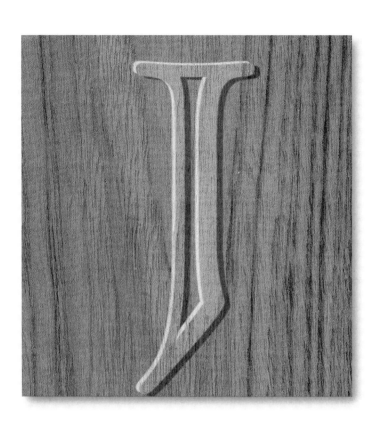

Jade

The ancient Chinese believed that jade was more precious than gold. However, Europeans did not discover its existence until the 17th century when the Spanish conquistadors brought it back from Mexico (not China, where a different type of jade is found). The Spanish nicknamed it *piedra de ijada*, which literally means 'stone of the side' because the Mayans believed the stone had the power to cure renal colic and relieve backache. Following suit, the Germans called jade *nierenstein*, meaning 'kidney stone'.

The Chinese attributed far greater virtues to jade, a symbol of dazzling beauty, but also of hardness, endurance and inner strength. They believed it was linked to eternity, so they reduced it to a precious powder and dissolved it in water to make both a miracle cure and an elixir of eternal life. It was also the custom for betrothed couples to drink out of jade goblets, thereby sealing their union forever. The importance of jade can be seen from Hexagram 50 of the I Ching, which is symbolically compared to a cauldron. The sixth line represents the jade carrying-rings that allow it to be hung over the fire: 'Jade is notable for its combination of hardness with soft luster. [...] Here the counsel is described in relation to the sage who imparts it. In imparting it, he will be mild and pure, like precious jade.' (*The I Ching or the Book of Changes*, translated from Chinese to German by Richard Wilhelm and from German to English by Cary Baynes, Princeton University Press, 1990 [1st Ed. 1950].)

It is unusual for jade to appear in a dream. When it does, it is always a sign of a surprising new development or factor that is about to have a positive or beneficial effect on the dreamer's life.

Jaguar

The ancient Mayans regarded the jaguar as the incarnation of a deity comparable to Mother Earth and the moon. As a result, it represents both the telluric, fruitful powers of the earth and the dark, fertile, magical forces of the moon. According to a myth believed by many native tribes in

South America, the last surviving jaguar, whose species had been hunted to extinction by mankind keen to rid the world of this flesh-eating predator, took refuge in a tree and begged the moon for protection. Since that day, the jaguar is reputed to be a nocturnal creature. Because of this, Mayan sorcerers, who were lunar figures, used to wear a jaguar skin and mask.

If a jaguar features prominently in a dream, the nocturnal and lunar symbolism surrounding it indicate that the same criteria apply to its interpretation as for the appearance of a wolf (see page 543).

Jester, clown

In the 16th century, the jester who had entertained the king and royal court, or the lord and his

entourage, in the castles of 13th-century Europe, became one of the main characters of Italian theatre. He was therefore both the king's jester and the Arlecchino (French Arlequin, English Harlequin) of the *Commedia dell'arte*.

In the 12th century, the French Arlequin was in fact written with an 'h' since it derived from the Old French *hellequin*, *halequin*, *herlequin* or *hielekin*, used to refer to a demon, imp or will-o'-the-wisp. The harlequin therefore shares certain characteristics with the Fool, the last or extra card in the Major Arcana of the Tarot.

However, the Fool can also be a representation of the king's jester and, as such, symbolizes our double, the reverse side of our personality, which always appears in a disturbing and paradoxical light, sometimes bringing us the stroke of luck,

the unexpected opportunity or way out attributed to the Fool or the Joker in a modern deck of cards or certain dice games. The term 'joker' derives from the verb 'to joke', i.e. to make fun or play tricks. The joker was therefore the fool, the jester, the trickster, the practical joker.

Whether harlequin, fool or joker, the jester was also sometimes wrongly identified with the clown. The clown is not in fact a trickster or a joker, but a clumsy, awkward, oafish and grotesque character who doesn't laugh at those around him like the jester or harlequin. The difference between the jester and the clown lies in the fact that the jester makes the king an object of ridicule, whereas the clown is himself an object of ridicule. The jester makes fun of other people, while other people make fun of the clown.

So, the interpretation of a dream about a jester or a clown will be very different. Usually, the jester is a representation or caricature of yourself. If you dream about a jester, you are making fun of yourself. This often happens when you are in or about to become involved in a situation where you risk taking yourself too seriously or becoming the victim of an over-inflated sense of self-importance, an

extreme exaggeration or an over-dramatization. Dreaming about a clown, on the other hand, is a warning that you are or may be overly naive or lacking in judgement or insight.

Jewel, jewellery

The English word 'jewel' is derived from the Old French *juel*, *joiel, joel* and possibly *jeu* (Latin *jocus*), meaning 'game' or 'plaything' and, ultimately, 'jewel' (*joyau* in modern French). It was also used to refer to a woman's sexual organs and sometimes her lover. Finally, it was associated with joy – which in 11th-century France had both masculine (*joi*) and feminine (*joie*) forms to distinguish between male and female joy – and pleasure (*jouissance*). Thus, in the minds and customs of our forebears, jewels were associated with play, joy and pleasure. Isn't it for these very reasons that we give jewels or jewellery today?

In 16th-century France, the term *joyau* was supplanted by the word *bijou*, which derives from the Celtic word *biz* ('finger') incorporated into the Breton dialect as *bizou*, meaning a 'ring for the finger'. So originally

Jewel,
jewellery

bijou referred to any form of ring but, like jewels and jewellery, its plural, *bijoux*, has come to refer to rings, necklaces, chains, bracelets, brooches, ear-rings, crowns and tiaras.

In the distant past, rings and necklaces were made from plants, flowers, wood, stones, the teeth and bones of wild animals, feathers and rare natural materials. For this reason, they were very precious and undoubtedly had the value of a talisman, amulet, sacred instrument or emblem that protected, deified or identified those who wore them. Today, we give a ring, bracelet or necklace to express our love, esteem and fidelity towards a particular person and tend to associate jewellery more readily with the etymological origin that links it to joy. However, in our collective ancestral memory, jewellery still has magical and sacred connotations. This may have something to do with the possibility that the common etymology of 'jewel(lery)' and *jeu* ('game') dates from a time when the tools of divination (stones and bones) were worn as necklaces by soothsayers and magicians.

The way in which we interpret a dream about jewellery, or the symbolic significance of jewellery we have found, been given or lost, depends very much on the type of jewellery. Each piece of jewellery has its own particular significance depending on where it is worn on the body, its shape, and the stones or metal from which it is made. Constraints of space make it impossible to consider them all, but you will find some of the symbolism in the following entries: *Buckle*, page 74, *Chain*, page 90, *Pearl*, page 415, *Ring*, page 430, *Sceptre*, page 446, *Silver*, page 456.

For example, being given a ring is always a sign of present or future joy, material benefits, profits or bonuses, but it can also symbolize a mission or a delicate or dangerous task to be accomplished. In this case it won't be so much a gift as a test or trial to be undergone, an obstacle to be overcome. If you put this or any other ring on your finger, it is important to consider which finger it is (see *Ring*, page 430, *Hand* (and fingers), page 214). Whatever is symbolized by this finger will be invested with power or assume great importance in your future life.

Finding a ring is a sign of future joy, while losing one means you will be deprived or cheated of joy.

Wearing bracelets tightly around your forearm is a sign of

dependence. A bracelet worn on the right wrist reveals a lack of flexibility and understanding and, on the left wrist, a morbid and inhibiting attachment to your past. However, if the bracelet is a metal ring that leaves the wrist free, this interpretation should be modified since it appears that these qualities are well integrated into the framework of your personality and do not interfere with your behaviour in any way.

Wearing a necklace is always a sign of a strong emotional bond. The looser the necklace and the lower it is on your chest, the stronger the symbol of fidelity, constancy of feelings and a full love life. However, if it fits closely round your neck, the emotional attachment is more constraining. A pearl necklace is a sign of wealth but also a sign of purity, honesty and loyalty.

Finding a necklace or dreaming you have been given a necklace is the symbol of an imminent reconciliation or the promise of a fruitful union.

Finally, we should not forget the association between jewellery and amulets and talismans. This is why people tend to dream about jewellery when they are going through difficult and testing times and are seeking help and protection.

Journey

Dreaming about a journey reveals an urgent need for escape and freedom. This type of dream shows that the dreamer needs to break free from routine: he or she feels fenced in by circumstances and has the impression of standing still or going round in circles. The dreamer wants to come into contact with other values, attitudes, ways of life and thinking, to initiate a process of inner change in order to see life from a different perspective, or to exploit qualities or inclinations that he or she possesses but that are either lying dormant or are unknown to the dreamer. A journey is not just an act of travelling through space, it is also a quest for new horizons. Someone who regularly dreams of taking a journey sees him- or herself as a traveller, a transient in life. Even when they have a stable lifestyle and circumstances, maybe even because of this, they believe that they are only passing through, that nothing lasts forever in this

world. To avoid stagnation and to continue their inner growth and personal development they have to keep moving.

Joy

Joy is not a symbol. It is a profound feeling that should not, however, be confused with gaiety or good humour, which are more superficial and short-lived. Real joy sometimes arouses contradictory emotions that can lead to tears.

However, it is worth including joy in a dictionary that aims, among other things, to deal with the symbols used by our dreams as a language to convey messages that are very important to us. In a dream, we may feel joyful, we may experience a feeling of intense joy that is not the result of any external event, that seems to come out of the blue, and we wake from this dream in a state of delight tinged with nostalgia. It is as if we had made contact with the purest, most unalterable and most inaccessible part of ourselves, the innermost depths that sometimes produce uncontrollable and overwhelming surges of emotion, a phenomenon widely and frequently described by mystics all over the world. Dreams like this can be regarded as a way of cleansing the soul. Dreamers who, on waking, still feel touched by the state of grace that descended on them, should not fight the feeling because it may have the same effect as bathing in the fountain of youth (see *Youth*, page 552).

Jupiter

Mesopotamian myths about Jupiter. This civilization – whose rich cultural and spiritual heritage has inspired many of the myths, legends and symbols that continue to haunt us to this day, so firmly rooted are they in our collective consciousness – provides the most perfect, complex and yet surprising portrayal of Jupiter's place in the zodiac.

In actual fact, ancient astrology had nothing to do with the influence of the stars and bore no relation to their physical presence. However, when physicists or mathematicians maintain – through ignorance or the wish to be keepers of a more absolute truth, one that is easier to demonstrate, less changeable and therefore more reassuring – that the forces and laws governing the stars are universal, that they should be understood in terms of radiance and gravitational pull and not, under any circumstances, in terms of effect and individual existence, they imply that the concepts behind astrology are null and void, baseless.

This implication is very wide of the mark. Any astrologer worthy of the name will never consider the appearance of Jupiter in the zodiac of a birth chart, for example, in terms of radiance, i.e. influence. Jupiter is seen as a symbolic representation of certain personality traits that are assigned to the planet Jupiter. To enable people to grasp all its richness and complexity, its significance and underlying meanings, the planet has been associated with certain myths, legends, symbols and signs. Together they form a language in its own right that fires our imagination, arouses our senses and stimulates our intelligence.

In Mesopotamia, Jupiter was Marduk, a mythical figure of the first order celebrated in the

Enuma Elish – literally 'when on high' – a religious poem made up of seven songs written to the glory of Marduk in the early 12th century BC but bringing together some much older mythical beliefs. According to this poem, Marduk was made the champion of all the gods. His task was to fight Tiamat, a primordial feminine deity symbolizing the abyssal waters and savage, destructive primeval chaos.

Marduk was given a bow, a club and a net to stand against Tiamat and vanquish her. According to the *Enuma Elish*, Tiamat attacked Marduk with an army of demons and mythical monsters, laden with splendours and resembling gods, each more brutal than the last. But Marduk succeeded in killing Tiamat by shooting an arrow through her stomach. He then cut her body into two halves, one of which became the vault of the heavens

From the Louvre Museum, Paris.

Jupiter

and the other the solid earth. The legend then recounts that the Tigris and the Euphrates, Mesopotamia's two rivers, flowed from Tiamat's eyes.

By rising up against Tiamat, a primordial deity, Marduk therefore released the world from chaos, from primeval disorder, and divided heaven and earth while preserving the links that bound them. He then created universal laws for this new world. Finally, his task completed, he handed Anu, man's great ancestor, the tablets of fate that were to become the Anutu, the talisman of supreme power.

Egyptian myths about Jupiter. If Marduk, a Sumerian god, is taken in conjunction with Nut and Geb, typical Egyptian deities, it is possible to deduce that Nut (the vault of heaven) and Geb (the earth) were the offspring of Tiamat, who had been cloven in two by Marduk. However, according to the hierarchy of the Egyptian gods, Nut and Geb were the children of Shu and Tefnut, who personified earth's air and moisture and were themselves a god and goddess sired by Atum, the creator god of

Heliopolis, who was later assimilated into the Sun-god Re. It was during the merciless battle which, according to Egyptian myth, was waged by Re against Apophis – who, like Tiamat in Mesopotamia, symbolized primeval chaos and was represented in the form of a great snake – that the victorious Re also created heaven and earth, day and night. As a result, Re-Atum can be regarded as a Jupiter figure in Egypt, as can his great-grandson, Set, the son of Nut and Geb, whose attributes were storms and rain. He was the great protector of ancient Egypt who journeyed with Re each morning, helping him to ward off attacks by Apophis.

Greek myths about Jupiter. In all probability, the Greeks drew their inspiration both from the myths of Marduk, Re-Atum and Set, to create the myth of Zeus, the 'bright sky' as he was called, who was the chief deity of Olympus. Zeus was not only the god of clear skies and light but also of heavenly phenomena: storms, lightning, rain. Zeus's thunderbolts, an expression of his vengeful and violent wrath, were manifestations of justice both in the kingdom of the gods and the world of mortals. However, judging by all the legends and adventures attributed to him, Zeus was far from being unfailingly just and upright. He had grave weaknesses, flaws and serious deficiencies, but his power and his supremacy were never really challenged. As for the excesses, overindulgence, profligacy, natural expansiveness and the enthusiastic, generous, prodigious *joie de vivre* that are all typically Jupiterian qualities in astrology, these are illustrated by a list, which is by no means exhaustive, of the offspring produced by Zeus's various liaisons: his daughters included Aphrodite-Venus, Athena, Artemis, Helen, Persephone, the Horae (the seasons), the Moirai (the Fates), the Muses and the Dioscuri; his sons included Apollo, Ares-Mars, Argos, Dionysus, Hercules, Hermes-Mercury, Perseus and Tantalus.

Kali

See Isis and Kali, page 281

Key

A key is used to open or close a door. As such, it is associated with the idea of mystery, secrets, obstruction, closure and death. On the other hand it also has connotations with opening, clarification, liberation and deliverance.

This dual nature often appears in dreams about keys and emphasizes the fact that it is not enough to have a key, you also need to know what you are going to use it for: to open or close something. Since it takes an act of will to use a key, it is therefore a symbol of choice and the exercise of free will. If you dream about a key, it means you are having to make a choice, or will have to make one soon after having the dream.

Because a key is inserted into a keyhole, psychoanalysts also see it as a phallic symbol. While this is one possible interpretation, it seems a pity that this analogy is often made automatically. However, it is worth noting that a key-shaped symbol was used during the palaeolithic period to represent the silhouette of a woman.

Kidneys

See Thighs, pelvis, lower back and genitalia page 490

King

A king is a constant feature of human societies throughout the world. The Latin *rex, regis*, from which the English words 'regal' and 'regicide' derive, denoted both power and riches, since *reges* was used to describe the moneyed classes. The Indo-European noun *reg* is at the origin of *rajan* ('king') in Sanskrit, which can be found in 'raja' and 'maharaja', referring to an Indian ruler or prince. In Celtic Europe, particularly in ancient Gaul, *rix* was the root of the name given to the king, as in the famous ruler Vercingetorix, for example, and in Albiorix ('king of the world'), the mythical character, honoured by the Gauls, who shared many traits with the Greek god of war Ares (the Roman Mars) as he is featured in the zodiac (see *Mars*, page 326).

All civilizations have their kings – whether it be the pharaoh in Egypt, heavenly emperor in

China, great king in Persia, tsar in Russia, raja in India, as well as sultans, caliphs, shahs or negus (title of the emperor of Abyssinia) – and these rulers symbolize unity. Vested with divine power, they unite and unify. For this reason, they are thought to bring their subjects strength, courage, power, wealth and prosperity. However, over the millennia, various successive kings who have reigned in countries all over the world have not always been equal to their task, their destiny, their role. Some appear to have fallen foul of the gods or of circumstances. Others have abused their authority, their divine or sacred power: there have been numerous tyrants and usurpers throughout the history of mankind. However, the principle of the supreme leader has persisted in people's minds as, even today, most countries feel the need to have or elect some

kind of ruler, whether it be a president, king or queen.

Originally, it was believed that the king was chosen by the gods and endowed with remarkable gifts that set him apart from his peers. As a result, the legendary kings who were paragons of bravery and heroism still epitomize the essence of royalty. This is because people still feel the need to identify with a supreme ruler who is capable of leading a nation and making people pull together, a true gift indeed, when human feelings and aspirations are so contradictory that they tend to drive people apart. This is why people often dream of their king or president, although this may only be a symbolic representation of that hunger for perfection and the absolute that, consciously or subconsciously, spurs us on.

Dreaming that you are in the presence of a figure of authority therefore often reveals a need to put your own house in order and unify your spiritual energies.

Kingfisher

As its name implies, this bird is a skilled fisher and very fond of small fish. It frequents Europe's increasingly rare unpolluted rivers and streams, uttering its distinctive piping call and plunging its long beak into the water to catch fish with consummate skill. When it is not feeding, the male courts the female by offering her fish. The pair dig a nest in the bank of the river or stream that they frequent. They both sit on the six or eight eggs laid by the female for about three weeks, but they can have up to three broods per season.

It is not unusual to see these birds flying together in pairs. This is probably why the kingfisher was regarded as a symbol of marital fidelity, a happy love life, and the joy of being part of a couple. It was also a symbol of beauty: the kingfisher has been nicknamed the 'flying jewel', sits dazzling bluegreen wings contrasting with the red plumage of its torso. It was not just native Americans who believed that the feathers of certain birds had beneficial, protective powers. In medieval England and France, it was commonly believed that wearing kingfisher feathers guaranteed providential protection. An early name for the kingfisher was 'halcyon', from the Latin *alcyon*, itself derived from the Greek *alkyon* meaning a mythical bird. According to Greek legend, Alcyone or Alkyon, the daughter of Aeolus, king of the winds, was changed into this fabulous bird, said to calm wind and waves. Unsurprisingly, the kingfisher was also called a diver. Jacobus de Voragine, a 13th-century Italian chronicler, tells us how the halcyon or diver came to be known as St Martin's Fisherman: 'On his way, he [St Martin] saw divers on the riverbank that were watching for fish and that caught several. "This is the behaviour of devils," he said: "the birds are trying to surprise the unwary; they catch them without them noticing; they devour the ones they catch, and the more they eat, the less satisfied they are." So he commanded these birds to leave these deep waters and go into desert countries' (Jacobus de Voragine, *The Golden Legend*).

Kiss

Symbolically, a kiss is a merging of breath, a fusion of spirits. This is why, by kneeling to kiss the ground, an individual unites his or her spirit with the great forces of nature that are the origin of all life.

In ancient Greece, this rite was performed by the initiates of the Eleusinian Mysteries of Demeter-Ceres, the earth goddess, when they came to worship in her temples. It was perpetuated by the early Christians and then by the Catholic Church, with worshippers kissing the robes, feet and hands of saints, bishops and the pope in token of reverence and devotion, or kissing relics and statues of saints to implore forgiveness or protection.

In the Middle Ages, vassals had to kiss the hand of their overlord to demonstrate their fealty and respect. This custom gave rise to the practice – which became widespread among the nobility – of kissing a woman's hand as a sign of homage and esteem.

It is impossible to discuss the symbolic implications of the kiss without referring to the kiss of Judas Iscariot. Although it has been the subject of much discussion and writing, the deeper meaning often eludes us. This is best illustrated in Matthew 26: 47–50: 'And while he yet spake, lo, Judas, one of the twelve, came, and with him a great multitude with swords and staves, from the chief priests and elders of the people. Now he that betrayed him gave them a sign,

saying, Whomsoever I shall kiss, the same is he: hold him fast. And forthwith he came to Jesus, and said, Hail, master; and kissed him. And Jesus said unto him, Friend, wherefore art thou come?'

This fatal kiss for which Judas is notorious is based on a misunderstanding and a distorted interpretation of an episode that can only be invested with its full significance by considering the symbolic implications of the kiss that Judas gave Jesus. Yehudah (Judah or Judas) is an extremely noble Hebrew name. The letters of the Hebrew alphabet that form it contain the tetragrammaton YHWH (Yahweh, God), plus *daleth*, which also means 'door'. Yehudah therefore represents the door in the name of God, or the door in time since, in Hebrew, the name Yahweh

(God) comprises the three modalities of time: HWH, *hawah* ('the present'), HYH, *hayah* ('the past') and YHH, *yeheh* ('the future').

The name Yeshua (Jesus) – derived from Yehoshua (Joshua) and transcribed into Greek as Yesuz and into Latin as Jesus – only has three of the letters of the tetragrammaton, YHW, from which it is impossible to reproduce the three modalities of time. In other words, Jesus is placed outside of time, he is timeless.

When Yehudah (Judas) kissed Yeshua (Jesus), he embraced a universal, immortal and eternal truth. His action therefore has fundamentally symbolic, spiritual and theological implications since, in this context, kissing or embracing has the dual sense of kissing someone you love and embracing something, someone's interests or a cause. This is a far cry from the kiss of betrayal.

If you dream you are kissing or being kissed by someone, you should always ask yourself what particular interest you have in that person or they in you, and in what way there could be a meeting of minds or spirits. This kind of dream is nearly always a good sign, so you can disregard the detrimental and distorted interpretation of Judas's kiss, one of those preconceived ideas that are hard to dispel.

Kite

The black kite is a bird of prey belonging to the same family as the falcon, goshawk, vulture, eagle or buzzard. It is found throughout Europe, in Scandinavia, southern Asia, Africa and Australia. A hunter of small vertebrates, it feeds by preference on carrion, dead fish or birds. The female lays only two or three eggs in April or May, and the last chick to hatch is often tossed out of the nest by the slightly older sibling chicks. The black kite lives near rivers and large lakes in company with heron colonies. It can grow as large as 50–60cm (20–24in), and is noticeable for its impressive circling flight and strident cry.

The kite was one of the birds dedicated to Apollo, the Greek sun god, symbolizing his gifts of farsightedness. According to the myth, Typhon, the monstrous son who hatched from an egg produced by Gaia and Tartarus, attacked the heavens, forcing the gods to take refuge in the Egyptian desert. Ares took the shape of a fish, Hermes that of an Ibis, Dionysus that of a goat, Hephaestus that of an ox and Apollo that of a kite, while Zeus and Athena battled with the supernatural creature whose head touched the stars and who had one hundred dragons' heads in place of fingers.

Knees

*See Feet, legs and knees,
page 183*

Knot

The knot is one of those everyday objects that has far greater symbolic significance than at first appears. Routine acts or events, ordinary gestures and familiar objects are often full of symbolic meaning because their simplicity makes them an excellent vehicle for subconscious messages. After all, who has never tied a shoelace, scarf, cravat, necktie or piece of string?

However, it is also true that, once human beings had acquired the ability to reason, they saw evidence of the gods and all that was sacred in the simplest of actions. There was something magical about making something happen by doing something else, or by creating or producing something that changed people's perception of reality or the world. This was the case with bread, for example, which was often used as a symbolic medium in various religions or mystical philosophies to illustrate something that was not found in nature but that could be created by processing, preparing and mixing pre-existing materials or ingredients according to certain rules. This also applied to the knot which, in ancient Egypt, for example, probably formed the basis for one of the most representative symbols of that learned and complex civilization which lasted almost three thousand years: the *ankh*. The *ankh*, ansate cross or cross of life, resembling a sandal strap, a shoelace, a looped belt or simply a knot topped by a loop, depicts three symbols in one: the cross, the key and the knot. The ansate cross in fact was often associated with the Isis knot, symbolizing eternal life.

Because the knot shares certain symbolic analogies with the cross and the key, it is also associated with the heart, which it often represents and which was regarded by our forebears as the seat of the intellect. Egyptian sorcerers and doctors placed great emphasis on the heart, sometimes according it excessive importance.

The fact remains, however, that the knot is always associated with density, tension and life. By its very nature, it begs to be untied: in fact, one of the main reference books of Tibetan Buddhism is evocatively entitled the *Book on Untying the Knots*.

As a result – and this holds particularly true in a dream – you should never ignore the fact that a knot can be untied. If you are in an awkward situation or confronted by a thorny problem in a dream and a knot plays a prominent role, or if you simply see yourself tying or untying a knot, you can be sure that your difficulties will soon be resolved.

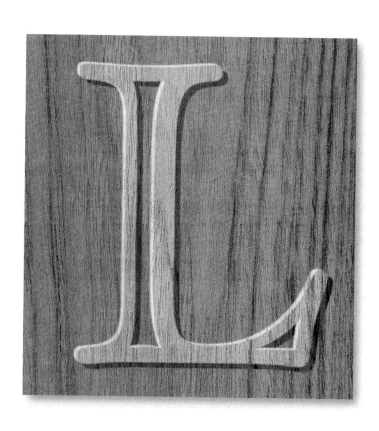

Labyrinth

Like the circle, cross and spiral, with which many analogies can be drawn (see pages 100, 134 and 306), the labyrinth is a universal symbol. Found all over the world, in all cultures and civilizations, it is most often found in Greece, where it appeared as early as the fifth millennium BC, particularly on ceramics, and earlier still on rock carvings dating from the sixth millennium BC, discovered in the Italian Alps. The labyrinth was also an important symbol for native Americans, particularly the Incas in Peru,

From Hermann Hugo, Gottselige Begierde, Augsbourg, 1622.

where immense labyrinthine diagrams were discovered on the high plateaux of the Andes Cordillera, in the Nazca valley. Some of these are up to 120m (131yds) long and are thought to have been realized between AD 300 and 600.

The labyrinth was also represented all over the world: in ancient Egypt, ancient Syria, India, Tibet, Africa, Europe and by the various tribes on the Austral Islands. More recently, labyrinthine motifs were used in many of the stained-glass windows for cathedrals and buildings of the Gothic period in Europe.

One of the most effective symbols of initiation into spiritual life. It is curious that, from south to north and east to west, neolithic men and women all shared the same view or interpretation of their world, of heaven and earth, universally represented by the circle, spiral, cross, labyrinth, etc. These symbols are so pregnant with meaning and have played such a key role in people's physical and mental perception of their environment, that their significance is immediately obvious, even if their purpose, use, language and main principles are no longer known. This is because we are subconsciously aware that they are at the root of all the languages we have formulated to name, identify or distinguish people and objects, thereby engaging in a dialogue with nature and our fellow human beings.

The labyrinth is an initiatory circuit. We enter it through a gate or – more exactly – we plunge into its midst with the aim of finding, understanding or doing something while we are there. We often leave by the same gate, but only after following a maze of corridors and chambers, some of which are dead-ends. This is why the symbolism of the labyrinth has numerous analogies to that of gestation, intrauterine life or order emerging from chaos, as well as to that of life battling against the destructive and chaotic forces of death.

The myth of the Labyrinth. The labyrinth appears in a famous Greek myth: the account of Theseus, who fought the guardian of the Labyrinth, the man-bull Minotaur, and won, battering him to death with his bare hands. He found his way out again with a ball of wool given to him by Ariadne, the daughter of Minos, King of Crete, and Pasiphae, his wife, nicknamed 'she who shines for all', the daughter of Helius, the sun. Bewitched by a spell cast by Theseus's father Poseidon-

Neptune, the god of the sea and the ocean, Pasiphae fell madly in love with a white bull, and gave herself to him, body and soul. The Minotaur, with a bull's head and a human body, was their offspring, whom Minos concealed at the centre of the Labyrinth. Everything comes full circle in this legend, set against the backdrop of the famous Labyrinth, and the children make amends for the mistakes of their parents. Theseus, the son of Poseidon, breaks his father's spell and repairs his father's wrongdoing by killing the Minotaur. He is helped in his task by Ariadne, Pasiphae's 'extremely pure' daughter, who, unsurprisingly, is in love with Theseus.

It is easy to see why the founders of psychoanalysis used Greek mythology to support their theories. As for us, what interpretation should be given to this symbolical myth? The first task is to establish who the Minotaur was or, more precisely, what he symbolized. In all ancient civilizations, and even earlier than that, in the palaeolithic era, the bull has always been regarded as a deity associated with fecundity, fertility, death and rebirth, similar to a mother-goddess. But, although this may seem paradoxical, primitive cultures believed this was a

male mother-goddess, a primordial, fertile, male principle with maternal characteristics, in other words a parental, protecting and reassuring entity. This is the symbolic universe connected with the sign of Taurus, the bull (see page 556).

This means that although seed is a female element, it is generated by the male principle. To produce fruit and new seeds, the seed must return to the maternal belly of the earth. The symbol of the labyrinth, therefore, represents this process of renewal in which one principle merges with another to create a third that returns to its point of origin in order to produce something new. However, there is always the risk that a link may break somewhere along the chain. This is because the mother-goddess is just as powerful a destroyer as she is a creator. She can make the earth

as arid as she has made it fertile, hinder growth or deliver the kiss of death. In the myth of the Labyrinth, Pasiphae undergoes this harrowing experience, since she is in the power of the Minotaur-mother-goddess, blinded by her love for him and held captive by her emotions. Theseus is therefore able to set her free by following Ariadne's thread, which could also be described as a spider's thread: the silk with which the latter weaves a natural labyrinth and which symbolizes both the thread that binds the soul to the body and the thread of fate. However, this thread is not to be trusted, because it is also often used to weave a web of feelings, emotions and hopes that can prove fatal. This is why in the legend, having accomplished his mission, the hero abandons Ariadne on a deserted beach.

This is probably to avoid being caught in the web she is weaving around him, which can be seen as a fresh labyrinth: that of thoughts, desires, feelings and ideas.

Ladder

The ladder is one of those wonderful symbols that, while based on a very simple principle, represent a stage in the human condition that is extremely important for the spiritual development of each and every one of us. According to the world's mystical traditions and ancient beliefs, man living on earth, the earthling dreaming of extra-terrestrials and guardian angels, is only 'passing through'.

If we dream of beings who come from another world or live in another dimension, it is because we feel constrained by our own vast world and hope there is some way out, that this universe, our universe, is not definitively closed, in spite of the fact that, according to astrophysicists, it is constantly expanding.

Our distant ancestors experienced the same anguish, thought the same thoughts and examined the same issues, which is why the questions we ask today can be found in the myths and symbols of antiquity.

Psychoanalysts and psychiatrists like Sigmund Freud and C.G. Jung were right: the finest archetypical representations of what they defined as 'complexes' can be found in the profusion of humanity's myths and symbols.

In the imagery of the ladder, the first example that springs to mind is the ladder in Jacob's dream: 'And Jacob went out from Beer-Sheba, and went towards Haran. And he lighted upon a certain place, and tarried there all night, because the sun was set; and he took of the stones of that place, and put them for his pillows, and lay down in that place to sleep. And he dreamed, and behold a ladder set upon the earth, and the top of it reached to heaven: and behold the angels of God ascending and descending on it.' (Genesis 28: 10–12.)

Without drawing any conclusions, it is worth pointing out that there is an immediate and obvious parallel between the angels ascending and descending the ladder in Jacob's dream – an account written *c.* 800 BC and inspired by much earlier myths and legends – and certain modern claims of extra-terrestrials ascending and descending the ladder of a spaceship.

When trying to interpret the significance of Jacob's ladder, we should bear in mind that every account in the Bible has a symbolic value and every character is mythical before being historical. Furthermore, their names are often indicative of an experience that would, in modern parlance, be qualified as 'psychological' but which will here be referred to as 'human'. This is quite simply because, regardless of our race, culture, social class or beliefs, it could be experienced by any one of us and, as such, is an experience that involves us all. Etymologically,

From **L'Échelle de Jacob ('Jacob's Ladder')** *Avignon School, 15th century, Musée du Petit Palais, Avignon.*

the word 'ladder' derives from the Old English *blædder*, related to Old High German *leitara*. It is defined as a portable wood or metal framework with horizontal steps or rungs for climbing up and down and, figuratively, as a hierarchy with a series of ascending levels or stages. Symbolically, the ladder, like the cosmic tree and the rainbow, is a path or link between heaven and earth. In this context, it symbolizes personal and spiritual development in the form of the ascension of the cosmic ladder, with each rung representing a different state or level of consciousness. The individual therefore progresses from the material world at the bottom of the ladder to the spiritual world at the top, a progression that leads to the opening of the consciousness and liberation of the soul.

In the same way, the ladder in Jacob's dream signifies that this development, represented by the ascent and descent of the angels, is only possible for mortals if the ladder is placed firmly on the earth below and linked to heaven above. In other words, the energies of heaven above and earth below must be able to circulate continuously along the ladder, in the same way as the energies that circulate freely – upwards and downwards, in an endless and uninterrupted cycle – within the body (see *Thighs, pelvis, lower back and genitalia*, page 489). If these energies are impeded in any way, there is a risk that we will falter on the path of our personal and spiritual development. This symbolic representation is identical to that of the Hindu concept of the kundalini (cosmic energy) that exists within each and every one us and is pictured as a coiled serpent lying at the base of the spine – the parallel between the ladder and the spinal column is obvious (see *Tree of life according to the cabbala*, page 501).

As can be seen from the above, a dream about a ladder is therefore of great symbolic significance and should be treated as a warning that the vital and primordial energies – ascending and descending – must be allowed to circulate freely, for within them lies the power of regeneration and the potential for spiritual development.

Lake

This is, first and foremost, a symbol of rest, tranquillity, peace and quiet, immediately evoking the image of clear, limpid water.

However, because the moon is reflected in it as if it

were a mirror and because the lake itself seems like a mirror placed on the earth's surface, it has often been metaphorically associated with the lunar symbolism of gestation, imagination, dreaming and the unconscious mind. Beneath the still waters of the lake, there is an entire world teeming with life, a world where something is hatching, stirring, growing and brewing. This is why in ancient times and the Middle Ages the lake was both the realm of nymphs and naiads and the home of the dragon. Although all these symbols are similar to those generally attributed to the sea, the key difference between the symbolic representation of the sea and that of the lake is that the former is linked to the sky and is therefore seen as boundless, active, regenerative, continually alive and in motion, while the latter is landlocked, closed in on itself; this receptive, passive expanse of water is always still.

As a result, to dream of walking alongside a lake or contemplating its clear, calm surface is a sign of complacency and self-satisfaction. The person involved in the dream is happy to be just as they appear – they are not concerned with what is going on beneath the surface. On the other hand, the dreamer who sees a lake with choppy waters, churned up by waves or seething with currents, is obviously beset by inner anxieties and mixed emotions that are in the process of surfacing and herald a change of mood or an essential realization. Last but not least, a lake in a dream may simply predict a birth, an act of creation or a new situation about to unfold.

Lame man

Everyone has heard of the riddle of the Sphinx, the mythological creature with a lion's body and a human head: 'What has one voice, and walks on four legs in

the morning, two at noon, and three in the evening?' The Sphinx posed the riddle to all who passed and devoured those who could not answer. No one could, except Oedipus, the hero of one of the most famous legends in Greek literature: 'A man, who crawls on all fours in infancy, walks on two feet when grown, and leans on a staff when aged.' Therefore, according to the riddle, a man inevitably ends his life lame. The image of the lame man is reminiscent of the combat between Jacob and the angel during which 'Jacob's thigh was out of joint'. Jacob said it was because he had 'seen God face to face' that he became lame (Genesis 32: 25–32). Another legendary lame man was Hephaestus, son of Zeus and Hera, who was the Greek god of fire and metalworking (whom the Romans identified with Vulcan). He was lamed when his father flung him out of heaven for coming to his mother's rescue during a dispute.

These various mythological accounts reveal that the lame man, by the very fact of his infirmity, has been touched by divine grace. He has acquired the supernatural gift of knowledge, awareness and understanding usually reserved for the gods whose mark he bears.

The lame man is therefore an initiate. This gave rise to the belief that meeting or passing a lame man is often the harbinger of a revelation, a realization, a test or trial to be undergone, an obstacle to be overcome, a period of conflict and difficulty from which we will emerge victorious but which will leave its mark. It will also involve some form of real moral, psychological or spiritual conversion.

Dreaming you are lame signifies that you will inevitably have to undergo some form of test or trial, be tested by circumstances or put yourself to the test in order to obtain what you want or desire in life at the time when you have the dream. It is an extremely significant dream, rich in symbolism, and should not be ignored. However, you should always modify and adapt its interpretation by taking account of the circumstances of your life.

Lamp

The main purpose of the lamp is to reproduce a celestial nocturnal phenomenon: night-time light, light conquering darkness. Symbolically, the lamp is a source of light, a sun or miniature star, because, like them, it generates and radiates its own light. The lamp was therefore initially a symbolic representation of the presence of a god, deity or household spirit, before it became an object lighting our way through the darkness. In this respect, it should be related to the symbols associated with the flame, candle, light, etc. (see page 515).

Because lamps are now electric, the dreamer must distinguish between the symbolic representation of an ancient lamp, with a wick and flame, and

the modern lamp, which can be switched on and off. The former often alludes to an indescribable, immanent and immortal presence, to the soul or spirit, while the latter is linked to a flash of light, the spark of life, a revelation or a realization. Nowadays, people switch a lamp on and off automatically, without giving it much thought. Because of this, the appearance of a faint glow brightening to a light that can banish the darkness has lost its magical, sacred quality, even though, deep within, we are still capable of working this type of magic.

Lark

This unassuming little brown bird nests in fields and meadows where it feeds entirely on insects. It is a member of the *Alaudidae* family, from the Latin *alauda* ('lark'), which gave the French *alouette* of the well-known children's song. The English name derives from the Old English *lawerce* or *lǽwerce*, of Germanic origin and related to the German *Lerche* and the Icelandic *lævirki*.

Although this insect-eating bird is extremely useful in controlling pests, it tends to be better known for its melodious song, which moves those who hear it to the very depths of their being. It is all the more impressive when you realise that the lark has a very small wingspan and that it sings while in flight – at heights of over 400m (1,300ft)! Its song has been seen as the expression of the joy of living, happiness and fulfilment. For this reason, the lark was sacred to the Gauls who saw it as a symbol of happiness and a bird of good omen. According to ancient Greek legend, the little songbird existed on earth and in the heavens long before the gods took up occupancy. It does have a negative side to its character and was sometimes seen as a symbol of carefree existence, infidelity and fickleness. However, this is eclipsed by William Blake's beautiful tribute to the lark:

> *His little throat labours with*
> *   inspiration; every feather*
> *On throat and breast and*
> *   wings vibrates with the*
> *   effluence Divine.*
> *All Nature listens silent to*
> *   him, and the awful Sun*
> *Stands still upon the mountain*
> *   looking on this little Bird*
> *With eyes of soft humility and*
> *   wonder, love and awe.*
>
> 'Milton', f. 31, ll. 7–11
> (The Birds and the Flowers)
> in *The Poetical Works of William
> Blake*, OUP, 1914, page 379

Left

*See Brain (right and left
sides of the), page 67 and
Senses, page 448*

Legs

*See Feet, legs and knees,
page 183*

Leo
(sign of)

See Zodiac, page 564

Leopard

This magnificent big cat, which according to the etymological root of its name is a hybrid between a lion and a panther, acquired a bad reputation in ancient times. In Egypt, it was renowned for its savage nature and embodied the forces of evil as represented by the god Set. The Egyptian priests wore a leopard skin in order to symbolize their victory over evil. In actual fact, this duality – embodied by the leopard's compound name, meaning lion-panther – is also found in the Chinese myth of the leopard which, depending on various Far-Eastern ancestral beliefs, either sprang from the moon, the forces of darkness or the shadowy places of the earth where it lived in order to bring about the birth of spring. Its dual nature was also recognizable from its spotted coat.

A power for good and a force for evil, the appearance of a leopard in a dream is always ambiguous. It indicates either that the dreamer needs to recognize and reconcile the different and opposing sides of their nature or that the dreamer concerned may be dealing with someone who is not all they appear to be.

Lerna
(the hydra of)

See Hercules, page 230

Libra
(sign of)

See Zodiac, page 569

Light

To understand how traditional magic has formed the basis for the world vision formulated by modern scientific investigations, we need only examine the history of light and, in particular, the episode relating to Giambattista della Porta. In 1558, this Neapolitan physician published a work called *Magia Naturalis* (*Natural Magic*), devoted to the wonders of the natural world. In it, he described an extraordinary experiment: when light was filtered through a lens placed in a dark room, he noticed that the images were inverted and reversed. Without understanding the process, he made an observation that was to lead to the invention of the camera obscura and the telescope, which in its turn was to revolutionize popular concepts about the sky, the cosmos and light.

However, the fact that we have succeeded in measuring the speed of light and have grasped the fact that light is an electromagnetic wave, of which only part of its field is visible, does not alter the fact that light was once regarded as the purest, most beautiful, most precious and most wonderful expression of life. This is why, in any given civilization, culture or religion, light is always associated with a joyful heart and soul, fulfilment, happiness, perfection, the first stirrings of a desire for God and faith, and the manifestation of divinity incarnate.

As a result, light was the ultimate symbol of life and, better still, of eternal life, to which mortals have always aspired. It was also the symbolic representation of the forces of good that dispel or destroy the forces of darkness. In this respect, light also represented salvation and supreme happiness for humanity, a divine light that

was visible to no optical instrument such as the human eye: on the contrary, mystics believed that this light could only be glimpsed by closing your eyes on the world in order to open the eyes of your soul, which were then dazzled by the light. So it can be said now, more than ever, that there is a physical light, that is both wave and particle, and a spiritual light, that is associated with the light described by the ancients.

When light plays an important role in one of your dreams, you must work out whether it is a physical or electric light or a symbolic light. Sunlight often indicates a necessary clarification, a realization or even, if very bright, a type of blindness that is preventing you from seeing clearly. Electric light is associated with the life force that can be extinguished at any time. However, a light that does not come from any external source, which is in some way supernatural, heralds a happy event, intense joy, inexpressible happiness or a feeling of sheer delight that may appear out of the blue. It is unusual to see a light like this in a dream, but when it occurs, it is a sign of a genuine spiritual experience that the dreamer may sometimes find hard to describe.

Lightning

Because of its sudden and unpredictable nature, lightning is a symbol of an upheaval or a sudden and unexpected event, and this how it should be interpreted when it appears in a dream. However, lightning never occurs in isolation since it is by and large a phenomenon produced by storms and, for this reason, is associated with natural phenomena of a cataclysmic nature. Because of its force and violence, and the potentially devastating effects when it strikes the earth, our ancestors usually attributed lightning to the anger of the gods – the famous thunderbolts of mythology. But since the gods only manifested their anger with such intensity when mortals had infringed their divine laws, our early ancestors lived in fear of incurring divine wrath. However, although the ravages of these storms were usually proportional to any transgressions, they were sometimes disproportionate since the gods themselves could be unpredictable and inclement. It was not just by

chance that the ancient Greeks – whose myths, legends and divine pantheon were inspired by those of Egypt, Mesopotamia and other ancient cultures – made thunder, storms, thunderbolts and lightning the attributes of Zeus, the chief god of Olympus. But storms and lightning also symbolized fertility in the minds of our ancestors, firstly because they were associated with rain, but also because the blinding flash of lightning was regarded as the manifestation of the divine seed falling from the sky and fertilizing the earth.

A dream about a storm, especially one in which lightning streaks the sky, is quite common among pregnant women who either do not know they are pregnant or are about to give birth. Furthermore, a dream about lightning that looks as if it has opened a breach in a sky darkened by storm clouds can be interpreted in one of two ways, either as the sign of a probable solution to a situation in which you have become inextricably embroiled, or of an imminent upheaval.

See also *Thunder*, page 493.

Lilith

*See Isha, Eve and Lilith,
page 279*

Lime tree

This legendary tree, with its healing, divinatory and medicinal properties, was originally, if the myth is to be believed, a beautiful woman called Philyra, whose name simply means 'lime tree'. Philyra was loved by Cronus, who was her uncle (since she was the daughter of Oceanus). However, they were surprised by Rhea, Cronus's wife. To prevent her from recognizing him and to escape her wrath, Cronus changed into a stallion and made love to Philyra in this form before galloping off. Their union produced a child, half man, half horse – the centaur, Cheiron. Disgusted and repulsed by the monster she had just brought into the world and that she would have to suckle, Philyra begged her father to save her. Oceanus acquiesced to his daughter's pleas and changed her into a lime tree. It was by feeding on the sap of the lime tree, his mother, that Cheiron learned all there was to know about the medicinal, soothing and fragrant properties of this tree as well as the properties of all plants and fruits.

He became a famous physician, scholar and seer and he always used his knowledge for the greater good and protection of mankind.

Lion (the Nemean)

See Hercules, page 229

Lizard

The lizard either represents a miniature dragon or the oldest creature, the great ancestor of all living species, associated with the iguana and the snake (see page 459). As a result, it was feared and worshipped by primitive peoples. However, the diminutive lizard that basks on the stone walls of houses or gardens in Mediterranean countries, drinking in the sunshine and snapping

up little insects, has become a familiar, protective creature, a symbol of domestic happiness. The Egyptians even regarded it as a benevolent spirit keeping watch over the house or hearth.

The appearance of a lizard in a dream can therefore be interpreted in two ways: on the one hand, it can be associated with the myth of the dragon and that of the snake, in which case the forces it represents can either be regarded as diminished, powerless and inoffensive or about to assume great importance for the dreamer; on the other hand, however, the lizard can simply symbolize domestic happiness and harmony.

See also *Salamander*, page 438.

Lotus

The Egyptians loved flowers, plants and trees. In ancient Egypt, flowers were an important part of everyday life: they were often given as gifts and were also offered up to the dead. Cornflowers, poppies, chrysanthemums, irises, jasmine, mallow, mandrake, larkspur and water-lilies were very popular but the place of honour was given

to the blue or white lotus, the most beautiful of the *nymphaea*. According to Egyptian legend, the great primordial, immortal serpent Nehebkaw was born from the heart of this sacred flower. He encompassed all the *kas* or vital energies of the earth and lived in Nun, the primordial ocean from which all life emerged. According to another Egyptian legend, the lotus gave birth to the sun every morning, allowing it to set off on its journey. Because of this, anyone picking a lotus flower without authorization could be severely punished. The sacred flower, which gave new life to the sun by opening its petals, was associated with the female sex organs and therefore linked to the continual cycle of birth and rebirth.

The generic name of nelumbo now signifies a type of aquatic plant with long leaves and a flower that is more often pink than white or blue. This flower emanates a sweet aniseed fragrance and contains a large seed-pod that swells and hardens to become almost egg-shaped.

The lotus was sacred in India and China as well as in Egypt. The Chinese not only associated the lotus flower, or golden lotus, with the vulva, but also with the highest wisdom, strength, wealth, marital happiness and eternal life. In India, *Padma*, the Sanskrit word for lotus, is the symbol-word used to represent the chakras. *Padma* also symbolizes pure beauty and holiness. Brahma, the Hindu creator god, and Vishnu, his avatar, a solar god – whose name literally means 'one who pervades' – are often represented sitting on a lotus in Indian iconography. The lotus was also used to represent the Buddha's throne. The *Padmasutra*, which literally means 'the lotus thread', is regarded as the key work of reference for the Buddhist doctrine. Finally, the founding father of Tibetan Buddhism, who lived in the eighth century, was called the *Padmasambhava*, which means 'lotus born'.

Lozenge

This shape symbolically represents the entrance to and exit from the world. In other words, it is one of the most common representations of the vulva or female sex organs. Possibly of Arab origin, the word may be derived from *lawzinag*, which was the name of an almond cake, from *lawz*, meaning 'almond'. The almond is also a symbolic representation of a woman's genitals, of the vulva and of creative energy (see page 24). However, in Latin, the name for a lozenge was a *rhombus*, from the Greek *rhombos*, which referred to a top, a tambourine, a spindle or spinning wheel that was used to utter magic formulas and cast spells. Another derivation may come from *lausa*, a Persian word meaning 'tombstone'.

The lozenge symbol is therefore far more complicated than it appears. It can be interpreted not only as a birth or a death, a transition or a symbol of the female sex, but also as an unconscious desire, if a lozenge-shaped object plays a key role in a dream, or if the dreamer protects himself by using a rhomb, or lozenge, as sorcerers did in ancient times. Lastly, it is also worth noting that the Christians used a lozenge before they began using a rosary.

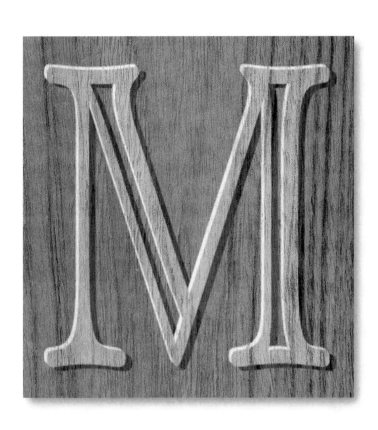

Magpie

The black-billed magpie (*Pica pica*), with its raucous chattering call, is the best-known and most representative species of magpie. It occurs throughout Europe, as well as in much of Asia, ranging as far as northern Egypt. It is easily distinguished by its black-and-white (pied) plumage and long tail. The magpie is happy to live near forests and water-courses and in meadows, fields and prairies, but it also frequents villages and cities, as it is a fairly sociable bird. In her treetop nest, the female lays five to eight eggs that she incubates alone for almost three weeks. She feeds on small rodents, molluscs, insects, fruit and grain, but she is also not above pillaging the nests of other birds for sustenance.

The reputation of the thieving magpie is well founded. This bird is known to steal anything that sparkles, burying its treasures in the ground with its beak. Another distinctive feature of the magpie is that it chatters all day. This loquacious-ness is said to draw its origin from the myth of Dionysus who, under the influence of drink, was prone to talk endlessly. Finally, the magpie has always been regarded as a bird of omen, as can be seen from the old rhyme:

> *One for sorrow, two for joy*
> *Three for a girl, four for a boy,*
> *Five for silver, six for gold,*
> *Seven for a secret never to be old,*
> *Eight for a wish, nine for a kiss,*
> *Ten for a marriage never to*
> *   be old.*

Mandala

In some respects, we all have our own mandala, although most of us are unaware of it. Deep within, we all have a space that is ours alone, a pure, sacred, secret and mysterious space that sometimes serves as a refuge. The mandala is simply a graphic, coloured and geometric representation of this inner place where, according to the Hindus, the soul is reunited with divinity or merges with it. In other words, an analogy can be drawn between the principle of the mandala and the key characteristics of the house: a place of rest, peace and quiet, the womb, etc.

Mandala means 'circle, arc, segment' in Sanskrit. However, as the square is contained within

the circle or implicitly represented by it, the mandala is often represented by a circle within a square, itself able to contain many other circles and squares, creating the dizzying impression of continual motion. As a result, when a mandala appears in a dream, it can be interpreted according to the criteria attributed to the symbols of the circle, square and centre (see *Circle*, page 100).

However, the Sanskrit word refers not only to the diagram, illustration or picture that serves as an instrument of meditation for Tibetan Buddhist monks, but also to the circle or cycles of hymns in the *Rig Veda*, the oldest of the four collections of Vedas – the Hindu equivalent of the Jewish Bible – that was probably written in the 12th century BC and that contains over a thousand hymns.

Whether it is a diagram or a hymn, the mandala is always an instrument of meditation and soul-searching, and a representa-tion of the self and the universe, the microcosm and the macro-cosm that both originate in the same principles or essence. The appearance of a mandala in a dream, therefore, has extremely spiritual connotations.

Maple tree

The maple tree has strong associations with Canada, a country where its leaf is the national emblem and maple syrup has become a national product. The syrup is made from the sweet-water sap – obtained from the tree during the dormant period – which is concentrated by evaporation in open pans to produce the characteristic colour and flavour.

It goes without saying that bees discovered the delicious sap and fragrant flowers of the maple long before human beings and,

from time immemorial, have gathered its pollen and nectar for their delicious, sugar-rich maple honey. But Canada does not have the monopoly on the maple tree. In ancient China, it was associated with the concept of honour, since the Chinese for 'maple' was a homophone of the verb meaning 'to confer an honour'.

In North America, as in all Anglo-Saxon countries, the maple is a symbol of longevity and vigour. It was also believed to ward off demons and nocturnal spirits and, for this reason, people placed small branches and sprigs of maple at the door of their house or the foot of their bed, in much the same way that the stork weaves maple twigs into its nest to ward of the bats that eat its eggs.

Mares of Diomedes (the)

See Hercules, page 244

Marriage

Every religion in every civilization in the world has its own hierogamy or ceremony devoted to the sacred union of a man and woman. In a world where marriage has become a social institution rather than a religious one, there are many economic or psychological reasons for it, but few that are religious in the true sense of the word, i.e. derived from the Latin verb *religare*, meaning 'to bind'.

In ancient civilizations, therefore, the union between the god and the great goddess imposed not only order and unity on primordial chaos but gave it a rationale. In other words, the marriage of a man and woman is an ideal way to ensure that they lead a more settled life, calming extreme, reckless emotions and impulses, confused feelings and destructive anxieties. The struggle for survival, which may be desperate and suicidal if waged alone, becomes a happy, salutary experience if undertaken together. Man and woman, who made a mistake, committed an original sin or were misled by evil spirits – depending on the various beliefs, myths and cosmogonies – possess the power to join forces and impose order where none appears to exist. This gives real meaning to the saying 'strength through unity'.

A representative example of this process is the mythical

marriage between Zeus – symbolizing divine omnipotence that is capable of acting without restraint and moderation, and breaking all the rules (Zeus's legendary unbridled passions and countless conquests are a case in point) – and Themis – the goddess of law, daughter of the sky (Uranus) and the earth (Gaia), who both emerged from the primordial chaos. This sacred union of two gods produced the Horae, originally goddesses of the seasons, then of the hours. These three sisters were called Eunomia, Dike and Eirene, or good order, justice and peace. Their three sisters, who were also daughters of Zeus and Themis, were the Moirai, Atropos, Clotho and Lachesis, who sat spinning human fate. This clearly shows that the marriage or sacred union between a man and a woman gives birth to order, justice and peace, as well as all concepts of fate and human destiny. As far as the Greeks were concerned, at any rate, marriage not only engendered social order but also bound human beings to their fate.

Without charting the historic, economic and social developments that caused the Church to institute religious marriage in the 12th century – a model still used for Western marriages today – it is worth noting that there have always been parallels between nuptial and funerary rites, wedding celebrations and funerals, even though they now

seem so different. However, in deep and secret places, the psychic zones from which our dreams well up, there are often close links between marriage and death, physical union and the soul's release, perhaps because the sexual climax resembles the ecstatic release of the soul.

Dreaming of marriage, therefore, may simply counterbalance a deep yearning, a hunger for renewed unity, togetherness, harmony, 'good order, justice and peace'. However, it may also indicate another much deeper craving: that of the soul which, when it unites with the divine, throws off the shackles of life, illusion and death.

Mars

Mesopotamian myths about Mars. The question is sometimes asked why there are twelve signs of the zodiac and only seven governing planets, although three supplementary planets have been added (Uranus, Neptune and Pluto). How can two signs have the same ruling planet, when their significance and their relationship to the seasons, among other things, are completely different?

Mars is a case in point: disregarding Pluto – acknowledged by contemporary astrologers as the second ruling planet of Scorpio, the eighth sign of the zodiac, if not its sole ruling planet – and taking Mars as the ruling planet of both Aries and Scorpio, it seems odd that the same planet should govern two such different signs of the zodiac, which – albeit complementary in some respects – diverge widely in many crucial points. To understand this, it is necessary to travel back in time and to observe how Mars was regarded in Mesopotamia, the birthplace of astrology. Nergal ('the burner') – who became master of Ku.Mal. ('field dweller'), the first sign of the zodiac, Aries, as well as of Gir.Tab. ('the scorpion') – was regarded as the god-king of hell or the underworld. His faithful servant, whom the Sumerians called 'Nergal's trapper', was none other than the figure of death. This is why Greek astrologers attributed to Nergal, the original Mesopotamian Mars, both Aries' fiery, impetuous qualities and Scorpio's association with death. Nergal, the ruler of Aries, was the victorious fire that purified everything and triumphed over death, while Nergal, ruler of Scorpio, was the sacrificial fire that abolished death. As a result, in Mesopotamia, Aries was originally regarded as the victorious man, while Scorpio was seen as the free man, since the former claimed to be stronger than death and the latter reduced death to servitude: death became his servant. Likewise, the vital energy that burns within us and that, symbolically and astrologically, is represented by Mars, either enables us to live or consumes, destroys or regenerates us, depending on the particular circumstances.

Egyptian myths about Mars. There is no ancient Egyptian deity with qualities similar to those attributed to Nergal, first by the Sumerians,

then by the Babylonians. Mars can therefore be seen in the warrior aspect of Horus: Heryshaf, the ram-god whom the Greeks identified with Hercules and who was often regarded as a hero with typically Martian qualities: courage, strength, daring, but also violence, brutality, sometimes even cruelty. Possibly the Egyptians regarded Mars as a mixture of Horus, the falcon-god, and Anubis, the jackal-god, since the falcon and the jackal were animals that, traditionally and astrologically, were associated with Mars.

Greek myths about Mars. Greek mythology, however, boasts a Mars-figure in the person of the god of war, Ares. This warrior-male was characteristically belligerent, violent and deadly, but also possessed the vigorous, primitive and vital qualities attributed to this ruling planet of Aries and Scorpio.

According to the Greeks, who were profoundly influenced by Mesopotamian myths when they created their own pantheon of Olympian deities, Ares was the god of war who gave his utmost on the battlefield and was invoked by soldiers seeking his protection before braving the carnage. Ares was therefore represented by a strong man, a battle-ready soldier, wearing a breastplate and helmet, with a sword at his side and a spear and shield in his hands. His giant stature and his terrifying war cries filled his enemies with fear. He was not therefore the typical image of a god or hero. He usually fought barefooted, but he also had a chariot pulled by four high-spirited horses. As if that were not enough, he employed the services of four horsemen who were also his children and demons, called Deimos (fear), Phobos (panic), Eris (strife) and Enyo (war). However, as well as the spear, sword and shield, he is also sometimes depicted brandishing a torch, symbolizing the power he was endowed with by the Greeks, as leader, showing or lighting the way forward.

This symbol is associated with Aries, who can play, variously, the role of a pioneer, instigator and visionary.

All the myths in which Ares plays a key role are warlike in nature. However, Ares was also regarded as an ardent and passionate lover who could be possessive and violent at times. Astrologers through the ages have therefore drawn various conclusions about the relationship between Mars and Venus in the zodiac from his stormy, passionate and clandestine love affairs with Aphrodite.

To this day, the symbol of Mars or Ares is used to represent man and that of Venus or Aphrodite to symbolize woman, and not just by astrologers. The love affair between Ares and Aphrodite led to the birth of a daughter, called Harmonia, a symbol of balance, concord, moderation, sympathy and peace. When the seemingly paradoxical but actually complementary qualities of Mars and Venus are brought together, the result is perfect harmony. As a result, it should be remembered that everyone, male and female, possesses the contradictory qualities of Mars and Venus that appear in their astrological birth chart and that these can be harmoniously integrated.

Mask

Masks were associated with agrarian, funerary and initiatory rites, long before they were used in carnivals and the theatre. In primitive societies, it was usually the men who wore masks during ritual ceremonies dedicated to the mythical gods they represented. In this sense, the mask was never regarded as an object to hide behind, as it generally is today. Instead, it was identified with the god, or occasionally the demon, embodied in the masked man to such an extent that he appeared to be possessed. As well as wearing the mask of the invoked god or demon, he would dance, utter incantations and participate in certain rites that put him in the appropriate state for summoning the god or demon. Because these actions blurred the boundary between visible and invisible, the world of the living and the world of the dead, the kingdom of good and the realm of evil, almost all primitive societies excluded women from these rites in a bid to protect them from the forces of evil.

Masks also represented the self: the god or demon, sometimes the combination of each, called the demiurge, which lies dormant in each of us. In Egyptian funerary rites, a death mask was fashioned to enable the deceased to embark on the perilous journey through the underworld and attain immortality. This mask was regarded as his true face. If some masks look terrifying, this was because they were expressly designed to exorcize demons, those monsters created by mankind: barbarity, destruction, murder, hatred, egoism.

Masks almost always have a salutary, liberating function. They should not be worn indiscriminately, though, because masks can cause the wearer to lose their grip on reality. If you see yourself masked in a dream, particularly with someone else's face, this usually indicates that you may be feeling a loss of identity. It can also be a symptom of mild schizophrenia – the uncontrollable feeling that someone else has wormed their way inside your head and has silently and insidiously taken the place of your own personality.

Masks can also represent a transfiguration in the true sense of the word. They are the face of a divine image that appears to us, or of the divine force that, according to universal mystic beliefs, lies dormant within each of us and is our very reason for living. In this case, the mask is radiant and entrancing, rather than contorted. Several hours after death, the dead often display an expression that was once regarded as the face of their soul. However, this is not to ignore the deceptive, hypocritical and dissimulating character of masks or, more pertinently, of the men or women who choose to hide their true face behind a mask.

As a result, when a mask appears in a dream, whether you are wearing it or are confronted by a masked person, you must differentiate between the funeral or death mask on the one hand and the affirmative, life-giving mask on the other. The former may herald a bereavement, sometimes symbolical, but also sometimes literal, while the latter may relate to an important realization about your own identity. You must also be on the look-out for the mask that represents dissimulation in all its forms as this often refers to a betrayal or a tendency to be taken in by appearances.

You should also remember the masks that represent demons. Terrifying or comical in appearance, these are symbolic representations of exaggerated feelings that we all feel but are forced to hide by a host of conventions, principles and unspoken laws. These feelings resurface, without our knowing it, though never by accident, in our dreams.

A discussion of masks would not be complete without mentioning the masks worn by modern heroes in popular literature and cartoons: Zorro, Superman, Batman etc. are all avenging heroes, eager to see justice done. They inhabit the world of our waking dreams and appear in ever-increasing numbers on our cinema and TV screens, watched avidly by children, teenagers and adults. We must not ignore the messages and ideas conveyed by these modern-day heroes, who represent a new mythology that may not be so weighty and richly varied as its time-honoured counterpart, but is just as revealing.

Mercury

Mesopotamian myths about Mercury. One of the defining characteristics of this planet is that it almost always stays in the wake of the sun. This means that it is virtually impossible to observe with the naked eye, apart from about once a year, for several hours, in Europe. This naturally has to be at twilight or just before sunrise, particularly in autumn and spring, when the meteorological conditions are just right: the sky must be hazy or slightly cloudy. The fact that this planet is so difficult to see is probably the reason why ancient astrologers endowed it with such an ambiguous, unstable and transient nature. Likewise, its role as a messenger between gods and mortals probably stemmed from the fact that it always followed in the wake of the greatest god of the sky (the sun), whose servant or attendant it may have been. However, in Mesopotamia, the circle of the zodiac, situated on either side of the ecliptic, was called the 'path of the sun and the moon' and all the planets were supposed to follow the path of Nanna (the moon), because this was a lunar astrology. As a result, Nabou (Mercury) followed the path of the moon. Nabou was the ruling planet of Mash.Tab.Ba or the Great Twins, who became Gemini, the third sign of the Mesopotamian zodiac, which did not acquire its definitive 12-sign format until early in the fifth century BC. Mercury was also called Shihtu, meaning 'he who rises'.

Egyptian myths about Mercury. The representation of the planet Mercury in the Ancient Egyptian pantheon of tutelary gods – which probably deeply inspired the Greeks – bears close similarities to the characteristics attributed by astrologers to this planet, both then and now. This was Thoth, god of scribes, astronomers, healers, accountants and the mysteries as well as sorcerer and scribe of the underworld. Thoth played a key role in the Egyptian divine hierarchy as an ibis-headed god, whose pointed beak symbolized practicality but whose shape also alluded to the crescent moon. In Egypt, despite attributes and attributions that have a great deal in common with those accorded to Mercury in astrology, Thoth was a lunar god. 'Decisions made by the supreme god first had to be dictated to Thoth to become effective. The latter drew up copies and was responsible for promulgating them. [...] Once a decision had been written down, Thoth personally ensured that it was implemented, either by informing the individual addressee or by telling the assembled gods, if it was addressed to more than one individual. This procedure involved quite a bit of coming and going, which explains why Thoth served as the necessary intermediary between the other gods, collectively or individually, and their ruler, or as a messenger, activities that were merely offshoots of his main duty.' (Dimitri Meeks, Christine Favard-Meeks, *Daily Life of the Egyptian Gods*, translated by G.M. Goshgarian, Cornell U. Press, 1996.) Thoth, the lunar god, exemplified all the professions that someone with a strong Mercury in the birth chart would relish: writer, secretary, correspondent, informant, messenger, go-between etc. Speech and writing are functions of the intellect. They were the duties carried out by Thoth and are also those associated with Mercury in astrology.

Greek myths about Mercury. The mythical Greek god identified with Mercurius or Mercury, Roman god of merchants, travellers and thieves, was Hermes. He was represented by the Greeks as a handsome youth wearing winged sandals, symbolic of levitation (probably a refer-

ence to the Babylonian god, Shihtu ('he who rises'), and a wide-brimmed felt hat with a low crown, called a *petasus* or *petasos* in Rome, that protected the wearer from rain and sun in Italy and Greece. As a result, whenever Greek artists drew or painted a traveller, they always depicted him wearing a *petasus*. This is also the hat worn by the figure on the first card of the Major Arcana of the divinatory Tarot pack, the juggler, who has typically mercurial qualities: intelligence, spirit of initiative, manual dexterity and cleverness. As the legend goes, Hermes was the son of Zeus and Maia, whose name means 'grandmother'; she was a daughter of Atlas, who carried the heavens on his shoulders and who, according to legend, was himself a son of Uranus. In other words, according to Greek mythologists,

Hermes was the grandson of Cronus on his father's side and the great-grandson of Uranus on his mother's side. Astrologically speaking, given that the Greeks were deeply influenced by the Egyptian and Babylonian culture in which they were steeped, it can be inferred that Mercury was a product of Jupiter and a by-product of Saturn and Uranus. On top of this, given the fact that the Egyptians regarded Thoth, whose attributes correspond to those attributed to Mercury by the Greeks and later by the Romans, as a lunar god, it is possible to see Maia, Hermes' mother, as a lunar figure and conclude that Mercury's qualities originate from the Moon and Jupiter on the one hand and from Saturn and Uranus on the other.

As can be seen by this example, studying the ancient myths of the planets and their history sheds new light on each of the ruling planets in the zodiac.

Merlin the Enchanter

Having played a role in Celtic legend for several centuries, Merlin reappeared in the 12th and 13th centuries, portrayed very much as he is today. Geoffrey of Monmouth, a Welsh scholar and bishop, author of a *Vita Merlini* (*Life of Merlin*) in 1148, and Robert de Boron, an Anglo-Norman poet who wrote *Merlin* in the late 12th century, were responsible for revamping the character of Merlin, until then a Breton prophet in Celtic legend; they transformed him into the son of a demon and a virgin, endowed him with super-natural powers and incorporated him into the legend of King Arthur by crediting him rather than Arthur with the formation of the Knights of the Round Table in the sixth century.

Merlin was allegedly born in Wales, around AD 470, a few years before Arthur. His father was a Roman magistrate and his mother had been a vestal virgin (a virgin priest-ess devoted to Vesta, the Roman goddess of

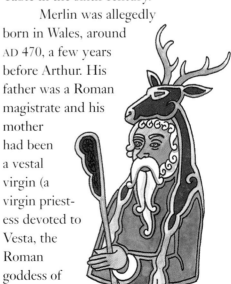

the hearth) until she renounced her vows. In the Roman Empire such behaviour was punishable by death so, in a bid to save her life, Merlin's mother claimed a supernatural conception, telling her judges that the baby she was carrying was chosen by the gods. When he was born, she named him Ambrosius, meaning 'immortal' (ambrosia being the mythical food of the gods).

Ambrosius subsequently became Merlin, who was not only a bard, poet, musician and singer, but also a druid, seer, magician and adviser to Ambrosius Aurelianus, the prince who freed the island of Britain, opposing the king and driving out his Saxon allies around the end of the fifth century.

As the legend goes, one day the king of Britain was warned by his seers and magicians that his throne was in danger. According to them, the person responsible was an evil spirit who was opposing his plans in the guise of a male child born with no father. The ruler's soldiers went in search of this child and brought before the king the boy, Ambrosius, the future Merlin, who then proceeded to make his first prophesy. Before the king and his seers and magicians, he revealed that there was a great lake beneath the castle

and at the bottom of this lake was a conch shell containing two serpents: one red, the other white. When his words were proved correct, the conch shell was shattered and the serpents freed. The white one then violently attacked the red, which was almost overcome on three occasions. However, the red serpent eventually gained the upper hand and drove off the white serpent. Ambrosius explained that the white serpent represented the standard of the king and his Saxon allies and the red serpent the standard of the Britons. He also predicted that after being subdued three times by the treacherous king, the Britons would rise up and drive out the tyrant and the barbarians. This indeed came to pass and was, according to Arthurian legend, Ambrosius's first wonder and his first true prophesy. Thus the Breton bard became the druid Merlin.

In the Celtic religion, a druid was not just a priest who worshipped trees, springs, stones, the mythical creatures of the forest and the spirits of fire, air, earth and water. He was also a doctor, healer, philosopher, astrologer, magician, seer, poet, musician and teacher and he had a great deal of political influence. This is why Merlin was regarded as a key figure in druidism.

Imagination and fantasy were to do the rest.

On the death of Ambrosius Aurelianus, the prince who liberated the island of Britain, Merlin became bard to his successor, King Arthur, fulfilling the role of seer, astrologer, magician and political adviser. He aided the king in the heroic war of resistance that ravaged the country in the sixth century and during which the Britons, who took refuge in Wales and Cornwall, drove out the Saxons, the Jutes and the Angles, barbarian hordes from the north who had invaded their island. King Arthur's victories were so remarkable that they amazed his contemporaries and were attributed to supernatural powers he had at his disposal.

Towards the end of his life, around AD 560, Merlin witnessed a fratricidal war between Welsh Britons and Scottish Britons, although this time he was powerless to help. This latest episode had a disastrous effect on his mental health and his faith in mankind. He returned to the wilds and died a hermit some time later in the forests of Cornwall, surrounded by nature spirits. Merlin the druid, prophet and enchanter became the stuff of legend, having predicted, among other things, the birth of King Arthur, the resistance of the Britons and the defeat of the barbarian invaders.

This legend soon travelled beyond the island of Britain and spread throughout the Christian world. Shortly after the death of Arthur and Merlin, Pope Gregory the Great sent some Benedictine monks to evangelize the Britons. During the subsequent century, the quest of the Holy Grail added a new dimension to the legend of Arthur and Merlin, becoming the supreme goal of the Knights of the Round Table. Killing two birds with one stone, the Christians intertwined the legendary exploits of the Arthurian heroes with Bible stories and used this material to spread the teachings of Christ.

Mermaid

When a mermaid or siren appears in a dream, you should pay particular attention to her song and what it symbolizes: auto-suggestion, bewitchment and hypnosis. Generally, when someone dreams about a mermaid, they are often fascinated or obsessed by something that is causing them to act irrationally. Like a sorceress, a mermaid is a sea witch who leads people astray.

However, there is another side to the mermaid, which is still ambiguous but much more beneficial. She is also a representation of the sea goddess, embodied, for example, by Aphrodite/Venus who, according to legend, sprang from the foam of the sea, born of the sperm of her father Uranus who, before being castrated by his son Cronus, ejaculated one last time on the surface of the water. In the Celtic legend the goddess/fairy Morgana also emerged from the waves: her name meant simply 'born of the sea'. Hence the mermaid should also be associated with the type of love that can keep a man spellbound, plunging him into a sort of trance, a type of bewitchment. An irresistible and dangerously alluring woman is therefore called a siren. However, since the soul and the subconscious have none of our sexist prejudices, whether you are a man or woman, a dream of a mermaid shows that you may just as easily be under the spell of your own powers of seduction and autosuggestion, a victim of your own illusions.

Mesopotamia (cosmogonies in)

See Cosmogonies in Mesopotamia, page 126

Midday and midnight

Working on the basis of a 24-hour day, midday and midnight are the two solstices. Midday is when the sun is at its highest, representing the summer solstice, marked by the longest day and shortest night of the year. This always takes place around 21 June and coincides with the first day of summer and the sun's entry into the zodiac sign of Cancer. Midnight is when the sun is at its lowest, representing the winter solstice, marked by the shortest day and the longest night. This always takes place around 21 December and coincides with the first day of winter and the sun's entry into the zodiac sign of Capricorn. In other words, the Cancer–Capricorn axis represent the highest and lowest points of the zodiac or the two poles of midday and midnight.

However, it should be remembered that the signs of the

DICTIONARY OF SYMBOLS, MYTHS AND LEGENDS

Mesopotamia
(cosmo-
gonies in)
Midday and
midnight

zodiac are read anticlockwise. As a result, going by the movement of the ascendant – which, together with the descendant that is in the opposite position and combined with the subject's birth location, indicates the exact location of the horizon line at the precise time of birth – the house corresponding to the highest point or midday in the birth chart, in other words the middle of the sky or mid-heaven, is analogous with Capricorn, while the House corresponding to the lowest point or midnight in the birth chart, in other words the bottom of the sky or *Imum Coeli*, is analogous with Cancer. As can be seen, therefore, the poles are reversed, and earth's midday corresponds to midnight for an individual and midnight on earth is equivalent to midday for an individual.

This seems to imply that when the earth is in full sunlight, when daylight reigns supreme, mankind is in darkness and that, on the contrary, when the earth is plunged into darkness and night takes over, mankind is bathed in light. In actual fact, this is the ancient symbolic and mystical interpretation of this astronomical phenomenon. According to ancient mystics, this world is an illusion. When it is flooded with light, we are blinded by its illusory nature. However, when it is plunged into darkness, we can see clearly and grasp the nature of reality. The mystics often described the physical world we inhabit as the 'dark night of the soul' and they called the soul's submersion in this dark night of the soul 'illumination'. In the Chinese symbolic tradition, midnight and midday represent the peaks of yin and yang. However, the Chinese also believed that there was a terrestrial yin and yang and a heavenly yin and yang.

Midday and midnight are brief, fleeting instants that mark the midpoint of the day and night. At midnight, there do not appear to be any observable celestial or physical phenomena. This did not prevent people in the past from regarding it as the darkest, most disturbing and most deadly time of the day. On the other hand, a remarkable phenomenon takes place at midday: when the sun is at its zenith there are no shadows on earth.

Midday or midnight in a dream often reveals that something important is happening or about to happen in your life. If it is midday, this can mean a crucial meeting, a peak, a pinnacle or a success; if midnight, it may herald a final stage that brings about a revival. However, as we have seen, the mystical notion of blindness associated with midday should not be ignored, nor should that of a revelation that can come at midnight, in the heart of darkness.

Milk

Unsurprisingly, milk is symbolically regarded as the drink associated with life, fertility, joy, happiness and abundance. This rich, magical, maternal drink contains all the energy-giving properties that are required by a child's body and organism, at least, until mankind meddles with the planet on a grand scale, thereby destroying the natural properties of mother's milk and transforming it into a latent poison.

Milk is a lunar symbol, like the lake (see page 311). However, it lacks the disturbing connotations that are occasionally attached to symbolic lunar images. Milk, because of its colour, and also because of its function, conjures up images of purity, sincerity and the naked truth, devoid of all ambiguity. Milk represents the joy and happiness of motherhood, as well as the contentment of a child, who has no need to worry about survival because it is guaranteed a constant supply of mother's milk, which is a symbol of abundance comparable to the famous horn of plenty (see *Horns and crowns*, page 262).

Dreaming of milk therefore signifies plenitude, fertility, gentleness, fulfilment and freedom from care.

Mirror

This symbol refers back to our forebears' singular vision of the world and of reality that, on close examination, may not be quite as absurd as first appears. Greatly simplified, this interpretation of the world posed the following question: what if the physical world around us, everything we see and touch, the ground on which we walk, the sky above us, everything that constitutes our reality, were just an illusion, a figment of our imagination, a projection of our individual and collective consciousness, a fantastic effect created by mirrors? Thus the mirror, which originally was no more than the reflection of an individual's face, seen when collecting or drinking water from a river, pond or lake, became a symbolic representation of the human soul. The Greeks regarded it as the *psyche*, meaning 'breath', 'life', 'soul', while *soma* was the body. Psychoanalysis literally means the study of the human soul. The word 'psychosomatic' refers to the influence of the mind or soul on the body. It is recognized that the mind can affect the body in such a way that it develops physiological, organic and biological symptoms or disturbances, most of which are caused by a state of mind, ill-adjusted behavioural responses or mental disorders.

People look at themselves in mirrors: they discover their own face and become more aware of themselves. Knowing what they look like and being able to recognize themselves in a mirror means that they can watch themselves. But do they

see themselves as they really are? They see themselves as others see them, of course, but there is an irresistible urge to improve on appearance, so the mirror reflects a more attractive, more gratifying physical image. The mirror offers people the chance to experiment with their reflection, to use it as a model to beautify themselves, put on fancy dress, present others with an image that matches the one they have of themselves. The mirror is therefore associated with the idea of wearing masks, lying, dressing-up and dissimulation (see *Mask*, page 329).

However, because the mirror knows everyone's true face, it has acquired a memory and has become associated with the human consciousness. Like us, it knows what we alone know: who we really are. This is why the verb 'reflect' is used to describe what the mirror does when it shows someone his or her own image. 'Reflect' is

derived from the Latin word *reflectere*, which means to 'bend back' or 'curve'. Used figuratively, to 'reflect' means to direct our thoughts back to an object or event in the past. As a result, when we view our reflection in the mirror, it seems as if we are projected back into our own past and that we are witnessing the effect of memory. The words 'reflection', 'reflect' and 'reflex' share the same etymology and carry the same sense of flashbacks.

This is generally the message conveyed by a dream in which you see yourself in a mirror. It indicates that you see yourself as you were and not as you are now. It also shows that people tend to live their present lives imbued with nostalgia for the past. On the other hand, to dream of looking in a mirror without seeing a reflection indicates that contact with the conscious self has been broken. This is a dream of psychic disassociation and it warns the dreamer of the danger of a psychological imbalance that could have serious repercussions. Last but not least, if the dreamer sees the reflection of someone else while looking in a mirror, this is often a sign of latent schizophrenic tendencies or a virtual split personality. It implies that this person may do things unwit-

tingly, without being aware of them, without even remembering them. The mirror can therefore play a key symbolic role in a dream.

Finally, there is the dream of passing through the mirror to the other side, which is often associated with dying. In other words, the mirror functions as a doorway leading from this world to the hereafter. However, all the above-mentioned interpretations are more likely to indicate a shift in appearances and consequently a new realization or changing viewpoint.

Monkey

The evolutionary theories of the illustrious English naturalist Charles Darwin created a considerable stir in the 19th century. However, what people say or think they know about the pioneering works of this learned man is generally based on hearsay rather than an in-depth knowledge of his œuvre. Thus, following in the great tradition of alchemists and adopting their language, Darwin, an immensely inquisitive and pragmatic man, alluded to a 'transmutation of species' while, as a humanist, he researched 'The Expression of the Emotions in Man and

Animals' and, late in life, as if to mark a return to simple, natural things, he wrote a work entitled *The Formation of Vegetable Mould, Through the Action of Worms*. Thanks to Charles Darwin's work, monkeys have been linked to man and it is generally believed that man is descended from the monkey. However, it seems that no one has thought to compare the principle of the evolution of the species, particularly the concept that the monkey is the ancestor of man, with the myths, legends, beliefs and symbols relating to the monkey. It should be pointed out, of course, that the puritanical Europeans of the 19th century did not favour the idea of an atavistic link, however distant – probably dating back to between five and ten million years ago – between the monkey with its unbridled sexual urges, and man, who was held to be a model of virtue and intelligence. It is also true that whenever monkeys appear in myths they are always rather unsavoury, cunning, greedy, lustful creatures, even if they are also recognized as having a certain degree of intelligence and great manual dexterity.

There is, however, one substantial exception to this rule and it is found in ancient Egypt. Thoth, the lunar god, lord of numbers and letters, mathematics and writing, god of scribes and sorcerers, inventor of the calendar, whom the Greeks identified with Hermes and the Romans with Mercury, was represented by a man who either had the head of an ibis or the head of a baboon. The Egyptians therefore identified the monkey with a lunar, mercurial god who was sensitive, intelligent and imaginative, although easily influenced and unstable. In India, Hanuman, the king of the monkeys, whose name meant 'strong jaws', was a fantastic animal with certain similarities to Thoth, since he could fly, he was a sorcerer and healer and he possessed many supernatural powers. The servant and assistant of Rama, the seventh incarnation of Vishnu, Hanuman could transform human emotions into spiritual energy.

As a result, the monkey generally symbolizes the instinctive powers that, placed in the service of the intellect, enable people to accomplish feats of mind over matter that appear to be magical in nature. This is often the most important

aspect of a dream that prominently features a monkey. However, you should never lose sight of the dual nature of this animal, which can be sly, cunning and unreliable. It represents all the qualities, strengths and weaknesses of the human mind, which can be intemperate, restless and destructive, or restrained, sublimated and redeeming.

Moon

Mesopotamian myths about the moon. This great ancient civilization provides us with an excellent representation of the deified moon. However, before going into further detail, it is worth pointing out that astrologers, and even occasionally mythologists, can and do mix up cultures, civilizations, beliefs and the deceptively simple underly-

ing meaning of certain myths, resulting in a confused and incoherent interpretation. This means that myths concerning the moon, Venus, the great goddess or Mother Earth are often jumbled together.

There is no doubt that these deities are easily confused as they are often associated with the same elements and share certain common or similar qualities. However, as we shall see, in Mesopotamia the moon, later transformed into a female god of time and the night, clearly differs from the goddess of love and fertility on the one hand and the great goddess, who is sometimes associated with the time of primordial chaos, on the other. The main difference between the moon and these other deities is the fact that this was not a goddess but a lunar god: Sin or Su-en, who later became Nanna, and had a wife called Ningal –

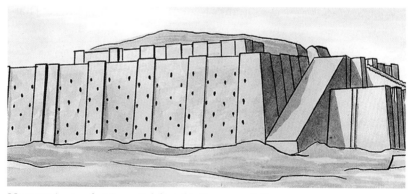

Mesopotamian temple (ziggurat) dedicated to the moon god Nanna.

evidence indeed that this was a male god and not a goddess. He should not be confused with Inanna, the goddess of love, who was associated with Ishtar, Astarte or Lilith (see *Inanna*, page 275). Nanna-Su-en was the son of Enlil, god of the air, himself the son of An, god of the sky.

In Mesopotamia, therefore, the moon was a male god. There was also a Hittite deity, who made her appearance in the first half of the second millennium BC, whose name, Arinna, meant 'mother-sun', and whose husband was none other than Menesis, the moon.

Egyptian myths about the moon. The crescent moon was sometimes regarded as the barque of Re, the sun-god. This is the case in some representations of Khons, the Egyptian moon god, whose name means 'the wanderer' or 'traveller'. He was sometimes depicted as a young man wrapped in a shroud, or more frequently as a man with a hawk's head, crowned by a crescent moon surmounted by a sun disc. Here again, the lunar god is male, not female.

However, the Egyptians believed that the sun and moon

were not related and were not a divine couple. The sun or Re reigned supreme and he is definitely a god, not a goddess. On the other hand, the moon was also identified with a god, as in Sumerian and Hittite mythology. In Theban theology, Re and Khons were related since, according to the priests of Thebes, Khons was the son of Amun, a tutelary god who was assimilated to Re, and of Mut, which means 'mother' in Egyptian. The moon god of Egypt was therefore the son of the sun and of Mother Earth.

Greek myths about the moon. Selene was the personification of the moon, the night star, whose name, derived from *selas*, meant 'light' or 'radiance'. According to the most prevalent Greek myth, she was the daughter of Hyperion, 'he who lives on high or above the earth', a Titan, himself son of Uranus, the sky, and Gaia, the earth. Hyperion and his sister-wife, Theia, had another son, Helius, the sun, and another daughter, Eos, the dawn. In other words, Hyperion, the sky's main source of light and Theia the divine, his sister and wife, produced the sun, moon and dawn.

According to another legend, however, Selene was the daughter of Helius, or the sun. In this personification, she was depicted as a beautiful young woman, crossing the sky in a splendid silver chariot pulled by two white horses.

The legend of Endymion concerns Selene. The moon fell madly in love with this charming and handsome shepherd, whose Greek name can be translated as 'he who is naturally charming'. There are various versions of this legend: some say that Zeus fulfilled Endymion's desire for eternal youth by plunging him into everlasting sleep, and Selene, captivated by his beauty, came every night to gaze at him; others that the moon herself kissed Endymion and plunged him into an endless state of dreaming so that he might stay young forever and so that she could love him for eternity. In any case, both versions refer to the notion of time, of sleep and of dreaming which are accepted as typically lunar qualities.

Besides this personification of the moon, Greece has another major lunar figure, Hera, the protectress and chief goddess in the pantheon of Greek deities on Mount Olympus. She was the sister and jealous wife of Zeus, the daughter of Cronus, god of time, and Rhea, the earth – not the planet Earth but the firm, cultivable surface of the earth. Like her brothers and sisters, Hades, Poseidon, Demeter and Hestia, she was swallowed by her father, Cronus, but regurgitated owing to the intervention of the Titaness Metis and Zeus, Cronus's third son, who had been hidden from his father by Rhea. The children then killed their father and Hera was supposedly adopted and brought up by Oceanus and Tethys, whose name means 'she who orders or organizes', or by the Horae, who were the goddesses of the seasons. As a result, Hera is immediately associated with the notions of time (Cronus), organization (Tethys), time passing and the seasons (Horae), and the water that covers the world (Oceanus): characteristics that are all also attributed to the moon in astrology. Hera became the protectress of married women. Her jealous scenes, anger and vengeance were famous. In Rome, she was identified with the goddess Juno, the personification of the lunar cycle.

The Black Moon

The Black Moon, or 'dark side', is not a planet but an imaginary point. What it shows in the

Lilith's many faces

Depending on the sign of the zodiac in which the Black Moon is found, it suggests characteristics belonging to one or several female mythical figures that correspond exactly. Because there is not enough space to list the qualities of each of these mythical goddesses here, they are simply listed in their order of appearance in the zodiac.

In Aries: Lilith assumes the appearance of a warrior goddess, like Athena or one of the Valkyrie, of German-Scandinavian mythology, whose name means 'she who chooses warriors destined to die in battle'.

In Taurus: she is Inanna-Ishtar or Aphrodite-Venus, but also Gaia, the earth.

In Gemini: she is Psyche, and perhaps also Isis, the great Egyptian goddess.

In Cancer: she is Calypso, the nymph, or Circe, the sorceress, but also Sleeping Beauty or the fairy godmother.

In Leo: she is Cybele, the mother of the gods or the great mother, as she was called in Asia Minor and Rome, who was symbolized by a black stone.

In Virgo: she is Demeter-Ceres or Antigone.

In Libra: she is Persephone-Proserpine, the daughter of Demeter and the wife of Hades-Pluto, or Sophia, wisdom.

In Scorpio: she is Artemis, sister of Apollo, or Hecate, or Lachesis, one of the three Moerae or Fates, who measured the thread of life.

In Sagittarius: she is Diana the huntress or Hippolyte, queen of the Amazons.

In Capricorn: she is Hera, daughter of Cronus-Saturn.

In Aquarius: she is Basileia, daughter of Uranus; she had two children from her union with Hyperion: Helius, the sun and Selene, the moon.

In Pisces: she is one of the Sirens, or Thetis, one of the Nereids, or Tethys, the sister-wife of Oceanus.

zodiac of a birth chart is so original and occurs so infrequently in the currently accepted order of things that astrologers now generally gloss over it, relegating the information it reveals and the questions it raises to an obsolete, fusty branch of astrology that lacks any serious basis.

Paradoxically, the concept of the Black Moon was revived by psychologists who, whatever the time, period, place or method of approach, have always analysed themselves in order to gain a better understanding of themselves and others.

What does the Black Moon tell us? It is impossible to refer to the myths and manifestations that have been attributed to the Black Moon since time

immemorial without first immersing ourselves in its universe, understanding its messages, what it represents and what it can tell us today. The Black Moon is in fact a topical concept, one that has endured over many millennia. It lives within each of us, but operates unknown to us, because we are rarely fully aware of who and what we are and how we think, act and live.

If we are to understand it, we must accept the fact that inside each of us there is an area of darkness, a shadowy, impenetrable area – hence the adjective 'black' – which is endowed with the female qualities of receptiveness, creativity and the regenerative power of chaos – hence the name 'moon'. This dark area is uncontrollable: it cannot be tamed or subjugated; and, although it can be ignored, repressed or inhibited, this does not cause it to disappear, because the more it is ignored, deliberately or unwittingly, the stronger and more powerful it becomes.

This dark area within us prevents us from accepting the unacceptable, from compromising or making concessions concerning certain fundamental things in our life. Thus it reveals that we all possess an inner force that prevents us from giving in, becoming resigned, stagnating or declining. It manifests itself during our everyday life as the kind of catalyst that can occur through accidents, unhappy love affairs, acts of madness or serious illnesses – unusual events that suspend normality and temporarily cause us to take leave of our senses – as if to remind us what really matters.

The subtle message conveyed by the Black Moon is that we should all know who we are, why we are here, what we are made of, what we think and why we act as we do. It is not enough to rest content with what is pleasant, reassuring or comfortable. The Black Moon breaks taboos and strips away masks, denouncing privileges, commonplaces and received ideas. It disturbs, provokes and demands sacrifices.

Lilith, the universal myth of the Black Moon. The Black Moon is personified by Lilith. She was initially a Sumerian goddess, probably earlier than Sin-Nanna, the moon, whom we have seen was a male deity, as was often the case in ancient times, contrary to the modern attributes of the Moon (see page 278). Lilith, however, was definitely a goddess and her attributes were both lunar and Venusian as well as even slightly Uranian and Plutonian. This is therefore a highly complex myth

that cannot be easily categorized. If the biblical legends associated with her are to be believed – it is known that the authors of the Bible were deeply influenced by Mesopotamian myths when writing some books of the scriptures – Lilith was a type of female Satan, in other words a fallen deity who not only had the effrontery to defy the Lord, but also to guess the divine, sacred meaning of the mysteries of his name, thereby assuming his power and ruling defiantly after acquiring her wings. In Sumer, she was also represented naked, standing on two recumbent lions, with a lunar crown on her head, two long wings sprouting from her shoulders and folded down her back. She also had lizard feet and was flanked by two owls. In her two raised hands, she held the symbol of Ishtar-Inanna-Aphrodite-Venus. The medieval cabbalists were certainly inspired by this figure when they created the 22 cards of the Major Arcana of the Tarot, particularly that of the Devil.

Mother

The appearance of a mother, our own or someone else's, in a dream, confronts us with real life, the reality we inhabit. The sea is the original, universal substance carried by the earth, which it rendered fertile in the same way as the waters of the womb ensure a woman's fertility. There is therefore an obvious link between the womb (see page 545), the sea (see page 447), and the mother. And each often refers back to the other(s), because each one plays the role of a medium or intermediary between everything that is invisible, unknown and formless and the real world.

Mother goddesses

See Athena, page 40,
Gaia, page 200,
Inanna, page 274,
Isis and Kali, page 281,
Venus, page 515

Mountain

An inaccessible place, a link with heaven and the gods, the mountain, whose mysterious summit is often wreathed in clouds, sym-bolizes the legendary axis of the world. The mountain is a bridge, a two-way passage between heaven and earth. Long thought to be a hostile, inaccessible place, at whose summit the elements were unleashed (the volcano's fire, the burning cold of ice and snow, storms and tempests), the mountain was primarily regarded as the earthly seat of the gods; it was also seen as the sacred place chosen by the gods for their descent to earth and as a holy place, forbidden to the profane, where gods appeared to mortals, or where the chosen or foolhardy human, who dared to scale the sacred mountain, came face to face with the god who had deigned to speak to him. In short, the summit of the mountain was where mortals and gods interacted.

Moses, Mount Horeb and Mount Sinai. The most compelling legend on this subject is that of Moses receiving the Ten Commandments from God on Mount Sinai. However, this myth was initially linked to the symbolism of the mountain because, according to the Bible, the burning bush was revealed to Moses on Mount Horeb. It was here that the prophet Elijah climbed up to God, 'unto Horeb the mount of God.' (I Kings 19, 8) and then Moses in his turn experienced the phenomenon of the 'burning bush' (Exodus 3: 2). Historically, there are several centuries between Elijah and Moses. However, the five books or scrolls of the Greek Pentateuch or Jewish Torah are known to have been written much later by a number of authors who drew their inspiration from different sources and created symbolic links between different events that probably had a historical basis although taking place at quite different times. What is interesting here, however, is the symbolism of the mountain in the minds of the Bible's authors, whether they were writing about Mount Horeb, Mount Sinai or even Mount Ararat, the mountain on top of which the ark finally came to rest, in the story of Noah's Ark. The name Ararat derives from the Hebrew word *aror*, meaning 'curse'. The scholarly authors of the Bible added the Hebrew letter *teith*, meaning 'buckle' or 'shield', to mark the end of the curse, since this indicates that, in some ways, the buckle had been fastened. Likewise, a rainbow, also a type of mountain, a bridge between heaven and earth, between God and mankind, appeared as a sign of the covenant between the Lord and Noah (see *Rainbow*, page 427).

This brings us to the purest symbolic meaning of the mountain, a place that links high and low, the pinnacle of reconciliation, of perfect, absolute union. It represents the fusion within human beings of male and female, which should not be regarded as opposites, as contrary sexes, but as two poles, two primordial, vital and original energy forces that have always governed all creation on earth. Each individual has these two sides, warring within, dividing and setting apart, so that humankind lives in a permanent state of duality, constantly wavering between good and evil. In Chinese culture these two primordial energy poles are represented by the Tai Chi Tu, the yin/yang symbol (see *Two*, page 365). Hexagram 52 of the I Ching, which we call Serenity, is therefore represented by the mountain. The image for this hexagram shows that the masculine principle is on top, following its natural direction, and the feminine principle is below, because of the direction of its movement. Thus an analogy is drawn between the mountain, the heart and the spinal column, while the six changeable lines of the hexagram allude to an ascent of the mountain that is bound to result in inner peace.

The mountain, axis of the world, pivot of the sky, navel of the earth. Similarities can also be drawn between the myths and symbols associated with the mountain and those relating to the tree of life and the navel or centre of the world. However, these myths and symbols can also be compared to those about paradise, which is to be found at its summit, the ascent to the seventh heaven being represented in particular by the rainbow, whose seven colours indicate the seven heavens that humans must scale to attain freedom, eternal life and supreme happiness. According to Arabic and Islamic mythology – which seems to have preserved a world vision similar to that of its ancestors, the Semites from Mesopotamia – the earth was shaped like a flat circular disc. On top of this floated the inaccessible mountain called Kaf or Qaf, made of green emerald. This is, in some respects, a representation of the pivot of the world, of earth and heaven, a kind of mother-mountain, just as there are maternal or primordial waters and a Mother Earth. The Muslims believe that Kaf is a link, a distant place, a boundary, and a doorway from this world into another. In this mythology we find all the beliefs, symbols and myths that are customarily associated with the mountain.

Sacred mountain, mountain of revelation, mother mountain, emerald mountain and white mountain are just some of the names featured in an almost endless list of the mountain myths and legends from all civilizations. Perhaps the mountain's most important role is the part it plays in the mystical account of the life of Jesus, from the Sermon on the Mount to Golgotha (meaning 'skull' or 'place of the skull' in Hebrew), by way of the Mount of Olives. The extent to which various beliefs and the different interpretations of their symbols have recurred over the millennia can be seen by the fact that, according to the Gospels of St Luke and St John, when Jesus was arrested on the Mount of Olives, Simon Peter had a sword in his hand, with which he struck Malchus (Luke 22: 50, 51 and John 18: 10, 11). 'Sword' in Hebrew is *herev*, a word also used to refer to Mount Horeb, where Elijah and Moses received their revelations. In addition, the sword is also the symbol of the word, the divine word, that was handed down to mankind on the mountain-top.

The story of Moses is primarily associated with the Ten Commandments. However, we should also see in it the moment when humans dared to use writing to express their beliefs and draw up their laws. If God wrote the Ten Commandments for his chosen people, it was because the written word could also convey matters of a sacred and divine nature. Once again, the mountain was the site of a revelation for humanity: the possibility of putting beliefs and laws into writing.

Mud

Although we tend to associate mud with things that are dirty or soiled, we nevertheless know that it also has wonderful therapeutic and curative properties that have been valued since early antiquity. Mud baths are particularly effective and are still widely used today in thalassotherapy centres. Falling into a mud bath, literally or in a dream, may mean you get dirty but it is also a sign of good fortune, happiness and prosperity.

Because mud is associated with the clay mixed with water from which the first human beings were made, it also has a sacred, magical and divine quality. It is the divine matter or *prima materia*, the original raw material used by the gods to create mortals. However, the combination of the pure elements of earth and water, can also have adverse effects at unformed, latent, uncreated levels, if it doesn't bring about an immediate transformation of their principles. We know, for example, that water fertilizes the earth and facilitates the growth of seeds and then plants. But mud has another, disturbing and monstrous aspect, since it can also absorb life, engender an involution (degeneration) as opposed to an evolution (development): a fixation at a lower level of life. In this respect, the expressions 'to wallow in the mud' or 'to drag somebody through the mud' have a clearly pejorative connotation, particularly as the Gallic and Welsh words – *borvo* and *bervi* – also meant 'mire' and 'filth'.

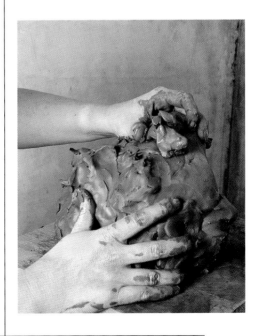

Etymologically speaking, there seems to be an association of the ideas of 'boiling' and 'heat' found in the Irish *berbaim*, the Welsh *bervi*, the Breton *bervo* and the Gallic *borvo* (French *boue*) and linked to the name of the Celtic god Borvo (the Gaulish 'Apollo') which connects him with the therapeutic powers of thermal springs. In this way, mud has always had a dual nature – beneficial or harmful, regenerative or destructive, depending on the context and circumstances.

Wallowing in mud in a dream can therefore be a sign of regeneration, cure and a beneficial transformation in your life or situation. It can also mean that you are about to enter a period in your life during which you risk being besmirched or dishonoured. However, you'll be pleased to know that, in our experience, the first interpretation is more common.

Mushroom

Due to its hallucinogenic or deadly properties and its phallic shape, the mushroom is always associated with carnal pleasures, visions and supernatural powers. There are more than a hundred thousand species of mushroom, many of which have curative, medicinal properties, while others are poisonous and deadly. Many also have a particular significance but these are far too numerous to list here. Suffice it to say that, by association with its properties and shape, a dream about a mushroom represents a false impression of which you are the victim, something that is poisoning your existence, so to speak, or, quite simply, a suppressed desire to assert yourself and gain recognition.

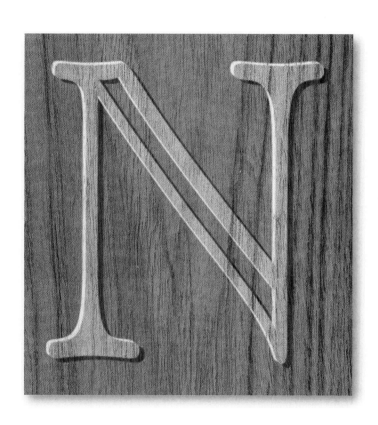

Nemean lion (the)

See Hercules, page 229

Nenuphar or water-lily

The nenuphar or water-lily and the Egyptian lotus have a great deal in common since they belong to the same family and are associated with similar qualities. They also share the same etymology because nenuphar is derived from the Persian word *nilufar*, itself taken from the Sanskrit *nilautpala*, meaning 'blue lotus', composed of *nila*, 'blue', and *utpala*, 'lotus flower'. Although the lotus was a sacred flower in Ancient Egypt (see page 319), this name is of Indian, not Egyptian, origin. The Latin for water-lily was *nymphea*, a name derived from the Greek *nymphe*, referring both to various plants, including the lotus and other water lilies, and to the nymphs, wood and water sprites in Greek mythology who had become fairies by the Middle Ages. The water-lily is therefore associated with fairies, fairyland, nymphs, the magic of nature, femininity, abundance and fertility.

In a dream, the water-lily either has sensual, romantic connotations, becoming the focus of the dreamer's desires, hopes or feelings of nostalgia, or a sacred meaning, revealing the dreamer's craving for the absolute.

Neptune

Mesopotamian myths about Neptune. Neptune, like Uranus and Pluto (see pages 512 and 420), was not originally a god/planet governing one of the 12 signs of the zodiac. The French astronomer Urbain Le Verrier, intrigued by the irregular orbit of Uranus, discovered Neptune's location in 1846 and the planet was seen by telescope for the first time by the German astronomer J.G. Galle on 23 September 1846. As a result, it was not included in the zodiac by astrologers until the second half of the 19th century, when it was made the ruling

planet of Pisces. In our opinion, however, Jupiter is still the chief ruling planet of Pisces and Neptune's role, although not negligible, is secondary in that it modifies, refines or emphasizes certain qualities associated with the original ruling planet of Sagittarius and Pisces.

In this respect, we can see there are similarities between these two zodiac signs in the fields of superior intelligence, spiritual life and high-mindedness. In actual fact, a superior, philosophical or religious turn of mind is commonly associated with Sagittarius, while practicality and sociability are characteristic of Gemini, the opposite star sign. Pisces is also linked with superior intelligence and an active inner life since it is associated with renunciation, mysticism, religious fervour, meditation, etc. It can also be seen that the Gemini–Sagittarius axis of the zodiac corresponds to a Mercury–Jupiter axis, as these are respectively the ruling planets of these signs. The same holds true for the Virgo–Pisces axis, since these two signs also have the same respective ruling planets.

These details are crucial if we are to understand the meaning of the Sumerian myth of the god Oannes, the Mesopotamian

bringer of civilization and an idealized representation of Neptune, a planet that frequently causes problems for the most experienced contemporary astrologers. Too often do they forget, in fact, that it was under the joint influence of Jupiter and Neptune during the last third of the Pisces era that our modern, technological civilization flourished. As described by the Chaldean priest, astrologer and historian, Berosus, who emigrated to Greece and founded the first school of astrology on the island of Cos around 300 BC, the god Oannes was a true bringer of civilization. According to Berosus, the human race was stagnating, leading a primitive, uncultured existence, when a

fantastic monster with the body of a giant fish, two heads one above the other and two human feet, emerged from the Red Sea. This creature instructed the human race in writing, science and technology, housebuilding, founding cities, irrigation and farming etc. In fact, if the legend reported by Berosus is to be believed, Oannes, the amphibian god from the sea, who lived with humans by day and returned to the sea at nightfall, taught the human race everything it knew. Later, Berosus wrote, other similar beings appeared and continued mankind's education. These marvellous, fabled sages were called the 'seven shining apkallu'.

Egyptian myths about Neptune. For obvious reasons, the Egyptians attached far greater importance to the Nile and its Delta than to the Mediterranean sea bordering northern Egypt or the Red Sea in the east. It is therefore impossible to find an Egyptian god directly equivalent to the Sumerian Oannes, the pioneering god from the deep. However, Ptah, the tutelary god of Memphis, and the fish-goddess Hat-

Mehit, associated with Banebdjedet, the ram-god of Mendes, were mythical figures who bore certain similarities to Oannes and therefore to Neptune. In fact, Ptah was an initiatory god, as his Egyptian name 'He who opens' suggests. He created the world by the thoughts emanating from his heart and the words emerging from his tongue. He was also associated with the invention of various sciences and crafts and, because of this, he became the protector of craftsmen. As for Banebdjedet, although he was a ram-god, his consort was a fish-goddess and he was regarded as the father of Harpocrates or Horus as a child, representing the rising sun, a symbol of eternal youth and immortality.

Greek myths about Neptune. In ancient Greece, on the other hand, the myths and legends about Poseidon are more or less directly analogous to those associated with the Mesopotamian god Oannes, although in Greek mythology Poseidon was mainly the ruler of the sea. He was regarded as a violent god with a stormy temperament who sired many offspring. In general, his was no longer a civilizing role. He was occasionally confused with Oceanus, son of Uranus (heaven) and Gaia (earth), the eldest of the Titans, whereas Poseidon was the son of Cronus and Rhea and therefore the grandson of Uranus and Gaia. This made him the older brother of Zeus, who rescued him after their father, Cronus, had swallowed him and his other siblings. However, Poseidon, who was depicted armed with a trident, the weapon used by tuna fishermen, and driving a chariot pulled by fantastic sea monsters that were half-horse, half-sea serpent, was every inch the ruler of the sea. Fabled Atlantis, supposedly founded by the giant Atlas, was Poseidon's island, a type of El Dorado, boasting splendid cities overflowing with riches. Its inhabitants were reputed to be highly sophisticated, well-educated and knowledgeable, a single reference to Poseidon in a civilizing role, bringing us back to the Sumerian myth of Oannes.

As a result, it is important not to forget the pioneering, civilizing aspect of the planet Neptune, regarded as the higher octave of Mercury, as can be seen by all the myths and legends associated with it.

Night

According to Greek legend, night was the daughter of chaos or, to put it another way, darkness originated from the world of cosmic forces and undifferentiated life forms. Nevertheless, light sprang from this primeval chaos, deep within the dark and shadows. For this reason, night is almost always automatically contrasted with day. However, the alternation of day and night creates a natural rhythm that mirrors the biological rhythm underpinning the world of nature, animals and human beings.

It can therefore be said that a dream about something that happens at night always underlines this rhythm and suggests the day that precedes or follows it. That is, of course, unless you are suddenly plunged into an impenetrable darkness that banishes all light. In this case, it is a question of darkness enveloping your conscious self, something that is essential if you are to see and appreciate the bright inner light. Focusing on a point of light in the dark or at night is obviously much easier than in broad daylight or bright conditions.

Nightingale

The name 'nightingale' refers in particular to the light brown Eurasian nightingale (*Luscinia megarhynchus*), whose mellifluous song can be heard in forests, farmland with hedgerows near water, and parks and gardens in towns and rural areas. The young male, which has an innate talent for song, makes an appearance in April or May, singing his full-throated song to attract the female. Just after the mating season, in May or June, she lays four or five eggs in her nest, built in a bush using grasses and roots. When the fledglings hatch after two weeks of incubation, she and the male feed them with caterpillars and fruit. In September, the nightingale migrates to Africa until the following spring.

The nightingale also features in Greek mythology. It first appeared in a legend that explains why its melodious song is so melancholy and nostalgic and why, like the swallow, it is a symbol of spring. Philomela, sister of Procne, queen of Thrace, was raped by her brother-in-law, Tereus, who was enchanted by her lovely voice. Seeking vengeance, Procne and Philomela murdered Itys, Procne's son by Tereus. Just as the vengeful king was about to run his wife and sister-in-law through with his sword, Zeus made a timely intervention, transforming Procne into a swallow and Philomela into a nightingale. The nightingale that sings through the night is therefore Philomela, the tragic sister of Greek legend.

Nine

See Numbers, page 388

Noah's Ark

Everyone knows the story of Noah and the ark he built single-handed, in the face of general indifference, to save the human race and the animal and vegetable kingdoms from total annihilation. It is a story in which Noah always comes across as a very likeable legendary and mythical hero. However, although the image of Noah as the saviour of mankind remains engraved in the collective memory and continues to fire the modern imagination, we are less familiar with the fact that Noah – who, like Moses, was chosen from among all men and 'saved from the waters' by Elohim (God) – is also the hero of a story that has major symbolic and psychological implications. Noah is a modern hero and the amazing story of Noah's Ark has given, gives and will continue to give each and every one of us food for thought.

The secret code of the Bible. By way of introduction to the interpretation of the myth and symbolism of the biblical legend of Noah's Ark, it is useful to point out that, long before Sigmund Freud started the 19th-century trend for psychoanalysis and the resulting psychological investigations that have more or less become part of our everyday lives, the cabbalists and early compilers of the Bible had already read and interpreted the biblical accounts on two different levels. On the one hand, there was the clear and simple secular interpretation of the stories, legends, adventures and historical facts associated with individuals or heroes who performed remarkable and exemplary deeds invested with religious significance. On the other, there was an esoteric interpretation that was originally transmitted only by

Illustration from a 10th-century manuscript, Gerona Cathedral library.

word of mouth and only to those initiated into its mysteries.

This second interpretation of the Bible, achieved using a code based on the letters and numbers of the Hebrew alphabet, enabled those who had mastered this secret language to decode the accounts and to isolate information concerning emotional factors and elements, deep-rooted psychology, moral behaviour and the eternal strengths and weaknesses of human nature. Contrary to what we are led to believe today, it was not a matter of using this secret code to predict inevitable and catastrophic facts and events, but to transmit information on the origins of the human race, its accomplishment, evolution and development. The great biblical accounts therefore often combine a romanticized historical narrative with strong religious connotations linking people in the same community through beliefs, and a more mysterious, esoteric, mystical and religious

construction which aims to link people with themselves. In other words, this more subtle interpretation of the accounts in the Bible using the cabbalistic code makes it possible to discover information that is useful for self-knowledge.

What do we understand by the term 'ark'? Two different Hebrew words were taken to signify 'ark' and each has a different meaning. The first, *ahron* or *aron*, was translated as 'ark' and refers to the Ark of the Covenant that housed the two tablets of the Law (better known as the Ten Commandments), given by God to Moses for his chosen people. This ark was eventually placed in the Temple of Jerusalem by King Solomon but disappeared when the Babylonian armies of Nebuchadnezzar destroyed the city in 587 BC. The Latin *arca*, from which the English word 'ark' derives, referred to a chest, box or coffer. It is also the root of 'arcane', which means 'secret or concealed mystery'. 'Ark' was also used to translate *tebah*, the word that referred to Noah's Ark. In this way, the translators of the Bible made the subtle connection between Noah's Ark and the Ark of the Covenant that symbolized the new alliance between God, Noah and his descendants.

This connection is valid both etymologically and symbolically. But it doesn't convey the exact meaning of the Hebrew word *tebah*, which, at a symbolic level, means 'all the created energies of life'. So, according to the interpretation of this account using the secret cabbalistic code, when Elohim (God) warned Noah of the great flood and told him to build a *tebah*, he was urging him to gather all his energies within him, to realize that he was in fact the receptacle of all the energy-creating and cosmic forces of life on earth. In other words, he was advising him to gather all the forces and energies contained within him in order to save them from destruction and death. In this context, the animals of the ark represent the primordial and instinctive energies within us, which we should preserve and save from the forces of destruction around us.

Creation and birth are often the products of chaos. Any new circumstance that implies that a page is being turned in our lives, that we are leaving our past behind to look or move towards the future, is often a source of anxiety. We become submerged by a flood of emotions that we cannot always control. However, change is one of the great principles of life, which is constantly

being transformed and regenerated, and we must therefore resign ourselves to this fact. In order to embrace change, turn a corner or cross a bridge in our lives, we must not only guard against the external influences that hold us back and entrench us in our past, but also against the whirlpool of emotions that threatens to submerge us and in which we run the risk of drowning.

If we bear this in mind when interpreting the myth of Noah's Ark, it becomes patently obvious that it is not simply an historic narrative or a religious story but the account of an age-old experience, of preoccupations that concerned our ancestors as much as they concern us today, and one which could well have many lessons for our modern way of life.

See also *Flood*, page 188.

Nudity

Who has not dreamed, at least once, of being naked in a public place or surrounded by correctly dressed people, without finding the experience disturbing or embarrassing? This is known as a recurring dream: one that occurs often and is common to all dreamers. We find the idea shocking because, in modern

Numbers

The number as a unit. This is not an examination of numbers in terms of mathematics or accounting, but as ancient symbolic archetypes, each forming an indivisible unit, a force, an energy source with its own specific associations. In this respect, therefore, numbers cannot be added up or subtracted from each other; each number is an indivisible unit, complete in itself.

1 – One

One is a unifying number, forming a whole. Here it is not a question of the first or base numeral, but of a symbol uniting various principles of existence. Some people believe that the universe is the reverse of the number 1; others believe that it is everything that converges on, moves towards or returns to 1. The etymological root of the word 'universe', the Latin *universus*, originally meant 'turned into one'. It seems therefore that the number 1 has always been regarded as a whole, an absolute principle, a final outcome and an end in itself. The concept of the whole contained in 1, and vice versa, can be found in the popular expression 'It's all one',

Western society, it is common practice to wear clothes and conceal one's body.

In a dream, nudity often refers to the original state of innocence in the sense that all men and women were born naked. This original innocence is represented by the Bible story of Adam and Eve, before they sinned.

For this reason, nudity also refers back to the myth of the androgyne (see page 26). According to this myth, nudity symbolizes not only truth, purity and authenticity, but also completeness, perfection and achievement. In fact, the androgyne, the primeval man-woman or woman-man, represents a fully realized human being, ideally both man and woman, who has no need for a third person to be him- or herself. Walking naked in a dream, therefore, sometimes indicates a subconscious desire to be complete in this way.

meaning it all comes down to the same thing.

The point of light. It seems as if 1 is both beginning and end, as if the beginning and end form a whole, an entity, a single unit. This principle is seen in the ancient diagram of the point of light at the centre of a circle. 'When the Unknown of Unknowns wanted to show himself', says the 13th-century Jewish mystical text, the *Zohar*, 'he began by producing a point of light.' If we imagine an empty, immaterial world in which nothing is visible, nothing exists, and in which a single point of light emerges from the unknown, we are suddenly brought face to face with the visible world. This visible light, which provides a focus for our attention and allows us to concentrate, also awakens and stimulates our awareness. This is how certain yoga exercises enable us, after adopting several positions designed to help us to relax and breathe properly, to create an inner void, pacifying or taming the natural restlessness of the mind, which can be regarded as a spirited young animal. When this void has been achieved, practitioners visualize a point of light. As well as being an excellent concentration exercise, this practice improves the powers of discernment, shrewd and objective

decision-making and, paradoxically, sharp-sightedness. In fact, people who practise yoga regularly find that, with time, their field of vision broadens and the point of light on which they are concentrating with closed eyes tends to grow, surrounding them and sometimes even absorbing them.

This phenomenon has also been described by people who have been in a deep coma from which they have sometimes miraculously awoken. Although these are completely unrelated cases, many different people have reported seeing a point of light growing larger and larger until it gradually enveloped them in a vibrant, beneficial glow that defied description.

Unifying symbols. Even if we are discussing an inner vision, it is impossible not to make a connection between the dot within the circle, which resembles the number 1 within the whole, and the iris at the centre of the eye. This dot or point of light at the centre of the circle also represents the astrological symbol of the sun, which appears like a blazing eye hanging in the sky. This was the Egyptians' perception of Re, the sun-god, whom they also represented as a magnificent cobra rearing up on its tail, with a single open eye that seemed to encompass its whole head. This was the Uraeus, often seen on the pharaohs' crown, which symbolized enlivening warmth, the breath of life. Thus the point of light, centre, eye, sun, heart and breath are all unifying symbols. Mention should also be made of the *sriyantra*, meaning literally 'instrument of the sublime'. This is a diagram used in Tantric Hinduism – a religious doctrine derived from Hinduism, centred around the awakening and mastery of basic energies and the fusion of opposites, which mainly uses kundalini yoga exercises – whose purpose is to focus the attention on the central point at the heart of the Whole and awaken the force that restores life or returns to the One. This diagram is a mandala that has a magical, unifying effect on the user.

Lastly, no discussion of this sort would be complete without referring to the monad, regarded as the major unifying principle and the soul of the world by alchemists, philosophers and practitioners of esotericism and the Christian cabbala of

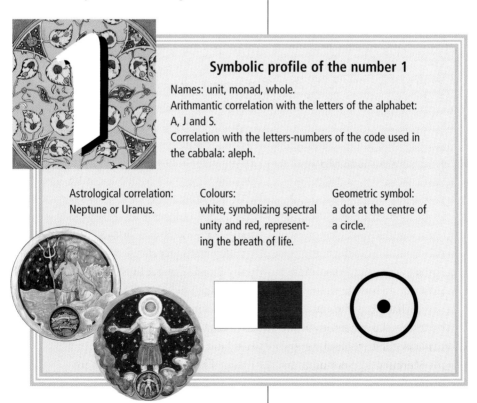

Symbolic profile of the number 1

Names: unit, monad, whole.
Arithmantic correlation with the letters of the alphabet:
A, J and S.
Correlation with the letters-numbers of the code used in the cabbala: aleph.

Astrological correlation:
Neptune or Uranus.

Colours:
white, symbolizing spectral unity and red, representing the breath of life.

Geometric symbol:
a dot at the centre of a circle.

Images and symbols relating to the number 1

Oinos is the Greek word for the ace in a game of dice. It is also the Indo-European root of the Latin word unus, meaning 'one, single, sole', from which words like 'uniform, unique, unity and union' are derived.

Hydrogen is the first atomic element in the periodic or Mendeleyev table, so-called after the Russian chemist who developed the classification of chemical elements. It is regarded as the most abundant element in the universe because it is the basic component of the stars. The nucleus of the hydrogen atom is formed of a single proton, orbited by a single electron.

Hydrogen is mentioned here more because of the structure of its nucleus, composed of a single proton and a single electron, than because of its position at the head of the atomic elements. In fact, there is a world of difference between the 1 that forms a single unit and the 1 that is the first numeral in a list. Something that comes first or forms the basis for something else does not necessarily form a unified whole.

2 – Two

The Tai-Chi-Tu or yin/yang symbol, the zodiac and binary rhythm are all symbolic representations of the unifying role played by the number 2. One of the most attractive symbols representing the perfect entity formed by 2 is undoubtedly the Tai-Chi-Tu from the Chinese Tao. It represents the underlying principle of Tao, a philosophy and religious doctrine dominated by the concept of perpetual change and transformation. Better known as the yin/yang symbol, it literally means 'the diagram of the supreme ultimate', or, more precisely, 'the diagram of supreme change'. This principle bears close similarities to that of the *prima materia* of the alchemists, since it is an image of the universal energy that governs all life forms.

The Tai-Chi-Tu is a perfect circle, divided into two equal parts by a central, vertical S that symbolically represents the primeval serpent or dragon of Chinese mythology. In the white section on the left, associated with the yang or great masculine principle, is a black yin dot. In the black section on the right, associated with the yin or great feminine principle, is a white yang dot.

The central dragon therefore both separates the yang from

the Renaissance. It was depicted by the English astrologer John Dee as a diagram inspired both by the tree of the Sephiroth in the cabbala and the symbol of the planet Mercury surmounted by the symbol of the sun.

and yet, as there are two of them, can reproduce continually and engender the multifarious forms of life found on earth and throughout the universe. It is also worth noting that the yin/yang symbol resembles those for the signs of Cancer and Pisces, and that there is an equal number of so-called masculine and feminine signs in the zodiac. The masculine signs are Aries, Gemini, Leo, Libra, Sagittarius and Aquarius; the feminine signs are Taurus, Cancer, Virgo, Scorpio, Capricorn and Pisces. In other words, all the fire and air signs in the zodiac are masculine while all the earth and water signs are feminine. However, grouped together in the zodiac, they form a coherent

the yin and creates perpetual movement between these two fundamental principles whose continual interpenetration is symbolized by a yin dot in the yang section of the Tai-Chi-Tu, and a yang dot in its yin section. This is how the Chinese view the continually changing nature of these two fundamental principles of life, which make up one entity

Symbolic profile of the number 2

Names: duet, double, duality, binary.
Arithmantic correlation with the letters of the alphabet:
B, K and T.
Correlation with the letters-numbers of the code used in the cabbala: baith.

Astrological correlation:
Saturn.

Colours:
black or brown, symbolizing visible matter.

Geometric symbol:
two points, two lines, one angle.

whole, each with individual attributes and properties that appear to influence the planets travelling through them, which themselves have a yin or yang principle depending on the nature of the planet in question. There is every justification, therefore, for saying that the zodiac is the Tai-Chi-Tu of the West.

Rhythm. It is not difficult to imagine how people became aware of rhythm, hearing that magical, sacred cadence in double time that was inspired as much by their heartbeat as by the natural rhythm of their footsteps when walking or running.

In fact, it is tempting to believe – although this is pure speculation, since there is no tangible proof to support this theory – that man grasped the concept of rhythm while walking and listening to the continual diastolic and systolic motion of his heart, endowing it with magical qualities since this inner rhythm seemed to correspond perfectly to various natural sounds, like the waves beating on the shore, certain birdcalls, the wind in the trees, the rain falling on the ground etc.

So, continuing this line of speculation to clarify the symbolism of 2, as perceived by our ancestors, it may have been a gradual awareness of the basic

> ## Images and symbols relating to the number 2
>
> The greatest paradox of 2 is that it represents the visible and the invisible worlds united, side by side.
>
> In fact, if 1 is represented by a point of light in the middle of a circle or a visible dot in the middle of a circle representing all that is invisible (see One, page 362), 2 shows a circle divided into two equal sections, the section on the left being white and the section on the right being black. As in the Tai-Chi-Tu, a black dot at the centre of the white section on the left indicates the appearance of the visible within the invisible, while the white dot in the black section on the right represents the gateway to the invisible in the visible.
>
> Helium is the second atomic element in Mendeleyev's periodical table. Its atom is composed of two nuclei, each comprising two protons and two electrons. Strangely, in 1868, the English astrophysicist Norman Lockyer named this second atomic element after the Greek word helios, meaning sun. We say strangely because the planet associated with the number 2 is Saturn and occasionally the moon as a great female principle, but never the sun.

binary rhythm of nature's masterful symphony that caused them to see everything in pairs: man and woman, heaven and earth, high and low, day and night, hot and cold, sun and moon, inside and outside, life and death, body

and soul and, much later, pure and impure, good and evil. We say much later because, a priori, these pairings did not necessarily involve the idea of duality or contrast, in the modern sense. In fact, 2 originally referred to a duet, a couple, a union, the double that is oneself. Duality is a key characteristic of anything that is doubled, not contrasted.

3 – Three

Whether it has the geometric appearance of a triangle or appears in the mythical, mystical guise of a trinity, 3 is a link and a creative principle.

The number 3 brings to mind the three major stages of human existence: birth, life and death. However, life is generally contrasted with death, since the former is characterized by the physical presence of an individual and the latter by their absence. This is tantamount to saying that, in terms of the concept of life and death, we are once again in the realm of duality, a realm marked by that fatal, insistent and eternal binary rhythm, a realm in which two contrasting yet complementary elements face each other without coming together and the entire world seems to balance on their opposition. However, the expression or existence of this polarity appears to be the result of the creative role played by a third element or factor. This is possibly the main characteristic of 3, which, whether revealed by the number 2, or by two opposing yet attracting numbers 1, is an additional, unknown element which, nevertheless, cannot be born, take shape or exist without this duality.

At a very simple, basic level of symbolism, it can be said that 1 is heaven and 2 is earth. Alternatively, 1 can be regarded as the nurturing father and 2 as the nurturing mother. The union of these two, who were probably separated at the beginning of time when they were originally a single entity, produces 3, the fruit. The fruit is life, the human race. This is why life appears in the middle of the three major phases of existence, birth and death being the gateways through which we make our entrance and exit.

The middle also represents the number 3. For example, if you draw a point or a line on the horizon that separates the sky from the earth, or the sky from the sea, you are in the sphere of 3, which simultaneously unites and divides two separate elements. In the realm of the number 2, we moved from one state to another without noticing. We were in the world of opposites that gives birth to the spark (see page 365). The number 3 is this spark, this inner energy, the flame that warms, enlightens and illuminates, the perfect symbolic image of the thinking mind and intelligence.

The Trinity. Thus, many religions have three deities that make up a single entity. For example, there is the trinity of the Hindu gods or *Trimurti*, meaning 'three forms': Brahma, the creator, Vishnu, the preserver, and Shiva, the destroyer. According to certain Hindu beliefs, the Supreme Spirit took Brahma from his right side to create the world, Vishnu from his left side to preserve it, and Shiva from the middle of his body to destroy it. The Christian Trinity, however, which unites the Father, the Son and the Holy Spirit in a single God, is less pessimistic. It is worth pointing out, though, that there is no mention of this doctrine or belief in either the Old or New Testaments, and it seems to have appeared around the 4th century AD. This suggests that it resulted from ancient beliefs and folk cultures produced by the combined influence of the Mesopotamian, Egyptian, Greek and Celtic civilizations. This vision of a deified trinity can be found virtually everywhere in the world and can simply be regarded as, first, a representation of the cosmos or universe, then of the human race and lastly of the psyche or consciousness, in other words, heaven, earth and mankind.

Tripartite form. Man is also a trinity: a soul, a body and a mind, or a head, torso and legs. According to ancestral beliefs and the physicians of antiquity,

mankind also has a triple body comprising the physical body, the etheric body, also known as the vital body, and the emotional body, also called the astral body. The etheric body is itself divided into three separate parts forming a single entity: vital ether, which is associated with sexuality, the will to live, the genitals, reproductive organs, the psyche and regenerative energy resources; light ether, governing the five senses and circulation, heartbeat and body temperature and reflecting ether, which controls intelligence, thought processes, reflexes, the will and action.

In the interests of thoroughness, the intellectual and philosophical principle of thesis, antithesis and synthesis should also be mentioned here. The first may be considered as life, in its original sense, the second as death, also in its original sense, therefore the third is seen as a characteristic of eternity, because life and death are not opposites: they are simply the two poles, visible and invisible, of the same reality, when taken together or regarded as a single entity.

According to this intellectual process, the number 3 – which is the first uneven number, just as the number 2 was the first even number, the number 1 being androgynous – has a creative role to play. It combines two conflicting elements that may be destined for destruction, possibly by each other, in order to produce something new.

Symbolic profile of the number 3

Names: ternary, triad, trinity, trio, triple, trivium.
Arithmantic correlation with the letters of the alphabet: C, L and U.
Correlation with the letters-numbers of the code used in the cabbala: gimmel.

Astrological correlation: Jupiter.

Colour: yellow.

Geometric symbol: triangle.

Images and symbols relating to the number 3

Although 3 can play a dynamic, creative role, it also serves as a link. For example, the line between two points is the third element without which these two points would not be connected or united. If we connect three points three times in twos, we obtain a triangle. This geometric figure is highly symbolic, because it has been used since time immemorial to represent the four primordial elements: the upright triangle, with its tip pointing upwards, represents fire, the male pole; the inverted triangle, with its tip pointing downwards, represents water, the female pole; the upright triangle, with a horizontal line through its middle, represents air, or spirit; the inverted triangle, also with a horizontal line through its middle, represents earth, or matter.

Since white and black are not colours, there are three primary colours: yellow, blue and red, and three complementary colours, resulting from three combinations of two primary colours: green, a mixture of yellow and blue, orange, produced by combining yellow and red, and purple, a mixture of blue and red.

4 – Four

The square and the cross are the two most faithful representations of the number 4, which is also a symbol of fate and free will. We are not interested in counting up to four here, even though counting and recounting – enumerating and relating – share the same etymology so it might be interesting to compare them, given the subject of this book. In fact, science, whichever way you look at it, is all the more fascinating because it enables us to understand and marvel at our world and the wonders of nature, not as if it were a perfect mechanism that we have learned how to operate to our advantage but like a fabulous book that we can peruse endlessly throughout our life, discovering new forms of life, new horizons, new worlds as the pages turn.

A perfect world. This introduction was a deliberate attempt to sum up all the pitfalls presented by the number 4, as well as all the opportunities it represents. This is because 4, with all its symbolic meanings, potentially allows us to exert

power and influence over the matter produced by the four primordial elements. However, in so doing, it boxes us into an unchanging physical reality, precisely because it underpins a closed, perfect universe, the basic structure of the cosmos as perceived by the Greek philosopher Pythagoras of Samos in the 6th century BC. At that time, it was thought that the world rested on four pillars, four columns, four sacred trees supporting the temple of the manifest world. It goes without saying that the four so-called bases of the world can also be compared to the four cardinal points.

Crossroads and territory. But let us go back to the vision our distant forebears might have had of their world, at a time when they were starting to discover and understand its principles, structure and order. They saw the sun rise at a certain point on the horizon, follow a set course through the sky, then disappear on the other side of the horizon. This enabled mankind to symbolize the great principle of duality: day and night, life and death, the visible and invisible world, high and low. However, if sunrise or daybreak can be observed, recorded and therefore anticipated; in other words, if it is

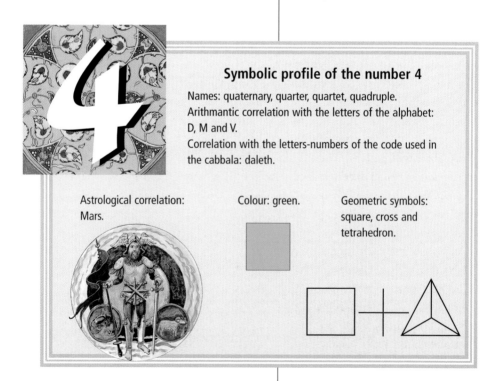

Symbolic profile of the number 4

Names: quaternary, quarter, quartet, quadruple.
Arithmantic correlation with the letters of the alphabet: D, M and V.
Correlation with the letters-numbers of the code used in the cabbala: daleth.

Astrological correlation: Mars.

Colour: green.

Geometric symbols: square, cross and tetrahedron.

foreseeable – because it always happens in the same place at the same time, every year – and if the same can be done with regard to sunset or nightfall, then a similar phenomenon, this time produced by the rising and setting of the moon, can also be established. Mankind therefore had the choice of four directions, four points revealed by the rising and setting of the sun and moon on any given day, in a certain place. In the same way, people can move forwards or backwards and turn right or left; in other words they can head in four directions, although they can only go in one direction at a time. This takes us into the symbolic realm of the crossroads. In short, the number 4 reveals two principles crucial to the early development of mankind's awareness and intelligence: the concept of territory or ownership, to use a more modern term, and that of choice, therefore of self-determination, free will.

Square and fate. In fact, by locating the four points of their world, as defined by the rising and setting of the sun and moon, our forebears established a closed universe belonging exclusively to them, even if they believed it was determined or governed by the gods. By joining up these four points one by one, they created the chief geometric

figure of the number 4: the square. Mankind believed that the earth was square and the sky round. It should also be pointed out that four points also define the first solid form, the tetrahedron, although these did not exist on the same plane, being composed of four triangles. A solid form represents physical reality, an event within the tangible world, something concrete. Thus, mankind exists within the realm of the number 4, which gives the square, that is four lines representing the boundaries of the world, his world. He is safe. Outside those four lines or points of reference is the unknown world, the forbidden. Although 4 encourages us to count our blessings and makes us feel safe, by the same token, it also limits and encloses us. By joining up each of these four points on the horizon two by two, not round the outside but inside, we create an additional point at the intersection of the two lines formed as a result. However, before moving

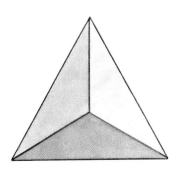

Images and symbols relating to the number 4

The Number 4 is primarily suggested by the cardinal points: the east or Orient, also called the Levant (meaning 'rising'), the point on the horizon where the sun rises; the west or Occident (meaning 'setting'), the point on the horizon where the sun sets; the north, easily located in the sky by means of the Pole Star in the constellation of Ursa Minor, less than one degree from the celestial north pole; and the south, naturally found opposite the Pole Star. These four cardinal points are comparable to the four equinoctial and solstitial points and, therefore, to the four seasons and the four elements that form the basic structure of the zodiac.

In the Old Testament, the name of Yahweh or Jehovah is written using four letters-numbers of the Hebrew alphabet: YHWH or Yood-Hay-Wav-Heith or 10–5–6–5 . It is therefore hardly surprising that the authors of the Bible should have come up with four major prophets: Isaiah, Jeremiah, Ezekiel and Daniel, or that, later, in the New Testament, there are four evangelists: Mark, represented by a lion, Luke, symbolized by a bull, John, who appeared in the guise of an eagle, and Matthew, personified by a man or an angel; nor is it surprising that, later still, the Church had four doctors: St Augustine, St Ambrose, St Jerome and St Gregory the Great. The four letters-numbers of the legendary, sacred name of Yahweh are obviously associated with the symbol of Christ's cross. The Bible also alludes to four rivers in the Garden of Eden and the Four Horsemen of the Apocalypse. There is in fact no doubt that the number 4 plays a prominent role in the Holy Scriptures.

on to this – because it brings us to the number 5 – man can himself be this central point, capable of heading for one of the four points. This puts him at the centre of a crossroads, able to choose the direction or path he wants to take. In this way, the number 4, the symbol of the square and the crossroads, is, by analogy, that of the destiny set before humans so that they can express their free will. When you are at a crossroads and you decide to take one direction rather than another, you are in fact deciding your fate.

5 – Five

Because human beings have five fingers on each hand, five toes on each foot and five senses to perceive the world, the number 5 represents mankind.

The fifth element does exist: it is not just an idea for a film dreamed up by a screenwriter and a film-maker. It was defined by the Greek writer Plutarch in the first century AD as follows: 'Supposing that the World in which we live is the only one, which is what Aristotle believed, it is itself, at least, composed of five worlds that comprise its Harmony: the first is Earth, the second Water, the third Fire, the fourth Air and the fifth Heaven, this last being called Light by some, Ether by others, and Quintessence, finally, by yet others' (Plutarch, *Parallel Lives*).

The five senses and quintessence. If, according to Greek philosophy, the harmony of the world was composed of five elements, the Hindus also believe that man – the microcosm – is made up of five main properties, comparable to the five major elements that make up the created, manifest world, the macrocosm. These five elements are called *skandha*, literally meaning groups or aggregates. They are as follows:

Skandha Rupa. Aggregate of matter or group of corporeality, composed of the four elements: solid (earth), liquid (water), warmth (fire) and movement (air). Each of these primordial elements is connected to one of the sense organs and its faculty: the nose and sense of smell for earth, the palate and sense of taste for water, the eye and sight for fire, the skin and sense of touch for air. The ear and sense of hearing are associated with ether, the fifth element.

Skandha Vedana. Aggregate of sensations or group of perceptions, composed of all types of feelings, whether pleasant, painful or neutral. For mankind, these are like doors opening onto the outside world.

Skandha Samjna. Aggregate of awareness or group of mental formations, broken down into six distinct sense objects: form, sound, smell, taste, physical sensations and mental perceptions.

Skandha Samskara. Aggregate of concepts and group of actions, bringing together all levels of psychic and instinctual activity, as expressed by desires, feelings, emotions, actions: attention, concentration, reasoning, judgement, will, spirit of initiative, the power to act, joy etc.

Skandha Vijnana. Aggregate of consciousness or group of knowledge, bringing together the six fields of activity of the consciousness or mind that encourage the acquisition of knowledge. Each of the sensory and psychic abilities is used as a tool or instrument for identification and learning. So we have awareness of smell (earth), taste (water), sight (fire), touch (air), hearing (ether or fifth element) and mental awareness.

This leads to the bold deduction that, according to the Hindu doctrine, mental awareness, which encourages self-awareness, may be what we in the West tend to call the sixth sense: the quintessential distillation of all the faculties, gifts, elements and qualities of the five senses.

This mental awareness is in fact a type of extrasensory perceptive faculty that enables us all to realize that the *skandha* or aggregates, as described above, are mere illusions. 'As stated in the preceding texts, the five Groups of Existence – either taken separately or combined – in no way constitute a real Ego-entity or subsisting personality, and equally no self, soul or substance can be found outside of these Groups as their "owner". In other words, the five Groups of Existence are "not-self" (*anattaa*), nor do they belong to a Self (*anattaniya*). In view of the impermanence and conditionality of all existence, the belief in any form of Self must be regarded as an illusion.' (*The Word of the Buddha*, compiled, translated and explained by Nyanatiloka.)

The cinquefoil and the pentagram. Medieval churches and cathedrals of Romanesque or Gothic inspiration were often decorated with stained-glass windows and sculptures in the shape of a cinquefoil. This is a geometric figure composed of a

Symbolic profile of the number 5

Names: quinary, fifth, quintet, quintuple and all names prefixed with pent, from the Greek pente, meaning five: pentagon, Pentateuch, Pentecost etc.
Arithmantic correlation with the letters of the alphabet: E, N and W.
Correlation with the letters-numbers of the cabbala: hay

Astrological correlation: Aries.

Colour: blue.

Geometric symbols: pentagram or five-pointed star and pyramid.

circle containing a five-pointed star and surrounded by five lobes that are actually circles whose centre meets each of the star's five points.

The cinquefoil was a symbolic representation of the pentagram, whose principle was established by Pythagoras. As Marie-Madeleine Davy wrote in her book on Romanesque symbolism: 'According to Pythagorean doctrine, ten is the perfect numeral; it represents unity and has always traditionally been the number associated with divinity. Mankind bears its image on his hands and feet [we have five toes on each foot, making ten in all, and five fingers on each hand, making ten in all]. If we take the Number 5 as the number for mankind, the pentagram becomes the emblem of the microcosm. As a result, the microcosm and the macrocosm, whose image it is, form the perfect number (5 + 5 = 10) for God.' (Marie-Madeleine Davy, *Initiation à la symbolique romane*, éditions Flammarion, 1964.)

This sum, from which results the perfect number for God, is actually a fusion, a union, a communion of the number 5 with itself. The cinquefoil, the symbolic representation of the pentagram, therefore represents not only humanity, the micro-

Images and symbols relating to the number 5

As we have seen, because humans have five senses (smell, taste, sight, touch and hearing) and five fingers – the thumb (associated with Venus), the index (associated with Jupiter), the middle finger (associated with Saturn), the ring finger (associated with the sun) and the little finger (associated with Mercury) – the number 5 was regarded by the ancient civilizations as the number for humanity. Correspondingly, the vertebrae of the spinal column were divided into five groups:

1 The seven cervical vertebrae supporting the skull. Each is associated with the seven ruling planets/gods of the zodiac.

2 The 12 thoracic or dorsal vertebrae, attached to the 12 pairs of ribs, each of which associated with one of the 12 signs of the zodiac.

3 The five lumbar vertebrae. The first four are associated with the four elements and the fifth with the fifth element: ether.

4 The five so-called sacral vertebrae, so-named because they are fused as the sacrum, which unites with the hip-bones to form the pelvis. The Muladhara chakra, encircling the cosmic energy force, the kundalini, is situated at the base of the spine.

5 This leaves the four vertebrae of the coccyx, which seem to form a single bone, perhaps the vestiges of a caudal bone.

cosm, in the guise of the five-pointed star which, naturally, symbolizes man standing upright, his arms and legs outspread, but also the universe, the macrocosm, in the guise of the five lobes corresponding to the five elements governing the world.

Last but not least, it should be noted that the pentagram, as its name suggests, is the fifth letter, that is the letter *hay*, in the alphabet of letters-numbers used in the cabbala. This was the symbol of breath, the essence of life, the seat and vehicle of the soul and the spirit. The Egyptian hieroglyph corresponding to this letter showed a man standing, his legs spread, raising his arms towards heaven.

6 – Six

The number 6 is the number of Genesis. Its two symbols, the hexagram and the Seal of Solomon, unite the elements and the ruling planets of the zodiac. Historically, it seems that the art of divination and the science of

numbers appeared in Sumer, in Mesopotamia, around the same time, *c.* 2900 BC, some five thousand years ago. Obviously, this raises an interesting question: did mankind begin to calculate before learning to write and did counting come before recounting, or vice versa? Although archaeologists and historians unanimously believe that the science of numbers derived from writing, they also agree that the principle of calculation predates that of writing. However, to examine the history of mankind and the early development of intelligence chronologically is a typically modern notion. For, while the historical traces of human discoveries, concerns and societies may indicate a certain chronology, there is nothing to say that these elements first appeared in that order. As a result, we believe that, like genetic memory, our history is inscribed within us: the path we have taken, the stages we have passed through, our gradually expanding awareness – all combine to create our distinctive vision of reality and the world today.

Genesis and the number 6. This path and this genesis are contained in the symbolic history of the number 6. However, before illustrating this further, it is important to stress a key point about science and symbolism as they were conceptualized by ancient civilizations. As shown by the symbols of the number 6, in comparison with those of the number 5 (see *Five*, page 374), numbers should be viewed in decreasing or descending order. Symbolically and according to the ancient science of numbers, 5 is larger than 6, even though this may be difficult to accept as we do not generally use numbers in this way. This chronological reversal illustrates the journey man must make within himself to get back in touch with his original essence and let his rediscovered consciousness take flight again, since it knows no bounds and recognizes no division. This takes us into the myth of paradise lost, which is found in all mythical cosmogonies.

So if we want to understand how, symbolically, the number 5 can be greater than the number 6, when mathematically and chronologically the opposite holds true, all we have to know is that 6 is the number for the human being developing in its mother's womb. In fact, biologically, a sixth-month-old foetus is fully formed. The remaining three months are simply to prepare the child for the physical, human existence waiting for it outside the womb. It is during these three months that the child's independent reflex memory develops, enabling it to react independently of its mother, and establishing the structure of its personality, which is outlined in diagrammatic, symbolic representation on its astrological chart, established at the precise moment of birth.

Therefore, the number for mankind at the first stage of development is 6, while 5 is the number for a fully-formed, fully-grown man, standing upright, as symbolized by the five-pointed star or pentagram (see page 378). This makes it easier to understand how 6 precedes 5 in the symbolism of numbers.

The hexagram and the Seal of Solomon. A hexagram is obtained by dividing a circle into six equal angles. A six-pointed star can be formed by connecting these six angles with horizontal, vertical and diagonal lines. However, a star is also formed by drawing two triangles inside the circle and the hexagon, one pointing up, the other pointing down. This star is a magical hexagram composed of the four

elements: fire, water, air, earth (see *Three*, page 368). Consequently, all the elements, as well as the properties associated with them, are distributed around the star-shaped hexagram. Fire is situated at the top, water at the bottom, air on the left, facing the hexagram, and earth on the right; hot is top left, wet bottom left, dry top right and cold bottom right. The seven ruling planets of the zodiac also have their place in the hexagram, as well as the metals associated with them: the moon and silver at the top, Mars and iron top left, Venus and copper top right, Jupiter and tin bottom left, Mercury and mercury bottom right, Saturn and lead at the bottom, the sun and gold in the centre. The structure of the hexagram of elements and planets therefore suggests that the science of numbers is not dissimilar to that of astrology, that the two agree and were probably created at the same time.

As for the Seal of Solomon, this differs from the hexagram in that the two inverted triangles that make up this star-

Symbolic profile of the number 6

Names: senary, sextet, sextuple, sextile.
Arithmantic correlation with the letters of the alphabet: F, O and X.
Correlation with the letters-numbers of the cabbala: waw.

Astrological correlation: Taurus.

Colour: indigo.

Geometric symbols: the hexagon and hexagram or six-pointed star.

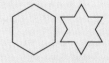

(see *Two*, page 365).

Images and symbols relating to the number 6

As 6 is the number of the first stage of man's development, it is easier to understand the meaning of the legendary six days it took God to create the world, according to Genesis. According to the Avesta, the sacred book of Zoroastrianism – whose earliest texts are contemporaneous with the earliest writings of the Bible, written by the Hebrews (c. 1400–1200 BC) – the world was not created in six days, but in six stages or phases:

- In the first phase, lasting 45 days, heaven was created.
- During the second phase, lasting 60 days, water was created.
- In the third phase, lasting 75 days, the earth was created.
- The fourth phase, lasting 30 days, corresponds to the creation of the plant kingdom.
- In the fifth phase, lasting 80 days, the animals were created.
- Last but not least, the sixth phase, lasting 75 days, saw the creation of mankind. This was the same number of days taken to create the earth. If we add together the number of days it took to create the world we get 365.

did build his famous Temple in accordance with the six degrees inscribed in this Seal, there is an obvious and striking similarity between this symbol uniting male and female elements and the Tai-Chi-Tu, the yin/yang symbol, the Chinese image of the absolute, whose underlying principle is reminiscent of the cosmic egg that generated the creation (see *Two*, page 365). As can be seen, the number 6 refers us back to number 2.

7 – Seven

There are seven days in a week, seven ruling planets in the zodiac, seven musical notes, seven colours in a rainbow, seven crystal systems etc. Symbolically, 7 is the number of perfection. 'And the Lord said unto Noah, Come thou and all thy house into the ark; for thee have I seen righteous before me in this generation. Of every clean beast thou shalt take to thee by sevens, the male and his female; and of beasts that are not clean by two, the male and his female. Of fowls also of the air by sevens, the male and the female; to keep seed alive upon the face of all the earth. For yet seven days, and I will cause it to rain upon the earth forty days and forty nights; and every living substance that I have made will I

shaped geometric figure are interlocking. As well as being associated with the elements and the planets, these two triangles represent man and woman, the closely linked masculine and feminine energies. If Solomon destroy from off the face of the earth' (Genesis 7: 1–4).

Seven pairs of clean animals, seven pairs of birds of the air, seven days' grace before the flood was unleashed upon the earth: the number 7 occurs frequently in the story of the flood in Genesis. And there is more: 'And he stayed yet other seven days; and again he sent forth the dove out of the ark; And the dove came in to him in the evening; and, lo, in her mouth was an olive leaf pluckt off; so Noah knew that the waters were abated from off the earth. And he stayed yet another seven days; and sent forth the dove; which returned not again unto him any more' (Genesis 8: 10–12).

Although number 7 plays an important role in the story of Noah, there are other references to this number, which the Jews and the first authors of the Bible felt symbolized a sense of perfection and completeness in the holy Scriptures. As a result, Solomon built the 'House of the Lord' in seven years (I Kings 6: 38). Elisha laid himself upon on a dead child who sneezed seven times and opened his eyes (II Kings 4: 32–35). Elisha instructed Naaman, captain of the king of Syria's army, to wash himself seven times in the waters of the River Jordan to cure his leprosy (II Kings 5: 1–14). The number 7 actually appears 77 times in the Old Testament and forms the

Symbolic profile of the number 7

Names: septenary, septet, septentriones, the Roman name for the constellation of Ursa Major, from the Latin referring to the seven oxen.
Arithmantic correlation with the letters of the alphabet: G, P and Y.
Correlation with the letters-numbers of the cabbala: zein or zayin

Astrological correlation: Gemini.

Colour: violet.

Geometric symbol: seven-pointed star, formed by the planets and the days of the week.

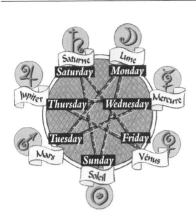

keystone of St John's Revelation, which close the New Testament and refers to seven churches, seven seals, seven angels holding seven trumpets, seven signs, seven plagues and seven vials!

The bow and arrow. The symbolic power of the number 7 can be understood best by returning to the legend of Noah, which predates the writing of Genesis (see *Noah's Ark*, page 359). This is because the flood ended with a treaty of alliance between the Lord and Noah, represented by a rainbow composed of seven colours, each of which, incidentally, is associated with a musical note: red for C, violet for D, indigo for E, blue for F, green for G, yellow for A and orange for B, if ascending the scale; red for C, violet for B, indigo for A, blue for G, green for F, yellow for E and orange for D, if descending the scale. It is impossible not to notice the similarity between the shape of the rainbow – which seems to form a

multicoloured bridge of light between heaven and earth, and also a drawn bow aiming at heaven – and the seventh letter-number of the Hebrew alphabet that forms the code used in the cabbala. *Zayin* or *zein*, meaning 'weapon', was originally symbolized by an arrow, whether it was written by the first Jews or the Egyptians. The bow and arrow are therefore the best symbolic representations of the number 7, the arrow resting on the bow illustrating, as it were, the seven stages, the seven steps, the seven heavens that mankind must scale to reach the gateway of the gods leading to immortality.

Seven, number for the gods and universal number. Whatever the belief, religion or civilization, the major elements of creation, the universe and mankind rest on the number 7. The Egyptians as well as the Hindus and, later, the Buddhists, believed that mankind was composed of seven primordial elements, identical to the seven original elements on which the created, manifest world is built. However, the *Enuma Eilish* or *Epic of the Creation* about Mesopotamian and Babylonian astrology – which generated a true religious cult in its time (see *Cosmogonies in Mesopotamia*, page 126) – written on seven tablets is of particular interest as it mentions the advent of the finest representation of this universal structure, which our ancestors perceived long ago and which, according to them, was the exact replica of the earth. The structure in question was the zodiac and the seven planets/gods, which shared the same name in Sumerian. Nanna or Sin and the moon, Shamash and the sun, Marduk or Dapinu (he of the dreadful glow), god of Babylon and none other than Jupiter, Ishtar or Dilbat (the white) and Venus, the great goddess of

Nineveh, Nabou or Shihtu (he who jumps) and Mercury, Ninurta or Kayamanu (the constant) and Saturn and, last but not least, Nergal (the burner) and Mars, together created the structure of the zodiac which, according to the Chaldeans, formed the basis of the world and a religion based on the concept of fate. Seven gods made the world spin round and governed the fate of souls, representing the completeness and perfection of the world created for mankind, but also showing the way to an eighth heaven, reached by passing through the gateway of the gods.

Images and symbols relating to the number 7

Although number 7 occurs very frequently in the Bible, it also appears in fairy-tales, which are often full of symbols. Thus, there are stories about seven brothers and of an ogre who wears boots with which he can take strides of seven leagues. Likewise, Snow White finds shelter with seven dwarfs, whose house she tidies. Both the seven brothers and the seven dwarfs in Snow White are representations of the seven stages of consciousness, the seven personality traits, the seven elements that make up man's existence, as we have already seen. These are instinct, emotion, intelligence, intuition, reason, will and awareness.

8 – Eight

A symbol of the infinite and eternity, the number 8 also represents the terrestrial and celestial energies that continually circulate from top to bottom and bottom to top and regenerate themselves. The symbols on the VIIIth card of the Major Arcana in the divinatory Tarot, Justice, take us straight into the realm of this magical, mysterious and somewhat disturbing number. The symbolism associated with this card emphasizes the primitive and primordial nature of the symbols to which it refers. These can be summed up as follows: when life is governed by necessity and personal survival or the survival of the species is at stake, both man and animal act without concern for morality or any other such considerations. This is the message encapsulated by the number 8: almost simultaneous capacity for life and for death, which nothing can control or stop. As a result, although Justice is associated with the sign of Cancer (the crab), as is the symbolic figure of the numeral representing this number (see *Symbolic profile of the number 8*, page 386), its basic mode of expression and the information it provides have greater affinity with the eighth sign of the zodiac, Scorpio, which also heralds a change (see page 572).

Transcending time. A simple exercise will help us to understand how our forebears managed to preserve their original interpretation of the world and existence and hand it down over the millennia, despite the vicissitudes of history. We suggest you employ the analogical system, a mental process used by our forebears to create the structure of the zodiac in order to organize their sophisticated science of signs and their world vision. The idea is to start with a natural phenomenon and try to establish potential similarities, links, direct or indirect relation-

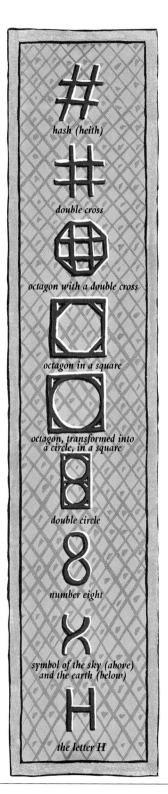

hash (heith)

double cross

octagon with a double cross

octagon in a square

*octagon, transformed into
a circle, in a square*

double circle

number eight

*symbol of the sky (above)
and the earth (below)*

the letter H

ships and interrelationships. Associations can be invented or imagined, although there should always be a meaningful, if not logical, explanation for them. We note in passing that this is the same principle, based on the association of ideas in this case, used by psychoanalysts with their patients. Our aim is to find and understand the link(s) that exist(s) between the number 8, Justice (VIIIth card of the Major Arcana of the divinatory Tarot), the capital letter H and the mathematical symbol for infinity. Once we have demonstrated that all these figures represent the same thing, we may have a vague idea of the way in which we might one day be able to tran-

scend time. This is not to enjoy time-travel, a possibility offered by certain science-fiction authors – setting us down in some weird and wonderful world – but to liberate ourselves from time and, in so doing, to free ourselves from death.

From infinity to eternity. Take Justice, the VIIIth card of the Major Arcana from a pack of Tarot cards. Place it near you and read the following closely: look at the box on page 385 and you will understand how we proceeded from a simple barrier or fence, the meaning of *heith* in Hebrew – which also indicates H, the eighth letter of the Hebrew alphabet as well as the eighth letter of the Western

Symbolic profile of the number 8

Names: octet, eighth, octave.
Arithmantic correlation with the letters of the alphabet: H, Q and Z.
Correlation with the letters-numbers of the cabbala: cheth.

Astrological correlation: Cancer (the crab), whose symbol is associated with the vertical, separate eight, and Scorpio, the eighth sign of the zodiac, whose dialectic fits the symbolism of the number 8.

Colour: red.

Geometric symbol: octagon.

Images and symbols relating to the number 8

A discussion of this number would not be complete without mentioning the eight basic trigrams of the I Ching. These eight diagrams, each composed of three whole or broken lines, are brought together in an octagon at the centre of which is the Tai-Chi-Tu, the Chinese yin/yang symbol, representing the primordial male and female energies that represent the capacity for life and the capacity for death and are mentioned in connection with number 2 (see page 362). The eight trigrams are related to the eight directions on the equivalent of the Western compass card.

In China, the eight-petalled lotus symbolizes the Eightfold Path to be followed for purification according to the teachings of Buddha.

alphabet – to a double cross and from this to an octagonal or eight-sided figure, contained in its turn in a square. This figure becomes a circle within a square and is then doubled while the squares disappear, giving the number 8. Last but not least, you can see how the sign representing a barrier has become the symbol of the letter H, a capital naturally, because the small 'h' has no symbolic significance.

If you now take a look at the Justice card taken from your Tarot pack, you will see that the woman holding a sword in her right hand and a set of scales in her left hand is sitting in a chair that is in fact a capital H.

It is also not surprising that the capital H is associated with the lungs, because the shape of these organs is similar to this letter. As a result, the number 8 is the symbol for the respiratory cycle, the act of breathing in and out that enables us to pass from

life to death continually, without noticing. This constant movement, this rhythmic breathing, bears certain similarities to the movement and rhythm of time. In fact, it was man who invented the measurement of time in seconds that are ticked off one by one at a regular, insistent pace. And how did he devise this system? Perhaps by referring to the heartbeat, the rise and fall of the chest when breathing? When people breathe in or inspire, they draw on life and its ideas, as in the saying 'to find inspiration'. When they breathe out or expire, they give up their soul, their spirit, their life and they die.

As a result, mankind standing upright, symbolized by the number 8, is a representation of eternity, just as the horizontal eight is a representation of infinity. In the horizontal position, mankind is merely physical matter, breathing in the air and the spirit of the earth. He is born, dies and is reborn *ad infinitum*, held captive by the capacity for life and the capacity for death mentioned earlier. But when he stands up, he is breathing in the air and spirit of heaven. He becomes a spiritual, immortal, eternal being. However, this involves a wrench, a break, a drastic change of behaviour and attitude, a change. This is why the number 8 is the finest symbol of man standing upright, spiritual man, man as spirit, man set free.

9 – Nine

The nine or Ennead (Greek *ennea*, 'nine') will help us to understand how numbers can come full circle, thereby heralding something new that will appear with the number 10. When referring to the number 9, it is hard to resist the temptation to play with words: *novem*, the Latin word for 'nine' shares its root with *novus*, 'new'. Following conception, a child remains in its mother's womb for nine months. It could be said therefore that the number 9 is the result of something new or, put another way, that it takes nine months to produce something new, nine months for a mother to give birth to her child. However, it should be pointed out that, in line with

age-old traditions, our forebears used lunar months, not the months in our current calendar, to make their calculations. As a result, the frequent miscalculations made by modern obstetricians are the result less of poor diagnoses or faulty predictions and more of a misunderstanding arising from the fact that 9 x 28 days adds up to fewer days than 9 x 30 or 31 days. The difference between the two is almost a lunar month.

Number 9, the sign of Cancer and the serpent. But this is not the only analogy presented by this number. For example, if we lay the number 9 on its side and place another 9, reversed, above it, we have the symbol for the sign of Cancer (the crab). We have seen, with regard to the number 8, that by visualizing the latter in a horizontal position, we gain a better understanding of the meaning of this astrological symbol which is formed of two similar, inverted loops, one below, the other above, the first creating the impression of being plunged in water, the second of floating or drifting on the surface (see page 387). The symbol for Cancer is derived from the fact that in early summer, the period of the year governed by the sign, the waters of the earth are warm.

Crustaceans or little fish come to the surface, while insects hover just above the water. This is what is represented by these two inverted loops, which also refer to the warmth of the water and the vapours rising from it. If we join these two loops together, we get the number 8 lying on its side and this is the symbol of infinity. This continual motion is exactly what occurs when heat causes water vapour to condense, forming clouds that sooner or later will turn into rain (see *Water*, page 528). We have come full circle. Everything suggests, therefore, that the symbol of Cancer is not composed of two 9s one above the other, but a 6 at the bottom and a 9 at the top. We have already examined the analogies between the number 6 (see page 379), and gestation, pointing out that the six-month-old foetus is fully formed. The child therefore has three more months of development within its mother's womb before being born at the end of the ninth month. This clearly shows how 6 and 9 represent two key stages in human development. However, there are two other phases between them, symbolized by the numbers 7

and 8. Pages 381–388, devoted to these numbers, demonstrate how the number 7 attains a certain level of perfection, while the energies at the top and bottom of the number 6 join and circulate to bring about a continual process of regeneration. Once more, we have come full circle. But there is still a remaining primordial stage to pass through. This is the stage represented by the number 9, which was initially symbolized by a serpent biting its tail, then by a coiled serpent. The serpent is not only a symbol of primeval chaos, but also of the primordial energies that can free the soul and the spirit from the tyranny of the body, the flesh and physical matter (see *Snake*, page 459). The serpent

389

instigates and enlightens; it releases creation from chaos, and perhaps, more simply, brings the child from its mother's womb.

Number 6, number 9, yin and yang. No discussion of the number 9 would be complete without pointing out that it indicates the changeable solid yang line of the hexagrams in the I Ching. However, once again, its relationship to the number 6 can be seen by the fact that the yin, according to the Chinese culture of the I Ching, is symbolized by the changeable broken line and corresponds to the number 6. The two other unchangeable middle lines are obviously the 7, a solid line, and the 8, a broken line. This reveals exactly the same symbolism, the same progression, the same pattern as those shown in the previous paragraph. We have come full circle yet again. Last but not least, it is worth noting that the expression 'we have come full circle' is repeated advisedly in order to illustrate the fact that the letter *teth* of the Hebrew alphabet, which corresponds to the number 9, was represented in antiquity, particularly in Egypt, by a sign representing the circular shield of an Egyptian soldier, the shape of which is reminiscent of the serpent biting its tail. It just remains to add that in the case of the number 6 the serpent

Symbolic profile of the number 9

Names: novena, ninth, ennead, nonagon. In ancient Greece, an enneatic festival was celebrated every nine years.
Arithmantic correlation with the letters of the alphabet: I and R.
Correlation with the letters-numbers of the cabbala: teth.
Astrological correlation: Leo, as well as Cancer, as we have seen.
Colour: red.
Geometric symbol: a square composed of four other squares, in which each of the nine intersection points can be seen. This figure can also be represented by a cube with a dot at its centre. A nonagonal figure with nine equal sides, or a star with nine points, four pointing downwards and five pointing upwards.

Images and symbols relating to the number 9

According to the celestial hierarchy drawn up by Pseudo-Dionysius the Areopagite in the 6th century AD, there were nine choirs or orders composed of eight angels, totalling 72 angels, each associated with a sector of the zodiac and linked to a group of planets that revealed its specific characteristics. These nine choirs were the seraphim, the cherubim, the thrones, the dominions, the powers, the virtues, the principalities, the archangels and the angels themselves.

It is worth noting that 72 = 7 + 2 = 9. The total of all the numbers from 1 to 9, reduced, also gives 9, as follows:
1 + 2 + 3 + 4 + 5 + 6 + 7 + 8 + 9 = 45 = 4 + 5 = 9.

Last but not least, the entire principle of arithmancy or divination by numbers is based on the resonance of the first nine numbers.

10 – Ten

The number 10 is an end in itself, a return to centre, to unity, a fresh start in terms of life and self-fulfilment. If the number 1 symbolizes the origin, the beginning or, as we might say nowadays, the initialization (see *One*, page 362), the number 10 represents a result, an outcome, an achievement. Whatever has been sown or conceived by the number 1 can be harvested or brought into the world with the advent of the number 10.

As a result, this number encompasses, unites and contains all the preceding numbers and, symbolically at least, demonstrates that achievement comes at the end of a cycle, marking the start of a new cycle in its turn.

This is because our forebears, who named the ten numbers before writing them in the sand or carving them in stone, believed that they had been inextricably linked since time immemorial, forming a chain like the one comprising the cycles of life. It should be remembered, after all, that the culture passed down in writing does not date back much further than three thousand years, although human beings, who had already mastered the art of making fire – as well as other skills and practices that have

has its head at the bottom: it is still developing. In the case of the number 9, however, its head is at the top as it is about to be born. Obviously, this view must be reversed with reference to intrauterine life, since a child is usually born head-first. And yet it is then in the position of the number 9. Perhaps the ancients wanted to imply that, in this world, we see everything back to front?

been forgotten – were socialized over half a million years ago.

Number 10, time, the cycle of eternal recurrence. The great underlying principle of all natural cycles, starting obviously with the seasons – of which there are four in Western civilizations, although there are only three in Egypt, for example – is that, paradoxically, they announce and bring about a change, a transformation, sometimes even a metamorphosis, through the repetition of a phenomenon that always remains the same. This is an important idea, because it reveals that ancient civilizations had a much more pragmatic vision of the world than is generally thought, a vision that was considerably more pragmatic than ours, in fact.

What do we do now? We measure, evaluate, assess, calculate, compare, codify and classify everything in the physical world with the aim of dominating and exploiting it, either for commercial reasons or to influence or control a particular domain. With this in mind, we have even pushed back the frontiers of the visible world, since we are able to observe things that are not visible to the naked eye: cells, for example. However, instead of opening our eyes to the world, to life, to others, we are left feeling that the more extensive and varied our knowledge is, the more progress we make, the greater our expertise and the more we distance ourselves from the simple realities of life, the more isolated from each other we become.

Symbolic profile of the number 10

Names: denary, decade, decalogue, decan.
Relationship with the letters-numbers of the cabbala: yood.

Astrological correlation: Virgo.

Geometric symbol: decagon or ten-pointed star.

Our forebears measured the world to gain a better understanding of its limits, believing that they and the world had been fashioned according to the same principle, the same design. And what better way was there to conquer time, to live outside or beyond its constraints, than to become its equal? The person who is equal to time is in harmony with nature and the cycles of life: he or she is set free. Such is the power of the number 10. By sending us back to the point of departure or square one, the number 10 paves the way for regeneration, a continual process of rebirth, since it heralds the end of a cycle. It allows us to be reborn by adhering to the cycles of life. We now know that we are governed by biological cycles and that there is no escape from them. Unfortunately, we never take this into consideration and the modern medical profession, apart from a very few exceptions, has completely lost interest in this phenomenon.

Once again, and this is just one of the paradoxes of our technological era, the more we find ourselves trapped in a routine that compels us to repeat the same actions, the same tasks, the same patterns endlessly, the less we live in the present and the less aware we are of the right moment to act.

Our forebears did not see any point in repeating an action, a task or a remark unless in a participatory context. They never acted alone. For this reason, their actions had a purpose and meaning that could transcend the act itself. They were exemplary. Modern man, on the other hand, has moments of feeling that everything we do is meaningless and of no particular benefit to anyone.

By symbolizing all the cycles of life and, therefore, the myth of eternal recurrence, the number 10 sends us back to the beginning, to square one, which is at the centre and which represents the centre. It is as if, by counting from one to ten, we are following an initiatory path back to the point of origin, the centre. This is why the number 10 is often represented by a circle, the magical symbol of the never-ending cycle, and a circular

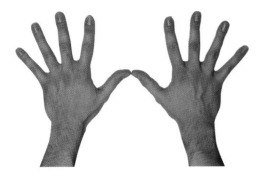

figure whose centre is indicated with a dot and whose meaning is: return to unity or unity regained. 'The "Centre" is therefore the site of the sacred *par excellence*, the site of absolute reality. Similarly, all the other symbols of absolute reality (Trees of Life and Immortality, Fountain of Youth etc.) are also found at a Centre. The path leading to the centre is a 'difficult

Images and symbols relating to the number 10

It is obviously no coincidence, since ten is the total number of fingers on two hands, that the hand is the symbolic representation and name of yood, the letter-number of the code used in the cabbala that corresponds to the number 10, or that Moses received ten commandments written by the Lord in fiery letters, on top of Mount Sinai (see Mountain, page 348). This is again a return to the 'centre' and to unity, an achievement, an eternal recurrence.

path' [...] The road is laborious, fraught with danger, because it is, in fact, a rite of passage from the profane to the sacred; from the ephemeral and illusory to reality and eternity; from death to life; from mankind to divinity. Access to the "centre" equals a consecration, an initiation; an existence that was profane and illusory yesterday is replaced by a new existence that is real, durable and effective.' (Mircea Eliade, *The Myth of the Eternal Return.*)

12 – Twelve

The number 12 was probably regarded as an ideal unit of space and time measurement in ancient times. At any rate, it represents the number of signs in the zodiac and forms the basis of the duodecimal system. Ancient history books suggest that our forebears counted and measured everything in twelves. For example, the Egyptians divided day and night into two 12-hour periods. Depending on whether it was after the summer solstice, when the days became gradually shorter and the nights longer, or after the winter solstice, when the days were longer, they decided that night and day in turn were composed of 12 long hours and 12 short hours – this enabled them to account for variations in the length of the day or night without having to divide them into an unequal number of hours.

Number 12 and the universal zodiac. In Egypt, the astronomer-scribes, keepers of the calendar, divided the year into 360 days with 3 seasons of 120 days. Each of these seasons was itself divided into 4 months of 30 days, each month itself divided into 3 periods of 10 days. This bears obvious similarities to the time measurements of the zodiac, with one difference: we now have 4 seasons instead of 3. That apart, there are 360 degrees in the zodiac, divided into 12 equal parts consisting of 30 degrees, making the 12 signs of the zodiac, each of which is divided into 3 equal parts consisting of 10 degrees or decans.

There are also countless allusions to the number 12 in the Old and New Testaments: the 12 Tribes of Israel, the 12 oracular gems, the 12 Apostles, the 12 gates of the New Jerusalem according to the Apocalypse, etc.

These references to the number 12 probably have a common origin, predating the writing of the Bible. The *Epic of Gilgamesh*, a long mythical Sumerian poem dating from early in the second millennium BC, is composed of 12 tablets, like the 12 signs of the zodiac. And the *Epic of the Creation*, or *Enuma Elish*, an Akkadian cosmogonic narrative from the end of the second millennium BC, was made up of seven tablets, like the seven planets/gods ruling the 12 signs of the zodiac. This latter narrative also contained the foundations of astrology.

There is nothing to say that the Indian and Chinese zodiacs, which followed the Egyptian zodiac, did not draw their inspiration from the same Mesopotamian source. This is why the number 12 crops up so frequently in all these civilizations, despite the fact that their social systems differed so widely.

The 12 links in the chain of dependent origination. The number for the perfect, unchanging cycles of nature and life everywhere was 12. The Buddhist chain of dependent origination also claims 12 main links in the chain of causation that leads to a soul's reincarnation. These links or causes are called *nidanas*, which can be translated literally as 'links, chains, or rings'. Each *nidana* has a name distinguishing it from the others and is represented by a precise symbolic image that illustrates the 12 causal steps or series of events that chain mankind to existence:

1 *Nidana Avidya*, ignorance or blindness, represented by an elderly blind woman, guided by a man. This shows how we are blinded by desire. The guide is actually man's fate, which must be followed.

2 *Nidana Samskara*, impulsive accumulation, represented by a man sitting before a potter's wheel, making a clay vessel. This image symbolizes the cycle of cause and effect as it relates to our existence.

3 *Nidana Vijnana*, conscious- ness, represented by a monkey climbing a tree whose top is too high to be seen or reached. This is an image of the intellect that leads the individual to identify with its ideas and actions, and ends up linked to them.

4 *Nidana Namarupa*, name and form, depicted as a man in a boat with no oars, drifting aimlessly with the current. This image symbolizes the invocation of a life form by means of its name, an act that creates the appearances and illusions that chain man to existence.

5 *Nidana Sadayatana*, the six foundations or six domains, represent- ed by a house with six access points: a door and five windows, symbolizing the sense organs according to the Hindus; the door is the

Symbolic profile of the number 12

Names: dozen and twelfth.
Correlation with the letters-numbers of the cabbala: lamed.

Astrological correlation: Libra.

Geometric symbol: the Egyptian sacred triangle, whose base measured 4, the side 3 and the diagonal 5, resulting in a perimeter of 12.

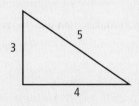

spirit and the five windows are the eyes, the ear, the nose, the tongue and the skin. This represents the consolidation of one's base of operations, the six senses and their respective sense objects.

6 *Nidana Sparsha*, touch or contact, showing a man working the land. This image symbolizes man's perception of the world's physical reality through his senses and the needs, dependencies and constraints that are created by physical imperatives.

7 *Nidana Vedana*, sensation or feeling, represented by an eye pierced with an arrow. This image symbolizes pleasure experienced through the senses, which continually awaken new desires and needs.

8 *Nidana Trishna*, thirst, aspiration or craving, represented by a man drinking a goblet of wine. This image symbolizes the thirst for living, which is never assuaged and which makes man want to possess, acquire and dominate in order to satisfy this need. However, if his craving is transformed into an aspiration, he is then able to free himself from the never-ending cycle of reincarnation.

9 *Nidana Upadana*, clinging, represented by a man gathering fruit in an orchard. This image illustrates man's continuing attachment to life and worldly goods, resulting from the thirst for living which is illustrated in the previous *nidana*.

10 *Nidana Bhava*, being or becoming, represented by a woman whose head and face are covered by 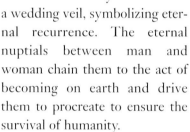 a wedding veil, symbolizing eternal recurrence. The eternal nuptials between man and woman chain them to the act of becoming on earth and drive them to procreate to ensure the survival of humanity.

11 *Nidana Jati*, birth, showing a woman bringing a child into the world. This is the natural continuation of the previous image and reveals that, at this stage, the individual is locked into the cycle of endless rebirth.

12 *Nidana Jara*, old age and death, represented by the body of an old man undergoing the Hindu ritual of cremation. This image symbolizes the final stage of life on earth, at least while the individual

remains blinded by desire and allows himself to be guided by fate, as shown in the first image.

13 – Thirteen

Superstitions die hard, as can be seen by the number 13 – regarded as unlucky by some, lucky by others – particularly when the fifth day of the week, Friday, falls on the thirteenth day of the month. This phenomenon derives from a logical mathematical process and can happen as many as three times in the same year. In 1998, for example, 13 February, 13 March and 13 November were all Fridays. Eleven years earlier, in 1987, 13 February, 13 March and 13 November were also Fridays. There is nothing extraordinary about this phenomenon as it is possible to forecast which Fridays fall on the 13th of the month. On the other hand, it does raise an interesting question.

What is superstition? As is the case for many words that have lost their original meaning, we must first examine what the term 'superstition' meant to our forebears and then how we understand it today. Originally, the Latin word *superstitio* meant 'to stand over, control, surmount, survive'. Superstition was therefore something that allowed man to surmount the trials and tribulations of existence, control his destiny and his instincts, overcome problems and weaknesses, survive, come what may. Nowadays, what survives of superstition is more to do with generally groundless belief in the particular value, influence or power of certain signs, actions or rituals. It is likely, however, that most popular superstitions have their basis in the original meaning of the word, which has become lost and distorted.

Friday the 13th. The story of the Last Supper, when the 12 Apostles shared his final meal with Jesus, is the main reason why Friday the 13th is thought to be unlucky. Historically, the Last Supper is said to have occurred on a Friday and, in view of what happened to Jesus – who was, after all, the 13th guest – after the meal, it is easy to see why this day would have been seen as unlucky by some. However, because Christ's Resurrection testified to his divinity, even though Friday the 13th heralded his temporal death it revealed his immortality and could thus be regarded as lucky. To ensure agreement on this subject, a perpetual hemerological calendar showing which Fridays would fall on the 13th was drawn up (see table on page 399). If the

Hemerological table of lucky
or unlucky Friday the 13ths,
depending on the year

Hemerology is an astrological system for identifying lucky and unlucky days in the coming year. This science, whose first written traces were found in Mesopotamia in the middle of the second millennium BC, is still used in India and persists in China – despite the ravages of the Cultural Revolution – where, formerly, no one would ever do anything before consulting their hemerological almanac.

When the first day of January falls on a Monday, day of the moon, a Wednesday, day of Mercury, or a Sunday, day of the sun, the Friday 13ths in the coming year are regarded as neutral. On the other hand, when 1 January is a Tuesday, day of Mars, or a Saturday, day of Saturn, any Friday 13ths in that year should be regarded as unlucky. Last but not least, when 1 January falls on a Thursday, day of Jupiter, or a Friday, day of Venus, the Friday 13ths in the coming year will always be lucky.

HERMEROLOGICAL TABLE

Friday 13 NEUTRAL	Friday 13 UNLUCKY	Friday 13 LUCKY
Monday 1 January	Tuesday 1 January	Thursday 1 January
Wednesday 1 January	Saturday 1 January	Friday 1 January
Sunday 1 January		

first day of the year fell on a day that was under the influence of a favourable planet, the Friday the 13th(s) occurring throughout that year would be lucky. On the other hand, if 1 January fell on a day that came under the sign of an unlucky planet, the Friday the 13th(s) in the coming year would be unlucky. However, going back in time, the Chaldeans, whose calendar comprised 12 lunar months, added a 13th lunar month every 6 years. During this 13th month, all activities ground to a halt because it was thought to be particularly unlucky – and this was 1500 BC!

Several other numbers

The major symbolic numbers are those from 1 to 10. An important role is also played by the numbers 12 (see page 394) and, to a lesser extent, 13, which is easy to understand when you consider that all the ancient calendar systems were inspired by the cycles of the moon and sun. The other teens – 11, 14, 15, 16, 17, 18 and 19 – are only of interest if they are being interpreted in connection with the Major Arcana of the divinatory Tarot. In that case, it should be remembered that these Arcana were originally symbolic representations of the letters-numbers used in the cabbala.

An examination of the symbolism of numbers would not be complete without mentioning the number that appears in St John's Revelation: the legendary 666 or Number of the Beast: 'And I beheld another beast coming up out of the earth; and he had two horns like a lamb, and he spake as a dragon. […] Let him that hath understanding count the number of the Beast: for it is the number of a man; and his number is Six hundred threescore and six.' (Revelation 13: 11 and 18.) Over the centuries there have been many attempts to solve this enigma, but no satisfactory explanation has yet been found.

O

The letter 'O' obviously has numerous analogies with the zero and the circle, which share the same origin and the same symbolic and mathematical value, since the Arabic word for circle was *zeroh* (see page 100). However, the symbolism of the letter 'O' differs greatly from that of the zero and the circle, which represent a void or an infinite space. The letter 'O', in fact, symbolizes a confinement or a withdrawal into oneself in a bid to elude the factors for external change, transformation and development. Further exploration of what is today known as graphology or the study of handwriting shows, therefore, that the letter 'O' is a symbolic representation of matter or the material world and, equally, of physical death or any ordeal that results in a type of symbolic death and inner transformation.

Thus, when a writer spontaneously forms an open 'O', this suggests he is undergoing an ordeal that will force him to grow or develop. However, if the 'O' is closed, it would seem that he is impervious to the idea of inner or outward change in his life. A closed 'O' suggests a form of rigidity, an arrogant rejection of physical and spiritual reality, a

type of death. This person may be very quick to anger when faced with circumstances or events beyond his control. As we can see, therefore, the letter 'O' represents the act of opening or closing, liberty or confinement, and this is how it should be interpreted when it plays an important role in a dream.

We have also noticed that dreamers who pay particular attention to the letter 'O' when writing or transcribing their dreams are often on the point of losing their temper, or are revealing feelings of suppressed anger that are likely to erupt at any minute.

Oak

Imagine a divine and sacred tree, the symbol of strength and wisdom, planted in the centre of the world and linking heaven and earth. The ancient Greeks made the oak the tutelary tree of Zeus, and the first sanctuary dedicated to the chief god of Olympus was in fact an oak forest – Dodona in Epirus, in the land of the Molossi – where people went to consult the oracles of Zeus and Aphrodite. It was therefore believed to be the voice of Zeus himself who answered through the intermediary of the leaves of the sacred oaks as they rustled in the wind. According to Greek mythology, the club of Hercules was made of oak.

The Celts also worshipped the oak. Their priests or druids – whose name derives from the Celtic *druvids*, meaning 'very wise', and who were known as the men 'knowing (or finding) the oak tree'– gathered mistletoe, the so-called 'flower of the oak', at the New Year. In this context, the oak symbolized new life, regeneration and the immortality of the soul. The local druid would set out in search of mistletoe, the 'flower of the oak', on the sixth day after the new moon. If he returned empty-handed, it was a bad omen for the Celtic or Gaulish village.

Finally, the acorn, the fruit of the oak, was often regarded as the symbol of fertility and

prosperity since our ancestors knew that the new tree produced by the seed contained in this tiny fruit would live for several hundred years.

Oil

'Why should ye be stricken any more?
ye will revolt more and more':

exclaimed Isaiah, the visionary prophet, when addressing the people of Israel,

'the whole head is sick,
and the whole heart faint.
From the sole of the foot even
unto the head
there is no soundness in it;
but wounds, and bruises, and
putrefying sores:
they have not been closed, neither
bound up,
neither mollified with ointment.'
(Isaiah, 1: 5–6).

In ancient Egypt and the Middle East, oil came mainly from the fruit of the olive tree and was used for a variety of purposes – fuelling the lamps that lit the houses at night, burning on altars and in temples, preparing food, anointing the body and steeping plants for herbal cures. As a result, oil has always been a symbol of purity, gentleness, clarity and prosperity, even though modern oils lack the original purity of those used by our ancestors. It should also be remembered that, according to ancient traditions, princes and kings were often anointed with oil as a sign of their sovereignty and/or their divine power.

A dream that you are bathing in oil, being given or touching oil, is often a sign of imminent happiness.

Olive tree

The fruit of this beautiful, prolific tree is an emblem of fertility, longevity and purification, while the olive branch is a symbol of peace and prosperity. In ancient Greece, the olive tree was dedicated to Athena, the war goddess, who was the daughter of Zeus and Metis. She was armed with a spear and wore a helmet, an aegis – a goatskin cloak or breastplate that enabled her to become invisible at will – and a shield with the head of the Gorgon Medusa in the centre that caused all who saw it to freeze with terror. However, despite her often fearsome, warlike appearance, the goddess Athena was also the protectress of the cities of Greece.

The olive tree was also dedicated to Apollo. Priests burned lamps filled with olive oil in the temples consecrated to this solar god. Greek myth also relates that Hercules' club was made of olive wood. Finally, in the Bible, the olive tree is regarded as the king of trees (Judges 9: 8), as a divine food and as a sacred salve (Deuteronomy 8: 8 and Ezekiel 16: 9).

One

See Numbers, page 362

Original sin

See Paradise, page 410

Oriole

The fluting call of this lively, very nervous little yellow bird, no bigger than a blackbird, with

brown wings and red eyes, can be heard in old trees in gardens and parks and on the shores of lakes and rivers. The golden oriole (*Oriolus oriolus*), which has colonized Europe, Russia and the East, returns in early May from equatorial Africa after migrating towards the end of August. It builds an intricately constructed nest out of leaves, grass and fragments of tree bark, lining the inside with wool and feathers. The female lays four or five eggs over a period of two weeks in late May/early June. The fledgelings remain with their parents until the next migration, which is unusual for birds. The oriole mainly feeds on insects, but it is very fond of red fruit.

Its beautiful song frequently led people to regard the oriole as a symbol of joy and carefree happiness. The Chinese often confused the song of the swallow and that of the oriole, both considered harbingers of joy, happiness and a happy marriage. The fact that the oriole's fledgelings do not leave the parental nest before they fly off to warmer climes for the winter also meant that our forebears saw this bird as a symbol of a close-knit family and a happy home life.

Ostrich

The ostrich (*Struthio camelus*) is a strange, flightless bird that can run extremely fast on its equally strange two-toed feet. In addition, it also has a long, featherless neck and head. Its name is derived from the Greek *strouthion*, itself a diminutive of *strouthos*, a term used to refer to all types of birds in conjunction with an accompanying adjective.

In neolithic Africa and the Near East (9000–6000 BC), the very tough shells of ostrich eggs were used as receptacles as well as for making beads and other jewellery. In ancient Egypt, the ostrich feather was one of the attributes of the goddess Maat, the symbol of cosmic harmony, universal order, the continuity of all life, law and truth. Maat was regarded as the 'daughter of Re' (the sun-god) and wore an ostrich feather in her head-dress. In the Hall of Judgement, the heart of the deceased was placed on the scales of justice and weighed against the feather of Maat (the symbol of truth) during the 'Weighing of the Heart' ceremony.

The ostrich's tendency to bury its head in the ground in the event of danger has given rise to the popular expression 'to bury your head in the sand', meaning to refuse to see problems or confront difficulties. The French expression 'avoir un estomac d'autruche' ('to have a cast-iron stomach') is based on the bird's remarkable capacity to eat anything that comes its way.

Otter

This small mammal, under 1m (3ft) long, lives in swamps, lakes and rivers and belongs to the same species as the badger and the mink. Like the latter, the otter has been so widely hunted for its water-resistant fur that it has almost disappeared. Only the sea otter has survived in California and Alaska, since a law was passed to ban hunting. An inoffensive and useful creature, the otter has webbed feet with five claws and can live under water and dive down as far as 20m (167ft) for up to six minutes at a time, by closing its nostrils and ears. The Irish, who called it the water-hound, attached the same symbolism to it as man's loyal companion, the dog (see *Dog*, page 150).

However, the otter's agility in its aquatic habitat and its ability to swim under water meant that it was regarded as a magical, lunar animal, associated with the cycle of rebirth and fertility. It appears and disappears in the water as the moon does in the sky. When the otter appears in a dream, its habitual game of hide-and-seek and its characteristic grace as it swims through the clear waters of a river are often a sign that the dreamer is about to produce something new or to experience or witness a birth. It can also mean that a new factor is about to surface suddenly from the unconscious mind, leading to a new phase in the dreamer's life. The appearance of an otter is always a good omen.

Owl

Because it hunts by night and hides away during the day, the owl became associated with darkness, night, sadness, solitude and death. In China, however, it is regarded as a terrifying and sacred bird, a symbol of lightning and the emblem of blacksmiths, dedicated to the winter and summer solstices, the rebirth and triumph of light. In ancient times, this bird of the night was also associated with the moon. In the Aztec and Inca cultures it symbolized the 'house of the night', while the eagle represented the 'house of the day'. When the owl is depicted as a symbol of divination or clairvoyance, the distinction is made between the barn owl – which watches over the legacy of the past and therefore the ancestral knowledge and wisdom that it imparts to those concerned – and the tawny owl in its role as guardian of the night, protecting mortals against demons or warning them if these demons appear or threaten them in any way.

Barn owl. The barn owl (*Tyto alba*) is a nocturnal bird of prey that feeds mainly on small

rodents such as mice and shrews. With its light-brown and white plumage, long legs and characteristic heart-shaped face, it is probably the best known of the genus *Tyto* (family *Tytonidae*). Its face, along with the absence of ear tufts, has earned it the nickname 'monkey-faced owl'.

The barn owl is usually a solitary bird, nesting in hollow trees, towers, old barns, lofts and ruins. The adults are about 30–40cm (12–16in) long and the female lays her eggs – two clutches of between four and six eggs each per year – on the ground. Unfortunately, the barn owl is becoming increasingly rare because its habitat and nesting places, especially towers and corn lofts, are gradually disappearing.

Eagle owl. The eagle owl (*Bubo bubo*) inhabits the countries of continental Europe, Asia and northern Africa, and is occasionally sighted in Great Britain. It is in fact a horned owl, any owl of the genus *Bubo* (family *Strigidae*) that has horn-like tufts of feathers. The eagle owl is a very impressive bird that can reach up to 1.7m (5½ft) in length. It is virtually impossible to see during the day when it hides away in trees or crevices in rocks. At nightfall you can often hear its characteristic hooting which becomes almost obsessive during the mating season, in February and March, when the female lays

three to four eggs in a nest usually built in the hollow of a tree. This owl is a formidable nocturnal hunter, swooping down on its prey of small rodents and other birds that it sometimes even attacks in their nests. It is also extremely fond of hares, partridges and pheasants. The bird's tawny plumage and round, luminous orange eyes add to its striking appearance.

Tawny owl. The tawny owl (*Strix aluco*) is one of the 11 species of wood owl – genus *Strix*, family *Strigidae* – found in the woodlands and forests of the Americas, Asia and Europe. The distinctive 'song' of the tawny owl – a plaintive and melodious hooting – is particularly insistent in February, during the mating season. The female lays between two and six eggs and sits on them for about a month, in March or April. She continues to stay with her chicks for another ten days, to protect them, while the male brings back the spoils from his hunting – usually a selection of small mammals and birds, frogs and insects. You may catch a glimpse of this sedentary bird – it is a year-round resident – at dusk, mainly in forests or on the edge of woodland near small towns and villages. In the dead of night, you may hear its characteristic hooting, but you will only see it when there is a full moon, which is ideal for hunting.

In medieval Europe, the tawny owl was believed to have evil powers and was associated by the Church with death, evil and witchcraft. This may have been because, much earlier in history, it was the symbol of clairvoyance and divinatory powers. It is easy to understand why people attributed such qualities to a bird of prey that hunted by night and concealed itself during the day, as if afraid of the light and the sun, and why some even saw it as an incarnation of the evil eye. But by then it had been forgotten that the owl was the bird of Athena, the sister of Apollo and the Greek goddess of war, but also and above all, the goddess of wisdom, fertility and the arts. Like Athena, the tawny owl is the embodiment of inspiration and initiation.

Paradise, Adam and Eve, Original sin

Although myths about paradise, the primordial androgyne and the first man and woman are universal, the concept of original sin is one of a kind. Our task here is to attempt to understand the meaning of certain Bible stories dispassionately, without any religious bias. It is not a question of whether it is right or wrong to believe in such and such a Bible story, but of shedding new light on these stories, based on the scientific discoveries made by contemporary archaeologists and historians. We will also take account of myths or legends that bear close similarities to this story and, with regard to the Bible, the sometimes complex information revealed by the secret code of the cabbala, which is as much the product of mathematics and logic as of inspiration and speculation. One point worth noting is the fact that the great Bible stories often contain a number of symbols, which, taken together, form a message. This message may be very instructive, since it was transmitted by people who experienced events that affected them so profoundly that they felt the need to hand them down to us. In fact, these accounts were written at a time when the art of writing was still in its infancy and the privilege of a chosen few. As a result, they are not only anonymous because all traces of their authors have disappeared over time, but also because of the sacred, taboo nature of writing.

Generally, if we take one of these Bible stories literally, it seems full of improbabilities. On the other hand, if we approach it in a poetic, mythical or religious way, depending on our convictions and beliefs, it reads very differently. With regard to the story of Adam and Eve, we will merely highlight several of the recurring, universal symbols found within it: paradise, the first man, the first woman and sin.

Paradise. Ancient civilizations often regarded paradise as the finest representation of the afterworld, frequently symbolized by a beautiful garden. This garden, situated at the centre of the cosmos, was mankind's supreme goal. However, in the Bible stories, it exists at the beginning of time, so it can be compared to the myth of an original golden age, which man once knew and which he will one day recapture. Eden, this garden of delights and paradise lost whose entrance remains to be rediscovered, can be compared to the symbols of the labyrinth (see page 306) and the Tibetan mandala (see page 322). However, its description by the first authors of the Bible was inspired by an earlier, Sumerian text, later reproduced by the Babylonian Semites, that referred to a 'land of the living' situated south-west of Persia and irrigated by four rivers. In Genesis 2: 10–14, it is written: 'And a river went out of Eden to water the garden; and from thence it was parted, and became into four heads. The name of the first is Pison [...]. And the name of the second river is Gihon [...]. And the name of the third river is Hiddekel [...]. And the fourth river is the Euphrates.' This clearly shows that the garden of Eden had a specific geographical location. It should also be noted that the cabbalists regarded the *Gan-Aeden* from the story of the creation as a place that Adam had to leave to avoid running the risk of stagnating. They viewed it as an excessively comfortable refuge, one that encouraged apathetic and immutable physiological and psychological conditions in themselves that prevented mankind from evolving or exercising will-power, free will and individual consciousness.

Adam and Eve. They form an apparently inseparable primordial couple. Historically, their coupling, regarded as a sin of the flesh, is mentioned for the first time in texts by the Jewish theologian Philo of Alexandria, who lived in the 1st century AD. However, because the numerous texts of the Bible were written at different times, there are two versions of the creation of Adam and Eve. The earlier one is called

Yahwist, because in it God is called Jehovah or Yahweh; the second, later version is called Elohist, because God is referred to as Elohim. In this second version, Adam and Eve are represented as the two halves of an androgynous being who has been divided. This is the version preferred by the cabbalists, who named the first man Adam, fruit of *adamah*, the earth. He was both man and woman and this brings us back to paradise lost, in the sense that, according to the cabbalists, this original man is also the person we must become.

Original sin. Mesopotamian physicians knew that certain illnesses could be transmitted by contact. They formulated numerous treatments, prepared remedies and commonly performed exorcisms. In fact, they thought that the bearer of an illness, besides being contagious, was the victim of an evil spell for which, in some way, he was responsible. He had therefore committed a sin and had broken the rules and laws governing their civilization. As a result, he not only had to be healed, but also absolved of this sin, particularly as he may well have committed it inadvertently or despite himself. This was the context within which the first Bible stories were written.

However, in the Old Testament this notion of unwitting transgression was completely altered. It could be prevented, simply by drawing up a list of laws. Any man or woman who kept these laws would not know evil, illness, or suffering. Unfortunately, however, it was not as simple as that because men and women with pure hearts and intentions still suffered without any obvious cause. There therefore had to be an initial reason, an original sin, committed by Eve, according to the Yahwist tradition, or by the androgynous Adam, according to the Elohist tradition and the cabbalists, to account for the torment and suffering of innocent victims. This is how the concept of original sin came about.

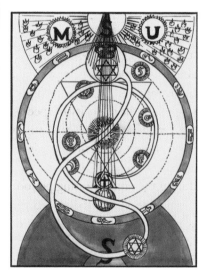

From **Alchimie et Mystique (Alchemy and Mysticism)**, *Taschen, 1997.*

Parrot

There are more than three hundred species of parrot, the majority of which live in Australia, central and eastern Africa, Egypt, the Middle East, India and southeast China. The budgerigar and the cockatoo are two well-known representatives of this perching bird, whose prehensile feet have two toes directed backwards, which enables them to maintain a strong grip on branches. With their thick, hooked bill, they can slice into fruit and tear off the buds they love, but they also feed on insects and their larvae. Like the dog, elephant or crow, the parrot appears to be able to respond to human language, and it is able to repeat words, being able to imitate the human voice by means of its thick, fleshy tongue. In the majority of species, the female lays from two to six eggs that she incubates alone, although parrots live as a pair during the entire nesting period.

The parrot, an exotic island bird, probably derives its name from the dialect French *Perrot*, a diminutive of the name *Pierre*, just as the magpie derived its name from *Magot*, the Middle English pet form of the given name Marguerite or Margaret, itself derived from the Latin *margarita*, meaning 'pearl', perhaps because the magpie is known to be attracted to anything white and sparkling. It is not known, however, why the parrot should have been named after the above-mentioned diminutive, although there are some who see a connection with the Old French *perore*, from the Latin *perorare*, which means 'to discuss, explain, speak for', or from *perorele*, which was Old French for a frivolous conversation.

Partridge

The most common species is the grey partridge (*Perdix perdix*), found throughout almost all of Europe, ranging as far as central Asia. It lives in non-migrant groups in the steppes, prairies and farmland to which it has adapted. Around the end of February, the birds mate and leave their group so that the female can lay 10 to 20 eggs, which she will incubate with the male over a period of nearly four weeks, between April and June. The mating pair of partridges is fairly inseparable. As they feed mainly on seeds, weeds and pests, they are very useful birds and their tender, gamy flesh is much appreciated.

In India or Iran, the partridge symbolized grace, charm and feminine beauty, while in China it symbolized erotic, lascivious and carnal love. In fact, this bird, which only leaves its family group to live as a pair, was seen by our forebears as a creature with very loose morals, all the more so because the male's halting courtship display in the mating season, which lasts over three months, leaves very little to the imagination. This is why the partridge is associated with the initiatory, erotic rites performed in spring.

Peacock

The best known of the species is the blue peacock (*Pavo cristatus*), with its vibrant blue train of tail feathers, studded with orange and black eyespots, that can grow as long as 2m (6ft). During the courtship display, the male ele-

vates and spreads his tail, uttering his characteristic raucous call. He will also fan his tail in the presence of another male. Native to India and Sri Lanka, the peacock was brought to the West by Alexander the Great and later taken to America. Initially popular as a domesticated ornamental bird, it was later appreciated as a tasty dish.

According to a Greek myth, Argus, whose name means 'bright one', was a prince of the kingdom of Argos, now in the north-eastern Peloponnese, in Greece. He had a hundred eyes scattered all over his body, which enabled him to see everything – his surname was Panoptes ('the all-seeing'). Hera, sister-wife of Zeus, charged Argus to keep watch over Io, a young girl from Argos whom Zeus loved and whom he had transformed into a cow to protect her from Hera's jealousy. However, on Zeus' orders, Hermes lulled Argus to sleep by playing his flute, then killed him.

To immortalize her faithful servant, Hera transferred the hundred eyes on Argus's body to the tail of the blue peacock. Since then, every time the peacock fans his tail, Argus is reborn and his hundred eyes open once more on the world.

Pearl

One of the characteristic features of the pearl, perhaps even the most prominent one, is its rarity. Something exceptional or someone dear to us is often called a 'pearl', which has become a bit of a cliché. It is nevertheless a matter of fact that pearls are very rare. They are produced by oysters, known as pearl oysters, attempting to reject a foreign object, like a grain of sand, a parasite or a fragment of shell, that has worked its way between the two valves of the shell of this mollusc or invertebrate animal, fossils of which have been found dating back to the Cambrian period. After several years, the intruder is covered by several concentric layers of a secretion produced by the oyster and is now a pearl. It is worth noting here that the oyster is traditionally associated with stupidity and spinelessness, while the pearl is associated with rarity and purity. This may seem paradoxical – the pearl can hardly be regarded as a pure product, given its method of formation – but people do tend to go by appearances.

Because of their appearance, shape and pearly whiteness, our forebears associated pearls with the moon; because they were fished from the bottom of the sea, they were also linked to principles associated with the mysteries and origins of life and to exclusively feminine qualities. In India, as well as in Europe in the Middle Ages, powdered pearl was thought to be a powerful aphrodisiac.

A dream of a pearl often reveals that we have rejected something essential that is capable of regenerating and revitalizing us and that must be retrieved from the depths of our psyche. However, it may also foreshadow an imminent discovery or an important realization. Last but not least, this type of dream can have extremely spiritual connotations. The pearl becomes a dreamlike representation of our soul, our most precious possession.

Pelican

The white pelican (*Pelecanus onocrotalus*) is a nomadic, migratory bird that lives in Asia Minor, Egypt, south-west Asia and India during the autumn and winter. In the spring and summer, though, it is found throughout the Danube delta. It tends to live near large lakes, lagoons or river deltas, because it feeds on the fish it attracts by beating the surface of the water with its wings, then scooping them up in its throat pouch. It eats around 3kg (6lb) of fish a day. The female lays two eggs in the spring, which she incubates with the male for around 33 days. Pelicans are always majestic and impressive in flight and they travel together in regular formations.

Why did the pelican become a symbol of charity, Christ and the Resurrection, particularly in heraldic bestiaries, the first of which made their appearance in Europe around the 12th century? Probably because the pelican is reputed to sacrifice itself to feed its young, just as Jesus sacrificed himself to save mankind, according to the Christians. According to medieval bestiaries, the pelican is fond of its brood but when the young grow they provoke the male's anger and he kills them. Three days later, the mother returns to the nest, covers the dead birds with her body and pours her blood over them, which revives them and they then feed on her blood. In the Middle Ages, the mythical, legendary phoenix (see page 417) was often depicted as a pelican.

Pelvis

See Thighs, pelvis, lower back and genitalia, page 490

Pentagram

See Five, page 374

Pheasant

The pheasant, which originated in Asia, is a member of the family *Phasianidae* (order *Galliformes*). There are many different species of pheasant, but the one found widely in Europe – the common pheasant (*Phasianus colchicus*) – was introduced by the Romans. It has a long tail, long body feathers, a dark green head and white

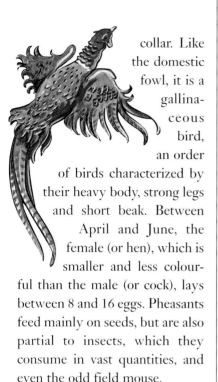

collar. Like the domestic fowl, it is a gallinaceous bird, an order of birds characterized by their heavy body, strong legs and short beak. Between April and June, the female (or hen), which is smaller and less colourful than the male (or cock), lays between 8 and 16 eggs. Pheasants feed mainly on seeds, but are also partial to insects, which they consume in vast quantities, and even the odd field mouse.

The term 'pheasant' derives from the Old French *fesan*, from the Latin *phasianus* and the Greek *phasianos ornis*, i.e. the 'Phasian bird', named after the river Phasis in Colchis which, according to Greek mythology, was the land where Jason and the Argonauts went in search of the Golden Fleece. However, the pheasant also plays a key role in the mythology of Asia, especially in China where its spectacular mating displays have made it the symbol of the cosmic awakening of the yang (or male principle) that occurs in spring, the luminous and solar forces announcing the advent of their supremacy. According to the Chinese, at the onset of winter, the yang pheasant is transformed into the yin serpent, and in this way punctuates the seasons of the earth and the life of the universe. It was to reflect this universal principle that the architects of the ancient pagodas built the roofs of Taoist and Buddhist temples in the form of pheasant's wings.

Phoenix

This legendary bird sprang from the fertile imagination of the ancients. The phoenix was originally an Egyptian deity who wore the crown of Osiris and represented this great Egyptian god, but was also associated with Re, the sun, the supreme god. According to various myths, Osiris and Re were both immortal and eternal. The phoenix was also a long-lived bird that rose again from its ashes after it had died, like Osiris after his initiatory journey through the afterworld, and in the same way that Re, the sun, reappeared every morning in his sacred barque. Writing in the 5th century BC, Herodotus described the phoenix as follows: 'Another sacred bird is the phoenix; I have not seen a phoenix myself, except in paintings, for it is very rare and visits the country [Egypt] (so they say at Heliopolis) only at intervals of 500 years, on the occasion of the death of the parent-bird. To judge by the paintings, its plumage is partly golden, partly red, and in shape and size it is exactly like an eagle.' (Herodotus, *The Histories*, translated by Aubrey de Sélincourt, Penguin Classics, 1954.)

Pigeon

The rock dove, *Columba livia*, the common ancestor of most domestic pigeons, has dark grey plumage and light grey wings with black wing bars. It occurs mainly in Europe and North Africa and Asia.

The stock dove, *Columba oenas*, on the other hand, has grey-blue plumage and is the pigeon found everywhere in Europe. This non-migrant bird lives mainly in forested areas and likes to nest in holes in trees.

The rock dove, an increasingly common sight on the European continent over the years, has adapted to urban life in the big cities of Europe, where it nests for long months in walls, on top of bell-towers and on the roofs of buildings. Mating pairs of stock doves and rock doves incubate the three or four clutches of two small eggs laid by the female between April and July for about two weeks, feeding mainly on seeds.

Because the pigeon is a gentle, monogamous bird that mates for life, it is regarded as a living symbol of gentleness and lasting love. This can also be seen by the expression 'pigeon pair', referring to boy and girl twins. It was once supposed that the two eggs laid by the pigeon produced a male and a female and that these twin birds lived together in love for the rest of their lives. Pigeons are also very easily caught by snares and, in the 16th century, 'pigeon' became the slang term for a dupe or very gullible person. The expression 'stool pigeon', referring to an informer or decoy, alludes to the former practice of tying or nailing a pigeon to a stool to lure other pigeons that were then shot by the waiting hunters.

Pine tree

In the first century AD, Pliny the Elder wrote the following lines about the pine tree: '...the most admirable is the stone pine: it bears cones that are ripening cones, others that will reach maturity the following year and others the third. There is no tree more eager to give unstintingly of itself: in the very month one harvests a pine cone, another ripens; the cones are distributed in such a way that not a month goes by without more ripening.' (Pliny the Elder, *Natural History.*) This shows how the Greeks came to regard the pine-cone as a symbol of fertility, reproduction, the eternal rebirth of life and continual renaissance.

In Greece, the pine tree was dedicated to Attis. In one version of this hero's complicated myth, he was loved by his own father, a hermaphrodite, who struck him down with a frenzied delirium. Under its influence, Attis castrated himself and died.

However, pine trees grew over his tomb and the continual growth of the pine-cones symbolized his everlasting life. In China, the pine tree is also regarded as a means of achieving eternal life,

and Taoist monks chew pine seeds, pine needles and pine resin while saying prayers, in the hope of becoming immortal.

Pisces
(sign of)

See Zodiac, page 583

Plough

Did the plough and chariot appear in Mesopotamia at about the same time, in the third millennium BC, as historians and archaeologists would have us believe? It is quite probable, since they are not only similar in appearance but are both related to death, as the chariot appears to have been used for funerary purposes before it was used for war and the plough is associated with the earth, the kingdom of the dead.

Be that as it may, the forerunner of the plough was the hoe, which consisted of a long wooden handle and a sharp metal blade. Like the plough, it was used for tilling the earth and marking out furrows. It appears that for a long time the hoe was the most widely used agricultural tool in Europe, where the plough did not appear until *c.* 1000 BC. In symbolic terms, both the hoe and plough are associated with fertility, since the use of the blade or ploughshare to penetrate and open the earth in order to plant seeds is symbolic of fertilization and the sexual act.

It is therefore relatively easy to interpret a dream in which a plough appears or plays a prominent role. But you should not assume that it automatically predicts the conception and birth of a child. The plough can equally well predict a circumstance, event or situation that is in the embryonic stage, beginning to take root or be created. Furthermore, it should be remembered that, as the tool used for turning the earth, the plough can also indicate that everything within us, our inner earth, needs to be turned over, so that what is underneath is brought to the surface and vice versa. This idea of 'turning over' and inversion should be borne in mind when interpreting a dream involving a plough.

Finally, the symbolic and mythical language of dreams is not without its humour and we should also take account of expressions such as the French 'mettre la charrue avant les bœufs' ('putting the plough before the oxen'), expressed in English as 'putting the cart before the horse'. For the French, at least, seeing a plough in a dream can simply mean that the dreamer is being too impulsive, acting too hastily and that he or she should wait for the right moment. In such circumstances, it is possible that English-speakers dream about a cart. This serves to reinforce the fact that, while some symbols and legends may be universal, many are culture-specific.

Pluto

Mesopotamian myths about Pluto. Pluto did not exist in either Sumer or Akkad. Therefore, when the Chaldean and Babylonian concept of the passage of the soul – the soul's journey through the seven spheres, just before taking physical form on earth, and in the opposite direction, just after physical death – made its appearance around the 7th century BC, it only referred to the seven primordial planets/gods. There was no reference to planets or astrological characteristics paving the way for modern astrological interpretations of Uranus, Neptune and Pluto. However, the principle of a primordial world of chaos from which all physical life came and to which it returned after death, as well as the cycle of life and death that met in a place that was both sacred and cursed, can be found not only in Mesopotamia, but also in every cosmogony in the world. These beliefs gave birth to the myth of Pluto and led to the definition of the key characteristics of this planet, which is associated with death as much as with life, according to a principle of perpetual regeneration. Nowadays, life and death are such opposites, so far apart from each other, that we find it hard to see death as anything other than an end – the end of everything we have known during our life. However, even though our forebears, like us, were distressed by death, and sometimes even obsessed by it, they did not set it apart from life. And the great principle of regeneration that often occurs in death or that results from it – and without which life, in nature, would not be able to continue or endure – was an integral part of their beliefs. This comes over clearly, for example, in a Sumerian poem that relates how Ishtar-Inanna (see *Venus*, page 274) dared to descend into hell, situated in the underworld, whose uncontested god was Enki/Ea. She was received there by Ereshkigal, guardian and ruler of hell, who

stripped her of all her talismans and powers, so that she would remain there, eternally dead. However, owing to the intervention of Enki/Ea, she came back to life and emerged triumphant and regenerated from the kingdom of the dead. For the rest of her life, however, she was condemned to live six months on earth and six months in hell. Greek mythologists drew their inspiration from this poem – which they knew, but which was only rediscovered by archaeologists and historians in the early 20th century – when devising the myth of Persephone, another representation of Venus and one which shares many of the characteristics of the sign of Libra. On the other hand, it is interesting to note that, according to this Sumerian poem, if the

Osiris, the Egyptian god of the dead.

god of the underworld was Enki/Ea, god of the 'fertilizing waters' which enrich the earth, hell, over which he also reigned, was guarded by a woman, Ereshkigal, whose husband was none other than Nergal or Mars.

Egyptian myths about Pluto. The god of the dead, the god who dies but whose soul lives for eternity after triumphing over numerous ordeals on the journey between the world of the living and that of eternal life, was Osiris, brother-husband of Isis. In many respects, Osiris resembles the Mesopotamian god Enki/Ea, because he was also a bringer of civilization and a god of vegetation, as plants are born, then die and are reborn every year. Osiris is often accompanied by Anubis (Inpw or Anepu in Egyptian), the protector of necropolises, guardian of the abode or land of the Dead, and inventor of mummification. He was depicted either as a recumbent dog or jackal, or a jackal-headed man with a square muzzle and long pricked ears.

Greek myths about Pluto. Anubis inevitably brings to mind Cerberus, the 'hellhound', who guarded the entrance to the land of the dead and would not let the living through. Cerberus means 'demon of the pit' and, according to vari-

ous myths, it was a giant dog with three heads, a terrifying serpent's tail, and a host of serpents' heads all over its back. However, it was Hades, or 'the unseen', who reigned over the kingdom of the dead, according to the Greeks. Hades was the son of Cronus and Rhea, and therefore the brother of Zeus/Jupiter and Poseidon/Neptune, among others. After Zeus had murdered their father, these three gods shared rulership of the world: Zeus took the kingdom of heaven, Poseidon the sea and Hades was given hell or the underworld. Like Ereshkigal, the Sumerian ruler of hell, Hades was a pitiless god. He strove to ensure that no one ever left the underworld once they had entered and was assisted in this task by numerous demons or evil spirits. One of them, Charon, was regarded as the ferryman of the souls of the deceased, taking them in his boat across the river that divided the land of the living from the kingdom of the dead.

Represented as a winged demon with shaggy hair intertwined with snakes, he was to become the 'death demon' of the Etruscans several centuries later. To pay for their crossing, the deceased had to give Charon an offering. For this reason, it was the custom in ancient Greece to place a coin in the mouth of corpses before burial to pay for their passage.

Poplar tree

The poplar has been a funerary tree since the most ancient times: headdresses made with poplar leaves have been found in Mesopotamian royal tombs dating from the end of the fourth millennium BC. The tree was also associated with the kingdom of the dead in Greece. Thus, having performed his 12th and final Labour, which involved descending into the infernal regions to capture Cerberus (see page 254), Hercules made himself a poplar wreath from the tree planted by Hades or Pluto in the Elysian Fields. This may be why, five thousand years ago, persons of royal blood were buried wearing a wreath woven of poplar branches. More recently, in the Middle Ages, this tree was associated with memory, nostalgia, regret and remorse, guilty feelings, sacrifice and expiation. The poplar can live to the ripe old age of three hundred years.

Puppets

Initially, puppets were statuettes with no moving parts that represented deities, goddesses or gods and were displayed during processions for various religious and sacred festivals. Over time, more sophisticated images were developed, which could speak, move and seem alive. They became mythical and symbolical

embodiments of human emotions – suffering, joy, happiness – or noble and heroic deeds or acts of petty-mindedness. They were worked by hand or by strings but, like the figure of Pinocchio – the wooden marionette who was eventually transformed into a little boy with his own body and soul – puppets could be seen as representations of mankind created by the gods out of clay.

In a dream, you should bear in mind the appearance of a shadow theatre and the interplay of illusions that often characterizes human relationships. The manipulation of puppets represents the way people tend to be influenced by others, lacking personal conviction and individuality. These images indicate that the dreamer needs to be aware of something important.

Quail

The quail, a member of the family *Phasianidae*, is similar to a partridge but usually smaller and less robust. It has a small, rounded body with brownish or greyish-beige feathers and some-times an attractive white 'collar' edged with black. Quails tend to be found among tall grasses and especially in cornfields where they are well camouflaged. They are highly prized game birds whose flesh is considered a deli-cacy. It is a little-known fact that these migratory birds can be easily tamed. The word 'quail' is derived from the medieval Latin *quaccula* and Old French *quaille* (modern French *caille*), in turn thought to derive from the Old German *kraka* ('crow') and its diminutive, *kwakla*.

In certain popular expres-sions, the quail is associated with comfort, well-being and affection. The French expression 'chaud comme une caille' means 'snug as a bug in a rug', while 'rond comme une caille' has a direct English equivalent in 'plump as a partridge'. The French *caille* is also used as a term of endearment ('pet' or 'honey'), a meaning that appears to have been combined with the game-bird image in the Everly Brothers' song 'Bird Dog' (1958) where the bird-dog in question is exhorted to 'stay away from my quail'.

In Greek mythology, the quail is associated with the birth-place of Apollo who, according to legend, was born on the island of Ortygia, the 'island of quails' (from the Greek *ortyx*, 'quail'). His mother Leto, who had been visited by Zeus, fled to the island to escape the jealous fury of Zeus' wife Hera. There she gave birth to Apollo and Artemis, and Apollo honoured the island by making it the centre of the Greek world and renaming it Delos ('illustrious').

Rain

Rain was regarded by many of our forebears as a blessing or gift from the gods. Who has not heaved a sigh of relief when the heavens open after a period of drought or when a storm breaks, lightening the heavy atmosphere that precedes it? However, rain

was also seen as an instrument of divine punishment, particularly the rain that caused the legendary flood described in the Bible (see *Flood*, page 188). Rain fertilizes; it is like seed falling from heaven. It also floods, submerging everything, making the waters of the rivers, lakes and seas rise until they swallow up entire tracts of land, drowning all forms of life.

Rain can therefore be an instrument of life or death. It can relieve, comfort or pose a threat, a mortal danger. How should we decipher the message delivered by a dream of rain? By understanding that this message comes from heaven, in other words, from the most highly developed part of our consciousness, and that we are therefore being bathed in spiritual comfort, whose beneficial action eases or fertilizes the physical, material world in which we live.

Rainbow

In legend and mythology, the rainbow is often seen as a bridge between heaven and earth. According to the biblical account of the great flood and Noah's Ark, it is also the symbol of an alliance or covenant. 'And God said, This is the token of the covenant which I make between me and you and every living creature that is with you, for perpetual generations: I do set my bow in the cloud, and it shall be a token of a covenant between me and the earth.' (Genesis 9: 12–13). Here, the 'bow in the cloud' (a literal translation), symbolized by the rainbow, represents the bridge rebuilt between 'God and every living creature of all flesh that is upon the earth' (Genesis 9: 16) after the fall that preceded the great flood.

The idea of a bridge or path linking heaven and earth, and used by the gods to visit the world of mortals, is a universal symbol. Some cultures believed it was an immortal who had been transformed into a celestial serpent, others saw it as a means of carrying mortals off to heaven. However, it was more often perceived as a sign of the gods' leniency and benevolence towards mankind.

The most beautiful mythological embodiment of the

rainbow is undoubtedly the Greek goddess Iris, the messenger of Zeus and Hera and the harbinger of good news, who came down to earth from heaven along the path of the rainbow. She was depicted wearing a dress of dewdrops in the sparkling colours of the rainbow, which is why her name was given to the iris of the eye. The seven colours of the rainbow were also associated with the seven 'heavens' or rungs of the cosmic ladder that initiates had to climb, one by one, to reach the eighth heaven of the revelation and liberation of the soul.

A dream about a rainbow can be interpreted in one of two ways. On the one hand, it can mean that you can look forward to a happy event, a promising future or great joy. On the other, it can symbolize difficult and testing times ahead – especially in the financial or material sphere – followed by a beneficial renewal, since a rainbow never predicts a disastrous situation or occurrence. It can also be the sign of an alliance or reconciliation if you are at variance with certain people when you have the dream. But most often, dreaming of a rainbow puts you in touch with yourself and plunges you into the very heart of your finest vital and spiritual energies. In this respect, it is a symbol of revelation, regeneration and personal accomplishment.

Raven

The raven is a passerine bird, i.e. it belongs to the *Passeriformes*, an order of birds – including larks, finches, thrushes and sparrows – characterized by the perching habit. The term is in fact derived from the Latin *passer* ('sparrow'). Like the sparrow (see page 464), the raven has four-toed feet – three pointing forwards and one backwards – enabling it to perch easily on branches, and a very short neck. However, the similarities stop there since, with a wingspan of up to 1 m (over 3 ft), the raven is much larger than the sparrow and has shiny black plumage.

The raven is also renowned for its remarkable intelligence and is said to be able to understand certain words, in the same way that the parrot, the dog and the elephant are supposed to do. However, this aspect does not appear to be borne out in *Aesop's Fables* (see *Animal*, page 31) where, in 'The Raven and the Swan', the raven envies the swan's beautiful white plumage and tries to wash the black from its feathers.

Today, the raven is generally regarded as a pest since, although it feeds on the carrion of other birds and small mammals, it is also extremely partial to cereal crops. However, it has not always had the bad reputation that it has today. According to the biblical legend, before releasing the dove from the ark (see *Dove*, page 154), Noah released a raven 40 days after the flood. It was therefore the raven that first discovered that the waters had subsided and, as such, was a symbol of renewal: 'And it came to pass at the end of forty days, that Noah opened the window of the ark which he had made: and he sent forth a raven, which went forth to and fro, until the waters were dried up from off the earth' (Genesis 8: 6–7).

In ancient Greece, as the bird of Apollo, the raven was believed to share the god's gift of prophecy and was generally regarded as the symbol of clairvoyance. It therefore became the companion and familiar of soothsayers and clairvoyants but, since their predictions were not always auspicious, it was not seen entirely as a bird of good omen, especially in the Middle Ages. This idea was reinforced by the fact that it fed on carrion and was often considered to be the harbinger of misfortune, pestilence and death. In the 19th century, it was immortalized in Edgar Allen Poe's poem 'The Raven' (1845).

Red

Red is the colour of life, fire and blood. It therefore symbolizes the bright, illuminating light of life and vital energy. For this reason, it is associated with action, vitality, impulses, desires and violent feelings, everything that encourages people to express themselves. It is also a sacred, secret colour, because of its connection with blood: sacred, because ancient cultures regarded it as the very substance of life and the soul – those who lost their blood lost their life and soul – and secret, because the blood that flows through the veins and arteries is invisible.

Although a symbol of life and vital energy, red is also a representation of death, supreme sacrifice and purification, in the mystical sense. Sunrise is red, but so is sunset. Red therefore not only indicates an awakening of the consciousness, but also the ultimate sacrifice, necessary for rebirth.

Red is also the colour of passion, of the extreme, often destructive, emotions and instinctive urges which men and women control as best they can or repress, as the case may be, but to which they sometimes fall prey, despite their best efforts. However, it should be stressed that these human urges are regenerative by nature and essential to life and survival.

That being the case, when this colour plays an important role in a dream, it should be regarded as a manifestation of your thirst for knowledge or power, or a need for action, for creativity. It could reveal an intense and overwhelming feeling of excitement that may be betrayed by your desires, urges and hidden passions or a hunger for living that sustains you but is not being given free rein. Dreaming of the colour red could also indicate the existence of a secret or mystery that is about to be revealed.

Right

See Brain (right and left sides of the) page 67, and Senses, page 448

Ring

The shape and appearance of the ring means that it has a number of points in common with the symbols for the circle and the wheel (see *Circle*, page 100). However, its distinctive characteristic lies in the fact that it is above all the symbol of an alliance, bond, union, association or attachment. For example, the papal ring, also known as 'the Fisherman's Ring' in memory of St Peter, the fisherman and founding father of the Church, symbolizes temporal authority and spiritual fidelity and is broken when the pope dies. Another example is the wedding ring exchanged by a couple on their wedding day and which they each slip onto the other's ring finger which, as its name suggests, is the finger on which the wedding ring is traditionally worn.

A ring is also the symbol of the indefinite, eternal, continuous and unchanging cycle as represented by the zodiac or zodiacal circle – from the ancient Greek name *zodiakos kyklos* ('circle of animals') since most of the constellations contained within it represent animals. By its association with the zodiacal circle, and therefore with the earth's orbit and the sun's annual path, the ring can also be seen as the symbol of the perpetual cycle of years and eternity.

According to legend, the famous Seal of Solomon (another name for the Star of David) was a ring from which the king drew his wisdom and power. In ancient and medieval times, doctors often gave their patients stone or metal rings to cure certain ailments. Today, beneficial powers and magical properties are still attributed to certain curative and lucky rings.

Sometimes rings were used for the purposes of bewitchment or casting spells, so that the person wearing an enchanted ring would become an object of desire for the one whose love they coveted. It was a common practice in medieval Europe, imported from the East where it was widely used by women who wanted to make themselves desirable.

Being given a ring in a dream symbolizes an imminent union. Finding or receiving an old or antique ring is the sign of a belated union. Losing a ring, on the other hand, is a sign of betrayal or disharmony in a relationship or friendship(s). A broken ring represents a broken promise, or a wish or desire that will not be fulfilled. A ring worn on the index finger symbolizes pride, on the middle finger, prudence, on the ring finger, union, and on the little finger, clairvoyance.

River

According to Greek mythology and the cosmogony of Hesiod (see *Gaia or the myth of Mother Earth*, page 200), Oceanus (Greek *okeanos*) was the personification of the great primordial river that encircled the earth, the ultimate river and father of all rivers, whose power rivalled that of Zeus. Oceanus married his sister Tethys – who became the mother of most of the world's river-gods

– and together they formed a divine couple. Just as the ocean was often regarded as masculine and the sea as feminine, so the rivers that flowed into the sea appeared in male form and their tributaries in female form. Rivers and their symbolism were central to the life and beliefs of all ancient civilizations, and they were virtually regarded as gods. Many of these civilizations were founded and flourished on the banks of great rivers – the Tigris and Euphrates in Mesopotamia, the Nile in Egypt, the Huang Ho (Yellow River) in China, and the Ganga (Ganges) and Indus in India – owing to the key role played by the annual floods that covered the land with their fertile silt. In each case, the river was regarded as a generous but powerful god in whose vicinity all sorts of divinities, spirits and water sprites represented the great forces of nature.

However, there are two other important symbols associated with rivers – time and the bridge. The river flowing from its source to the sea is very evidently a representation of time passing from past to future without interruption, of human life progressing inexorably from birth to death. The bridge that makes it possible to cross from one side of the river to the other

is the symbolic bridge between life and death, between the visible world and the hereafter. Thus, although following the course of the river as it flows to the sea symbolizes the path of life that leads from birth to death, we are still present in life. By contrast, crossing the river to the opposite bank is the equivalent of passing from the reality of the visible and tangible world to another, unknown world, a world of which we have no certain knowledge.

River water also evokes everything that follows a natural, normal and obvious course, that 'flows' in the right direction. In this context, the Swiss psychologist and psychiatrist C.G. Jung referred to the 'natural penchant' – a strong inclination or liking, from the French *pencher* ('to incline') and the Latin *pendere* ('to be suspended') – with which we associate the river. Water flows in the direction in which the earth slopes and is propelled by the movement of the earth's rotation. Similarly, we also have natural penchants, like the function of the dream, for example, or the urges that drive us to satisfy desires or vital needs. In physiological terms, our blood always flows in the same direction within our veins and blood vessels. It is therefore probable that psychic energies follow the same identical and continuous movement and that, in this way, they too are associated with our natural penchants. While following the course of a river back to its source is an act invested with powerful spiritual or mystic symbolism (see *Source*, page 461), ancient wisdom tells us not to 'swim against the current' of the river, but to 'go with the flow' and follow the natural course of things, i.e. the course of existence. But this doesn't mean letting yourself go or relinquishing control of your life so that you no longer hold the reins of your destiny.

Interpreting a dream in which a river appears or plays a key role requires a great deal of subtlety. For example, swimming with the current of a river can mean one of two things, depending on the dreamer's state of mind and situation. It can either signify a tendency to let yourself go or let everything in your life 'go with the current' (which in French also has the figurative meaning of 'going to rack and ruin'), or it can symbolize your wisdom, humility and acceptance of the destiny that carries you along but which does not delude you. Conversely, swimming against the current, in more or less turbulent waters, is often

a sign of dangerous temerity, presumption and pride, although this dream can also be interpreted as a major realization of the need to resist certain destructive elements that are dragging us along.

Rod, staff

The rod or staff can take many forms. As a cudgel it a powerful weapon, as a staff a means of support and as a wand an instrument of magic. However, whether it is a hunter's or warrior's cudgel, a pilgrim's staff, a schoolmaster's cane, a sorcerer's or magician's wand, a shepherd's crook, a blind man's stick or a bishop's crosier, the rod or staff always symbolizes the power and authority of the person wielding or holding it. This power and authority may 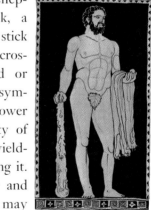 have been conferred by initiation, or by supernatural powers, or it may be an innate gift.

Because a staff or stick is used for support when walking, it is associated with both the human who leans on it and the earth on which it rests. In this sense, it is the axis of the world linking earth and heaven, a conductor of subterranean telluric currents and celestial electric currents.

The rod also corresponds to the vertebral column and the symbolic image of the serpent, found for example in the kundalini (cosmic energy). As such, it corresponds to all energy currents circulating between earth and heaven but also between heaven and earth. The rod is more than a magical attribute, it is an instrument of divine revelation. One obvious example of this is the biblical account of Moses' rod (which was in fact Aaron's): 'And the Lord spake unto Moses and unto Aaron, saying, When Pharaoh shall speak unto you, saying, Shew a miracle for you: then thou shalt say unto Aaron, Take thy rod, and cast it before Pharaoh, and it shall become a serpent. And Moses and Aaron went in unto Pharaoh, and they did so as the Lord had commanded: and Aaron cast down his rod before Pharaoh, and before his servants, and it became a serpent. Then Pharaoh also called the wise men and the sorcerers: now the magicians of Egypt, they also did in like manner with their enchantments. For they cast down every man his rod, and they became serpents:

but Aaron's rod swallowed up their rods' (Exodus 7: 8–12).

The serpent-rod is the attribute of Asklepios (or Aesculapius), the Greco-Roman god of medicine, whose staff with the coiled serpent became the symbol of medicine as the representation of the movements of the energy-giving and psychic currents that flow through the human body. It should not, however, be confused with the caduceus carried by Hermes, the Roman Mercury and messenger of the gods; although often used as a medical emblem, the latter has no medical significance.

In the divnatory Tarot cards, the rod in the Minor Arcana is clearly a cudgel-like weapon, while the staff of the Hermit, the IXth card in the Major Arcana, is more like that of an initiate, a spiritual master or guide.

Dreaming about a rod or staff very often refers either to the principle of vital, energy-giving psychic currents or the concept of a guide. If a rod or staff features prominently in a dream, it can be a sign that you are experiencing or about to experience a period in your life when you will need to be guided, directed and enlightened. Alternatively, it can mean that you would be well advised to look to your vital, energy-giving psychic resources, which you are wasting rather than using wisely and to the best advantage.

However, since the rod is also a symbol of power and authority, seeing a rod in your dreams can signify a transfer of power, meaning that you will either be required to exercise firmness or to submit to certain rules and regulations, otherwise you will incur a penalty or fine.

Rose

The rose is the lotus of the West since all the symbolic values attributed to the lotus in Egypt and Asia are represented by the rose in Europe. It is therefore the epitome of the mystical flower, a symbol of birth and rebirth, Christian resurrection and eternal life. Nevertheless, most species of this beautiful flower are native to Asia.

The rose was also very popular in Greece. The species that grew on the island of Rhodes, among the oleanders or rosebays and the rhododendrons that bear its name (the Greek word for 'rose' was *rhodon*), was famous, as was rose oil, one of the most highly prized perfumes from Arabia. The wind rose, a guide on mariners' navigation charts showing the directions of the eight principal winds, was later combined with the compass card. This took the form of a 32-pointed star corresponding to the 32 rhumbs or points on the sailors' compass, and is reminiscent of the eight-petalled lotus.

The ideal symbol of womanhood, beauty, purity and holiness, the rose was regarded by Christians as an attribute of the Virgin Mary. Thus, the word rosary or *rosarium*, which literally means 'rose garden', and which referred to the crown of roses worn by statues of the Virgin Mary, was given to a chaplet used to count prayers to Mary; it has now become the name of the prayer recited while counting the beads, in the same way that Hindu and Buddhist monks, on the other side of the world, recite the mantras, liturgical texts and hymns that are their instruments of meditation.

The Rose of Jericho, or Resurrection Plant, is a small plant native to Syria that curls into a ball when dry, appearing dead, but uncurls its branches when exposed to moisture. This characteristic feature caused numerous legends to spring up around this plant that, from East to West, was regarded as a miraculous flower whose properties were associated with the common rose. Many species of rose were probably introduced into Europe in the 12th century by the Crusaders, who brought rose bushes back with them. The famous red rose of Provins, in France, widely cultivated by the counts of Champagne, particularly by Henry II, king of Cyprus, then of Jerusalem, was native to Damascus. It was this rose that, in the 13th century, was made the badge of the house of Lancaster by Edmund 'Crouchback', younger son of Henry III of England and suzerain of Provins.

However, as far back as the first, second and third centuries AD, the Greek physicians Dioscorides, Galen of Pergamum and Theophrastes cultivated roses as much for their beauty and perfume as for their medicinal properties. The infusion of rose petals has been renowned since early antiquity for soothing sore throats and stimulating pulmonary activity. Rose water is also an ultra-effective lotion for cleansing and toning the skin and, for this reason, was reputed to have genuine youth-giving qualities.

Rowan tree

The rowan, also known as the mountain ash or sorb apple, wields strange powers over spirits, phantoms and lost souls, if our forebears are to be believed. According to ancient Celtic beliefs, driving a rowan stake through the chest of a corpse helped it to regain its soul and settle its spirit, thereby preventing it from haunting the place where it had once lived. This was the source of the legend that driving a stake through the heart of a vampire would put an end to it. The rowan was known as the witchen or witchwood because it was believed to ward off witches, as in the old saying: 'Rowan tree or reed/Put the witches to speed.' This tree has certainly always been wreathed in mystery: it was thought that demons were summoned and consulted under its branches and that it provided protection against fatal diseases and wild animals.

Sagittarius
(sign of)

See Zodiac, page 575

Sail

This word denotes a taut piece of material fixed to a mast in order to catch the wind and propel a sailing boat. The sail swells,

stretches, sways or cracks in the wind. It is receptive, embracing, taming and imprisoning the wind. It therefore creates a physical resistance that results in a powerful forward movement. Seeing a sail in a dream is not only a sign of escape or a journey, but can also reveal inner drive and strength.

Salamander

As suggested by the Latin etymology of its name, derived from the Greek *salamandra*, the salamander was first and foremost a large lizard. It is a mystery, however, why people in the 16th century attributed the qualities of a fire spirit to this amphibious lizard which tends to live in damp places and whose glossy black skin with bright yellow markings is covered with a poisonous mucus. In fact, the alchemists believed that salamanders were fabulous, indestructible creatures that were able to live in fire, although, unlike undines or water sprites, they were not able to enter into a direct relationship with humans for fear of burning them. However, they were not demonic by nature, and performed the role of fire guardians. 'This fabulous lizard simply denotes the central, incombustible and fixed salt that retains its nature even in the ashes of charred metals and was called "metallic seed" by the ancients.' (Fulcanelli, *The Dwellings of the Philosophers*, 1930.)

However, much earlier than this, the Greeks identified the salamander with the myth of the phoenix, the mythical bird that was thought to survive the flames and rise again, reborn, from its ashes (see page 417). Also, for obvious reasons, the salamander was associated with the fire-breathing dragon. Whatever the case, however, an analogy is always drawn between this

animal and fire. As a result, dreaming of one or more lizards may either herald an imminent problem or signify a happy home life, as we have already seen earlier (see *Lizard*, page 318). However, to dream of a salamander is either a sign of passionate feelings and emotions, or of a radical change, a drastic and unavoidable inner transformation that is about to take place or is already under way.

Salmon

The Celts believed that the salmon had similar characteristics to those of the wild boar (see page 63). It was regarded as a sacred food, worthy of the gods: anyone who ate its flesh was bound to be stronger or more powerful. However, because it could swim upriver, leaping high cascades and fighting rapids, the salmon was considered to be magical by nature. That being the case, catching and eating a salmon was thought to make one wise and omniscient, capable of achieving eternal youth or travelling back in time to the kingdom of the ancestors, as well as possessing the gift of prophecy.

The salmon is therefore unlike any other fish; it is magical, and if one appears in your dream, it indicates that you need to recharge your batteries by revisiting the past, that you should retrace your footsteps to find what you really need, perhaps even a solution to your problems.

Salt

Sometimes when a child asks an innocent question and you answer just as simply, you may catch yourself putting the world to rights. It is the same when, childlike, you consult your dictionary to find out where salt comes from and learn that it is formed by sodium chloride and found everywhere in the natural world. Does this answer your question? No, because it does not explain *where* salt comes from or why it exists. You then consult an encyclopaedia, which gives you additional information such as the fact that salt is formed of ions of opposite signs: anions and cations. Does this tell you anything about the origins and uses of salt? Not at all. There is no point in perusing a dictionary or encyclopaedia in any more depth, because these works rarely approach information from your chosen standpoint.

However, one fact may put you on the right track to find the answer you seek: you learn that human blood – your blood – contains about the same proportion of salt as does seawater and that any decrease or increase in the level of salt in your blood can cause serious organic disorders.

Not only is salt found everywhere in nature, therefore, but it is also essential to maintain the balance of your vital organs. This is why, throughout history, salt has always been a symbolic instrument of life or of destruction, depending on how it was used. In ancient times, for example, salt was used as currency to pay the wages of peasants, labourers or soldiers. In fact, the English word 'salary' is derived from the Latin *salarium*, which denoted a Roman soldier's allowance to buy salt. However, Jehovah used salt and sulphur, key alchemical ingredients, to destroy Sodom and Gomorrah as a means of punishing these cities' sinful inhabitants (Deuteronomy 29: 21). Then, having defied his instruction not to look back at the ruins of Sodom and Gomorrah, Lot's wife was transformed into a pillar of salt (Genesis 29: 26). Lastly, salt was often associated with bread. In Hebrew, the letters of the word 'salt', *melah*, can be rearranged to form the word 'bread', *lehem*, with the difference of just one vowel, and offerings made to Jehovah almost always contained salt. Taken from this angle, therefore, salt is life. You should always bear this in mind when salt plays an important role in a dream. This is because the opposite of salt is bitterness and dreaming of salt often shows that you need to rediscover this vital element within yourself. After all, a physical or spiritual salt deficiency is wholly detrimental.

Saturn

Mesopotamian myths about Saturn. The Sumerians called Saturn Kayamanu, 'the constant'. In Akkad, he was called Ninurta, although it seems that Ninurta was more often associated with the principles and qualities of Nabou (also known as Ninurta) or Mercury, who was called Shihtu ('he who jumps') by the Mesopotamians (see *Mercury*, page 330). However, Mesopotamian myths and legends are less hierarchical and less tightly-structured than those in Greek mythology, the characters often appearing in different guises and their qualities, functions and properties tending to merge or become interchangeable depending on the myth.

Saturn

There is therefore a clear distinction between Kayamanu, Saturn, who is a representation of the planet as it appears in the zodiac, and the god(s) whose characteristics, loves and adventures can be associated with our concept of the ruling planet of the zodiac sign of Capricorn. However, in Greece, as we will see, Cronus and Saturn were interchangeable.

Whatever the case, Kalakh (modern Nimrud), the second capital of ancient Assyria, was the site of the temple of Ninurta, the god identified with Saturn, not Mercury. An important myth relates how Ea (Enki in Sumerian), who was lord of the abyss, the sweet waters in the earth, and the sea, ruler of the infernal regions and one of the three main gods in Mesopotamia with An (Anu), the sky god, and Enlil (Bel), god of the earth and air, summoned Ninurta, son of Enlil, to fight the thunderbird Ansud. This swift, powerful bird acted as messenger between Enlil, the supreme god, and the other gods, and was supposed to assign to each god the role and duties designated by Enlil. However, Ansud, taking advantage of his privileged status, usurped his power to determine the

fate of the gods and mankind, in a clear parallel with the Bible story about Satan, the fallen angel. Ninurta's weapons were powerless against Ansud, who brandished the tablets of fates that enabled him, for example, to order the wood of Ninurta's bow to return to its tree and the bow's cord to return to the sheepskin from which it was made. Only a storm finally put an end to the demon, whose wings were cut off by Ninurta, thereby reinstating Enlil's supreme power.

This mythical account shows that Ansud and his attributes have a great deal in common with Cronus, then Saturn. However, the latter was identified with Ninurta, probably because of his patience, perseverance and tenacity, and even his pugnacity, typical Saturnine qualities that enabled him to vanquish Ansud.

Egyptian myths about Saturn. Strictly speaking, there is no god in the Egyptian pantheon that is completely representative of the planet Saturn, as it appears in the zodiac. This is not really surprising, because astrology originated in Mesopotamia, not ancient Egypt, and later exerted a profound influence on Greek attitudes and culture through the Chaldeans. However, the gods Set and Thoth do bear certain similarities to Saturn. Set because he fought Apophis, the great serpent of the night, and therefore aided the supreme god of Egypt, Ra, who could thus be reborn every morning. This legend has many points in common with that of Ninurta and Ansud. Thoth was a lunar god, but also lord of time division, the calendar and learning, qualities that tend to be associated with Saturn. This does not, however, discount the fact that Thoth also bears many similarities to Hermes/Mercury (see *Mercury*, page 330).

Greek myths about Saturn. Cronus, who became Saturn in Rome, was a Titan, son of Uranus, the personification of heaven. Cronus was therefore the son of heaven/Uranus, just as, in Mesopotamia, Ninurta was the son of the air/Enlil. According to a now famous myth, Gaia, the earth, who had countless children by Uranus, persuaded her youngest son, Cronus, to kill his father by castrating him. The parricide

became lord of heaven and married his sister, Rhea. But his dying father prophesied that Cronos would one day be dethroned by one of his children, therefore Cronus devoured them one after the other as they were born. When she was about to give birth to Zeus, her sixth child, Rhea went into labour in secret and gave the newborn baby into the care of the Curetes, children of the earth, the nymphs, and Amalthaea, a she-goat that fed him with her milk. Rhea then wrapped a stone in swaddling clothes and gave it to Cronus , who devoured it without any inkling of the deception. When Zeus grew to manhood, he waged war against Cronus, whom he defeated. However, according to the less well-known Orphean religious tradition, Cronus and Zeus eventually made their peace, and Cronus is described as a great king, full of goodness and wisdom, whose reign was a golden age. 'First of all, the deathless gods who dwell on Olympus made a golden race of mortal men who lived in the time of Cronos when he was reigning in heaven. And they lived like gods without sorrow of heart, remote and free from toil and grief: miserable age rested not on them; but with legs and arms never failing they made merry with feasting beyond the reach of all evils.' (Hesiod, *Works and Days*, translated from the Greek by Hugh G. Evelyn-White.)

Scales

Scales are above all the symbol of divine and temporal justice but also of balance and harmony. The symbols and myths associated with scales fall into one of two categories – those attributed to Libra (the scales) (see *Zodiac*, page 569) or to Justice, the VIIIth card in the Major Arcana of the Tarot.

When you dream about scales, it often signals that you feel a need for order, balance and harmony, or that justice will intervene in your life in the near future.

When the two sides of the scales are perfectly balanced, it is often a sign that you can trust your own sound and well-balanced judgement or that you are psychologically and morally well-balanced.

If the scales are tipped to the right, your balance is only skin-deep. It relies far too heavily on rational, realistic and emotional values and this is weighing you down. If the scales are tipped to the left, on the other hand, you are weighed down by your dreams and illusions.

Scales to feathers (from)

In the beginning there was the serpent. Then the fish and the bird, the symbols of clairvoyance and divination, appeared simultaneously. To understand all the myths and symbols inspired by birds or associated with birds by our ancestors, we must first draw a parallel between the fish that inhabit our seas and oceans and the birds that populate the skies.

Myths of the fish-woman and bird-man. There is a number of striking similarities between fish and birds. Fish are covered with scales and have fins that enable them to navigate the marine depths and currents with ease and agility, and at sometimes truly amazing speeds. Birds are covered with feathers and have wings that allow them to fly in the sky and negotiate the air currents with equal ease and agility and often remarkable strength. These marvels of the natural world have always been a source of fascination and wonder for mankind and, although modern man can now plumb the depths of the oceans and fly through the skies, these skills do not come naturally. Human beings have had to call upon all their skill and expertise in their attempts to imitate nature, although they have never actually equalled it. This is why we are still fascinated by myths about the fish-woman, i.e. the mermaid or the siren, and the bird-man in the form of Icarus or the angel. At one time or another, most of us have dreamed of swimming freely in the vastness of the ocean depths or flying like a bird, high in the sky.

Certain palaeontologists – palaeontology is the study of plant and animal fossils – have advanced the theory that birds appeared in the Jurassic period, 150–200 million years ago. Others believe they were an animal species that developed after the extinction of the dinosaurs, some 60 million years ago, and that these 'fearful lizards' – 'dinosaur' derives from the Greek *deinos* ('fearful') and *sauros* ('lizard') – which hold such fascination for us today, were in fact the ancestors of the birds. But however many years ago birds appeared on the earth, all modern scientific theories of evolution agree that they are descended from reptiles. But where did the reptiles come from, if not the waters from which they apparently emerged during the Devonian period, some 400 million years ago? Scientists have theorized that fish and birds share the same origins since it would seem that amphibians – creatures that could live both in water and on land, in the same way that the frog does today – provided the link between branchiate fish (with gills) and terrestrial amniotes (reptiles, birds and mammals). One cannot help wondering whether our distant ancestors were aware of this fact, since the myths and symbols they attributed to fish and birds are often very similar. Did they in fact make this link long before 20th-century scientists demonstrated that fish and birds could have been 'cast in the same mould' and gone on to follow

two distinct evolutionary paths and develop the many different species that we know today? It is unlikely that our ancestors were aware of it as such, but they certainly sensed the similarities and, almost without knowing, made the subtle connection between fish and birds.

In many ancient civilizations, and even in Christian imagery, the scale was used as a symbol of the doorway to the kingdom of the gods, the heavens or heaven. For example, Christ was sometimes depicted walking on ground covered with scales, or the scale might be associated with the eyelid to symbolize the 'doorway' of vision in the sense that, when the scales fall from his eyes or his eyes are opened, man can see. He doesn't see what everyone else sees, but what his sensitive inner eye – which has a sort of invisible, protective scale – knows and sees. In this sense, the scale is similar to the shell in that it protects the raw flesh of the sensitive organ or organism inside but, when opened, frees and liberates the emotions. As their name suggests, emotions – the word derives from the Latin *movere* ('to move') – are the motors of life and can either submerge or enlighten us, depending on the circumstances. Man is therefore like a fish, swimming in the ever-changing waters of his emotions, from which he draws his inspiration and motivation.

According to the Babylonian priest Berosus, the fish-god Oannes – the ancestor of the sea gods Poseidon and Neptune – taught mankind the sciences of medicine, astrology, architecture and agriculture. Some ten thousand years ago our ancestors sculpted heads of fish-like beings which no doubt represented divinities but whose meaning and symbolism is lost to us today. Finally, when we take account of the fact that the feather is associated with the gifts of clairvoyance and divination – which was why shamans and medicine men often wore or carried feathers – the connection between scales and feathers, between fish and birds, becomes immediately obvious. Both are the 'guides'

of mankind, representations of the soul swimming in the depths of the oceans or flying high in the sky. The soul identified with the fish or the bird is visionary in the sense that it can see within and from within, in the darkest regions of the earth, the depths of an ocean as yet unexplored by man, or in a privileged position that gives it a superior and panoramic view of reality, an 'overview'. What is more, like the fish and the bird, which appear to have evolved from an earlier common source, the creation of the soul also seems to have pre-dated that of mankind. Finally, because the bird was invested with the qualities of clairvoyance, divination and spiritual freedom, it is easy to understand how, over the ages, men inter-preted the appearance of the many species of birds as a prolif-eration of signs and omens.

Sceptre

This regal attribute symbolizes supreme authority, either tempo-ral or spiritual. As it is probable that it was originally a rod or staff, a sceptre featured promi-nently in a dream carries the same meaning as a rod (see page 433). This is because both repre-sent not only the act of dispens-ing justice and exercising power but also, and most importantly, the divine right to do so. How-ever, in this context, right also carries the sense of duty.

It is often the case that those who dream they are holding a scep-tre are facing a period of their life when they have to assume numer-ous responsibilities, tasks and oblig-ations.

Scorpio
(sign of)

See Zodiac, page 572

Scythe

See Sickle, page 456

Sea

The sea is not just creative (see *Womb*, page 545), it is also regenerative. It generates life and absorbs it in the same way. It is not enclosed like the womb, but a constantly moving, endlessly changing world in a continual process of formation. It teems with life that becomes richer and more prolific with every passing second.

Being in the enclosed space of the womb is like being inside a fruit stone, in an intermediary world, as could be seen from the symbolism of that word. Being in the sea, although you may be swimming in possibilities, you are also in an intermediary situation. If we accept that all animate life on earth has emerged from the sea, then it can be regarded as the great womb of nature. The sea is

therefore also a womb and when it appears in a dream, it should be regarded as such. It remains the representation of a natural principle, but not a mother figure, simply a part of the great universal maternal entity that is generally seen as an earth goddess. All the mother goddesses to whom ancient peoples dedicated similar cults – Ishtar or Astarte, Isis or Aphrodite, Kali or Gaia, Rhea, Hera, Demeter etc. – were primarily earth goddesses.

As a result, the appearance of the sea or ocean in a dream is associated with everything that is chaotic and undifferentiated. It may indicate something that we have not realized, something that is perhaps in the process of taking shape or about to be born, but that is also liable to change at any time. This great original principle is of infinite richness and resides within us. We can bathe in it to revive ourselves, but we may also find ourselves out of our depth or in danger of drowning (see *Mother*, page 348).

Seal

The seal was one of the first imprints, marks or signatures made by humankind. Was it really a means of indicating man's power, authority or strength?

Although this is the commonly held view of pre-historians, who assume that it was always the male who exerted his supremacy over human communities, we tend to disagree, and we are not the only ones. Nevertheless, the realization by the hominid, male or female, that he had left a trace of himself behind was probably a fundamental stage in the development of his self-awareness. In all likelihood, however, this was not necessarily done to establish any feeling of supremacy but to mark out territory, find bearings in a place that they hoped would become familiar to them. It is possible that originally only the mark-maker could identify his mark. After all, it is no accident that the seal has become a symbol of secrecy.

As a result, a seal in a dream always represents a distinctive and important mark for the dreamer. If the design seems obscure or secret, try to remember it and draw it, as its geometric shape may be a valuable clue to the message contained in the dream. For example, there is obviously a correlation between the famous Seal of Solomon and the symbolic meanings of the number 6 (see page 378).

Senses and the hands
(the five)

Our body is capable of acquiring a spiritual knowledge of the world. This is something that Westerners find hard to imagine or believe, because they come from a repressed and inhibited culture that frowns upon sensuality. This mindset, which has held sway for many centuries in Europe, is less the result of

Judaeo-Christian religious beliefs, as some suppose, than the fanaticism and sectarianism of a select few and the naivety and passivity of many others. Nevertheless, the body has a mind, so to speak, and can think for itself.

The senses and cognition. The senses are not just the mechanisms that enable us to perceive the external world. Some individuals have better sensory faculties than others. One person will have sharp eyes and excellent vision, another may have such a keen and discerning sense of hearing that he can identify the slightest dissonance or the most infinitesimal discord of a musical instrument that would be missed by most people; others, with particularly discriminating taste buds and sense of smell can recognize a flavour or a perfume with their eyes closed, sometimes even at a distance. Our senses enable us to perceive the external world and it is this awareness of its shapes and colours, smells and perfumes, changes in temperature, noises and sounds etc., that teaches us about our own limits, and awakens what we call our consciousness. This consciousness is made keener by the fact that we can distinguish between the sensations of pleasure and pain. One last point that should be made is that there is an obvious analogy between taste and knowledge, because we assimilate or digest both the fruits of the earth and new concepts or ideas. After all, words like 'see', 'perceive' and 'sense' can be used both literally and figuratively. There are many expressions in English that use the senses in a more

metaphorical way: 'to follow one's nose' means to trust to instinct, while a 'soft touch' is someone who is soft-hearted and easy to impose on. Human beings therefore have a true sensory intelligence and their bodies can think for themselves. To oppress this intelligence by inhibiting its senses is therefore tantamount to cutting yourself off from the external world and stifling your consciousness. Thus, the fact that religions have made so much of conscience over the centuries is because, on the whole, people lacked it, or kept it on a tight leash or fought against it, giving rise to examples of all kinds of perverted and murderous excesses that have gone down in history and that, unfortunately, still exert an evil influence over our lives today.

The hands and love. However, it is never too late to feel at peace with ourselves, to regain the feelings of harmony, happiness and well-being that we crave and that are described in the myths of the golden age, paradise lost and mysterious

civilizations that are the stuff of fantasy: Atlantis, Mu etc. We can only find this inner peace if we love ourselves, and that means loving others. Thus, in Hebrew, *yada*, which means both 'I know' and 'I love' is derived from the root *yad*, hand. This helps to explain why Adam was meta-phorically said to have 'known' Eve. In Hebrew, the spoken language of the Bible, particularly Genesis, at a time when the Hebrew alphabet was very new and still preserved its original, symbolic semantics, the analogy between the hand, suggesting the verbs 'to grasp' and 'to seize', and the verbs 'to know' and 'to love', was very meaningful.

The hand is never innocent; it enables people to know and be known. *Yad*, derived from the letter-number *yood*, is linked to the process of self-identification, the moment when human beings become aware of their own unique, separate identity. According to the symbolism of the body, as it was viewed by the cabbalists, someone can only become aware of their own identity through their physical desire to know the external world and be known by it, and this knowledge is love.

Left hand or right hand? This train of thought naturally leads us to pose a sexist question

that goes far beyond the concepts of equality that prevail in modern society. Is the hand that represents knowledge and love the right hand or the left hand? This question actually never comes up. We ask it because we have established an artificial normality that does not really exist and that makes the right hand better than the left. The former is randomly associated with the masculine principle and the latter with the feminine principle. If we examine the Hebrew word – which, as we have just seen, is derived from *yad*, hand, and means 'I know' and 'I love' (and not 'I know you' and 'I love you') – we can deduce that it refers to what is called the 'heart hand', which is the left hand. It should be remembered that most of the early alphabets and writings were written or inscribed from left to right. Furthermore, *yada*, 'to know' is derived from the root *yad*, hand, plus the letter-number *ayin*, meaning 'eye'. Thus, 'to know' in Hebrew equals 'the hand that sees', in other words, knowing is synonymous with touching and seeing. That being the case, the reality of the external, material world can only be truly perceived by the left hand, the heart hand, the hand representing the feminine side of the individual, whatever his or her sex.

Set square

See Compass, page 106

Seven

See Numbers, page 381

Shadow

In ancient times, the shadow was both a representation of the soul and an image of the double. This identification of the shadow with the soul originated in the role shadows once played as man's guides. The direction, size and shape of the shadow of a tree or mountain, for example, tend to change depending on the hour of day and the sun's position. For this reason, it is likely that man, who has been navigating by the stars for thousands of years, also used the shadows formed by natural objects and his own body to find his way. It is also worth noting that the divinatory art of geomancy draws its inspiration in part from the shifting positions of shadows: the natural interplay of light and shadow produced by the sun and the configuration of things on earth.

It is therefore easy to understand how, owing to their role as guides, shadows came to be identified with the soul, which also acts as a guide. However, shadows are also associated with all that is hidden, dark, mysterious or gloomy. As a result, according to the Swiss psychologist C.G. Jung, everyone's psyche has a shadow side with all the personality traits that are denied or suppressed. Shadow, as it is defined by Jungian psychoanalysts, can therefore be detected astrologically by the position of the black moon in the birth chart (see *Black Moon*, page 344).

As a result, seeing yourself pursued or covered by a giant shadow in a dream is often a sign of repressed feelings that are threatening to overwhelm you. However, if you dream of walking in broad daylight or bright sunshine with no sign of a shadow, this can be interpreted in two different ways: either it is midday, the sun is at its zenith and your dream indicates self-

fulfilment, success and happiness; or it suggests that you are in denial, refusing to see, assimilate and accept all that is shadowy, dark, covert and hidden. As a result, dreaming of shadows should never be taken too lightly.

Shell

The ovoid or oblong shape of the shell, whether it is an eggshell or a seashell, is reminiscent of the shape of the female genitalia. As such, it is associated with pleasure and fertility, wealth and prosperity, and, more specifically, with conception, life in the womb and birth. All these characteristics are directly related to the moon through the cycles of fertilization, the tides and the weekly and monthly cycles that favour conception.

Furthermore, as the seashell and eggshell can be hermetically sealed and are therefore impenetrable, they are often associated with mysteries and secrets, and, above all, the universal myths of creation. According to these myths, a primordial egg or original shell (the cosmic egg) concealed something new – hidden from the

general view or which could only be seen on pain of being blinded – that would cause the world to emerge from chaos.

These images of life, birth and pleasure should be taken into account when interpreting a dream about a shell, which predicts that a new event, or possibly that a new feeling or emotion, is about to occur in your life. It indicates that something unprecedented, pure and spontaneous is 'hatching' within you, something with which you are, so to speak, 'pregnant' and that – unbeknown to you – is developing slowly but surely within you.

However, the seashell and eggshell can also be wonderful symbols of the soul. In this sense, a dream about them can have significant spiritual and psychological connotations in that they can herald a realization or a major discovery that will aid your inner development. A broken or empty shell, on the other hand, symbolizes a project or desire that has not been or will not be realized.

Shepherd

In myth and legend, the shepherd is a pastor, guardian and guide who tends his sheep with care and leads them to graze in green pastures. He is accustomed to being alone in the natural world with his flock and is therefore familiar with the slightest movements of the wind, knows the names of the stars and the names and properties of rare plants. He sometimes even speaks to the angels, has visions and hears heavenly voices. But he is above all renowned for his great care and vigilance in protecting his flock from wild animals, lions and bears.

This paternal and protective image of the shepherd is thousands of years old. According to one school of thought, the flail and crook-like sceptre that were the symbol of pharaonic power in ancient Egypt were inspired by the shepherd's fly whisk and crook. Christians are of course familiar with the pastoral scenes of the Bible and the image of Christ the good shepherd: 'The Lord is my shepherd; I shall not want. He maketh me to lie down in green pastures: He leadeth me beside the still waters ...' (Psalms 23: 1–2).

The pastoral theme in literature, which depicts the shepherd's life as carefree and idyllic, can be traced from ancient Greece (Bion, Moschus) and Rome (Theocritus, Virgil), through the Middle Ages, when shepherds, magi and sorcerers were often interchangeable, to the pastoral poetry of the Renaissance (Dante, Petrarch) and the pastoral romance novels of the 16th and 17th centuries (Miguel de Cervantes, Honoré d'Urfé). Within the context of the romantic idyll, evening was seen as a propitious time for lovers and may well have given rise to the French term 'l'étoile du berger' – the evening star or Venus (the planet associated with the goddess of love) – which appeared as the shepherd returned to the fold with his flock. Another French expression 'la réponse du berger à la bergère' ('tit for tat') – a remark used to end a discussion – may have derived from the pastoral convention of 'singing matches' that took place between two or more shepherds.

Dreaming about a shepherd often has romantic connotations and may be a harbinger of love, or it may predict the imminent solution to a problem that has been worrying you, thus putting an end to a 'discussion'. Finally, you may also dream about a shepherd at a point in your life when you feel uncertain and are in need of guidance, advice, help or protection.

Shield

As already stated (see *Buckle*, page 74), the term 'buckler' or 'shield' derives from the Old French *bocler*, in turn derived from *bocle*, meaning 'shield boss'. It is, of course, a symbol of protection and self-defence. Because it helped them to defy death by parrying the blows of the enemy and so remain unvanquished in battle, the warriors and soldiers of ancient times invested the shield with magical powers. For this reason, it was often covered with magic symbols intended to terrify the enemy.

The protective symbolism of the shield can be associated with the signs of Cancer and Capricorn. The characteristics of these two signs of the zodiac correspond to defensive attitudes linked to fear or hypersensitivity in those born under Cancer, and to mistrust and a tendency to rely solely on themselves in Capricornians.

One of the most famous myths associated with the shield is that of the slaying of Medusa by the Greek hero Perseus. Medusa, one of the three snake-haired monsters known as the Gorgons, turned all who beheld her to stone. Perseus had the idea of polishing his shield and using it as a mirror. When Medusa saw her own reflection in the polished shield, she was rooted to the spot (French *méduser*), and Perseus was able to cut off her head without looking directly at her.

A dream about a shield can be the expression of a need for help or protection. It can also represent a tendency to be self-protective, on the defensive and mistrustful of the outside world. In this sense, it can symbolize feelings of vulnerability at the time when you have the dream. Because the shield has magical associations, it may also symbolize providential protection that will help you in a difficult situation or make you invincible. It is therefore an encouragement to fight or defend yourself.

Shoe

The shoe was originally a wood or leather sole that covered the ball and heel of the foot and was worn by kings and nobles. For this reason the symbolism of the shoe relates to that of the foot and especially the heel.

The Hebrew word *aqov* ('heel') forms part of the name Yaaqov (Jacob). In the Bible, the story of Jacob tells how he was born holding the heel of his twin brother Esau. The Hebrew for 'hand' is *yad*, and together *yad* and *aqov* (the hand and heel) form the name Yaakov. In symbolic terms, the gesture linking the hand to the heel represents the ability of human beings to apprehend, grasp and understand the primordial energies that move within them, thus preventing them from being lost.

The legend of the Greek hero Achilles is also associated with the symbolism of the heel. Achilles' mother, the nymph Thetis, plunged her son into the waters of the Styx, the river of Hades, to make him invulnerable. However, as she immersed him in the river one part of his body, the heel by which she held him, remained dry. Thus, according to Homer's *Iliad*, after killing Hector at the siege of Troy, Achilles was in turn killed by Paris who wounded him in the heel. The legend gave rise to the expression 'Achilles heel' which refers to a small but fatal weakness.

In many cultures, the heel is regarded as a weak point in the human body and, according to an age-old tradition whose origins are obscure but which is found in a number of myths and legends, it is through the heel that a person's soul and life leave their body at the moment of death.

The shoe therefore has great symbolic significance and, for obvious reasons, is usually envisaged as part of a pair. This brings us back to the myth of the twins (see *Androgyne*, page 26) and, among others, to the twins Jacob and Esau.

In our dreams, shoes always appear in pairs, although we often dream we have lost one of the pair or are wearing odd shoes. This type of dream indicates a psychological imbalance, a loss of energy and a state of weakness. However, to dream of wearing a lovely pair of comfortable shoes is a sign of self-control, inner strength and self-assurance. Shoes that are too small mean you are feeling uncomfortable, agitated or confused, or possibly ill at ease in or deeply disturbed by your present situation. Clogs, pumps, boots, sandals ... each type of shoe has its own particular significance that corresponds to the situation or function it represents. This should be borne in mind when interpreting a dream about shoes.

Sickle, scythe

Although the sickle and scythe are similar in appearance – the sickle is in fact a smaller version of the scythe – they have different etymologies and different, if not opposite, symbolism. While 'sickle' derives from the Old English *sicol*, from the Latin *secula*, related to *secare* ('to cut'), 'scythe' derives from the Old English *sigthe*, related to the Old Norse *sigthr* and Old High German *segansa*. Because of its crescent-shaped blade, the sickle is associated with the moon. It therefore represents the lunar qualities of femininity, sensitivity and fertility and symbolizes harvest, abundance and the fruits of the earth. In view of this, a dream about a sickle always alludes to the fact that we reap what we sow and that, depending on the nature of our actions, the harvest will be either good or bad. Although the scythe is also associated with harvest, it is a very different type of harvest since the scythe is the attribute and instrument of death – also known as the 'grim reaper' – and mortality. In this context, it cuts and 'reaps' with devastating and inexorable effect. The XIIIth card in the Major Arcana of the Tarot – often referred to as the 'card with no name' due to the age-old terror inspired by the idea of death, to which no one remains indifferent – depicts a skeleton holding a scythe, in a field covered with the heads of dead men. The image represented by the card is deliberately macabre, in order to make an impression. However, just as the appearance of a scythe in a dream does not announce our own imminent death or that of someone close to us, the XIIIth card of the Major Arcana merely indicates that a radical change is necessary or about to occur in our life, a change that is vital if we are to be able to pursue our personal development. Thus the scythe and the Tarot card are invested with the same symbolism and bear the same message.

Silver

Because of its whitish colour, silver is a metal associated with the moon, while the yellow colour of gold links it to the sun. Silver's white, luminous appearance and ability to reflect light also made it a symbol of purity and wisdom. For the ancient Egyptians, it was a much rarer and more precious metal than gold since they obtained it from a

Sickle,
scythe
Silver
Six
Skeleton
Sky

gold-bearing ore mined in Nubia that contained only about 24 per cent of the metal. The Sumerians, who imported it from the so-called silver mountains of Elam (modern-day Lebanon), also regarded it as the richest and most precious of metals. They made silver ingots, which they used as a form of currency in their various trading activities. In fact, they were probably the first people to use silver as a currency in its own right, and Mesopotamians who possessed silver were regarded as wealthy.

The Latin word *argentum*, used to refer to the metal, silver plate and silver coins, was derived from the word *arguus*, of Indo-European origin, meaning 'brightness' or 'whiteness'. *Arguus* also gave rise to the verb *arguere* meaning 'to put in a clear light' and, by extension, 'to declare, prove or argue'.

Modern English, like the Latin, uses 'silver' to refer both to the metal and the coinage and this should always be borne in mind when interpreting the signs and symbols connected with silver. The metal is often associated with lunar myths and symbols relating to the moon: femininity, fertility, receptiveness, purity (see *Moon*, page 342). Silver coins can be associated with either prosperity, luck and

happiness or with envy, uncontrolled greed, miserliness and cunning. However, it has often been observed that dreams about silver, whether in the form of metal or coins, have meanings related to death – not the real, physical death of a person but a symbolic death, an important change in someone's life or situation. Furthermore, if we see ourselves with handfuls of silver coins, it is not so much a sign of prosperity or wealth as the need we will almost certainly experience to 'declare, prove or argue' to obtain what we want. Finally, losing silver is a sign of losing means or powers, of not being 'up to' a particular situation or of not believing you are capable of dealing with it.

Six

See Numbers, page 378

Skeleton

See Bones, page 65

Sky

You only have to look at the sky and feel its impressive and immeasurable vastness to understand how it fired the imaginations of our ancestors and led to the inspiration, belief and, finally, the certainty that the sky was the kingdom of the gods. The sky was the epitome of immensity for human beings who needed to live and feel safe within a limited and enclosed space with well-defined territorial boundaries that they blighted with interdictions, the better to protect themselves from the unknown. We should always remember that our vision and perception of the sky was handed down to us by our ancestors and that this perception persists, whatever people say, and in spite of the investigations, research, discoveries and speculations carried out and made by modern astronomers and astrophysicists. The sky still holds the same mysteries and questions for us as it did for our forebears. Like them, we look to the outermost limits of our universe to discover the echoes of its creation.

For there is no doubt that the universe had a beginning, the famous and inconceivable 'big bang' from which everything was created. Yet every beginning automatically implies an end. This is a principle that human beings, however sophisticated they may be, find it impossible to disregard – which explains the feeling of anxiety and disillusionment that a discovery of this nature engenders in the consciousness or the collective subconscious of the human race. It is a scientific reality that poses the problem of the primordial and ultimate void, the absolute nothingness from which the universe was created and to which it must inevitably return.

The sky is always disturbing, even more so nowadays than in the past, since we have given ourselves the means to scan, search and measure it. The ancients were in no doubt – since they subscribed to age-old beliefs – that the sky was populated by gods who presided over human destinies. Today, many believe that the sky is populated with extraterrestrial beings, most of whom have developed technologies and capabilities far superior to our own. Some of us are convinced that, good or bad, they are out there, watching and waiting, that they are helping or hindering us without our realizing what is happening.

This belief in the existence of extraterrestrials is not so far removed from the belief in angels. Angels, too, live in the sky and come down to earth, usually unbeknown to us, although there are just as many reports of people claiming to have seen or encountered angels as there are of sightings and contact with aliens.

Where does reality end and the dream begin? How do you distinguish between a visionary and someone suffering from hallucinations? It is impossible to give a categorical answer to these questions. What is certain, however, is that, from time immemorial, the sky has been the preserve of the dreams, fantasies, hopes and fears of human beings, who have invested it with their idealized, mythicized and figurative vision of their world, themselves and their lives. The vault of the sky is therefore like a huge curved mirror placed above the earth, in which human beings see and look at their own reflection, recognize themselves or identify with a god who resembles them but who, of course, lives above and beyond their reach.

All this has to be taken into account when the sky features prominently in a dream. It is usually quite simply a dream of revelation, without complicated symbolism, interpretation, identification or personalization. If the sky is threatening, laden with storm clouds, it means that the threat comes from within you, not from some form of external catastrophe.

Snake

This limbless reptile, with a long scaly body and a highly mobile jawbone that enables it to swallow prey larger than itself, has been the subject of many myths and cults. In all civilizations, it was a symbol of life and death combined, in other words, a symbol of regeneration.

It was selected in China as one of the 12 signs of the zodiac. Quetzalcoatl, the creator-god of the Aztecs, was portrayed as a feathered snake who was a bringer of civilization. The monsters of Greek mythology, such as Cerberus or Medusa, often had snakes grafted onto their body or head. Inanna/Ishtar, the great Mesopotamian goddess who was the source of inspiration for Aphrodite/Venus, was often represented with a serpent curled around her body (see *Venus*, page 274). In Egypt, Apophis, a symbol of primordial chaos, was represented as a huge serpent, the god of evil and the night. He was regarded as the mortal enemy of Re, the Sun-god, whom he fought every night. The Greeks

were probably inspired by this Egyptian myth when describing the battle between Apollo and Python, child of the earth, who fled to the oracle at Delphi before the sun-god killed him with his deadly arrows and took his place. Lastly, everyone knows the ambiguous but initiatory role played by the serpent in the story of Adam and Eve (see *Paradise*, page 410).

Dreaming about a snake often indicates that your psychic, instinctive and primordial energy is stirring and has assumed this guise to reveal itself to you. Whatever its appearance and colour, and whatever part it plays in your dream, a snake always has great symbolic significance. It may denote a revelation, a crisis of conscience, a realization, or an awakening or liberation of your instinctive urges.

Sorcerers

See Witches and sorcerers, page 542

Soul

The soul always conjures up the idea of an invisible power, a life other than earthly life, a consciousness other than the consciousness of the mind, body and the five senses with which we apprehend the external world. The concept of the soul has been interpreted in various ways, according to the beliefs of civilizations throughout the world, and a number of myths have been attributed to it. The present article focuses primarily on the concept of the 'soul' according to the beliefs of ancient Egypt.

According to the Egyptian civilization, the individual was made up of five distinct parts: the body, the *ba*, the *ka*, the name and the shadow. The *ba*, represented by a bird with a human head, comes closest to the Western idea of personality but is often translated as 'spirit'. The *ka*, represented by the crested ibis, was the creative life-force (sometimes translated as 'sustenance') of each individual, the essential component that distinguished the living from the dead and, by its presence within that individual, conferred 'protection, life, continuity, happiness, health and joy'. For the Egyptians, the *ka* was more than and other than the soul. It was an immaterial 'double' which, like the individual in whom it resided, had to have its own name. For example, according to the royal titulary (series of titles) of the 18th-dynasty pharaoh Thutmose III (*c.* 1479–1425 BC): 'the living *ka* of the Lord of the Two Lands [is called] Mighty Bull, Appearing in Thebes'.

The human-headed *ba*-bird is much more closely associated with the body and memory of the individual and is reminiscent of the restless spirit of the deceased still haunting the places where he or she once lived. The *ka*, on the other hand, suggests that the 'soul', or what Western civilizations refer to as such, continues to live on in the afterlife. According to Egyptian belief, it was the union of the *ba* and *ka* in the hereafter that brought about the transformation of the individual, immediately after death, into an *akh*, one of the 'blessed dead'.

The French word for soul (*âme*) derives from the Latin *anima* ('breath', 'air' or 'wind'), in turn derived from the Sanskrit *aniti* ('breathe' or 'blow') and the Greek *anemos* ('air' or 'wind'). However, in Latin there was a distinction between a masculine principle – *animus*, meaning 'spirit', which translated the Greek *thumos* (the seat of the passions) – and a feminine principle – *anima*, which translated the Greek *psyche* meaning 'breath' or 'soul' but also 'butterfly'.

Air, wind, birds (see the representations of the *ba* and *ka* above) and butterflies are common universal images for the soul (see also *Bee*, page 55).

See also *Air*, page 19.

Source

The source or spring is a symbol of purity. Returning to the source is tantamount to regaining one's original purity, rediscovering the sense organ of the soul. A spring is extremely rich in symbolic and mystical significance. Physically, it is an essential link in the water cycle. After living underground in the phreatic or

groundwater zones (i.e. to the area of saturation, beneath the water table) of the earth, the source gushes out, becomes a brook or rivulet, then a stream that swells to a river that widens even further before flowing into the sea and continuing its course in the many cross-currents that overlap and intertwine in the ocean. It then changes into water vapour once more, rises into the air and falls back down as rain, flowing over the earth or soaking deep into it to emerge here or there as a spring (see *Water*, page 528).

Source, birth, life and death. The unchangeable and constant cycle of water illustrates perfectly that of human rebirth on earth. It is easy, in fact, to draw an analogy between rain and fertilization, the sky being a representation of the father or the great masculine principle and the earth the mother or the great feminine principle, both omnipresent and at the origin of all terrestrial life. The rain is the seed of the sky that impregnates the fertile earth. In its womb, that is in the phreatic zones, the source grows – it is in gestation. It is just as if the earth were pregnant with a spring that finally spurts out of the mountainside or at its foot. This can be compared to the birth of a child, which then grows: the source represents the

baby, the brook or rivulet the small child, the stream the teenager and the river the man, whose entire life seems to be charted in this way and can be followed and understood by observing the course taken by a water source that has grown to a river on the earth's surface. Its course is man's destiny. However, the stream or river does not flow in a straight line towards the sea, but appears to be winding its way along like a snake, because the earth is spinning and this rotation influences the course of the water. However, the river water can only head towards the sea, just as man is destined to die, to return to the great original principle from which he came. This is because, symbolically, if the bowels of the earth can be compared to the mother's womb, then the sea represents the primordial waters in which the individual gestates and the foetus develops. All the sources or springs that have become rivers flow into the sea. Likewise, the unique, incarnate soul, represented by the solitary source, sooner or later joins all the souls that merge to form the ocean of life. This is why, since time immemorial, our forebears have regarded the source or spring as a symbol for the birth of mankind, the primeval waters as the essence of all life, and the ocean as a representation of the primordial chaos into which the disembodied souls plunge after their time on earth, while awaiting a new life (see *Sea*, page 447).

The return to the source. As we have seen, the source is at the origin of everything that begins, is born and takes shape. Symbolically, therefore, a return to the source is synonymous with a spiritual or mystical quest that involves rediscovering our original condition. To our forebears the source was divine, sacred, magical, pure and virginal in character, just as when a child is born, the soul is still pure. The principle of the soul is hard to conceptualize, because it cannot be apprehended intellectually. We must shed the desires, impressions and contradictory feelings that beset us at all times and come between us and the reality of the world in which we live. This is why a return to the source, the mystical quest that has featured in all religions and beliefs, necessitates a stripping-away of everything extraneous. It is an initiation into what can be

called a new consciousness. This means that we must take control of our awareness, although we are ordinarily controlled by it and are therefore at the mercy of our thoughts and actions. If we follow the course taken by the source to the ocean, a course that illustrates man's destiny, his life on earth, it is clear that by returning to the source, we defy death and the cycle of rebirth. Although reincarnation is a comforting concept, allowing us to glimpse life after death and a possible rebirth on earth, it still entails an inexorable, endless cycle, whose purpose and justification is questionable. In this respect, the concept of reincarnation and the cycle of rebirth bears similarities to that of the myth of the labyrinth, a place from which one can only escape if one possesses an Ariadne's thread (see *Labyrinth*, page 306). The only possible means of escape from this apparently eternal cycle of reincarnation is therefore to return to the source, to the original condition. In this respect, numerous stories and accounts abound throughout the world concerning the life of the mystics, which describe their childlike behaviour. They held their somewhat naive beliefs with such sincerity, such simplicity, that they could not be challenged. It was precisely because of this quality that these individuals impressed anyone who spoke to them. That being the case, everything points to the fact that this original condition, which can be rediscovered by defying death and returning to the source, is none other than the sense organ of the soul to which the Hindus and Buddhists refer.

Sparrow

There are several species of sparrow, but the most common are the house sparrow (*Passer domesticus*) – which could be described as metropolitan, since it now forms such an integral part of city life – and the tree sparrow. Apart from the fact that the latter is found exclusively in rural habitats since, unlike the house sparrow, it needs greenery, they are as alike as two peas in a pod. They also have similar habits, although the former nests beneath the windows or gutters of houses or buildings, in crevices in walls, and

sometimes on chimneypots, like storks, while the latter prefers holes in trees, where the male and female build a nest of straw and twigs. Their brood comprises four to six eggs. In cities and the countryside, the sparrow, whatever its species, is a valuable friend to man, as it feeds exclusively on insects.

This little bird, abounding in cities and rural areas, was equally familiar in Roman times, when it was associated with the protective, household deities of the hearth and pantry, probably because it protected their food from insects.

Sparrowhawk

The Eurasian sparrowhawk (*Accipiter nisus*) has a number of points in common with the goshawk, although the latter has a larger wingspan and is a sedentary bird, whereas the northern sparrowhawk tends to be migratory. In spite of its predilection for small passerine birds (such as sparrows), which it hunts by swooping down and taking them by surprise, the sparrowhawk is very much a family bird. Each year, the female lays a clutch of four or five eggs and sits on them continuously for 30–35 days. She also continues to keep her chicks warm after they have hatched while the male hunts and brings back food for his family.

This exemplary mother impressed our ancestors who saw the female sparrowhawk as a symbol of matriarchy and female supremacy. As can be seen from the above, she is an excellent mother, but she is also a better flyer and hunter than the male since she is larger and more powerful.

However, in spite of its innate sense of family, the fact that the sparrowhawk preys on small birds – perceived as innocent and defenceless in human terms – means that it has never enjoyed a particularly good reputation. Thus, although our ancestors regarded it as a bird of good omen – the harbinger of some form of advancement or union – it was also seen as an incarnation of the Devil that was able to cast a spell over its victims the better to devour them.

Spear

The spear, like the arrow, is primarily a solar symbol. In the past, it was associated with the sometimes deadly rays of the sun beating down on the earth or on those who had broken the divine laws. The vengeful sun despatched its arrows and fiery spears to punish mankind. However, the spear was also regarded as a phallic symbol. In classical Chinese literature, the male sexual member was named the 'jade spear', as jade was a symbol of the yang principle, of strength and perfection combined with gentleness. The seal of the Emperor of China was made of jade (see *Jade*, page 288).

In Greek mythology, the spear was one of the attributes of Athena, along with the helmet and the aegis. This goddess, the daughter of Zeus, sprang from her father's head when he asked Hephaestus to split it open with an axe. Athena was a war goddess, who played a prominent role in the *Odyssey* alongside Odysseus. However, she was also the goddess of reason, the arts and literature, therefore there is a certain ambivalence about her, because she held a masculine attribute, the spear, but she also fulfilled an entirely feminine role, that of muse for the arts. The outcome of this strange combination of qualities, which may seem opposites but are in actual fact complementary, was the birth of reason.

Reason can therefore be seen as a shaft of wit scoring a timely bull's-eye. This idea is worth remembering when a spear appears in a dream because, although the latter can simply be taken to represent the male member, mounting energy levels and manly strength, a spear thrown or caught often reveals an apt thought or a sudden realization. Although the spear can wound, it can also symbolically cure wounds: lancing an abscess is obviously painful but at the same time this action drains the abscess of pus and so helps to cure it.

Sphere

The Greek word *sphaira* referred to any round mass or object such as a ball or globe. However, the Latin word *sphaera*, derived from the Greek, referred exclusively to the heavenly bodies or planets, before coming to mean the vault of the heavens or firmament. The original Greek word for 'sphere' seems to be linked to the verb *spairein*, meaning 'to palpitate' or 'vibrate'. Thus, it is possible that the sphere was initially a symbolic representation of life.

After all, in the Greek tradition, the visible and invisible world, the earth and the heavens in the mythical sense, were represented by two interlinked concentric spheres. Many of the sphere's meanings are analogous to those of the circle (see page 100), therefore it also symbolizes perfection, the absolute, a whole, or a single entity. Ancient civilizations held that the most perfect representation of the universe was spherical in shape. The first known depictions of the world to be found in all civilizations were circles symbolizing a sphere. The zodiac itself was only created by our forebears because they imagined a heavenly sphere enlarging and encompassing the sphere of the earth.

Therefore, the presence of a spherical object in a dream often alludes to the generally subconscious desire of human beings to unite or combine all aspects of their personality. It reveals a craving for perfection and unity. However, a sphere rolling along solid ground or moving through the sky is never still, so the sphere should also be seen as a symbol of the dreamer's complete and absolute evolution.

Spiral

A symbol of the perpetual motion of life and the impermanence of things, the spiral represents eternal life or self-fulfilment. The result of a natural phenomenon, it is produced by a circular, centrifugal or centripetal force. In this respect, therefore, it is associated with the circle and its attendant symbolism (see page 100). Centrifugal force creates a movement away from the centre of a circle, whereas centripetal force involves a movement towards the centre. If you stir your finger around the centre of a basin of water, for example, you will see that the water eddies away from the centre towards the rim. On the other hand, if you make a circular movement with your finger around the rim of the basin, you will see that the water eddies towards the centre.

The spiral frequently occurs in nature and the universe, being one of those innate shapes found everywhere, from plants to galaxies, including the shells gathered on the beach at the seaside.

This fact did not escape our forebears who were at one with their natural habitat and generally identified with it. They found in the great book of nature the shapes and forms they used for symbols, creating a language with which they could interrelate with others, and communicate, even commune with nature. This is why Europe is dotted with megaliths, monumental blocks of stone erected during the neolithic period and engraved with spirals. In all likelihood, the presence of this symbol of a common natural phenomenon on neolithic gravestones indicates an early belief in the hereafter and eternal life, as the spiral represents an endless, evolutionary process.

The spiral, symbol of eternal life or self-fulfilment. Simply put, the spiral can be described as a symbol of evolution. However, the evolution in question will be different depending on whether we are referring to a centrifugal spiral, moving outwards from a central point, or a centripetal spiral, moving inwards from an external point.

In this respect, the spiral relates to the symbols connected with the circle and the labyrinth (see page 306). The Venus figures sculpted in the upper palaeolithic era – ranging from around 35,000 to 9500 BC – were often portrayed with a spiral on the belly or a vulva shaped like a spiral. This spiral was a symbol of fertility and life, the natural, magical processes of life as perceived by our forebears, who saw this as an obvious way to represent this phenomenon of natural evolution.

The centrifugal spiral was therefore both an emblem of life – the formation and evolution of life on earth – and evidence, so to speak, of eternal life, when it was also found on a megalith. Moreover, it seems that in the neolithic period, which followed the upper palaeolithic, the mother-goddesses described above, the famous Venus figures, were identified with the megaliths, being featured on some of them. Thus, to our forebears, life and death, or life after death, formed a con-tinuum that was perfectly symbolized by the spiral.

The centrifugal spiral is reminiscent of the circle and the centre but, because of its perpetual motion away from the centre, it departs from the circle of life, transcending the visible world to enter the invisible world. It is therefore also analogous to the symbol of the wheel and this explains why it also represented the passage of both the sun and the moon through the sky, as well as the impermanence of things (see *Circle*, page 100).

However, although the spiral moves outwards from a central point when it is centrifugal, representing the growth of life in nature, it can also be seen from another angle or, more precisely, from the opposite end. It can be envisaged as moving inwards from an external point, this time evoking the course of life or destiny that guides an individual towards the centre from the outside. This is the centripetal spiral, which relates to all the symbols associated with the

labyrinth, in other words, to the journey man must make towards his core, his inner self, uniting all aspects of his personality, focusing everything he is and everything he does on the central point that is the origin of everything. This spiral represents self-fulfilment, the journey that man must make within himself to return to his core. This spiral represents an act of soul-searching.

The spiral, ladder and kundalini. There is another spiral that relates to the symbolism of the ladder (see page 309). This one represents the continually moving, interpenetrating energies that fertilize, transform and constantly regenerate each other, as can be seen in the water cycle on earth (see *Water*, page 528) or along the vertebral axis, where the primordial energies of the kundalini, itself represented by a snake, circulate from top to bottom and from bottom to top.

Square

The square has obvious associations with the number 4 (see page 371), especially with the four cardinal directions, which, in all ancient civilizations, were guarded and symbolized by tutelary divinities. In Egypt, for example, Thoth was the guardian of the North, Sepa the guardian of the South, Horus the guardian of the East, and Set the guardian of the West. In the Buddhist tradition of India, their counterparts were Vaishravana (North), Virûdhaka (South), Dhrtarâstra (East) and Virûpâksa (West).

As well as being a universal symbol for the earth, the square is also closely connected with the circle (the symbol for heaven) of which it represents an organized structure (see *Circle*, page 100). In this context, the square is contained within a circle, which can in turn contain another circle, in which there is another square containing another circle, and so on to infinity.

This is the principle on which the *mandala* (Sanskrit, meaning 'circle') is usually based. This symbolic image, composed of circles and squares placed inside a square, was and is still

used as an aid to meditation by Indian and Tibetan Buddhists.

Last but not least, there are the famous magic squares that are the equivalent of talismans. These squares are found in all civilizations but were originally used for ritual, religious, magical and divinatory purposes by ancient Chaldean priests and later in Arab cultures. Each of the seven principal magic squares corresponds to one of the seven stars governing the 12 signs of the zodiac and was therefore believed to be invested with the protective power associated with that particular star. In the Middle Ages, these squares were known as 'seals', for example the seal of the sun, the seal of Mercury or the seal of Saturn. They were also used for ritual and divinatory purposes by astrologers and alchemists, especially during the Renaissance, and enjoyed renewed popularity in the 17th century.

Today, the concept of the square tends to refer to anything that is perfectly coherent and logical. As such, it is a concept that inspires feelings of reassurance and security, but also implies constraint since, as well as protecting, the square also limits and encloses. As a result, the square always represents an enclosed area in which you can feel safe from any form of intrusion or external danger, but in which you are also imprisoned.

Through its age-old association with the earth, of which it was the symbolic representation in ancient times, the square corresponds to earthly life, material reality, the tangible values of the world, everything that is concrete, established, unchanging and permanent.

If you dream you are in a square, whether it is a courtyard, a garden, a field or any other area in the form of a square, it may well be a sign of security, order and protection. However it can also represent a feeling of imprisonment, a situation from which you are unable to escape or extricate yourself. For example, logical reasoning based systematically on the same criteria and always leading to the same conclusions may well be represented in a dream by a square. It is up to you to work out whether the square is beneficial and positive or whether, on the contrary, it encloses and isolates you and hinders your personal development.

Stables of Augeas

See Hercules, page 237

Starling

The starling is a passerine bird, i.e. it belongs to the *Passeriformes*, an order of birds – including larks, finches, thrushes and sparrows – characterized by the perching habit. It is a member of the family *Sturnidae*, whose most widely found member is *Sturnus vulgaris*, about 20cm (8in) long, with iridescent black feathers and a long, sharp beak. It is particularly vocal in early spring when it can be heard 'singing' its head off with its beak wide open. It is at this time, in February or early March, that it returns to its breeding ground. Starlings nest in hollow tree trunks and crevices in walls and, for about a month, the male and female take it in turns to build a nest of twigs and raise their young. Interestingly, starlings are very particular about the materials they use for building their nests and don't use the first twig, root or piece of straw that comes to hand … or beak.

The French use the term starling (*étourneau*) in the same context that the Americans use 'birdbrain'. This is possibly because the bird's rapid and erratic flight – they fly in flocks – often gives the impression that they don't know where they are going, which is certainly not the case. It was the starling's excessive 'chattering' and especially its gift for mimicking other birds that earned it a reputation as a messenger or a magician. In the past it was even believed that it could recite magic formulae.

Stars

Astrophysicists are fond of telling us that 'we are all born of the stars'. This is a metaphorical and poetic way of saying that all the ingredients of the great concoction of life on earth are to be found in the stars scattered throughout the universe. The culinary analogy – the idea of combining different ingredients that were not necessarily intended to be put together – is not fortuitous. It was first made by the German astronomer and astrologer Johannes Kepler (1571–1630).

It appears that, as he watched his wife making his favourite cake, Kepler observed that she systematically used the same ingredients, without ever appearing to measure them, but always obtained the same, delicious results. After due reflection, the future father of modern astronomy drew an analogy between this intelligent, natural and spontaneous method of cooking, without apparent rules or any form of recipe, and the organization of the solar system, the universe and life on earth. He concluded that, just as the delicious cake, concocted from dissimilar ingredients whose combination defied all logic, would not have existed without the intelligence and skill of his wife, so the strange and inconceivable harmony of the world would not be what it is without the intervention of a divine hand.

As they looked at the stars, our distant ancestors soon observed an order, a relatively unchanging system of reference that provided them with some very useful points of reference. It is therefore reasonable to suppose that Polaris (Alpha Ursae Minoris) – also known as the Pole Star, North Star and Alroukaba (from the Arabic for 'knee') – existed in the sky of our ancestors long before it acquired these names or became the brightest star in the constellation of Ursa Minor ('lesser bear') or The Little Bear.

In actual fact, the sky moves and is continuously transformed, even though these changes cannot be seen by the naked eye during a lifetime. Thus, in around 7,600 years' time, Polaris will no longer occupy the role and position of the Pole Star in the earth's sky. It will have been replaced by Alderamin (Alpha Cephei) – from the Arabic *al-dhira al-yamin*, meaning 'right forearm' – the

brightest star in the constellation of Cepheus. In the past, civilizations throughout the world based astronomical figures, signs and forms (constellations) on the apparent fixity of the sky and the relative position of the stars. It was this stability that made all the more impressive any movements or phenomena that occurred in the sky and were witnessed by man.

While Johannes Kepler used deductive reasoning to conclude that there must have been some form of divine intervention to have created this inconceivable order out of the chaos of elements that form the universe, our distant ancestors reached the same conclusion by observing the sky and contemplating the stars. For them, the stars were guiding principles, the celestial signs of the gods, and if they saw in the sky what they regarded as the most beautiful, most powerful and most wonderful aspects of their life on earth, it was their way of raising their reality and human existence to the level of the gods.

By following a similar line of reasoning, Jewish cosmologists identified the stars, and especially the constellations, as groups of celestial spirits, in which each star was a benign spirit or an angel in its own right,

one of the many guardians of the world and of mortals. Thus, each of us has our own protective star (or guardian angel) somewhere in the sky. According to other, even more ancient cosmologies, the stars were the souls of the dead and the luminous intensity of each star was proportional to the spiritual development of the soul it represented.

All these visions and interpretations of the sky should be taken into account when trying to understand the meaning of a dream about stars. However, there is no need to explain the meaning of a dream in which we are following a star or see a star in the sky that appears larger and brighter than the rest. In such a dream, the star is quite simply a guiding principle we have called upon or which has been sent to us, a symbol of our destiny, or the sign of an important event that is about to occur in our life. The star of Bethlehem or the evening star (the planet Venus) appeared in this way to the Magi, the three wise men, who were also astrologers. Thus, the image of this star shining more brightly than the rest to announce the birth of Jesus is a symbolic way of saying that the three Magi had made the astrological prediction that an important event would occur in a particular place, on a particular day, under an exceptional astral configuration: 'and, lo, the star, which they saw in the east, went before them, till it came and stood over where the young child was' (Matthew 2: 9).

Stick, wand

The stick or wand is associated with the rod (see page 433) and the serpent (see page 459). Like the rod, it symbolizes wisdom, clairvoyance and divination. Like the serpent, it represents psychic powers and the instrument that invokes occult forces and subdues demons.

The wand or stick is the attribute of the magician, the sorcerer, the soothsayer, the fairy or the witch (see *Witches and Sorcerers*, page 542).

Dowsing or water divining is the art of the sorcerer who uses a hazel wand (a slender supple stick) to detect underground water. Rhabdomancy – from the Greek *rhabdos* ('rod') – is the art of divining water or mineral ore, sometimes even buried treasure, by means of a wand.

Palomancy is the art of throwing sticks or twigs to predict the future. In China, the I Ching was consulted as a book of oracles using yarrow stalks. Fairies and magicians use a magic wand to cast spells and bring about amazing transformations, while sorcerers use a wand to put curses on people or bring about monstrous metamorphoses.

Whether its powers are divinatory or magical, the stick or wand is the instrument of supernatural forces and powers that the user can exert over all living creatures and inanimate objects. Like the rod and the sceptre, it is a symbol of power.

Seeing yourself in a dream holding a stick or wand reveals your (conscious or subconscious) power to transform the circumstances of your life, to bring about a change in your situation, not by intervening directly in events or in the lives of those around you, but by seeing them in a different light, from a different point of view, and developing your view of the facts and circumstances of your situation.

Since a stick (in this instance a 'baton') is also used by a conductor to conduct an orchestra, it can also represent a responsibility or burden to be assumed, or symbolize the leading role you must play in your life to 'conduct' it in a harmonious manner.

Stone

Stone is associated with a belief in the continuance and durability of objects in contrast to the ephemerality of human life. Man early realized that stone was the one thing that remained relatively unchanged, at least in appearance, in the natural environment. It was probably this ability to withstand the ravages of time, rather than its hardness, that made it the ideal base for signs, symbols and drawings. We should not forget that it was this process – that archaeologists call glyphography or the art of engraving stones – that inspired our forebears to create the seal. Examples of seals, which were carved in intaglio (incised) and used to make a positive imprint on a soft material such as clay, have been found dating from the sixth millennium BC, eight thousand years ago, in Asia Minor and Mesopotamia. These seals served as imprints, signatures, proof of existence – they were not only the earliest form of written expression, the earliest letters so to speak, but also the first writings.

It is therefore true to say that the oldest and most durable natural element – although it is far from being eternal, since not even the earth and the stars are eternal – was the one that reflected people's wish to live after death, to mark their presence by leaving something behind, a trace, a souvenir, that ensured they lived forever in the memory of their children. Hence, man identified himself not with stone but in stone, by carving on it signs by which he could be recognized. The signature is still the best method of distinguishing one person from the next, of allowing someone to make his mark.

However, ever since man was able to fashion and alter the natural appearance of stone, it also became the abode of a god or the one God. Square, rectangular, and oval stones assumed a magical, sacred and divine aura. They represented the first temples, the home of the gods, then of the supreme God. The betyls, sacred stones honoured by the Semites, whose name meant 'the abode of the gods' – a term that could be translated now by 'the house of the lord' – were found everywhere in ancient times. Etymologically, the word 'betyl', from *bethel*, was formed initially by *bet*, which was probably at the root of *beith*, the second letter of the Hebrew alphabet, that can be translated here by 'house', and joined with El, a Babylonian and Semitic deity who appeared in the Bible under the name of Baal (also called Bel, but usually known as El), and who inspired the first authors of the Bible to refer to God as Elohim. Later, stone, the abode of the god, became a deity or divine power in its own right, then a cornerstone. The famous cornerstone mentioned so often in the Bible was Christ: 'The stone which the builders rejected, the same is become the head of the corner' (Psalm 118: 22, also Isaiah 28: 16 and the Gospels of Luke, Mark and Matthew). Stone has therefore retained its magical, sacred power for the Christians.

For this reason, a dream about a distinctively shaped stone is always magical and mystical in nature and can represent the purest, most precious and most durable human attribute: the soul. This is therefore a dream with a richly symbolic meaning.

Stork

This magnificent migratory bird, with its black and white plumage and long red beak, winters in central and southern Africa and spends the summer in India, Europe or the Middle East, depending on the species. The stork is, quite literally, a high flyer and the species that migrates south from Siberia via India flies over the high peaks of the Himalayas, which reach altitudes of over 6,000 m (19,685 ft)! Storks are also 'waders' which means they have long legs, a long neck and often a long beak, designed to enable them to wade and feed in shallow water and marshes.

In the past, these birds often nested in villages, on the roofs of houses and sometimes even on chimneystacks. Unfortunately, it is a sign of our modern times that, along with many other migratory birds, storks are tending to abandon the villages of Europe where they were once a common sight.

In Europe and Asia, the stork has always been regarded as a bird of good omen, a symbol of fertility, filial affection, wealth and, of course, conception and birth. There is any number of tales and legends throughout the world in which the stork is the harbinger of a birth or quite simply the messenger carrying a newborn baby, wrapped in a blanket, suspended from its long beak. For the Romans, the stork was the symbol of Juno, wife of Jupiter, the counterparts of Hera and Zeus in Greek mythology. As such, it was the personification of the great feminine principle.

Storm

See Lightning, page 317, Thunder page 493

Strawberry, raspberry

It is impossible to consider the strawberry and raspberry separately since they have a number of points in common. They have a similar appearance, shape and texture and their medicinal properties are much the same, i.e. they are full of goodness, are purifying and laxative, rich in Vitamin C, and the nature of the sugar they contain – laevulose, also known as fructose or fruit sugar – means they can be eaten and enjoyed by diabetics. Did you know that crushed strawberries also make an excellent toothpaste that is better tasting and more effective than chlorophyll? Before the human race developed the pollution and over-production that distort the taste of fruit and vegetables and lead to food mountains and waste, it was considered a crime to wash strawberries or raspberries before eating them since this removed all their fragrance and flavour. Nowadays, unless you grow your own fruit, you would be well advised to wash them first if you don't want to risk ingesting as much, if not more, insecticides and pesticides than Vitamin C.

Because strawberries and raspberries used to grow wild in woods and forests, they were often associated – symbolically – with fairies and witches, woodland sprites and gnomes. This is why baskets of strawberries and raspberries often feature in tales and legends. Because of their colour, they were also said to be the blood of a wounded angel or supernatural being which, as it fell to earth and coagulated, was transformed into these red fruits. For these reasons, strawberries and raspberries have a flavour of childhood, dreams, gentleness and tenderness that usually makes them beautiful and reassuring images when they appear in a dream.

However, it is important to understand that the symbolic language of dreams is expressed on a level where the past, present and future merge, where the dimensions of time and space that govern our everyday lives are turned upside down, in short, where anything is possible. As a result, the language of symbols, which is also the language of dreams, not only incorporates contemporary elements and phenomena with which our forebears were unfamiliar because they did not exist in the past – for example, the train, plane or automobile (see *Automobile*, page 45) – but also modern expressions which are themselves metaphors.

For example, a dream about a raspberry could have connotations with the phrase 'to blow a raspberry' which means to make a spluttering noise with the tongue as a sign of displeasure or contempt. This may be an allusion to the fact that you feel the need to express your contempt or displeasure at something or someone. Alternatively, as for all other fruit, a dream about strawberries and/or raspberries can simply be interpreted in terms of the fruits of the earth, fecundity and fertility.

Stymphalian birds (the)

See Hercules, page 240

Sun

Mesopotamian myths about the sun. The sun, Shamash in Akkadian and Utu in Sumerian, was, according to the Mesopotamians, the conqueror of night, illuminating the whole world and chasing away darkness. The governor of the heavens and the underworld, the destroyer of evil, he was worshipped, venerated and acclaimed by all. Although this was a genuine deification of the sun, Shamash/Utu was never a supreme god, as Ra was in Egypt. He was no more important than Nanna/the moon,

Detail of a Mesopotamian work from the 19th century BC.

or Inanna/Venus, for example. It should be pointed out here that the Mesopotamian astrologers, whose first known observations of the heavens date from the end of the fifth millennium BC, did not think that the seven (as they believed) planets governing the zodiac exerted any influence over mankind. They thought that the harmonious or disharmonious movements of the heavens formed a language in its own right that could be decoded by means of their astronomical observations. This language was that of the gods.

Egyptian myths about the sun. In Egypt, the sun was a supreme god: Re was the chief god of ancient Egypt and the great god of Heliopolis, whose name meant 'city of the sun' in Greek. The pharaoh was regarded as the 'son of Re' who, according to numerous Egyptian legends, created the entire universe. The myths relate that Re would cross the heavens each day in his barque and that, every morning, as he emerged from the darkness of the underworld, he was attacked by the mythical serpent Apophis, who lay in wait for him, threatening to plunge the universe into chaos. However, Set, the son of Geb (the earth) and Nut (the Vault of the heavens), helped Re to conquer

Apophis daily. Father of the gods, Re was syncretized with other deities although they never replaced him. Among them was Amun, who became Amun-Re, the god of the New Kingdom in Egypt, whose priests and upper clergy, based in Thebes, were very powerful until the fall of this great city in the seventh century BC when it was captured and sacked by the Assyrians. There was also Re-Horakhty, whose name means Re-Horus-in-the-horizon, one of the earliest monotheistic figures, since Akhenaten (tenth pharaoh of the 18th Dynasty, 1352–1336 BC) was inspired by his name to create his own, which means 'glory of the sun-disc'. The evening aspect of the sun was represented by Atum-Re, regarded initially as the creator god of Heliopolis, where he was depicted as an elderly man, glowing like the setting sun; he was probably worshipped in Thebes before Amun-Re. Khnum-Re was first regarded as the *ba* or soul of Re, then identified with him, being represented as a man

From an Egyptian work of the 14th century BC.

with a ram's head, whose job as creator of human life was to fashion a child out of clay on his potter's wheel. There were many other deities, although they cannot all be listed here. However, as we have seen, sun worship was found everywhere in ancient Egypt, although it is impossible to identify the symbolic characteristics attributed to the sun in the zodiac today.

Greek myths about the sun. The myths about the sun that sprang up in Greece are closest to modern astrological perceptions of this planet. Mention should first be made of Helius who, according to the Greeks, was both a god and a demon. A Titan, brother of Eos (dawn) and of Selene (the moon), Helius was a direct descendant of Uranus (heaven) and Gaia (earth). In

Detail from a Greek sculpture of the 7th century BC.

Greece, Helius was represented as a young man, whose golden hair symbolized the sun's rays around his head. It was he who, heralded by Eos and woken by the crowing of the cockerel, his tutelary animal, crossed the sky in his fiery chariot drawn by four dazzling white horses. Helius had the power to see everything on earth and was described as the eye of the world. He bore certain analogies to Re, but he was far from being a supreme god and was swiftly dethroned by Apollo, whose myths also share certain similarities with the astrological attributes of the sun. The sun represents the individual's instinctive will in a birth chart and also indicates the qualities of courage, determination, dominant strength, authority, kindness and generosity. It is also the ruling planet of the fifth sign of the zodiac: Leo. According to Greek mythology, Apollo was the son of the Olympian god, Zeus. He was the god of music and his instruments were the flute and the lyre – which he is said to have invented; he gave the lyre to Hermes who, in exchange, gave him his flock. He was a god of divination and, as his oracles were often delivered in the form of rhymes, he was also the god of poetry. However, he was also a warrior god, capable of killing

Swallow

enemies from a distance with his bow and arrows. The laurel was his oracular plant and it was the leaves of this plant that his priestess used to chew before entering a trance and delivering oracles. Numerous animals were sacred to him: the roebuck, doe, wolf, swan, kite, crow, vulture and particularly the dolphin (*delphis*), whose name evokes Delphi, site of the most famous temple erected to the glory of Apollo.

Swallow

The term 'swallow' covers 74 species of birds belonging to the family *Hirundinidae* (order *Passeriformes*). Some swallows are also known as house martins because they like human company and often nest below, above or in the corner of windows, on balconies, in cracks in the walls of houses, and below eaves and gutters. The sight of swallows returning from Africa in or around April, to the same sites they occupied the previous year, is a sure sign that spring has arrived. Each year, they build their nests using little pellets of mud covered in saliva to bind the grasses or pieces of straw picked up from the fields. They usually hatch two clutches of five eggs per year, sitting on them for around two weeks.

Swallows snap up the insects on which they feed in their beaks, in full flight, which can mean at speeds of up to 80km/h (50mph). Towards the end of September, they can be seen congregating on overhead power cables before flying off to Africa for the winter.

Although the swallow's tendency to hatch two broods per year makes it an emblem of fertility, it is first and foremost a symbol of clairvoyance. According to the encyclopaedic *Natural History* (AD 77) of the Roman writer Pliny the Elder (AD 23–79), the swallow restores the sight of its blind nestlings by feeding them sprigs of the greater celandine, commonly known as swallow-wort, a plant whose name derives from the Latin *cheladonia* ('celandine'), from *cheladonius* ('of the swallow') and the Greek *khelidon* ('swallow').

Furthermore, because this little bird returns to the same nesting site each year, it has come to be associated with happiness, fidelity and birth. For this reason, our ancestors believed that killing a swallow brought bad luck and even blindness.

Swan

The swan is a large aquatic bird belonging to the genera *Cygnus* or *Coscoroba* and the same order, *Anseriformes*, as the goose. Although some species have black plumage, notably in Australia, the most common image of the swan is that of a large white bird, with its long, slender neck and orange beak surmounted by a black nodule known as a tubercle. At times, it can be extremely aggressive, spreading its wings, arching its neck and emitting a piercing cry. Otherwise, its vocal range extends from a loud high-pitched honking to a low, muted sound.

The swan is invested with symbolism in cultures throughout the world and, over the ages, has fired Eastern and Western imaginations alike. Like the immaculate whiteness of its plumage, the swan is above all a symbol of purity and perfection. In Western Europe, it inspired philosophers and poets – even today William Shakespeare (1564–1616) is known as the Swan of Avon – while the bird's unhurried movements as it glides gracefully on the water have most probably given rise to the rather negative expression 'to swan around', meaning 'to wander idly'. However, it appears that the peoples of Asia invested the swan with the most beautiful symbolism – prudence, courage, nobility, elegance, purity and beauty. In Greek mythology, this last quality earned it the honour of being one of the attributes of Apollo and the form assumed by Zeus in order to seduce Leda. Its cry was perceived as both a song of love and death, and the 'swan song' that a dying swan is said to sing has come to mean the last appearance, publication or exhibition of a public figure, writer or artist before retirement or death.

The swan also inspired 'The Dying Swan', one of the most beautiful and moving pieces of 20th-century choreography, created to the music of Camille Saint-Saëns's *Carnival des Animaux* (Carnival of the Animals) by the choreographer Michel Fokine. It was performed for the first time by the Russian prima ballerina Anna Pavlova, in St Petersburg, in 1907.

Table

The table is a symbol of sharing and union. Sitting down at a table to share a meal or talk something over shows a willingness to join forces with others, hear someone else's point of view or reach a compromise. As a result, symbolically speaking, a meeting around the negotiating table or peace table is a sign, if not of alliance, then at the very least of arbitration or reconciliation. The expression 'round table conference', which alludes to the legendary table made by Merlin for King Arthur to preclude jealousy among his knights, was coined in the 19th century and is still used to refer to a conference in which no participant has precedence and matters are settled amicably with the maximum amount of give and take.

However, the word 'table', which originally denoted a flat surface, draws its origin from the Latin word *tabula*, derived from the word for the stone tablets on which the first scribes, who were probably Mesopotamian, not Egyptian, inscribed their cuneiform or wedge-shaped characters. Subsequently, *tabula* was used to denote any flat, rectangular manuscript as well as a rectangular or square wooden bench, and sometimes even a plot of land or a vineyard in Roman times. On the other hand, *mensa*, the correct Latin word for table, seems largely to have disappeared, except as the name of an international organization for individuals of high IQ, another allusion to the round table at which all members have equal status.

When a table features prominently in a dream, it is always a symbol of meeting or union, because it is the one object that perfectly represents community life, the family or clan. Dreaming about a table, therefore, shows that the dreamer craves togetherness, a sense of communion with his or her loved ones. If the dreamer is sitting at a table with a group of people, then the place he or she occupies is

important. However, this type of dream may also emphasize the dreamer's need to confide in someone, express certain feelings, confess to wrongdoing or a guilty secret, perhaps, in order to ease his or her conscience. Finally, there may also be an allusion to the Tables of the Law, which may give the table(s) appearing in a dream the sense of mortal or divine justice, as the case may be.

Tail

Although we no longer have caudal appendages or tails, our direct descendants probably had, hundreds of thousands of years ago. The tail is therefore associated with a variety of primitive instincts that are buried deep within the human psyche and have not yet been entirely expunged. These deep-seated, mysterious and sometimes even dangerous forces, which have the primitive savagery of animal instincts in their disregard for the rules, laws and taboos of civilized society, exert a subtle, subconscious influence on the behaviour of the individual. Although it is rare to dream about a man or woman with a tail, it is not unusual to dream about a mermaid or siren: a fabled creature,

half-human, half-fish, that inhabits the world of fantasy and imagination. A mermaid is really a woman with a tail and, if we understand the ocean as the primordial chaos that spawned every living thing on earth, the mermaid of our dreams therefore represents a fantastic being, capable of living in this enchanting yet harrowing primeval world of chaos.

According to the Swiss psychologist C.G. Jung, dreaming of a mermaid, being one in a dream or seeing any other animal with a prominent tail, such as a lizard or crocodile, shows that you are in touch with the inmost recesses of your psyche or that you are exploring them without assimilating them into your consciousness. Jung named the hidden side of the human psyche the 'shadow': 'Taking it in its deepest sense, the shadow is the invisible saurian tail that man still drags behind him. Carefully amputated, it becomes the healing serpent of the mysteries.' (C.G. Jung, *The Integration of the Personality*, 1939.) Viewed in this light, it is possible to see a direct link between the current craze for dinosaurs, which disappeared from the earth around 65 million years ago, and the shadow that, according to Jung, we all possess deep inside.

Tambour

It seems likely that the word 'tambour', denoting a type of small drum, originated in ancient Persia, where it originally meant a stringed instrument more like a lute than a percussion instrument. Even today, musicians often mark the beat or *tempo* by hitting their stringed instruments. It later came to signify a hollow wooden or terracotta instrument with a dried animal skin stretched across its head, like the African tom-tom. The tambour and the tom-tom are often confused, even though the former was an instrument of war and death, while the latter is the ancestor of all modern Western communication devices. In fact, to put it simply, the African or native American tomtom could be described as a type of mobile telephone, able to send a message over very long distances.

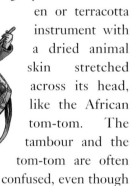

Therefore, hearing a tambour in a dream has a completely different meaning from hearing a tom-tom. The sound of a tambour could reveal an impending crisis, conflict or difficult period in your life or it could also be an early warning of some distant danger, as the tambour can be heard from a long way off. However, when you hear the staccato beat of a tom-tom, you should expect to receive some important news, a message informing you of an event or situation that concerns you personally and that will be delivered very quickly. The tom-tom can sometimes symbolize a rumour that is spreading very rapidly.

Taurus (sign of)

See Zodiac, page 556

Teeth

Hypnos, the Greek god of sleep and twin brother of Thanatos (death), was represented as a winged figure, a sort of angel, holding a tooth – the symbol of assimilation – in one hand and a horn of plenty in the other. As such, he symbolized the benefits of sleep and the regenerative assimilation produced by dreams.

Teeth therefore represent everything relating to the assimilation of earthly and spiritual nourishment. This is borne out by the expression 'to bite deeply into life', meaning to live life to the full. Etymologically, 'bite' is derived from the Old English *bitan*, which is related to the Latin *findere* ('to split').

Because of the obvious analogy with nourishment and assimilation, teeth were very early on associated with the principles of aggression and vital energy. By wearing necklaces made from the teeth of the wild animals they hunted, our ancestors assumed their aggressive and instinctive power and became stronger, more resilient and more alive. They knew that, when an animal showed or bared its teeth, it was a sign of aggression. Even today, the expression 'to show one's teeth' means 'to threaten', especially defensively, and to act 'in the teeth of', i.e. to act in opposition to or against something, is almost certainly derived from this symbol of aggression. There are many other expressions associated with the teeth – for example, 'to grit one's teeth' is a sign of determination or endurance, while our teeth 'chatter' when we are extremely cold or afraid – but they all tend to be associated with symbols of vital and aggressive energy, strength or death.

A dream about losing your teeth – a common dream that most of us have at least once in our lifetime – often signifies a loss of vitality or a lack of tone, self-defence or aggression. It can also represent a temporary – physical or moral – depression or a period in our life when we lack strength and energy and feel less resistant. It can also symbolize an inferiority complex or a feeling of guilt that makes the dreamer impotent.

Finally, according to the most ancient traditions of oneiromancy, and especially those of ancient Egypt, dreaming about losing a tooth means we are about to lose someone dear to us, while losing them all signifies that the dreamer will survive the people present in his or her life at the time of having the dream. It goes without saying that all these interpretations refer to healthy teeth. If, on the other hand, we dream about the loss or extraction of a bad tooth, this indicates an imminent liberation or release. However, it also means that we are undoubtedly responsible for the 'bad tooth' that is extracted or falls from our mouth in the sense that we allowed it (i.e. the situation) to degenerate. An excessively large tooth that falls out spontaneously is a sign of birth or creation. If it is pulled out, this means that the birth or creation will occur against our wishes or that we will need help to enable it to happen. Finally, a healthy tooth that is pulled out always represents a necessary sacrifice.

Temple

The temple is an earthly representation of the heavenly abode of the gods, not only those that are known, but also the inaccessible, omnipotent deities that created the world and ensure its continuity. However, it was originally an observatory for studying the gods, from which the planets and celestial phenomena that influenced terrestrial and natural phenomena were carefully scrutinized and studied by the astrologer priests and seers when making their predictions, forecasts and prophecies.

The predecessor of the temple, synagogue, mosque and church was the legendary Mesopotamian ziggurat, which was used to observe the heavens as well as make contact with the planets/gods. Although it is difficult to see the priests of the past as the counterparts of modern-day astronomers, and their temples as observatories, these things are preserved in our so-called unconscious memory.

As a result, to dream that you are entering a place consecrated to a god, a place of meditation and prayer, does not necessarily mean that you need to find God, convert or seek sanctuary. It is more likely to reveal a longing to understand and perhaps master the forces that govern your life, the many events that seem meaningless and arbitrary. In other words, those who dream of a temple hope to exercise their free will by becoming masters of their fate, identifying the means to recognize and read the signs that influence it. Like the carpet or rug (see page 82), the temple is also a place that encourages soul-searching and self-awareness.

Ten

See Numbers, page 391

Temple
Ten
Thighs,
pelvis, lower
back and
genitalia

Thighs, pelvis, lower back and genitalia

Our body is a reflection of what we are. Were we interested enough to take a few anatomy lessons to learn something of this science of the human body, while simultaneously immersing ourselves in the symbolism of the body developed, with great subtlety and precision, by our ancestors, we would be able to understand our symptoms, i.e. to read and interpret the language of the body.

The body has its own language and always has something of interest to 'say' to those who know how to read and interpret its various symptoms. As evidenced by its etymology, the term 'symptom' does not automatically imply illness since it derives from the Greek *symptoma* meaning 'chance' (a synonym for 'coincidence') from *sumpiptein* 'to occur'. A symptom is therefore an occurrence or coincidence of signs. In medieval French, for example, 'to be astounded or dumbfounded' was expressed as 'tomber en symptôme'. As has already been pointed out, the etymological origin of words is an indication of their true meaning, which has often become distorted over the ages, providing alternative meanings that ultimately constitute a popular counterculture. However, it should also be borne in mind that etymology is also culture specific and that the origin of a French word, for example, may often be different from its English counterpart, depending on whether the word in question has a Greek, Latin or Germanic root. Sooner or later, our curiosity often leads us to investigate the origins of words, to delve into the truth, or at least what we perceive to be the truth, since there is nothing more changeable than the truth. Perhaps the only real verity is that of the present, the exact moment at which we perceive it.

Thighs. When human beings walk or run, they use their thighs, legs, feet and, of course, their entire body. But the impulsion and power that motivates their legs comes from the thighs.

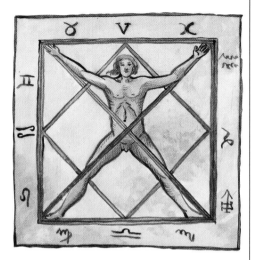

Thus, while the seat of the urges and desires is found in the lower back (kidney area), the seat of the impulsion that controls forward movement is located in the thighs.

Pelvis. In human beings, the pelvis is central to the mechanisms associated with the act of walking, the way in which we walk and our posture. The cabbalists referred to the pelvis as the doorway of the human body. It is through this 'doorway' that the energies have to pass as they circulate upwards and downwards, in an endless cycle, within our body. One of these circulating energies is the blood that flows through our veins and arteries. When it cannot flow freely, when there is a break, an interruption or a disruption in the pelvic area, it often causes arterial and venous problems. It

should also be remembered that below the pelvis lies an extremely important – vital and regenerative – energy centre that corresponds to the *muladhara chakra*, located between the genitalia and the anus, and regarded as the centre of mental energies and physical urges. In other words, the body's primordial energy centre, which nourishes and regenerates the mind, which in turn contains all our vital and creative forces, is located below the pelvis, at the base of the spinal column. If the pelvis is not positioned correctly, the individual is deprived of this primordial energy and its creative and regenerative forces. By observing the way someone walks, you can tell at once whether the pelvis is free or obstructed, i.e. whether the energies are circulating freely, upwards and downwards, around that person's body, or whether they are being obstructed. In this case, lying on the ground, relaxing for a few minutes and then moving the pelvis by arching and un-arching your lower back, is an excellent therapeutic and preventive exercise that enables you to maintain the flexibility of the pelvis and promote the free circulation of these energies.

Lower back. A supple pelvis enables you to control

your primal energies through the balance and strength of your lower back or kidney area, whose shape (i.e. kidneys) make it possible to draw a number of analogies with the feet (see *Feet, legs and knees*, page 182). For example, although a person stands upright by placing their feet on the ground, they are also standing and supporting themselves, symbolically, by means of their kidneys or lower back, the seat of their physical, material and moral balance. Furthermore, the shape of the kidneys resembles that of the ears and everyone knows the important part played by the ears in perceiving the sounds of the external world and achieving and maintaining balance. Thus the link between the ears, kidneys and feet plays a key role in controlling physical and mental balance. A person who knows how to listen, both literally and figuratively, is well-balanced and bearing and posture are indicative of a person's behaviour.

Genitalia. If a person has good bearing and posture, they therefore have a strong back and a relatively supple pelvis that facilitates the free flow of vital energies. They will also be able to contain their urges and will not expend these vital energies in trying to control their sexuality, which can therefore become a qualitative rather than a quantitative experience. This transformation is extremely important for personal development since the genitalia, or their symbolic representation, stand for 'to have' and 'to be'– the first being quantitative and the second qualitative. To get straight to the point and spare readers the need to explore relatively complex issues that would require an initiation into the cabbalistic code, the progression from 'to have' to 'to be' or from quantity to quality is illustrated by two situations represented in the Bible:

• the famous 'Be fruitful, and multiply' pronounced by Yahweh (Genesis 1: 28);

• the covenant of circumcision established between Yahweh and Abraham (Genesis 17: 10–14).

In symbolic terms, the first situation represents a depletion of the primordial energies that, used solely for procreation, weaken and impoverish the being. The second situation, on the other hand, represents controlled reproduction, which makes it possible to assimilate this vigour or seed with creative energy so that the individual can direct and control it towards and within himself in the same way as the disciples of Tantrism.

Thirteen

See Numbers, page 398

Thread

In Greek mythology, thread symbolized human destiny. It represented the course of a person's life that was spun, measured and cut by the Fates (*Fata*). In medieval Europe, there was a popular saying that a pregnant woman was 'spinning or weaving her child'. But thread is also associated with the chain in the sense of what links us to life, i.e. the thread that links the soul to the body, as expressed in the phrase that someone is clinging to life by a thread. However, the linking thread is also the guiding thread of which we should not lose sight, since it is the thread that enables us to go where we have to go and do what we must do. This is the lesson to be learnt from the Greek legend of Theseus and the Minotaur, since Theseus would not have been able to find his way out of the Labyrinth without the thread spun by Ariadne (see *Labyrinth*, page 306).

The appearance of a thread in a dream is therefore of great significance, especially if we lose hold or sight of it, since this means we are losing the thread or sense of our life and that we need to regain control. A dream about tangled threads or skeins of thread or wool means we are experiencing a certain confusion and are projecting ideas, feelings, desires, hopes and fears that together form a kind of labyrinth in which we feel imprisoned. It is up to us to find the sense or direction of our life among all these tangled threads.

Three

See Numbers, page 368

Thrush

The thrush is a passerine songbird, i.e. it belongs to the *Passeriformes*, an order of birds – including larks, finches and sparrows – characterized by the perching habit. It is of the same family as the blackbird (*Merula turdus*) or common thrush, but is a member of the subfamily *Turdinae*. With their brown plumage and characteristic spotted breast, the best-known European thrushes are the mistle thrush and the song thrush (*Philomelos turdus*). The latter's distinctive song is similar to that of the blackbird, although the thrush tends to repeat different motifs several times. The thrush – or 'throstle', to give it its poetic name – is about 20–22cm (7½–8½in) long and feeds mainly on fruit, insects and the occasional worm or snail (most of us have heard a thrush cracking open a snail shell against a rock or stone). Most thrushes build open, cup-shaped nests and lay between three and six pale-coloured eggs, sometimes tinged with blue. At the end of summer, they migrate to the warmer regions of southern Europe and North Africa.

From time immemorial, the thrush's song has been regarded throughout Europe as the harbinger of rain. For this reason, this familiar little bird played an important forecasting role for our forebears, who also regarded it as a symbol of long-evity and believed that eating thrushes would extend their life. Its resonant song was so distinc-tive and melodious that it made a great impression on the imagina-tion of the people of medieval Europe who associated it with the Christian imagery of the bird as the symbol of the human soul aspiring to return to par-adise, its eternal home.

Thunder

Thunder is the rumbling sound heard after the lightning flash. Caused by the expansion of rapidly heated air, it can be so loud and powerful that it makes the ground shake and seems to represent the unleashing of some supernatural force. We now know that thunder is a physical phenomenon that always follows a flash of lightning. Nevertheless, the build-up of atmospheric pres-sure preceding a storm is so great that the thunderclap following a lightning flash is often invoked to signify the inevitable disruption or salutary crisis that occurs when tensions, conflicts or clashes are so great that a con-frontation is unavoidable. An analogy was therefore often drawn between thunder and war, yet in the end, when the storm has broken, when the lightning has struck and the thunderclap has rolled, we experience a feel-ing of relief, serenity and well-being that we had almost forgotten existed.

However, when interpret-ing a dream, one crucial phenom-enon related to thunder and lightning should not be over-looked: there is no telling where lightning will strike or when thunder will be heard, and you can do nothing to prevent either.

That is why the rumble of thunder, and its attendant trembling and shaking, often symbolically represent the sudden appearance of the divine, the wrath of a god that mere mortals can only hope to mitigate through prayer and humility, a new awareness, a liberating crisis without which it is impossible to restore order.

As a result, hearing the sound of thunder or the earth rumbling in a dream almost always heralds a major upheaval, either physical or psychological in nature. However, in each case, the thunderclap is essential for self-development and personal growth.

See also *Lightning*, page 317.

Thunderbolt

*See Lightning, page 317
and Thunder, page 493*

Tiamat

See Venus in furs, page 515

Tit

The tit, an attractive little bird, is only 20cm (8in) long and is a common sight. There are many species – including blue, coal, long-tailed, marsh, alpine or crested – but the best known and most familiar is the great tit (*Parus major*), found in urban parks and gardens. Depending on the species, the female lays between 10 and 20 eggs in two broods, on which she sits with the male. Tits are happy to build their nest virtually anywhere: a mating pair is just as likely to use a hole in a tree as a letterbox or empty jam jar.

With its trusting, fairly tame nature, the tit soon became a symbol of sociability, simplicity and spontaneity. Like the kingfisher, this little bird is seen as an exemplary figure of marital bliss and fidelity because it often travels with its mate, and the male and female seem inseparable.

Toad

The etymology of the word 'toad' is obscure. It is thought to derive from the Old English *tadige* (of unknown origin) and the 15th-century *tadde* ('toad').

The toad is an anuran amphibian, an order of vertebrates (frogs and toads) characterized

Thunderbolt
Tiamat
Tit
Toad

by long hind legs adapted to hopping and the marked absence of a tail. It belongs to the class *Bufonidae*, which includes the European common toad (*Bufo bufo*). Although similar to the frog, the toad tends to be larger, has a dry, warty skin and spends more time on land than in the water.

In English, the term 'toad' is used figuratively to describe a vile, loathsome person and has given rise to the adjectives 'toadish' and 'toadlike', while 'toady' refers to an ingratiating person or sycophant and the verb 'to toady' means 'to fawn or flatter'.

For our ancestors, the toad was a creature that moved in dark, shadowy regions and was therefore associated with the great earth-goddess and with the moon. This probably also had something to do with the fact that it is a nocturnal creature and that it hibernates by burrowing underground, where it remains without eating or drinking for months on end. Its association with shadows and darkness

means that it appears in many tales and legends about witches who were reputed to use the toad's venom in the preparation of evil spells and poisonous potions:

> *Round about the cauldron go;*
> *In the poison'd entrails throw.*
> *Toad that under the cold stone*
> *Days and nights has thirty-one*
> *Swelt'red venom sleeping got,*
> *Boil thou first i' th' charmed*
> *pot!*

> (Macbeth, act 4, scene 1,
> William Shakespeare).

The toad was therefore perceived as one of the primeval creatures that existed when life emerged from the original waters of chaos but which, because it can live in water as well as on land, has remained at an intermediary and therefore primitive stage, as if fixed and refusing to evolve.

All this has to be taken into account when interpreting a dream about a toad. It should above all be remembered that the toad is, first and foremost, a representation of the great female principle and, as such, the Chinese naturally associated it with the female element (yin) related to coldness, darkness and the earth. They also regarded it as a symbol of the moon and believed that lunar eclipses came

about because the toad swallowed and then regurgitated the moon.

In a dream, the toad's amphibious nature, but also its ability to live buried in the ground for months on end without eating or drinking, can signify that the most obscure and the most luminous psychological forces arise from the same principle. In simpler terms, whether our thoughts are dark and negative or enlightened and positive, they are what we are. A dream about a toad therefore encourages us not to reject any part of ourselves, whether positive or negative.

Train

Like the motorcar and airplane, the train is obviously a modern symbol (see *Automobile* page 45 and *Airplane* page 22). As can be imagined, a train would hardly have appeared in the dreams of the Egyptians, Chinese, ancient Greeks, or even the people of the Middle Ages or Renaissance. However, we cannot be certain that they did not dream about a train: they may simply not have known what it was, when recalling the content of their dream. After all, we often dream about monsters, objects, instruments,

even landscapes or beings that do not exist: these have sometimes been portrayed, drawn or painted, and are simply regarded as products of the human imagination. Certainly, no images have been found to suggest that our ancestors had premonitory visions of a train. On the other hand, some believe that certain figurative representations by the Mayans, Aztecs, Akkadians, Egyptians, Indians or Chinese depict modern inventions like space shuttles or flying saucers. In the late 15th century, the painter Leonardo da Vinci had already drawn up plans for what, centuries later, would resemble the airplane, helicopter and submarine. Also, if we are to believe the theories put forward by certain psychoanalysts and physicists who posit the existence of a universal memory or consciousness within which a continuous space-time distortion may occur, the past, present and future can sometimes merge. If this is true then certain parts of our mind that are not ordinarily used

would be capable of travelling through space and time. Although we have no fixed opinions on this subject, we do believe that anything is possible.

Whatever the case, trains do exist nowadays and they have a symbolic significance. The train obviously represents a journey, but particularly the act of travelling from one point to another without being able to deviate from your course. In this respect, the interpretation of a dream about a train differs according to whether you are one of many travellers or whether you are driving the train. In the first case, you are not in control of the events in your life at the time when you have this dream. In the second, on the contrary, you are in control, you know what you are doing and where you are headed; you may even have a specific goal that you wish to attain at any cost.

Missing a train is a fairly recurrent dream. This often represents a lost opportunity or else a refusal on your part to involve yourself in a situation or go in a certain direction. Waiting for a train at a station may herald an imminent journey or move, or simply an anticipated event that is a long time coming. Lastly, witnessing a rail crash indicates that your life may be turned upside down by something that will, symbolically, cause you to go off the rails.

Treasure

Treasure often has the connotation of a mystery revealed and is associated with the discovery of something inaccessible, miraculous and unexpected. All the legends and tales that feature a great treasure involve extraordinary circumstances, covetous men and women who want to possess the prize at any cost and who end up possessed by it. In fact, the treasure in these stories appears to have less importance than its eventual use. This is because treasure is synonymous with riches, fortune, abundance, opulence, magnificence, luxury, authority and power. However, finding a treasure trove is so unusual, so difficult, that it has become the subject of a symbolic quest akin to the search for the soul, the most precious treasure possessed by man and the essential component that makes him what he is.

As a result, although dreaming of finding treasure may well herald a period of prosperity that exceeds all your expectations, it is generally a sign that you are about to experience a

happy event, a time of great joy that has nothing to do with material considerations, even though its cause is very real. This dream may also prompt a realization. You may be on the point of discovering that you possess inner riches, whether they are intellectual, spiritual or even emotional.

Lastly, people will often describe someone they love as a real treasure. The treasure in your dream could therefore represent this highly valued person.

Tree

See Christmas, page 97

Tree of life

Trees are a vital element of the natural world and life on earth. It is a well-know fact that, without them, the air we breathe would not contain the oxygen we need to live. This has led to forests being described as the 'lungs of the earth'. From time immemorial, trees have been a central preoccupation and focal point of human life. However, the primordial, magical and fundamental bond forged between human beings and trees seems to have been dangerously ruptured in recent decades. Trees have become a rare sight in our modern cities, which have been taken over by concrete, steel and cars. They have also been sacrificed to the interests – and profits – of large multinationals that have actively encouraged deforestation on a massive scale, thereby accelerating the desertification of vast areas of the planet.

In spite of this, the tree is still regarded as sacred in our primitive consciousness and, although trees are no longer worshipped in Western cultures, planting or felling a tree gives rise to very strong emotions. We are still filled with awe when contemplating a centuries-old tree or the depths of a forest that is both an inviting haven of peace and quiet and a mysterious and disturbing unknown world.

The ancient belief that anyone who planted a tree would enjoy long life is still very much alive in certain parts of the world. In modern-day Turkey, for example, Anatolian peasants are firmly convinced that, if they fell a tree, they will also sever their line of descent.

Primitive cultures identified as readily with the spirit of a tree as with the spirit of an animal (see *Animal*, page 31) and, as in the case of the animal, the qualities and characteristics of the tree reflected various aspects of the behaviour and character of the person in question. Trees were worshipped, had prayers addressed to them and were associated with the great spirits and mysterious forces of nature. It is therefore hardly surprising that many of the gods and goddesses in the myths and legends of ancient civilizations were associated with or emerged from a tree.

In ancient Egypt, the falcon-god Horus emerged from the acacia and, according to the Book of the Dead, 'twin sycamores of turquoise' stood at the eastern gate of heaven from which the sun-god Re emerged each morning. One of the most ancient tree cults was dedicated to the cow-goddess Hathor, creator of the world and 'lady of the sycamore'. The sycamore was also a manifestation of the sky-goddess Nut who shielded the dead Osiris and 'rejuvenated his soul among her branches'.

In ancient Greece, the oak was the tree of Zeus and the olive

the tree of Apollo. In the ancient Sumerian city of Eridu (Mesopotamia) stood the Kiskanu, a sacred tree whose roots, planted in the centre of the world, were the home of Enki (or Ea), the god of water and 'the source of all life', and his divine mother Bau, goddess of fertility, flocks and herds. The early writers of the Bible were inspired by this mythical and historical tree which appears in Genesis in the form of the tree of the knowledge of good and evil planted in the centre of the Garden of Eden by Yahweh.

The tree of life or cosmic axis of the world, the seat of a divine or spiritual entity, is a recurrent theme in the beliefs of

From a 16th-century Persian miniature

peoples throughout the world. Even today, the Tartars of the Altai Mountains still subscribe to the ancient belief that the largest tree on earth – a giant pine whose summit touches the dwelling place of the great god – grows from the navel of the world, at the centre of all things.

Over the ages, human qualities, weaknesses and virtues have been attributed and assigned to trees, probably well before the signs of the zodiac came into being. The Celts used this principle to establish a very elaborate calendar based on the phases of the moon. Each period of the year corresponded to the properties of a particular tutelary tree and an individual born during this period shared a number of characteristics with that tree.

In some cases, the similarities between mortals and trees

were taken a step further. For example, according to one of the most famous passages in the *Mahabharata*, which could be regarded as the Hindu equivalent of the Bible: 'When this mighty tree [the Ashwattha] is finally cut down [...], in spite of its strongly fixed roots – then the destroyer of that tree shalt seek for that place from which there is no more return to rebirth ...' (*Bhagavad Gita* 15: 1–3). According to the beliefs of the pre-Aryan Indus civilization, the Ashwattha was a sacred tree whose roots were planted in the sky and whose branches extended downward so that its leaves covered the earth. This inverted tree has a number of points in common with a human being: the roots = the head, the branches = the limbs, the trunk = the torso, the heart = the heart, the leaves and fruit = good and evil. Thus when a yogi practices the *sirsasana* (headstand), he is in fact replicating the position of the sacred tree whose roots plunge deep into the earth to draw on the life and energy that form the sap, and the parallel between the tree and the human being becomes clear.

A similar belief is found in the *Sefer ha-zohar* ('Book of Splendour'); traditionally attributed to the Jewish mystic and rabbi Simeon ben Yohai (fl. 2nd century AD) – although modern scholars credit most of it to the Jewish cabbalist Moses de León (1250–1305) of Spain – it describes the tree of life as an all-illuminating sun extending from heaven to the earth below.

From time immemorial, justice has always been meted out beneath a tree, but trees have also been the favoured site for fertility rituals and sacrifices. Thus, before becoming an act of barbarism or the price to be paid for a felony or crime, hanging was regarded as a sacred and totally symbolic act. The XIIth card (the Hanged Man) in the Major Arcana of the divinatory Tarot cards represents the ultimate, voluntary sacrifice of hanging. It symbolizes oblivion and the gift of self in favour of the fertility of the immortal soul and the liberation of the eternal and divine spirit present in each individual.

On this card, the branches of the two trees that support the beam serving as the gallows have been lopped and the trees are covered with scars left by the cut branches. The analogy between the tree and the human body is obvious since it is the two trees that are damaged, not the Hanged Man. Furthermore, the position of the Hanged Man, head downwards, is reminiscent of the position of the cosmic tree, the Hindu Ashwattha and the tree of life of the cabbala.

In medieval times, it was believed that mandrake, the equivalent of Chinese ginseng – whose humanoid roots were widely used for their magical aphrodisiac, soporific and analgesic properties – grew from the semen of hanged men that fell beneath the gibbet.

Tree of life according to the cabbala

Each and every human being is a potential tree of life. In the Jewish cabbalistic tradition, the sacred tree of the sephiroth (Hebrew *sephira*, number) is a perfect representation of this. The tree of life is a recurring and universal theme. For example, the mythical tree that inspired the biblical description of the tree of life – 'And out of the ground made the Lord God to grow every tree that is pleasant to the sight, and good for food;

the tree of life is also in the midst of the garden, and the tree of the knowledge of good and evil' (Genesis 2: 9) – must surely have been the black Kiskanu, the sacred tree deified by the Mesopotamians. Its roots reached to the centre of the world, the underworld and the home of Enki (or Ea), the god of water and 'the source of all life' (see *Tree of life*, page 498).

It should, however, be pointed out that, with regard to this passage from Genesis, a tendency to generalize has led to the confusion of the tree of life and the tree of the knowledge of good and evil, which are self-evidently not the same. It is 'the tree of life [...] in the midst of the garden'

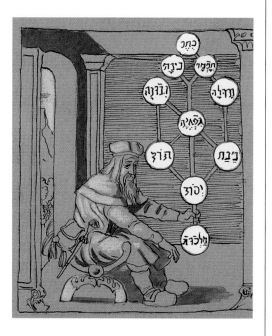

and not the tree of the knowledge of good and evil that is associated with the Mesopotamian Kiskanu. And the Lord's (Yahweh's) interdiction did not apply to the tree of life but to the tree of the knowledge of good and evil: 'Of every tree of the garden thou mayest freely eat: but of the tree of the knowledge of good and evil, thou shalt not eat of it: for in the day that thou eatest thereof thou shalt surely die' (Genesis 2: 16–17).

The confusion is further reinforced by the close association of the two trees. For instance, when Adam and Eve (and therefore the human race) have eaten of the tree of the knowledge of good and evil, they are driven from the Garden of Eden and can therefore no longer eat of the tree of life. In other words, the knowledge they have acquired has cost them their life and cut them off from their original sustenance. They now know the world, but no longer know themselves. They are disorientated, they have lost their way and their *raison d'être*, and 'till [they] return unto the ground' out of which they were taken (Genesis 3: 19), they will walk in darkness and live in ignorance. To rediscover their way and their direction, they have to climb the ladder that leads to the opening

Tree of life
according to
the cabbala

of their consciousness, the ladder that, in all world religions, bears such names as the Way, Truth, Life, Revelation and Illumination.

This cosmic ladder and the 'rungs' that the individual must climb one by one to rediscover his or her state of grace are wonderfully symbolized by the chakras (the psychic-energy centres of the body) and the awakening of the kundalini (cosmic energy) described in the Hindu religion. Six of the seven main chakras are located along the spinal cord and the seventh above the crown of the skull. The tree of the sephiroth is based on the same elements and principles. It can be said that the principles of the chakras and the sephiroth symbolize the tree of life, each in its own way and according to its own particular culture.

In this context, it is important to understand that each of us is an unconscious tree of life, and that it is down to us to regain our lost paradise. This Garden of Eden, paradise lost, golden age or promised land – call it what you will – is not a physical, external place but is within each and every one of us. And at its centre, at the very heart of what we are, is the tree of life, wonderfully well represented by the cabbalistic tree of the sephiroth.

The tree of the sephiroth. In Hebrew, *sephira* (pl. *sephiroth*) means 'number'. According to the esoteric Jewish mystical tradition known as the cabbala, the tree of life comprises the ten sephiroth, the emanations, or powers, by which God the Creator is said to become manifest. The concept first appeared in the *Sefer Yetzira* ('book of creation') where the sephiroth were the ten ideal numbers. In the cabbala, each sephira contains a divine energy to which it is difficult to give a name without resorting to schematization. 'Archetype' would seem the most appropriate term to convey or, at least, give a general idea of what is represented by each sephira.

That said, 'archetype' should not be understood in the sense of a typical, perfect and original symbol that can only be apprehended intelligibly by the soul and which constitutes the very foundation of all symbolic language – i.e. the language of dreams but also the language of omens and portents, as has been frequently stressed in the present work. It should rather be understood as pure, original energy that nothing can change or modify and that cannot be other than it is. It is impossible to envisage any form of deception or manipulation in respect of what is embodied by the sephiroth, which is why the human race was deprived of them when Adam and Eve chose to change direction and follow an alternative path. But, as has been stated with regard to the passage from Genesis 2: 16–17, even though human beings can no longer eat of the tree of life, they can at least envisage it and be aware of its existence, before being able to experience it.

For it should be clearly understood that, although the diagram of the tree of the sephiroth, as presented here, is intellectually very exciting, it is worthless until each of us has experienced it at first hand.

This experience is not without its dangers, since it implies deep and sometimes total personal commitment. It can be approached by attempting to understand the subtle links between the archetypal components of the diagram above and the human body. Thus, by comparing the male or female body to the main points of the diagram, it is possible to glean extremely valuable information regarding the strong and weak points of an individual, both in respect of their physical constitution and their psychic and psychological make-up, since the two aspects are closely interrelated.

The composition of the tree of the sephiroth.

• At the top is the first sephira – *kether* ('supreme crown'). But above *kether* is *ain soph* which translates literally as 'there is not', 'without end' or 'non-being'. *Ain soph* is not a sephira but represents the highest degree of consciousness (divine substance) to which it is possible to aspire.

• Below *kether* are *chokmah* ('wisdom') and *binah* ('intelligence'), the second and third sephiroth.

• Then come *chesed* ('grace' or 'mercy') and *geburah* ('strength'), the fourth and fifth sephiroth.

• Below them, in the centre, is *tiphareth* ('beauty), the sixth sephira.

• Then come *netzach* ('victory') and *hod* ('honour' or 'glory'), the seventh and eighth sephiroth.

• Finally, below *yesod* ('foundation'), the ninth sephira, and at the base of the tree of the sephiroth is *malkhuth* ('kingdom' or 'reign'), the tenth and last sephira.

Tunnel

Many analogies can be drawn between the hole and the tunnel, because the latter also represents a passageway or transit point. However, unlike the hole (see page 259), the tunnel is a long corridor with an entrance and an exit or an opening at either end: a tunnel always leads somewhere, although it can be a path into the unknown. That is why the route between earth and heaven, the land of the mortals and the home of the gods, was often represented as a tunnel of light, while the one leading down into the kingdom of the dead or the underworld was represented as a dark, terrifying corridor. One way or another, however, both the hole and the tunnel are initiatory in character. Someone falling into a hole is in the same position as someone walking through a tunnel, irrespective of whether it is light or dark. They must emerge from it transformed in some way or having grown in stature. In this respect, the most powerful symbolic interpretation of the tunnel is as a passageway leading to another life.

When interpreting a dream of walking through a tunnel, it is important to take note of its appearance: Was it light, dark, deserted? What was in it? What were you doing? A dream like this can sometimes simply be interpreted by the saying 'seeing the light at the end of the tunnel', meaning that you are finally coming to the end of a difficult period. However, you should never forget that the tunnel is primarily a passageway between two worlds and thus perhaps between two periods of your life, two levels of consciousness, or even between two sides of your own personality. As a result, a dream like this can represent a necessary transition, a route you need to take to be at peace with yourself.

Turkey

The turkey (*Meleagris gallopavo*) is a large North American gallinaceous bird – i.e. a domestic fowl and therefore of the same family as the cockerel and the hen – with iridescent copper-coloured plumage tinged with green and russet. The term 'turkey' is a shortened form of Turkey cock (or hen), meaning the African guinea fowl (which apparently spread through Turkish territory), and was later wrongly applied to the American bird. The turkey is extremely prolific and lays five or six eggs at a time, with clutches of up to 25 eggs. It is quite a fierce bird, and defends its young with spirit and aggression.

For the natives of North America, the hen was a symbol of fertility, while the cock was a symbol of virility. These beliefs continued to survive in Europe where the turkey was introduced in the 16th century. However, its unpleasant character and defensive and aggressive attitude soon earned the turkey a bad reputation, all the more so because there is something haughty and presumptuous in its bearing that makes it rather unappealing. This obviously inspired the expression 'to strut about like a turkey-cock', which has a direct French equivalent in 'se pavaner comme un dindon'. The French also associate the turkey with stupidity since a stupid woman is often referred to as *une dinde* (female turkey) – where the English would refer to a 'silly little goose' – and 'être le dindon (de la farce)' means 'to be cheated or outwitted', a popular expression coined following the successful 19th-

century play, *Le Dindon*, by Georges Feydeau. In the United States, however, 'to talk turkey' means to discuss something frankly and practically, yet another example of imagery and symbolism being culture specific.

Twelve

See Numbers, page 394

Twelve labours of Hercules (the)

See Hercules, page 224

Twins

See Androgyne to twins, page 26

Two

See Numbers, page 365

Umbrella, parasol

It might be thought that the umbrella is a recent, modern invention and therefore that it did not appear in our forebears' dreams, but nothing could be further from the truth. In fact, umbrellas appear on Chinese miniatures dating from the 2nd century BC. However it was not until the 18th century that the umbrella made its appearance in Europe, popularized by an English traveller and writer, Jonas Hanway, who initially encountered no end of ridicule as he carried it through the streets of London. It took many years for it to be accepted in Britain, despite the somewhat variable weather.

The parasol, on the other hand, is much older, because great ancient civilizations, like those of Mesopotamia and Egypt, were more accustomed to sunshine than rain. The tree was the first natural parasol, particularly the sycamore in Egypt, or the palm tree in other sun-drenched regions of the Middle East and North Africa.

Although the parasol and umbrella both symbolize protection, the former from the sun's rays, the latter from the rain, this artificial protection is not always a good omen in a dream. In fact, by sheltering us from something that comes from the sky, these devices, while very useful in everyday life, may symbolically deprive us of blessings from heaven and therefore of all types of positive energy.

This is worth bearing in mind, especially if you have a dream about an umbrella, as this is more likely to reveal a tendency to deprive yourself of beneficial and regenerative energies from heaven rather than a natural need to protect yourself from the sun's rays or the rain. After all, when you consider that heaven was once regarded as the abode of the gods, to shelter under a parasol or an umbrella is tantamount to cutting yourself off completely from the divine.

Unicorn and dragon

Numerous legends, fables and fairy-tales are based around these two mythical creatures, living symbols that have taken hold of the human imagination.

The unicorn. The popular representation of the unicorn closely resembles the one in the famous series of six late 15th-century tapestries, *The Lady with the Unicorn*, that are on display at the French museum of medieval arts and crafts in Paris, the Musée de Cluny. The unicorn is a fantastic, unreal animal with the body of a horse, cloven hooves and a goat's head with a long horn projecting from its forehead, hence its Latin name, *unicornis*. The English word 'unicorn' is derived from the Latin via the old French *unicorne*.

The myth of the unicorn appeared for the first time in the writings of the Greek historian Ctesias, physician to King Cyrus the Younger (423–401 BC), then to King Artaxerxes II Mnemon (404–358 BC), two rival brothers who plunged the Persian empire into chaos. As a result, the origin of the myth of the unicorn is often attributed to the Persians. In his account, Ctesias, who had travelled with Artaxerxes to Egypt and India, made mention of the medicinal properties attributed to the horn of this fabled animal, which was actually none other than the white Indian rhinoceros. Like the legendary unicorn, the rhinoceros is a fairly solitary, timid and completely herbivorous animal that lives in marshy areas and has one or two horns on its forehead. It is also virtually impossible to get close to the rhinoceros due to its extremely well-developed sense of smell. Powdered rhinoceros horn is said to have aphrodisiac powers and the unicorn, despite its apparent grace, frailty and the

female characteristics sometimes attributed to it, is a male ithyphallic symbol.

Whatever the historical origin of the unicorn, it became a popular mythical creature in the Middle Ages. As a symbol of purity and chastity, it was taken to represent the Virgin Mary. However, owing to its timid, untameable nature and the legend that it could only be approached and tamed by a virgin maiden, it was also seen as a representation of the baby Jesus. According to an 11th-century legend, drinking from a unicorn horn protected the drinker from all types of poison. Later, alchemists associated the unicorn with the stag, forming the perfect pair. A strange inversion thus took place that, while still faithful to the myth of the unicorn, recalled the fact that people in ancient times, particularly in Egypt, believed that the sky was female, represented by the goddess Nut, and that the earth was a male principle, embodied by the god Geb. The alchemists believed, therefore, that the unicorn represented the mind, sulphur and the male principle, while the stag symbolized the soul, mercury and the female principle. This meant that their union could produce the divine being.

The dragon. Without wishing to confuse two ideas or bend over backwards to find analogies and connections between various past beliefs and those that continue to haunt the imagination to this day, there are definitely many similarities between the myth of the dragon, a legendary creature, and the dinosaur that, although it once existed, seems no less fantastic. In some ways, there is something even more unreal about the dinosaur than the dragon because over 100 million years have passed since this creature walked the earth. Human beings, who have an average life span of around 70 or 80 years, find it very hard to imagine a period of

Unicorn and dragon

100 million years. Could that great reptile of the mesozoic era be the ancestor of the dragon? Or is it possible that human beings have preserved, in the recesses of their psyche, subconscious memories of the existence of this huge reptile? It is impossible to know for sure. All we know is that, for all their intelligence, human beings will never use more than ten per cent of their mental capacity and that their life span will not exceed around 100 years, even though they have enough grey cells to last 1,000 years.

Whatever the case, although we do not know if dinosaur skeletons were found in ancient times, one thing is certain: the iconography of the dragon often shows a fantastic, fire-breathing creature resembling a massive reptile with wings or fins, a long tail, long feet sometimes with talons, sometimes webbed. This is how it is portrayed, in the West at least.

On the other hand, in China, the dragon is a mythical creature, symbol of the yang, fertility and activity, represented by a large serpent coiled at the centre of the earth and responsible for the creation of the world. The sky and the constellations were also often represented by a large serpent covering the earth, both in the West and in China.

Symbolically, the myth of the dragon has been assimilated to and identified with the potential for primordial energy – creative and destructive, heavenly and terrestrial – that human beings carry within them and share with the earth. It is as if an incredible, unimaginably powerful force is being held captive both in the bowels of the earth and deep within the human being.

As a result, killing the dragon has become a human quest to master those primitive primordial forces that keep human beings locked into the endless, infernal cycle of birth and death, followed by a new birth and a new death, etc. The myths and symbols relating to the dragon were also incorporated into alchemical symbolism. Like the stag, the great female and mercurial principle, the dragon had to be sacrificed so that sulphur, the great male principle, could be extracted from him.

The unicorn and the dragon were not regarded as monsters or freaks of nature in primitive cultures. Even if they had been regarded in this way, however, it is worth remembering that, in ancient times and the Middle Ages, monsters were considered divine, precisely because they were monstrous, extraordinary and rare. Their specific qualities made them the terrestrial messengers of the gods. Therefore, while they may not have been honoured, their appearances were highly regarded and their presence was well-received. This is why the hunt for the unicorn or the dragon became a mystical quest. One does not hunt a dream, a legend, or a myth. In the search for either one, man sought to find himself; it was a quest for light, truth, love, purity and happiness: all the things for which people have always searched and always will.

Uranus

Mesopotamian myths about Uranus. In the cosmogony of this ancient civilization, the birthplace of many cultures, writing, the science of numbers and astrology, there were seven planets/gods. As a result, although it is relatively easy to find analogies in Assyrian myths with the characteristics attributed to the sun, moon, Mercury, Venus, Mars, Jupiter and Saturn in astrology, it is more difficult with regard to Uranus. However, given that the Greek myths, which are still a source of inspiration today, were themselves

drawn from Akkadian and Babylonian legendary and mythical sources, it should be possible to find myths and characters whose adventures and characteristics present analogies to Uranus. This holds true for the sky god who reigned over the heavens and who was called Anu by the Akkadians and An by the Sumerians. According to the Akkadian cosmogony or creation myth, Anu created the heavens. In an astrological treatise dating from the third millennium BC, we learn that Anu, Enlil and Ea, the great gods, determined in their council (*purhum*) the designs (*usurati*) of the heavens and the earth and gave them to the major gods. According to the *Enuma Elish*, which we discussed under *Jupiter* (see page 293), Anu did not intervene when Tiamat threatened to plunge the world into chaos. It was Marduk, the Mesopotamian Jupiter figure, who succeeded in vanquishing Tiamat and returned the stolen tablets of fate to Anu. According to the Epic of Atrahasis, known as the 'most wise', whose myth is a flood story predating that of Noah in the Bible, Anu was the father of the seven Anunnaku, the great gods whose slaves and servants were the Igigi, lesser gods who could be regarded as the ancestors of mankind (in

some texts the positions are reversed). It was Anu who defended the Igigi when they, exhausted by their toil, rebelled, and the sound of their wailing rose to heaven. As we have seen, Anu could not withstand chaos, but he stood by those who worked, suffered, complained and rebelled. These are all typical Uranian characteristics.

Egyptian myths about Uranus. If Uranus was identified with the sky, as was Anu in Mesopotamia, and later, in Greece, regarded as the personification of heaven, then Nut, the sky goddess, might be thought to be the Egyptian representation of this planet. However, Nut denotes only the vault of the heavens, while her brother and husband, Geb, represents the earth. These two representations of heaven and earth were separated by their father, Shu, as also occurred in the Assyrian myth when Marduk pierced the body of Tiamat with a deadly arrow (see *Jupiter*, page 293). We must therefore look further back in the hierarchy of the divine pantheon of ancient Egypt. Shu, the cosmic god, was the personification of the air, often represented standing with his arms raised to support Nut, the sky, his daughter, while Geb, the earth, his son, lay between his legs. However, the air cannot fully represent the elements evoked by Uranus. Shu and his sister, Tefnut, who symbolized moisture, were the first divine couple created by Atum, the creator god *par excellence*, who was later associated with Re, and became a sun god. It is therefore Atum, in his earliest presentation, before he was syncretized with Re to become a representation of the setting sun, in whom we can identify an Egyptian correlation with Uranus.

Greek myths about Uranus. Uranus was nicknamed by the Greeks 'King of the Mountains', because he was the personification of heaven. He was sometimes the son, sometimes the brother and sometimes the husband of Gaia, the earth. Uranus fathered many on Gaia, until she, weary of her fertility, persuaded one of her sons,

Cronus, to castrate his father (see *Saturn*, page 440). However, although this mythical misdeed is the best-known version of the story of Uranus, another version is of greater interest. It relates that this god was the first ruler of the Atlantieans, king of the famous and fabled Atlantis of which, to this day, no reliable archaeological and historic traces have been found. The Atlantieans were reputed to have possessed great wisdom and learning, and it was Uranus who is said to have brought them civilization and culture, teaching them, for example, the secrets of the calendar and the movements of the planets, as well as how to make forecasts from them. (In another myth, of course, it was Atlas who ruled over Atlantis; see *Hercules*, page 224). Like Anu in Mesopotamia, Uranus also possessed a tablet of fates that enabled him to foretell the future, and the Atlantieans have numerous points in common with the Anunnaku.

Vampire

There are countless phantasmagoric representations of the terrifying vampire and the fantastic world that serves as a backdrop for its evildoings. This creature has featured in countless novels and films, such as *Nosferatu*, made in 1922 by the German film-maker F.W. Murnau, which was the first screen treatment of a vampire, or in the character of Count Dracula, created by the novelist Bram Stoker, who was the subject of more than 30 films in under 50 years. Quite apart from the folk imagery, steeped in persistent superstitions, beliefs and ancient fears, that surrounds the vampire in the same way as Count Dracula wraps himself in his flowing cloak, the vampire was primarily a symbol of contamination. Before our forebears had any scientific knowledge of the formidable power of viruses, they were well aware of the fatal, terrifying processes of contagion, against which they were often powerless. Is it any different today, in fact, in a world plagued by a new virus that is wreaking havoc and can survive for over 60 years in white blood corpuscles? However, before novels created the image of the vampire as a fanged monster that drank its victims' blood in order to live forever, the contamination initially symbolized by this myth was psychic and spiritual. It was linked to the despotic powers of certain individuals who sought to dominate and feed off others, influencing them to follow their every wish or obey their every command.

Symbolically, the vampire represents the dominant individual who refuses to adapt to the world, to change or transform himself, who wants the world and other people to submit to him, and who has enough power or strength of will to succeed. The terrifying thing about this kind of person is that he cannot live simply by being himself: he needs other people to survive. Thus, in ancient times and the Middle Ages, all over the world and in every civilization, numerous demons displayed all the attributes of the vampire. And the real danger was always that once someone came into contact with a blood-sucking demon, he became, in his turn, a potential demon himself.

The myth of the vampire therefore symbolizes dependence or slavery, a refusal to adapt, change, metamorphose or live simply, and also a refusal to die, death being the ultimate metamorphosis according to numerous ancestral beliefs, a

truly inevitable process, against which human beings are powerless. Dreaming about a vampire must therefore be interpreted from this angle because, in a dream, it embodies everything that, within or around you, rejects regenerative change, which is the fundamental principle of life on earth.

Veil

A veil is a protective piece of fabric that can obscure the vision. The veil is associated with lying, concealment, a refusal to see something, as in the expression 'to draw a veil over', which means to conceal something from the knowledge of others, as a veil conceals a woman's face. Dreaming of a veil often reveals that the dreamer is a victim of self-imposed restrictions.

Venus

Mesopotamian myths about Venus. In the 1840s, when excavating at Nimrud, now in Iraq, the English archaeologist Sir Austen Henry Layard discovered numerous statuettes in the remains of the palace of King Ashurnasirpal II. These figurines, which all dated from

the 8th century BC, were of the goddess whom the Babylonians called Ishtar and who was also the Semitic goddess Ashtart or Astarte. However, the origins of this goddess, whose virtues and qualities closely resemble those attributed to Venus in astrology, probably date back much earlier, although there are so many possibilities that they have become confused and muddled. This is hardly surprising because, in the zodiac, Venus has a dual nature, being the ruling planet of both Taurus and Libra and, as such, presents two interpretations of the feminine. Ishtar is therefore sometimes identified with Inanna, the great Sumerian goddess who was occasionally, and wrongly, confused with Nanna, the Sumerian god of the moon (see *Inanna, Ishtar, Astarte, Aphrodite and Venus*, page 274). Inanna/Ishtar was credited with lunar qualities specific to Nanna/Sin, qualities with which, to some degree, she could be identified, although they were not, strictly speaking, hers. Lunar and Venusian qualities can easily be confused, since they are very similar and have many points in common, in so far as they are purely feminine properties. However, Nanna/Sin, god of the moon, and Inanna/Ishtar, goddess of love, were two very different entities. What is more, Inanna was not just a goddess of love in Sumer, but also a war goddess:

Haughty ruler, Inanna,
Skilled at starting wars,
You lay waste to the earth and
conquer countries
With your long-ranging arrows!
Down here and up there, you
roared like a wildcat,
And struck down the nations!

Taken from a poem attributed to the daughter of the great Sargon of Akkad (2334–2279 BC), Enheduanna, priestess of Nanna in Ur, at the time of Naram-Sin (2251–2218 BC).

Thus, the Babylonian goddess Ishtar, who served as the Greeks' inspiration for the myths of Aphrodite and Persephone, was originally the Akkadian goddess Inanna, as well as Dilbat, the morning star, which was none other than the planet Venus. Although it is sometimes thought (wrongly) that Venus is only the first star visible to the naked eye in the evening, in fact, Venus can also be seen in the morning, although the brightness of the sun may prevent us from seeing it in the dawn sky. Anahita, a Persian female war deity and the multiple goddess featured prominently in the sacred writings of Zoroastrianism, the Avesta, may have been another source of inspiration for the worshippers of Ishtar, whom the Jews called Ashtoreth, 'the shamed', and whom the Christians, much later, regarded as one of the right-hand women of Satan, the fallen angel. However, as well as being a warrior and an avenging goddess, Ishtar was also a goddess of love, a sacred prostitute and a sky goddess, who caused the planets to move, which is why the Babylonians called the zodiac 'the girdle of Ishtar'. Likewise, anything related to divination, oracles and magic was her domain.

Egyptian myths about Venus. Although numerous female deities were associated with fertility, magic, death and war in Egypt, the supreme goddess who best incorporated and synthesized their qualities was Isis the sorceress, sister-wife of Osiris. There is no doubt she played a vital role in the minds of the clergy in Egypt, where the priests were as powerful as the pharaoh, sometimes even replacing him or ruling the country behind the scenes. She certainly held a key position in the hierarchy of the tutelary deities that were so numerous in ancient civilizations and eventually came to be identified with some, taking their place. Furthermore, the influence of this goddess, to whom the Egyptians attributed exceptional properties and powers, was felt far beyond Egypt. In Greece, Cyprus and Crete, the qualities attributed to Artemis, Hecate and Persephone were assimilated with hers. And in Rome, in 80 BC, the emperor Caligula erected a temple on the Capitol consecrated to Great Isis. Isis could be comforting or dangerous: she could protect, perform acts of kindness, save lives and bring the dead back to life or, alternatively, she could end life by casting evil spells or using black magic, in which she was well versed.

However, she was generally regarded as a loving woman with undeniable human qualities.

Greek myths about Venus. The Greek goddess Aphrodite was the model for Venus, the Roman goddess of love. However, as we have seen, Aphrodite, the sacred prostitute, was merely an aspect of Ishtar, even if the Greeks distinguished between Aphrodite Urania, embodying spiritual love, and Aphrodite Pandemos, symbolizing carnal love. In Greece, however, there was another goddess who, according to her myth, lived through what was a veritable descent into hell, the underworld, when she was carried off by Hades, the god of the dead, whose wife she became. The abduction of Persephone, whose name means 'bringer of destruction', caused Demeter her mother, who was beside herself with rage at losing her daughter, to make the earth barren. Lastly, there was the warrior aspect of Ishtar that, in Greece, was embodied by Athena, whose name is derived directly from Anahita, the imperious female deity who appeared long before Ishtar.

See also *Inanna, Ishtar, Astarte, Aphrodite, Venus*, page 274.

Venus in furs to Tiamat (from the)

The above-mentioned goddesses were the most typical representations of the great goddess who has been worshipped and venerated on earth for millennia. Our relatively short lifespan prevents us from having an all-encompassing view of the world and of life. We have to look at our immediate surroundings from where we are standing and our field of vision is obviously restricted by the horizon.

We cannot comprehend everything that is happening around us at any given moment, even though we may think about it. *A fortiori*, we are totally incapable of imagining what the past was really like and we find it hard to accept that men and women in ancient times may have been fundamentally different from us. To arrive at some understanding, we need points of reference and instruments as well as remains and traces of their lives. However, even when we examine objects produced by a structured society, with habits and customs dating back two, three, four or five thousand years, we cannot help studying them from a modern viewpoint and bringing all our contemporary preconceptions into play.

As a result, there are almost as many versions of man's history as there are historians and, apart from the historical facts, events and dates about which we are more or less certain, the rest is pure conjecture and subjective interpretation. The further back we go, the truer this is.

The oldest known myth of a mother-goddess. In 1908, at Willendorf, in Austria, archaeologists unearthed a statuette, 11cm (4½in) tall, of a naked woman with pendulous breasts, a protuberant stomach and prominent buttocks, carved from limestone. There were still traces of red ochre in some of its hollows dating back to when it was made, at least 20,000 and possibly 40,000 years ago. Since then, specialists in the palaeolithic era, followed closely by journalists, have speculated freely. This

statuette was the first of over 200 prehistoric carvings of female figures to be found on the European continent throughout the 20th century, along a line stretching from the Pyrenees deep into the heart of the southern Russian steppes. The oldest, which has been dated fairly accurately, was sculpted about 30,000 BC. It was also unearthed in Austria, at Galgenberg, and the figure seems to be dancing. Conditioned by modern beliefs, we think of these crudely carved stone figurines as grossly obese women, which experts, drawing inspiration from the Roman goddess of love, have nicknamed, somewhat jocosely, Venuses in furs – because some of them seem to be wearing a kind of animal skin garment. However, to this day, we have no positive, tangible and irrefutable proof that these figurines of naked women, which are not all obese, represent any goddess of love worshipped or venerated by our distant forebears. Also, when we peruse the numerous theses and theories produced and published exclusively by men (archaeologists, palaeontologists, researchers, historians and even gynaecologists), we realize that at no time has the idea apparently crossed the minds of these researchers that these figurines could have been made by women, not men, nor that the customs, motivations and beliefs of these palaeolithic communities could have been different from ours. We should also consider the fact that the art of making these figurines seemingly persisted for at least 20,000 or 25,000 years, at a time when people were nomads, hunters and gatherers. The myth of the great goddess, who was to take on various guises, but whose sacred or divine functions and attributes remained more or less identical, did not appear until much later, when men and women, progressing from hunting and gathering to farming, had abandoned their nomadic lifestyle to settle permanently in one place. In all likelihood, therefore, the famous 'Venus in furs' originally had greater significance as a symbolic object than as a mythical one. It may simply have fulfilled the same role as a photograph today. Each statuette may have been a representation of a much-loved wife or mother, her image carved by her nearest and dearest so they would not forget her.

Tiamat, the goddess of primordial chaos. We have to go back much further in time to discover the goddess who may have been the first great mother of the world, although there is nothing to say that an even earlier mythical goddess will never come to light. According to the *Enuma Elish*, the Babylonian cosmogonic poem (see *Cosmogonies in Mesopotamia*, page 126) Tiamat was a divine entity symbolizing the primordial waters or the sea. These waters mingled with Apsu, another mythical god representing the sweet waters of the springs and rivers on earth, and created the gods of the Mesopotamian divine pantheon, who waged a savage, fratricidal war for supremacy. Their father, Apsu, disillusioned and furious at his children's behaviour, decided to do away with them. However, one of them, Ea, murdered Apsu, his father. To avenge the death of her husband, Tiamat then gave birth to a host of monsters, which represented the raging elements of the primordial waters. Rising up against them, Marduk, son of Ea, split open Tiamat's womb and liberated the primeval gods she had engendered with Apsu. He then used the limbs of Tiamat's corpse to create the world. Consequently, according to this myth, which may date back three or four millennia BC, Tiamat was the great goddess who, according to the Mesopotamians, not only created the gods but also, despite herself, the world.

Vessel

The shape and usefulness of the vessel – be it urn, jug, pot, bowl – make it a female symbol of conception, creation and birth. It is symbolically thought to contain treasure: life. The vessel has therefore always been regarded as sacred, because it was designed to hold various precious products of the earth: water initially, then milk or wine. Thus, for millennia, vessels have been used for ritual purposes in numerous religions. Neolithic examples have been found, decorated with bands, squares and triangles, which were used on altars by our distant forebears for religious or funerary purposes. Even today, particularly in the Christian liturgy, the chalice and ciborium are regarded as sacred

vessels. Furthermore, the fairly complex Latin etymology of the noun 'vessel' (*vascellum*, small vase or urn) refers equally to the receptacle that was used to collect water from a stream and to a container for the ashes of the deceased.

It can therefore be said that the vessel symbolizes birth and death. This is particularly true in a dream because, when a vessel features prominently, it can be seen as a presage of a birth, a new era or an imminent rebirth. However, it may also allude to the end of a situation. In this case, the dream refers to the final drop of water that causes the vessel to overflow and reveals the need for change.

Virginity

This strange word, whose origin is Latin, denotes a peculiar concept that has no equivalent in Indo-European languages. This is why the sixth sign of the zodiac, later named Virgo (see page 556), was called the 'young girl' in Babylon and Chaldea. However, it is hard not to notice the similarity between the Latin words *virgo, virginis* from which 'virginity' and 'virgin' are derived, and *viragine, viriginis*, that are at the root of 'virago', denoting a woman with manly strength and courage. This noun is derived from the Latin *virare*, meaning 'to wave, brandish, throw, make vibrate', all verbs with a masculine connotation, since *virare* itself derives from *vir*, 'man', which is the root of 'virile' as well as 'virginity'. As a result, a virgin was originally thought to be a woman who was the equal of a man, a man-woman, so to speak (from *vir*, man, and *gina*, woman), rather than a chaste maiden who had not yet had sexual relations with a man. If we approach the concept of virginity from this point of view, it no longer means what

it did in the minds of religious fanatics in Europe who tried to use the term to exercise their totalitarian power and curb their baser instincts. In actual fact, seen from this standpoint, virginity is essentially the principle of the sacred union between the male and female halves of the personality, whether a person is a man or a woman. This is therefore an important ancient mystical and religious concept, that bears close similarities to that of the primordial androgyne (see page 26). This is why, in ancient civilizations, the virgin, a woman with manly strength and courage, was often a courtesan or a sacred prostitute. She belonged to no man in particular, but to all men. She was a figure of universal love and enjoyed great privileges that were inaccessible to other women and men. She was initiated into the mysteries of the gods, magic, the sciences; in her turn she was a priestess and initiator and wielded great power. That being the case, she was worlds apart from the women, particularly in Europe, who, in later times, renounced their natural urges to dedicate themselves entirely to their faith or their God as nuns, some of whom, vulnerable and repressed, became hysterical or mad, suffering from hallucinations that they believed were mystical visions or prophecies. In fact, in one of the strange parallels revealed by the correlations between the letters-numbers of the cabbala, the planets and the zodiac signs, the letter-number *yood* is associated with the sign of Virgo. *Yood* is regarded as the great positive and creative masculine principle that presides over creation and the development of the intellect, the principle that selects, evaluates and organizes, typical characteristics of people born under the sign of Virgo.

As a result, an allusion to virginity in dreams often has to do with an initiation, one that is primarily an introduction to your inner self. People who dream of their own virginity subconsciously know that purity, truth and self-knowledge cannot be acquired without total self-abnegation and without tight control over their instincts, urges and intelligence. As for appearances of the Virgin Mary in sleep or while daydreaming – which occur fairly frequently all over the world, sometimes during genuine collective hallucinations – they may be manifestations of the famous 'white lady', the great mother-goddess who has haunted human consciousness since time immemorial and may represent the soul of the world,

the soul of humanity, part of which we possess within: our own soul.

Virgo (sign of)

See Zodiac, page 556

Vulture

The most representative species of this diurnal bird of prey is undoubtedly the griffon vulture (*Gyps africanus*). This bird has a long neck covered in white down, a short black tail, a reddish brown body and long, wide wings, giving it a wingspread of about 2.5 m (8 ft) in flight. Its area of distribution is in southern Europe, Asia and North Africa. This non-migratory bird lives in the mountains and arid flatlands and feeds on the corpses of dead animals, ripping them apart with its hooked bill. In a nest made of small branches and dry grasses, built into the rock face or a crevice, the female lays one egg per year between January and March. She incubates it with the male for seven to eight weeks although the fledgeling does not actually leave the nest until it is three months old. It takes four years for the young griffon vulture to become fully-grown.

Nekhbet, the vulture-goddess of Upper Egypt, was the protectress of childbirth and newborn babies. She was identified with Isis, 'great of magic', who became the heavenly mother, represented by a vulture with outstretched wings, with power over life and death, birth and rebirth, and therefore resurrection. Later, in Greece, Isis was associated with Eileithyia, goddess of childbirth. As a result, despite the vulture's well-earned reputation as a carrion eater, this bird of prey has a maternal side that was esteemed by our forebears.

Wagtail

The wagtail is a distinctively patterned, passerine songbird of the *Motacillidae* family. Its common name derives from the fact that it has a very long tail that wags continually as it walks and searches for food. It is found on beaches, in meadows (often in the vicinity of sheep), and near streams and riverbanks.

There are several species of wagtail – the yellow wagtail, the white wagtail, the grey wagtail and the pied wagtail (the species found widely in Great Britain). It is a sedentary bird that usually nests on the ground – sometimes against a wall or under bridges – and lays between five and seven eggs around May.

In Greek mythology, as an attribute of Aphrodite, goddess of love and beauty, the wagtail was a symbol of spells, bewitchment and love potions. As already mentioned, it was also a close companion of flocks and shepherds, who saw it as a protective spirit. For this reason,

they never harmed or killed a wagtail for fear that, in return, it might put a curse on their sheep. There are a great many legends and superstitions related to the fact that it wags its tail while walking. According to one of these, which presumably stems from the association with Aphrodite, anyone who sees a wagtail wagging its tail near their house in May will fall in love by the end of the year.

Walnut tree

This tree is associated with caryatids, stone statues of women, usually goddesses, which sometimes served as columns to support temple roofs.

In fact, according to Greek legend, Dionysus, the god of mystical ecstasy – who became Bacchus, the Roman god of wine and orgiastic festivals – was in love with Carya, a princess of Laconia. She had two sisters who, out of jealousy, exposed the couple's guilty affair by telling their father. Thirsty for revenge, Dionysus changed them into stone statues but Carya, who loved her sisters, died of grief. So Dionysus turned Carya into a walnut tree which, in Greek, is called *karuon*, *carya* or *caryo*, meaning 'nut', but also 'kernel'.

The walnut was also regarded by our forebears as a divinatory tree, sometimes devoted to Diana-Artemis, the huntress, and sometimes Proserpine-Persephone, Demeter's daughter, who became queen of the underworld, having been abducted by Hades-Pluto, its king. It was therefore regarded as a disturbing tree beneath which it was never a good idea to doze off or spend the night.

Warbler

Like the falcon (see page 180), there are many species of warblers, small songbirds belonging to either the family *Sylviidae* or *Parulidae* (order *Passeriformes*). From May onwards, their melodious, piping song can be heard throughout Europe. One of the best known is the garden warbler (*S. borin*), which, as its English name indicates, nests in the bushes of gardens and parks, but also in cemeteries and on the banks of streams, rivers and lakes. It is a delightful little bird that feeds almost entirely on insects. The female lays four or five eggs that she hatches, with the help of the male, for about two weeks. In September, having delighted us with its enchanting song throughout spring and summer, the garden warbler flies off to warmer climes.

The warbler and its song are associated with the mysteries of the night in the fairy-tale world of the Middle Ages. In fact, the garden warbler is often depicted in medieval floral and animal art, perched on a flower.

The Orphean warbler, usually found in woodland, is one of the few birds that can be heard singing at nightfall. Its name derives from its delightful song – the adjective 'orphean' means 'melodious' or 'enchanting' – and its association with the Greek poet and lyre-player, Orpheus, who tried to rescue his wife Euridyce from Hades (hell) after her death. His bid failed and he was soon afterwards killed by a band of Thracian women.

The warbler's distinctive method of building its nest, by 'threading' twigs through holes pierced in leaves with its beak, made it the patron of seamstresses.

Water

From spring to stream, stream to tributary, tributary to river, river to sea, sea to ocean, ocean to sky, and sky to earth, water is the cycle of life. The cycle of water evokes the myth of eternal renewal: water falls from the sky, penetrates the earth and rises to the surface in the form of springs, streams, tributaries and rivers that flow into the seas and oceans. The heat and warmth of the sun bring about the evaporation of water from the seas and oceans, the saturation and condensation of air and the formation of clouds – composed of particles of liquid or solid

water – which are driven along by the wind. Under the effect of atmospheric pressures, water is returned to the earth in the form of precipitation, i.e. rain, snow and dew.

Rain makes the earth lush and fertile. If rain does not fall, the earth becomes dry, arid and sterile. In this respect, water is the source of life. If rain does not penetrate the earth, there is no fermentation, roots cannot grow and seed cannot be transformed into grain. In this respect, water is the great principle of regeneration and metamorphosis.

Thus, water follows a relatively unchanging cycle – from liquid, through vapour, to the solid state – which, according to scientific observations, occurs approximately 34 times during the terrestrial year.

Water is the sensory organ of the earth or, to be more precise, it makes the earth sensitive and receptive. By evaporating and saturating the air with moisture, it also makes the air sensitive and receptive. Furthermore, due to the combined effects of gravity and the earth's rotation as it spins on its axis, water shapes the surface of the planet. The course of the rivers winding across the earth's surface, and the myriad currents that make water flow, are the result of the earth's rotation and gravity. But they are also a product of the moon's movements around the earth since the waters of the rivers, seas and oceans are subject to a subtle interplay of intermingling, swirling and continuously moving currents.

Rivers and primordial waters. The great civilizations of the ancient world were founded and developed on the banks of rivers, for example the Tigris and Euphrates in Mesopotamia and the Nile in Egypt. To mark the occasion of the new year, the Chinese emperor, known as the 'son of heaven' (*t'ien-tzu*), made sacrifices to the four great rivers of China – the Huang Ho (Yellow River), Yangtze Chiang, Huai Ho and Hsi Chiang (West River). In India, the Ganga, better known as the Ganges, is the white river of salvation, while the Yamuna is the black river of origins. For the Hindus, these rivers are associated with the gods Vishnu (the 'pervader' or 'sustainer') and Shiva (the 'auspicious one') who, along with Brahma, the creator god, form the Hindu trinity or Trimurti. According to Jewish tradition, the 'river on high' is the river of celestial grace and influence.

All these ancient civilizations shared the same belief in the celestial and divine origin of rivers. Since water was the original element *par excellence* and the great principle of life on earth, creation myths throughout the world refer to the separation of the waters on high (celestial waters) and the waters below (terrestrial waters) that gave rise to the rivers and seas, following an initial flood or chaos. In these creation myths and cosmogonies, water is the element of chaos – i.e. of undifferentiated life or of all possible forms of life – from which life as we know it emerged. The German philosopher Georg W.F. Hegel (1770–1831) described water as the element of abnegation, the element of perpetual 'being for others' that had no other being than the fact of being for others. According to Hegel, its determination was not yet being determined in

any way, which is why it used to be known as the mother of all determination. (*The Religion of Nature in Lectures on the Philosophy of Religion, Vol. II: Determinate Religion*, edited by Peter C. Hodgson, University of California Press, 1987.) Hegel is in this instance referring to the original and nourishing mother liquids (waters of the womb, the primordial waters).

Because water is the source of life, by drinking or immersing ourselves in it, we revitalize and regenerate ourselves, wash and purify ourselves. Natural spring waters and thermal waters are renowned for their therapeutic effects and some are even believed to have magical properties, like the so-called waters of youth, which, as their name suggests, have the ability to restore

youth. From time immemorial, the sudden appearance of a spring has been regarded as a miracle, a supernatural event and a gift from the gods. The drying up of a stream or river, on the other hand, has always been seen as a curse.

Water is also a symbol of fertilization, blessing, purification (e.g. baptism), wisdom, eternity, infinite and eternal love, and spiritual life. Rivers, fountains, pools, lakes, ponds, marshes, seas, oceans, rain, well water, streams, springs, mountain streams and waves are all invested with symbolism and meaning related to water as the source of life, purifier and regenerator.

Water and the signs of the zodiac. The characteristics of the signs of the zodiac are governed by their element. Cancer (the crab), Scorpio and Pisces are water signs and their characteristics are therefore emotional and intuitive. *Cancer is a cardinal water sign:* its water is the pure and purifying water of the gushing spring and the refreshing fountain, at a time of year when the sun is at its height. It is also the sign of the primordial waters that contain all possible forms of life. It is the sensitivity of the surface of the waters, born of the intermingling of warm and cold currents. It is the movement of the waves caressing the shore, punctuated by the rhythm of tides influenced by the moon. *Scorpio is a fixed water sign:* its water is the still and mysterious water of pools, marshes and lakes. It is the water that ferments, penetrates and regenerates the depths of the earth. It is the moisture buried deep within the earth, the water of wells and water tables, the secret water hidden beneath desert sands inhabited by scorpions and serpents. It is dormant, silt-rich water, the potential source of new life. *Pisces is a mutable water sign:* its water is the water of chasms, marine depths and vast oceans, the unleashed, chaotic water of torrential downpours, tempests and floods. But it is also the water that washes, soothes, cures, blesses, makes sacred and deifies. It is the pure, clear, smooth water of the lake in which man sees his reflection, discovers his soul and either becomes immersed in himself or sees the light. It is the water of life, the celestial water into which he plunges in order to be born or reborn.

Water-lily

See Nenuphar, page 354

Waterfall

A waterfall is the ultimate source. In ancient times, because waterfalls tend to occur high in the mountains, their waters were regarded as celestial, fertilizing and regenerating, divine and magical. By standing under a waterfall, it was believed you could cleanse your soul as well as your body and, as such, this was an act of purification. Furthermore, there were often caves behind waterfalls, secret places that gave rise to the belief that the waterfall invested those who bathed in its refreshing and invig-

orating waters with the power to make themselves invisible.

Throughout the world, there are tales and legends in which the waterfall is regarded as magical and purifying. For example, in the *Nibelungenlied* ('song of the Nibelungs'), an anonymous German epic poem written *c.* 1200, the hero Siegfried becomes immortal by bathing in the clear, pure waters of a waterfall.

Dreaming that you are bathing in the waters of a waterfall always has invigorating and stimulating implications. On one level, this dream, which symbolizes the immortality of the soul, is mystical and spiritual. On a more practical level and by association with the fact that its waters spill forcefully from high in the mountains, the appearance of a waterfall in a dream can represent the imminent occurrence of a series of events and circumstances that will bring about a renewal or change, or introduce something new into your life.

Weasel

The weasel often appears in popular legend and initiation lore disguised as a woman – a fairy or witch, magician-goddess or seductress, depending on the legend. As such, it symbolizes

female cunning taking advantage of male naivety in order to achieve its own ends. The weasel uses its female charms to distract its male prey and achieve its goal. In this role it appears to be the European equivalent of the fox in China and Japan since, in Japanese legend, it was the fox that often appeared dressed as a priest or a woman. (See *Fox*, page 197).

In Chinese legends, a cunning or deceitful woman also often disguises herself as a vixen with superb russet fur in order to seduce or distract a man from the quest he is pursuing. In European tales the woman assumes the form of a weasel. This belief was so firmly rooted in certain European countries that it was believed that a weasel's bite could paralyse the victim

In modern parlance, to weasel one's way into someone's affections or 'good books' means to gain affection or approval by devious and underhand means. The expression 'weasel words', which originated in the United States, is now widely used to refer to a deliberately evasive or misleading statement or speech, while 'to weasel out' of something means to evade responsibility or renege on a commitment.

Dreaming about a weasel can therefore represent either the cunning that you tend to use in order to get what you want or a desire that you dissimulate and conceal from yourself, or a person with whom you have or will have dealings whose intentions may not be open and above board.

Well

'Oh Lord, there are many around the well, but there is no one in the well' (Logion 74, *Commentary on the Gospel according to St Thomas*).

The well contains a spring providing a constant supply of pure water that can slake the thirst of anyone who wishes to drink deeply of the truth. This is the original spring from which everyone should drink (see *Source*, page 461). However, according to the *logion* or saying attributed to Jesus, quoted above, although there are many people around the well, few plunge in to partake of its refreshing spring waters. In this example, the well is a symbol of revelation, knowledge, truth and light, but it can also represent a fall into the abyss, darkness and nothingness. It is then a bottomless pit.

However, the image of the well is generally synonymous with inexhaustible spiritual riches or sustenance that increase the more you draw on them. As a result, Hexagram 48 of the I Ching, whose symbol is the well, is illustrated by an inexhaustible spring at which all can drink at will.

Dreaming of a well often indicates a need to recharge your batteries, to get back to basics, back in touch with the true, simple, natural values that form the very essence of life and are essential to relieve our often tormented minds. A dream like this may also herald a meeting with a cultivated person or a personal discovery. Falling into a well may indicate a desire or need for extensive self-examination.

Whale

Nowadays, everyone knows that the whale is a mammal and not a fish. However, in the past it was regarded as a marine monster (the Greek *phallaina* also means 'monster') that was only distinguished from other 'fish' by its vast size. This assimilation of the whale with a monster was not so much due to its gargantuan proportions as to the tragic accidents caused

by whales when human beings began to sail the seas. It was quite common for one of these huge creatures to swim into and damage a boat or ship, causing it to capsize or sink. It is easy to understand why, in ancient times, this ungainly and monstrous animal was regarded as a hostile and supernatural being, sent by the gods to punish mortals. It was to defy the gods that the ancients began to hunt the whale.

Later, they realized that a wealth of resources could be harvested from its body, which still continues to provide vast quantities of oil, blubber, meat and whalebone – used mainly in the food and cosmetics industries – not to mention the tonnes of fish swallowed by a whale and found, almost intact, in its stomach.

This inevitably brings us to the famous biblical legend of Jonah who 'was in the belly of the fish for three days and three nights. Then Jonah prayed unto the Lord [...]. And the Lord spake unto the fish, and it vomited out Jonah upon the dry land' (Jonah 1: 17; 2: 1, 10). Symbolically, the legend refers to a rite of passage or an initiation, a necessary regression undergone by an individual in order to achieve spiritual development.

Jonah's descent into the whale's belly, where he is plunged into total darkness for three days and nights, represents a return to our origins in the depths of life.

In this respect, the whale is another symbolic representation of the great mother-goddess – Isis for the Egyptians, Demeter for the Greeks, Cybele for the Romans, Kali for the Hindus – who gives life but can also take it away without warning. The whale-mother-goddess therefore took Jonah into her entrails to enable him to be reborn, to achieve awareness and enlightenment.

Of course, the period of three days and three nights

during which he had to remain in the whale's belly also has a symbolic significance. Three is the number of the union of heaven and earth, whose fruit is the spirit. It is a perfect number, the expression of totality and completion (see *Three*, page 368). It is also the length of time between the death and resurrection of Christ, as he himself predicted when addressing the scribes and Pharisees: '[...] for as Jonahs was three days and three nights in the whale's belly, so shall the Son of man be three days and three nights in the heart of the earth.' (Matthew 12: 40.)

Dreaming about a whale means that you are in need of a period of gestation in your life or that you are about to undergo a test or trial, which will offer an opportunity for personal development and enable you to live a happier, more fulfilled life.

The appearance of a whale in your dreams can also indicate a need to 'plunge' into the depths of your being, to turn inward in order to gather your strength and revive yourself. If you are at a point in your life where you are too absorbed by external considerations, chance happenings or social and material obligations, the whale you see in your dream(s) is warning you that it can emerge at any moment

and overturn everything. A dream about a whale is always of great symbolic significance and has an important message concerning you and your personal balance and development.

Wheel

See Circle, page 100

Wheelbarrow

Originally, the barrow was a handcart with two wheels. Symbolically, there is a strong association with the cart and chariot due to the fact that, in the Middle Ages, a small two-wheeled cart or 'sedan chair' was used to transport people. The single-wheeled barrow or wheelbarrow, used by European peasants to transport crops and produce, did not appear until the 16th century.

The user moves the single-wheeled barrow by holding the two handles and pushing it ahead, thereby transporting the load from one place to another. Because it was moved entirely by an individual act of will, it was soon regarded as a symbol of the human condition.

For this reason, a number of parallels can be drawn between the symbolism of the wheelbarrow and that of the Chariot and the Wheel of Fortune, the VIIth and Xth cards in the Major Arcana of the Tarot.

If you dream about a wheelbarrow, it always symbolizes a need for awareness. This involves taking your destiny in hand, assuming your responsibilities and taking charge of the burden of your life or the weight of your obligations in order to move forward, develop, make progress and, possibly, even move on. In this last event, the wheelbarrow may be a symbol of moving house.

White

White is the symbol of purity, innocence and perfection. It is not a colour as such but rather a potential colour or a synthesis of all the colours in the solar spectrum. This is why white is a symbol of unity as well as of everything contained within it.

For the Chinese, white is the absence of colour. By analogy, it also symbolizes virginity, the soul delivered from the torments of the flesh and passion, beauty stripped of all adornment, nudity, transparency, light, sincerity, virtue, peace, justice, truth and incorruptibility.

In the natural world, anything white is always wonderful and magical, pure and sacred – snow, milk, flour, linen, ivory, lilies, white roses and the moon, of course, which appears white in the heavens, especially when it is full.

White is often associated with silver (see *Silver*, page 456), crystal and pearls. It is also associated with the pure light of the aureoles (halos) of angels and saints. Last but not least, white hair is the symbol of old age, but also of venerability, wisdom and benevolence.

The etymological root of the word 'white' is of Germanic origin – Old English *hwīt*; related to Old Frisian and Old Saxon *hwit*, Old Norse *hvítr*, Gothic *hveits*, Old High German *hwīz*

White
Willow tree

(German *weiss*). Whit Sunday is most probably derived from the Old English *hwita sunnandaeg* ('white Sunday') probably due to the custom of wearing white robes at or after a baptism. The perception of white as a non-colour accounts for its association with things that have no form, are invisible or have not yet been revealed or manifested.

The strong presence of white in a dream may represent a situation that has not yet developed, or an absence of emotion and even a feeling of indifference. It can also reveal a certain coldness or a tendency to absorb everything without reacting. Although dreaming about white is always reassuring and calming, it is important to take account of the circumstances surrounding the appearance of this colour, which seems primordial in a dream. For example, dreaming about a white horse can be a symbol of the uncontrolled licentious feelings that assail and threaten to engulf us. It can sometimes also represent death, although this is rarely a physical but rather a symbolic death – the death of desires, feelings, behavioural reflexes, habits that should be checked or purified. Similarly, dreaming about a woman in white can equally well be a symbol of birth or a representa-

tion of death. As the latter, she is often known as the 'white lady'. Ghosts also appear dressed in white robes or a white sheet. However, dreaming about a white garment, catching hold of it, touching it or putting it on can be a sign of birth or a guarantee of purity, sincerity, frankness and innocence. To correctly interpret a dream in which white seems to play a key role, it is important to associate it with the object, animal, person or place with which it appears. Only then can we try to invest it with its full meaning, bearing in mind that the context of the white in question distinguishes it and gives it a special significance.

Willow tree

This tree is probably called a 'weeping willow' because it has trailing, leafy branches that droop down to the ground and along which raindrops trickle like tears. One of its distinctive characteristics is that it remains green throughout the year. This fact did not escape the Chinese, who regarded it as a tree of immortality, wisdom, spiritual inspiration and communication with heaven, or the Tibetans, who believed it to be the tree of life. According to Chinese legend, Lao Tzu, the presumed author of the Tao-te Ching, the book that inspired Taoism, loved to meditate in the shade of a willow tree in the sixth century BC. It was also under a willow that the younger Confucius had his famous interview with Lao Tzu, afterwards telling his disciples: 'I know how birds can fly, fishes swim, and animals run. But the runner may be snared, the swimmer hooked, and the flyer shot by the arrow. But there is the dragon – I cannot tell how he mounts on the wind through the clouds, and rises to heaven. Today I have seen Lao Tzu, and can only compare him to the dragon.' (Ssu-ma Ch'ien, *Shih-chi* or Historical Records.)

Wind

The wind is the hand of fate. When it blows, it serves as a vehicle for the spirits, the messengers of the gods and sometimes even for divine wrath. The raging wind scours the land in a storm, sweeping aside everything in its path, carrying water, fire and earth along with it, because no element can withstand the fury of the wind. Our forebears, who saw wind spirits everywhere, feared and respected the great mysteries of nature all the more because they appreciated its benefits. They knew how capricious, changeable and unpredictable the wind could be, although certain warning signs enabled them to anticipate and predict changes in the wind's direction or imminent tornadoes, cyclones and hurricanes. It is probably from such observations that the popular expression 'see which way the wind blows' derives. When you know which way the wind is blowing, you can head in the right direction, as sailors do to achieve optimum speeds by catching the wind in their boat's sails. However, a weathercock, which tells you which way the wind is blowing, is also a term for someone fickle and easily influenced.

As well as being the beneficial or destructive instrument of the gods, the wind also carries their voices and those of the spirits of the dead. When the wind blows in mountains or valleys, deep in the desert or in the midst of the ocean, its voices can be enchanting or frightening, depending on the circumstances. Odysseus heard the song of the sirens carried on the sea winds and, having ordered his sailors to tie him to the mast of his boat, managed to resist their blandishments.

The wind can be cooling, soothing and calming, like the gentle breeze or soft spring wind, or destructive and deadly, like the typhoon or tempest. When the wind blows through our big modern cites, scouring their streets and roads, city-dwellers can breathe freely at last. Without these gusts of fresh air, urban pollution would have made towns uninhabitable a long time ago. On the other hand, since the wind spreads anything it finds in its path, like pollen and germs, it also carried the radioactive fallout from the nuclear power station of Chernobyl. It is still not known what the long-term consequences of this disaster will be for what is now called the environment and what our forebears described simply as nature. Times change like the wind, which, with time, scatters everything, including the dust we all become.

It is more usual to dream about a tempest, storm or hurricane than a soft, gentle breeze. A dream like this can be interpreted as a sign that conflicting feelings have reached such a pitch that, if we are not careful, we will be completely overcome by them. It can also herald an imminent upheaval that will sweep aside everything in its path.

See also *Air*, page 19.

Wine

Wine is a product of the grapevine. Without the fruit of this natural wild plant, ancient civilizations would never have been able to produce this drink, which then acquired a divine, sacred character. In fact, the wild vine appears to have grown throughout Eurasia since time immemorial. Our prehistoric forebears appreciated grapes for their taste, fragrance and beneficial properties: grapes are now thought to be energy-giving and fortifying, they stimulate the muscles, the nervous system and the hepatic, cooling, diuretic, laxative and digestive functions, and they are rich in potassium, vitamins A, B and C and sugars that can be directly assimilated by the human body – unlike the industrial sucrose that we consume to excess today and that has depleted our bodies of essential minerals. To avail themselves of

all these benefits, therefore, our ancestors merely had to gather this wild fruit in the great garden of nature.

It is not known exactly when and how man conceived the idea of making wine by squeezing out the juice of a fruit that had been eaten for centuries. One story in Genesis provides some information on this subject, attributing the planting of a vineyard and the production of wine to Noah: 'And Noah began to be a husbandman, and he planted a vineyard: And he drank of the wine, and was drunken; and he was uncovered within his tent.' (Genesis 9: 20–21.) This text places particular emphasis on the wine's effect on Noah, who becomes drunk and removes his clothes. The story goes on to say that Noah's son, Ham, was shocked by his father's nudity and alerted his brothers, Shem and Japhet, who covered his body with a garment, averting their faces so that they did not see him. This good turn caused Ham's descendants to be cursed by his father (Genesis 9: 22–27). This story has resulted in some people making the rather hasty deduction that Noah was a drunkard. This is to forget, however, that nudity symbolizes truth, purity and simplicity. The naked man is as he was when he came into the world, as he was before original sin. So, by cursing his son for refusing to see him as he became after drinking wine, Noah was showing that he thought his children were refusing to see the naked truth, to see man as he really is. Wine was therefore regarded as a magical, sacred drink, whose properties enabled man to attain the divine, reveal the supreme truth and appear in his true colours without false modesty, hypocrisy or deceit. 'In vino veritas', said Alcibiades in Plato's *Symposium*: in wine there is truth.

Wine therefore became the symbol of the essence of life and, as such, was identified with human blood. However, the tendency towards drunkenness inherent in man, who longs for happiness and ecstasy, has always gone hand in hand with his fear of truth. What is more, since earliest times, history has shown that truth and justice have far too rarely prevailed. Therefore, wine, while preserving its sacred character, has always been regarded as a dangerous and addictive product that can encourage all types of excess and even prove fatal. Of course, it is important to distinguish between the inebriation, rapture, ecstasy and the feeling of well-being engendered by a moderate consumption of this remarkable drink and the excitement and artificial euphoria experienced by those who have drunk too much alcohol and are no longer themselves. The same distinction can be made between the intoxication of love that inclines the lovers to be kind and tolerant, and the all-consuming passion that blinds them and makes them intolerant and uncompromising.

Dreaming that you are drinking wine in moderation is often a sign of joy, enthusiasm, positive energy and well-being. However, it can also reveal a hunger for truth and justice, as we have seen. On the other hand, if you feel inebriated in a dream after drinking a large quantity of wine, you may not be yourself and you may be allowing yourself to be carried away by your relationships, your business dealings or even your ideas. You are gradually losing control of your life and allowing your activities or the outside world to lead you astray. If you dream you are standing among vines or taking part in a grape harvest, this is a sign of potential joy and happiness, but you must gather or harvest the grapes yourself. The dream's message is clear: rejoice, because everything you have been seeking is within close reach.

Wings

Wings are the symbolic representation of the soul and the intellect since they imply soaring flight, weightlessness and liberation. They are also a symbol of freedom, supernatural power and adventure since they make it possible to escape the pull of gravity, rise skywards, fly over mountains and move freely between one place and another by simply making the effort required to move them. Wings often represent the power of concentration that liberates and elevates the mind.

For example, the Greek god Hermes (Mercury in the Roman pantheon) had wings on his ankles or heels to emphasize the agility, rapidity, cleverness and ethereal nature of his mind.

Witch and sorcerer

Immortality is also represented by wings. You only have to think of angels and archangels, the earthly representatives of God whose task it is to serve, help, guide and enlighten mortals.

Temperance, the XIVth card in the Major Arcana of the divinatory Tarot cards, is depicted with wings as the symbolic representation of the regeneration and permanent transformation of the natural elements.

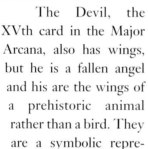

The Devil, the XVth card in the Major Arcana, also has wings, but he is a fallen angel and his are the wings of a prehistoric animal rather than a bird. They are a symbolic representation of the desires and passions that condemn the soul to be imprisoned by and dependent on worldly goods.

On the VIth card (the Lovers) in the Major Arcana, a cherub hovers on the wings of love above three people, preparing to shoot his arrow. In this instance, wings represent the expression or manifestation of a unique, privileged and absolute emotion that has the power of a magic spell.

Nowadays, it is generally accepted that sorcerers and witches are the fictitious figures of fairy-tales and legends with, as any reasonable and sensible adult knows, no basis in reality. Although there is historical evidence of witch-hunts during the Middle Ages, these have been largely dismissed as springing from malicious fantasies or a form of puerility on the part of our ancestors than a hunt for actual demons, since it is now generally agreed that demons do not exist. But can we be certain of this?

Witches and the Inquisition. If we want to give tangible form to the demon or what we take to be such – the Devil, the forces of evil, the powers of darkness – then we must look to the

past and refer to the images of the so-called witch-hunts and hunts for demons carried out in 15th- and 16th-century Europe.

Driven by the same religious fanaticism that inspires – albeit subconsciously – modern fundamentalists of whatever persuasion or religion, inquisitors of all ranks and levels of importance tortured, burnt and massacred men and women who, in their opinion, did not conform or subscribe to the rules, laws and accepted standards of the prevailing religion. These abominations were committed in the name of love and faith throughout Europe – especially in Germany and Spain – during dark ages that have left their mark on our collective imagination and memory.

When we depict or refer to witches, we always picture them as women who were forced to describe themselves, under torture, having been denounced, hunted down and condemned before being tried. Thus our image of witches – naked or dressed in black, riding a broomstick or some form of monstrous animal, concocting and casting evil spells, having signed a pact with the Devil whose marks they bore on their body – is a legacy of the second half of the 15th century, in the aftermath of the Hundred Years' War.

From **Le Dictionnaire des sciences occultes,** *Pygmalion,* **1986.**

It is worth mentioning that the term 'witch-hunt' is still used today to refer a campaign to expose political, commercial or social 'dissenters', always on the pretext of safeguarding the public interest. See also *Fairies*, page 176.

Wolf, she-wolf

It seems that all the evils on earth have been laid at the wolf's door. It has been blamed for many of man's misfortunes and, even to this day, we continue to be afraid of the beast that lurks within and is embodied by the wolf. In the Middle Ages, there were numerous accounts of ravening wolves attacking sheep, cattle, sometimes even children and adults in the European countryside. People were even terrorized by packs of wolves venturing into the towns during extremely harsh winters. It is hardly surprising that the wolves liked the dark, narrow lanes of medieval towns and villages, as this was where the villagers dumped their refuse: not only could they find all sorts of food but also an excellent place to hide. After all, wolves are well known for their cunning. The fear of wolves dates back much earlier than the Middle Ages, however, and wolves have existed on earth since time immemorial.

According to palaeontologists, the wolf's ancestor may be at least 40 million years old and fossils of wolf skeletons dating from around two million years ago have

been discovered, showing that the beasts roaming in packs in ancient times were very similar to the animals that are seen much more seldom now.

It is also common knowledge that wolves and dogs are very similar. However, although dogs are known for their obedience and loyalty, wolves can rarely be tamed. They have been driven out of the countryside so effectively that, in Europe, they have virtually disappeared. There is still the occasional story of a wolf attacking a ewe or sheep, because there have been attempts – despite ancestral fears and hatred – to reintroduce them into some regions in Europe. However, we are more likely to be knocked down or killed by a car than to be savaged by a wolf. Police and forest wardens have therefore replaced the former masters of the wolf-hunt who, in the Middle Ages, assessed the damage caused by packs of wolves and drove them away from the villages.

Nevertheless, the wolf is still on the prowl in our nightmares and the reason why this is so terrifying may simply be because, in the words of Plautus, a Latin dramatic poet writing in the third century BC: 'Man is a wolf to another man'. After all, the wolf is hardly a likeable animal: ferocious, voracious, cruel, cunning, sometimes carrion-eating, sometimes literally rabid, it has also been a plague-carrier in the past.

Likening the wolf to a human being is therefore tantamount to saying that the latter is capable of the worst. Indeed, there are people who, driven by ambition, greed or the need to satisfy their desires at any cost, are capable of absolutely anything. So the wolf embodies the inner forces of evil to which we sometimes yield free rein. A fear of wolves is therefore a fear of our own inner impulses: the creature represents the destructive instinct, which leads to uncontrollable desires and urges. For this reason, the concept of lycanthropy, or the notorious transformation of a person into a wolf, most probably dates back to a time when sorcerers or shamans wore a wolfskin to experience the instinctual animal impulses that all humans possess deep within. This extreme experience served as an exorcism, expelling the age-old demons of savagery, voraciousness and cruelty that lie dormant in everyone.

The wolf is thus a necessary evil. It brings about a revelation and provides an extreme, crucial and liberating experience that consolidates man's human-

ity. This is perhaps why, in many myths and legends about the foundation of cities and civilizations, the founding children are helped, adopted, fed and protected by a she-wolf, who in this instance symbolizes great Mother Nature, the *alma mater*, who is not only the creator of all life but also the great devourer of life. Rome's founders, Remus, a mortal, and Romulus, an immortal, were foster-children of a she-wolf.

Womb

The word 'womb' has a host of associations that include conception, preparation, mysterious inner alchemy, deep-seated regeneration, formation of life, creation, future birth, embryo, intrauterine life, foetus, seed and new beginnings. The womb is the starting point for all life, often represented by the primordial waters in world creation myths, those cosmogonies which, each in its own way, describe the separation of the waters above from the waters below. The first account of the creation in the Bible, for example, states that 'the spirit of God moved upon the face of the waters'. It continues: 'And God said, Let there be a firmament in the midst of the waters, and let it divide the waters from the waters. And God made the firmament, and divided the waters which were under the firmament from the waters which were above the firmament: and it was so. And God called the firmament Heaven.' (Genesis: 1, 2, 6, 7, 8.)

In the original text, the word translated as 'water' is the Hebrew word *maim*, meaning 'original, undifferentiated waters', which can be described as the waters of the womb. The word translated somewhat succinctly by 'heaven' was *shamaim*, which embodies a concept that might be conveyed by a fruit stone, which simultaneously connects the inside and the outside, yet separates them from each other. The current tendency to examine, search, probe and analyse the sky implies that we see the stone and ignore the fruit, thereby getting further and further away from the tree that produced it. In other words, the fruit stone is regarded either as something that connects or something that divides, separates and isolates; it is either seen from the inside by the heart's eye or from the outside using a telescope.

The womb contains the universal substance symbolized by the original waters into which the seed was thrown. Their union produces life that forms deep within the womb. That being the case, the womb is nothing but an empty mould or matrix without its waters, which are generally represented by the sea, the mother of all life, universal womb and substance.

Wood

A wood is essentially a group of trees, a reassuring place where you can feel secure, gather your thoughts, pray or meditate. In myth and legend, woods were often sacred groves, dedicated to benign divinities, in tune with the forces of nature. By contrast, forests were vast, mysterious places whose dark, wild depths were associated with initiation lore. While forests are sometimes associated with the symbols and myths related to the labyrinth (see *Labyrinth*, page 306), walking

in a wood always has positive connotations and symbolizes a time of peace when you can turn inwards and be at one with yourself.

But wood is also a material, the flesh of the tree so to speak. Magicians, sorcerers and diviners made their wands and rods from wood (see *Stick, wand,* page 474, and *Rod, staff,* page 433), while branches and bark were used to make amulets. It should be stressed, however, that magical instruments and protective talismans were not made from just any tree. For example, sorcerers' magic wands were made exclusively from hornbeam – no other tree would do – while oak, yew, mountain ash, hazel, birch, apple and pine (see pages 402, 552, 37, 219, 58, 34, 418) were often used in the magic and religious rituals, rites of initiation and divinations practised by the our Celtic ancestors.

Finally, in the Chinese zodiac, wood is one of the five agents or elements, the others being earth, fire, water and metal.

The presence of wood in a dream is always a good omen and a symbol of protection. But it is important, if possible, to identify the type of wood (i.e. the tree that it comes from) in order to understand its full significance.

It is also interesting to note that 'touching wood' is a superstition dating from the time when people began to venerate holy relics (*c.* 10th century). It originated with the belief that you could ward off fate by touching divine grace, represented by a piece of wood from the cross of Christ.

Wood owl

See Owl, page 406

Woodpecker

The green woodpecker, which has a beautiful olive-green plumage, and the grey-headed woodpecker, with its grey-green plumage, grey head and neck, are both found in nearly all parts of mainland Europe. In the early spring, this small bird becomes a true woodworker, chiselling a hole in a tree trunk with its strong, slender bill, to build a nest. It also uses its bill to forage in anthills, as these insects are its favourite food. Between April and May, in a tree trunk in a copse, avenue or orchard, the female lays between five and seven eggs that she incubates with the male for just over two weeks.

According to the myth relating to the birth of Rome, it was a green woodpecker (*Picus viridus*) that helped Remus and Romulus to survive by bringing them food in its bill. This belief probably reflected the fact that, in Greece, the woodpecker was the sacred bird of Ares or Mars. In Rome, the gifts of divination and prophecy were also attributed to the woodpecker. As a result, it was designated protector of farmers, hunters and travellers, because it foresaw both impending danger and imminent rain-storms.

Wren
(Goldcrested)

The European golden-crested kinglet (*Regulus cristatus*), also called the gold-crested wren and golden wren, is a small passerine bird weighing no more than 6g (¹/₄oz), which ranges through-out Europe as far as central Asia. Between October and March, although it regularly flies from south to north, it never strays from its area of distribution, where it tends to live in coniferous woodlands and flatlands. Its well-hidden nest, a dense sphere made of moss, lichen, grass and cobwebs, is suspended high in the branches of deciduous trees. The female lays between eight and eleven eggs in April or May, then another five to eight eggs in June. She incubates them alone for about three weeks, but both parent birds feed the fledgelings with small insects.

The male wren's crest gives it an erudite, scholarly appearance and this may be why the Celts saw this bird as a symbol of the druid while also associating it with the crow, which for them represented the warrior. Some believe the Irish Gaelic word for wren (*dreoilín*) derives from *draoi éan* or Druid bird. In any case, it was because of its regal crest that this bird, a species of kinglet, was regarded by the Greeks as the living symbol of the passing years. The Greeks, then the Romans, and lastly the Celts, hunted this bird around the time of the winter solstice to discover the wren of the new year.

Year, new year
(annual, anniversary, birthday)

A year is first and foremost the time the earth takes to make a complete revolution around the sun. It was according to this principle that ancient astrologers measured and established the concept of time on earth. While they counted the days and months by observing the different phases of the moon, they established the calendar and yearly cycle by following the apparent movements of the sun in relation to the earth. This annual cycle was characterized by a fatidic or prophetic day (the last day of the year) and a day of renewal and renaissance that marked the new year. For a long time New Year's Day was one of triumph for the sun, marking the point of the year when the days started to grow longer than the nights. This makes perfect sense if you remember that, in ancient times, the new year was celebrated at the time of the spring equinox (today 21 March). Interestingly, the English word 'year' is associated with the Polish *jar*, meaning 'springtime'.

However, with the advent of Christianity, it was no longer the triumph but the rebirth or resurrection of the sun that was celebrated at the time of the winter solstice (21 December), the turning point at which the days start to lengthen after the longest night of the year. Thereafter, the new year and all other anniversaries based on the annual cycle (from the Latin *anniversarius* and *annuus* meaning 'taking place each year') were associated with the triumph of life on earth, light revealed in the world, the triumph of light over darkness and life over death. The new year became a symbol of resurrection, revelation, the beginning of a new life and a new era.

A dream about New Year's Day or Christmas Day (which were both, along with the winter solstice, originally on the same day) or an anniversary or birthday can be interpreted as the prediction of some form of triumph or success in your life. It can also be seen as the awareness of a renewal, the end of a cycle or a particular situation, a 'door' or a stage to be passed through in order to enter a new period in your life.

Yellow

This colour was regarded either as a symbol of truth and authenticity – a solar colour which, combined with sky-blue, represented the sun and sky – or as a symbol of betrayal, depending on whether it was associated with the forces of light or the forces of darkness. As a result, yellow was chosen either as a sign of victory, triumph, joy, happiness, loyalty, sincerity and honesty or as an indication of deceit, treachery, adultery or pretence. Yellow is also often linked with the most precious metal of all: gold. However, in that case it demonstrates that all that glitters is not gold, in other words, it is not advisable to set too much store by appearances. It is also common knowledge that gold arouses covetous feelings, bringing out the worst in men and women. Because of this, yellow is also associated with strife, dissension, miserliness and greed.

As can be seen, yellow can be interpreted in a host of different ways, depending on its relationship to the other elements

of your dream. It is therefore essential to pay close attention to the context in which the colour yellow appears and the nature of the object, flower, animal, man or woman with which or whom it is linked.

Yew tree

It tends to be forgotten that, like the Romans, Celtic warriors who were unable to accomplish their mission – or simply to defend their beliefs and convictions to the bitter end – and whose honour was therefore compromised, killed themselves by falling on their sword. The sword would be set in the ground beneath the sacred yew tree, dedicated to the kingdom of the dead, since, for the Celts, the yew was a symbol of immortality.

It may be because our Celtic ancestors used its wood to make their shields that they invested it with magical powers that offered protection against death. The Romans referred to the Celts of north-western France, Britain and Ireland as the *Eburovices* ('combatants by the yew'), one of the three branches of the *Aulerci*, a people of Celtic

Gaul. The name has survived over the ages and the inhabitants of the town of Évreux, in Normandy, are still know today as 'Ébroïciens'. According to Celtic mythology, the first druid Hu Ar Bras and, later, his disciple Mug (Mog or Mogh) Ruith (Ruth or Roth) – described as the 'devotee of the wheel' and 'god of the seasons' – consulted the oracle and the gods using a wheel made from the wood of the yew, which was regarded as the wheel of rebirth, human destiny and the end of time. By the Middle Ages, all that remained of these Celtic beliefs and the yew as a symbol of immortality was its general association with death. For example, it was firmly believed that if you sat down or fell asleep under a yew tree, you ran the risk of being carried off by a fatal illness or falling into an eternal sleep.

Yin and yang

See Two, page 365

Youth

Youth is not a symbol. Youthfulness is regarded either as a stage of life ranging from childhood to maturity, or a state of mind, since people say colloquially that someone is or has remained 'young at heart'.

However, the image of youth is generally contrasted with that of old age, and the fear of growing old, of losing our looks and strength makes us nostalgic for youth in general and our own in particular. This is probably at the origin of the myth of the fountain of youth that, according to the most prevalent legend, was the chief quest of Alexander the Great who died prematurely, at the age of 33, without having found it. This fountain of youth, also known as the elixir of life or the philtre of eternal youth, enabled anyone drinking its waters to stay physically young, never ageing and never dying. If examined closely, this telling metaphor illustrates a state of mind rather than a physical condition. In actual fact, the very principle of life on earth depends on the continual regeneration of life forms, which in itself implies a decline. However, regeneration is not death but a way of renewing pre-existing organisms that undergo a contin-

Yin and yang
Youth
Zodiac

ual process of transformation, dying in order to be reborn. In this way, life goes on unaltered, despite the apparent changes taking place on the earth's surface. There is every reason, therefore, to believe that we all carry the seeds of youth within.

In our dreams, therefore, we often see ourselves as we were in our youth and find nothing unusual about this. However, such dreams are not so much the result of nostalgia as a call to order issued by the dreamers to the part of themselves that never dies, to their ever-present consciousness or soul, which sees them as they really are, whatever their age, their thoughts, the way they regard themselves. This is because, deep down, we are all aware of our true nature and, in the last analysis, if we are prepared to admit it, we know exactly who we are.

Zodiac
(the 12 signs of the)

Although it is common knowledge that the zodiac contains 12 images representing the 12 signs of the zodiac, it is less well known that each of the three ten-degree divisions or decans of a zodiac sign is also represented by a separate symbolic image.

These symbols are traditionally identified with myths that illustrate the major characteristics of the 12 zodiac signs and generally refer to the various exploits and misadventures of the Greek gods. These stories were exploited, interpreted and even adapted to the zodiac by astrologers, alchemists and Renaissance followers of esotericism. The pioneers of psychoanalysis also drew on these sources to come up with new readings.

It is natural to be curious about the origins of these myths and symbols and the reason why some rather than others were chosen to designate, elucidate or illustrate a particular zodiac sign. After all, these choices were not made arbitrarily or haphazardly but to reflect subtle correlations between certain aspects of life and human nature. To clarify the underlying significance of these myths and symbols, we will examine the three symbolic images that represent the three decans of each zodiac sign. These images, widely used in the West in the Middle Ages, were directly inspired by Greco-Chaldean astrology, itself a product of the complex science practised by Sumerian, Akkadian, Assyrian and Babylonian astrologer priests.

Aries

The first decan of Aries, from about 21 to 31 March: this is symbolized by a ram that is standing up and seems to be walking calmly, its head turned to look behind, perhaps to keep an eye on what is happening. There is something human about the way it is holding its head, bringing to mind a person who is figuratively always harking back, filled with nostalgia for the past. The sign of Aries governs a period that begins on the day of the spring equinox, which announces day's supremacy over night, the triumph of light over darkness. Although Aries faces the future squarely, impatiently rushing ahead, the first ram is walking slowly, looking back

over its shoulder. In Babylon, the first month of the year after the spring equinox was the month of sacrifice, when an offering of a lamb was made to the gods. Thus, our first ram is a sacrifice or, more accurately, has to sacrifice its past, the primordial waters of winter out of which it emerged – the previous three zodiac signs, Capricorn, Aquarius and Pisces, are actually winter signs – if it wants to be able to turn to face the future that is its birthright and make good use of the smouldering primeval inner fire that threatens to consume it from within, burning it to ashes. Thus, first-decan Arians are very spirited, but their fire is internalized. They advance, but somewhat blindly, because they cannot stop looking back at the past, meditating on their origins, even drawing inspiration from them to build or create something new. Their vision of the future is still firmly rooted in the past.

The second decan of Aries, from about 1 to 11 April: this ram is the one usually chosen to represent the sign in its entirety. This animal is shown standing up, in profile, and walking confidently from right to left, in other words, heading in the same direction as the zodiac signs. Its left hoof and head, whose muzzle is pointing towards the ground, form a straight line extending between the ground and the sky. The visible eye is also fixed on the ground. This ram is not looking ahead and is also advancing blindly or, more accurately, it gives the impression that it does not need to look where it is going. The carriage of its head suggests such determination, strength and inflexibility that we can only assume it is able to move forward without having to raise its eyes. In some representations, the shadowy outline of one of its fellow creatures or perhaps its mate can just be made out at its side, to emphasize that the ram is the male sheep or leader of the flock. The Merino ram depicted below took its natural place at the head of most Western flocks after the Merino breed, native to Iran and northern India, was imported into Europe and used extensively as foundation stock in the creation of many strains of

sheep. This role as leader and, by analogy, as pioneer or hero, is attributed to people born in the second decan of Aries, called the 'charisma' decan, because they possess a natural charm and influence that fascinate others and encourage them to follow in their wake.

The third decan of Aries, from about 12 to 20 April: this ram is reacting violently to something, rearing up on its hind legs with its forelegs raised and kicking forward. This time, its strength, energy, impetus and momentum no longer come from its head, but from its hindquarters and back. It seems to want to overcome an obstacle or reach a goal that is invisible or incomprehensible to us. Arians born in this decan, the so-called 'passions' decan, often fall prey to uncontrollable instinctive impulses and reckless feelings that may cause them to leap before they look. These fiery individuals, who are erratic in their behaviour and prone to sudden enthusiasms, tend to throw themselves heart and soul into everything they undertake.

Taurus

Each of the three decans of Taurus, the second spring sign, is represented by a bull whose bearing is indicative of a specific type of character and temperament.

The first decan of Taurus, from about 21 to 30 April: this bull is shown lying down, with half its body and hindquarters hidden behind a bush, the other half emerging from it. Its head is turned to the right or, in other words, towards the sign of Aries that comes before it in the zodiac (see page 554). The slightly tilted head seems about to move, while the eyes are looking straight ahead and therefore to our right, in the opposite direction to the movement of the planets within the zodiac. Its left leg is stretched out in front and slightly bent, its hoof on the ground as if the bull is preparing to stand up, while its right leg is tucked under its side. Although its stature leaves us in no doubt about its strength and power, these qualities seem passive and restrained. This bull primarily conveys an impression of peace, calmness and tranquillity, and its widely spaced horns are pointing outwards, giving no indication of any aggressiveness. This is therefore a peaceful bull that wants a quiet life and security and relaxes in its serene, contented strength. It only leaves its place of rest to satisfy its needs and it never makes any more effort than necessary. It is wearing a fixed expression. First-decan Taureans often have a great deal of common sense, but are inclined to have fixed ideas.

The second decan of Taurus, from about 1 to 11 May: this bull is depicted standing up, its bearing proud. Its head is slightly raised towards the sky and surmounted by two horns that together form a magnificent crescent moon tilted backwards. This bull appears to be walking confidently in broad daylight, from right to left – in the direction of the zodiac, this time – in a lush meadow, its right foreleg bent, its tail flicking up towards the sky. It blends in perfectly with its surroundings and forms an integral part of the landscape. It is in its element. It knows where it is going, what it wants and what it is doing. However, despite its obvious strength, its bearing suggests a certain light-heartedness that reflects its receptive state of mind, the fact that it lives in harmony with nature and that it is in tune with the instinctive urges awakened by this period of the year devoted to procreation. Here, the combined symbols of the moon and the lush earth, which are feminine in character, and of the bull firmly planted in this landscape, which is a masculine principle, are representations of 'fertility', which is the name given to this decan. This image therefore brings together the feminine and masculine psychological and sexual polarities that are about to be united. This bull is reminiscent of Apis, the sacred bull associated with the Memphite creator-god Ptah in Egyptian mythology, whose cult was fostered by Menes, the first recorded pharaoh, in order to unify Lower and Upper Egypt around 3000 BC.

The third decan of Taurus, from about 12 to 21 May: the position adopted by this third animal may seem surprising, at least at first. However, it perfectly matches the elements revealed by the third decan of this sign. This time we are shown a bull whose body seems less robust and less powerful than the bull of the second decan but which creates the impression of heaviness, mass, brute strength and weight. It is standing on its hind legs with its forelegs tucked under its body, as if in the process of lying down, and its forequarters pressing down on the ground. The surrounding landscape is less abundant than that of the second decan, as if to focus our attention exclusively on the bull. Its eyes are gazing at the ground and, on its head, its two horns, which are close together, point towards the sky. The impressive mass of its body, its posture which suggests it has collapsed, its bent hind legs firmly braced against the ground, revealing the strength of its back, are all elements that bring to mind the weight and intensity of Saturn, the ruling planet of the third decan, which endows people born at this time with a sense of realism, a down-to-earth turn of mind, strength of purpose and unshakeable convictions.

These symbolic representations of the second zodiac sign are clearly a far cry from the Minotaur, the mythical Greek monster with the body of a man and the head of a bull that devoured seven youths and seven maidens every year and guarded the Labyrinth until it was killed by Theseus with the help of Ariadne. It is also a very different figure from the raging bull that makes the ground shake when it charges.

Gemini

There are three multifaceted pairs of Gemini twins, although each pair is unique in its own way, as can be seen by the three symbolic illustrations for this sign. Gemini myths always allude to man's dual nature. The Mesopotamians called them the 'great twins'. These two individuals, similar in appearance, often symbolize the spirits of good and evil, although nothing in their physical appearance differenti-

ates them. The promptings of a good conscience or an evil spirit often speak in the same voice: our own. Thus, we realize that there are always two possible courses of action, two speakers with one voice, whose arguments may seem identical, but whose intentions are completely different. Many cosmogonies accept and illustrate the androgynous nature of the human being. The following Eskimo legend, for example, recorded by the Danish-Inuit explorer Knud Rasmussen, bears certain similarities to the birth of Eve in the Bible: 'It is said that in the past the world broke into pieces and that every living thing was destroyed. Torrential rain fell from the sky and the earth itself was destroyed. Then two men appeared on earth. They came from the hills of the earth; they were born like this. They were already adults when they emerged from the ground. They lived together like husband and wife and soon one of them was with child. Then the man who had been the husband sang a magic song: "A human being here, a penis there. May her opening be wide and spacious. Opening, opening, opening!" After these words had been sung, the man's penis ripped open with a great noise and he became a woman, and gave birth to a child. By these three humanity multiplied.'

The first decan of Gemini, from about 21 to 31 May: the two people representing the zodiac's first pair of twins are shown naked, side by side, and tightly clasped together. There is no doubt that this is a couple, with the man on the right and the woman on the left. The woman's right arm is hidden by the man's body and the man's left arm is hidden behind the woman's body, in such a way that his right arm and her left arm, which are bent and upraised, form 90-degree angles. These two figures seem to constitute a single body with two heads and could almost be Siamese twins. What tells them apart, however, is the strength indicated by the man's head and the gentleness radiating from the woman's face. On the other hand, the man's right leg is slightly bent, while both the woman's legs are straight. Clinging to each other, they remain upright, but their bodies are lean-

ing to the left, forming an angle of approximately 70 to 80 degrees, and one wonders how they avoid falling over in this position. This is simply because, like Neptune, the ruling planet of this decan, they are supported by the waves. They are following the stream of thoughts and ideas characteristic of Mercury, the ruling planet of this sign, and create the impression of being undifferentiated, in other words, they have not yet entered the realm of duality. They are real twins, clinging together in the same original egg.

The second decan of Gemini, from about 1 to 10 June: duality makes its appearance in the second decan, although this representation shows something more than duality, perhaps even a conflict, battle, fight or ritual dance, whose outcome will probably be fatal. The twins of this

decan are two youths who look alike and who are fighting. The man on the left is about to fall and his companion, leaning over him, is either holding him up or pushing him to the ground – it is hard to be sure, because the illustration shown here is ambiguous. Is this a depiction of violence and struggle, or complicity and kindness? Should we be thinking in terms of hostile brothers, like Cain and Abel, for example, whose symbolic story obviously has greater significance than a simple tale of a murderous quarrel between brothers, or the confrontation between the angel and Jacob who is, in fact, battling with himself? In this respect, it helps to know that, in the original Bible story, the word used to describe the wrestling match between Jacob and the angel can also refer to an embrace. That being so, it is easier to understand the ambiguous nature of the illustration representing this decan, which may depict two

figures wrestling or embracing, fighting or dancing.

The third decan of Gemini, from about 11 to 20 June: the image symbolizing the third decan is the one usually chosen to represent this dualistic sign. It shows a young man and a young girl standing up, the young man's left hand resting on the girl's right shoulder, the girl's right hand resting on the young man's hip. These two figures naturally bear a striking resemblance to each other. The young man's hand on the girl's shoulder alludes to the various symbolic meanings of the shoulder: man's goal, the promised land, knowledge revealed, the new dawn. The girl's hand on the young man's hip, on the other hand, emphasizes the fact that, just as Jacob dislocated his hip when wrestling with the angel (Genesis 32: 25), man is lame. He is missing part of himself and what is

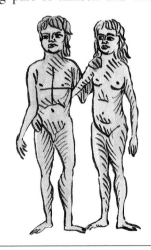

symbolized by the woman's shoulder is represented in this case by the hip.

Thus, the three decans of this sign represent an evolution that starts with the original, undifferentiated couple, touches on duality and concludes with a meeting of opposites that fundamentally resemble each other. This is a world in which the narcissistic interplay of relationships reigns supreme. However, like Jacob's battle with the angel, in this game, the loser wins.

Cancer

Whether represented by the crayfish or crab, people born under this sign are governed by the element of water, although there are differences depending on their decan. It is worth pointing out here that the planets in the zodiac and the 12 zodiac signs move in the same direction as water on earth. There is a physical explanation for this: the rotational movement of the earth is shared by the movement of the planets from east to west and the streams and rivers flow in one direction rather than another precisely because the earth is spinning on its axis.

What is most interesting, however, with regard to the symbolism of the sign of Cancer is this directional flow of water on earth and the fact that the three crustaceans representing the three decans of this warm, sensitive water sign, are swimming westwards. Despite Cancerians' deep attachment to their past in particular and the past in general – which is one of the key characteristics of this sign – the two crayfish and the crab are swimming in the right direction; they never seem to swim against the current in a bid to get back to their source.

Admittedly, this seems completely paradoxical. There are similarities in this respect between these images and those for the sign of Taurus, which bear no resemblance to the concept of the raging or sacrificial bull (see *Taurus*, page 556). In the same way as the zodiac does not represent a bullring for Taurus, the sign of Cancer, revised and corrected by European cultures, does not feature the crab with aggressive-defensive claws that

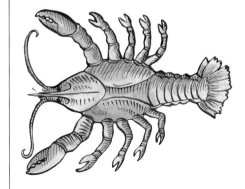

swims backwards or walks sideways. It only depicts two crayfish and a crab, all three in virtually the same position, swimming with the current, therefore anticlockwise or, in other words, travelling back in time.

And that is the way this sign advances: by going backwards. But when, like any self-respecting crayfish, it takes it into its head actually to swim backwards instead of forwards, it is going against the current and, as a result, regresses.

The first decan of Cancer, from about 21 June to 1 July: the first illustration of the sign of Cancer is a splendid crayfish with a long, plump body. Its caudal fin is well developed, which proves that it is perfectly able to retreat in case of danger. However, the most noticeable aspect of its shell is its roundness and its gentle curves, which give no sign of any aggression. This absence of violence is also accentuated by the fact that, although its two claws are obviously

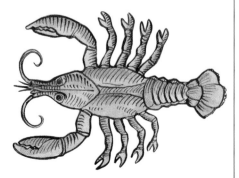

strong, they are closed and depicted in such a way that they resemble someone opening their arms in welcome, offering a hug or embrace. Lastly, this crayfish has two very long antennae. They begin at its eyes and almost join the tip of its claws, although they do not touch them, since the two ends curl round, symbolizing gentleness, receptivity and hypersensitivity, key characteristics of this sign. The creature's overall posture suggests passivity and immobility: it allows itself to be carried along by the current, living tranquilly on the surface of the water and exuding an air of gentleness and well-being. This representation of the first decan of Cancer, which is called the 'emotions' decan and whose ruling planet is Venus, is in the realm of pure emotion, as can be seen by the fact that the creature is depicted in harmony with its surrounding environment. This immobile crayfish is bathed in the waters of the past and, by staying where it is, keeps a grip on the present. It is very careful not to move forward or advance into the future.

The second decan of Cancer, from about 2 to 12 July: another crayfish represents the second decan of this sign, but it is smaller than the former, with a thin, elongated body. Unlike the

Zodiac:
Cancer

previous crayfish, the head of this one is not rounded. It forms an acute angle and its eyes are on the sides. Its antennae are much shorter and curl inwards. Its two forelegs, with closed claws pointing ahead, are no longer open; they virtually form a 90-degree angle with either side of its body. Lastly, its caudal fin is much more defined. It has three sections that resemble the three leaves of a clover or three half-moons stuck together. Our attention is drawn to the fin in this way to underline the fact that a species with a caudal fin like this has great defensive abilities, because the crayfish uses its fin to retreat when it senses danger. The posture of this crayfish suggests that it is less receptive and less part of its surroundings and implies a certain internalization, some cerebral activity perhaps, as if this animal were just about to act, as if it were thinking, meditating, or waiting for a sign. This second decan is called the 'revelations' decan and its ruling planet is Mercury.

The third decan of Cancer, from about 13 to 22 July: the third living symbol for Cancer is no longer a crayfish, but a crab. This difference in representation is very important because the crayfish is a crustacean inhabiting freshwater streams, while the crab lives in the salty water of the sea. However, the shell of the crab representing the third decan of Cancer is not as angular as that of crabs generally found on Western beaches. It is rounded and egg-shaped. Its eight legs are curved into a crescent moon shape and its claws are open, the front ones being disproportionately large and threatening. Its head is round and its eyes are hidden by short antennae that are curved to the side. Its caudal fin looks like a late addition, grafted onto its shell, and its six conjoined sections are reminiscent of a bird's tail feathers. This is a strange crab: its rounded shell suggests a great deal of gentleness, but its posture clearly emphasizes its defensive-offensive stance. It is a perfect illustration of the characteristics of the third decan of this sign. The ruling planet of this 'sensitivity' decan is the moon that encourages Cancer's receptive qualities.

Leo

Three magnificent, noble and majestic lions, whether wild or tame, reign supreme over the fifth zodiac sign. 'Lucky is the lion that the human will eat, so that the lion becomes human. And foul is the human that the lion will eat, and the lion will still become human', said Jesus in the Commentary on the Gospel according to St Thomas. The lion to which this gospel refers is not the noble, regal lion symbolizing Leo in the zodiac, but a representation of the Devil who, through temptation, endeavours to consume man entirely.

In fact, Leos are often characterized by a physical strength and imperious power coupled with an appetite for instinctive behaviour tempered by a certain self-control which can also prove to be instrumental in appropriating and fixing the energies confined in the endless cycle of rebirth.

Leos are often people who immediately exert a powerful influence over their surroundings. Furthermore, Leo is a fixed sign that stabilizes the qualities it reveals in people born under this sign. In this case, it is fire, the element associated with this sign that is fixed, even though the function of fire is not to stay still, but to burn in order to produce energy and heat, transform and purify.

Thus, like Prometheus, Leos are inclined to appropriate the divine fire that burns within and make it work to their advantage by diverting it from its divine purpose, harnessing it to dominate and rule the world. But the message of the seventh Logion from the Commentary on the Gospel according to St Thomas, quoted above, is that, in the last analysis, it is impossible to stop this divine fire from performing its primary and ultimate function, which is to free man from death.

It should also be remembered that the sign of Leo coincides with the harvest season, symbolized by the sickle or scythe of death. By selfishly using the divine fire to dominate the world, like the Devil, Leos are, symbolically of course, harvesting death. In so doing, their energy is dissipated.

Nevertheless, both Re, the Egyptian sun-god, and Christ were frequently represented by a mythical lion. This lion, by the force of its will and the divine breath it possesses within, attains immortality by refusing to divert the primordial energies from their purpose or, more accurately, by allowing theses energies to circulate freely so that, by a continuous process of self-regeneration, they regenerate man, making him immortal and victorious.

The first decan of Leo, from about 23 July to 2 August: the first image is that of a lion radiating tranquil strength as well as a certain heaviness and sadness. It is a handsome beast, but not remarkable. It is shown walking on its own through the savannah, its right leg raised slightly from the ground and its three other legs placed firmly on the ground, which suggests that it is advancing with a heavy tread. However, there is nothing heavy-looking about its body. It displays a certain nobility, with a beautiful mane forming four distinctive waves that curl over its neck and down its back and are so long that they almost brush the ground beneath its head. But its pace creates an impression of bulk and heaviness. Its head is bowed. Its expression seems sad and it seems to be grimacing or wincing, although it also appears strangely peaceful, as if it were

carrying the weight of the world with all its harsh realities on its shoulders, but was resigned to doing so. This is the saturnine, domineering and egocentric Leo, the most introverted of all those born under this sign who, although appearing composed on the surface, may display extreme behaviour.

The second decan of Leo, from about 3 to 12 August: a cheerful, sensual, playful and jovial lion follows this sad and intense creature. It radiates *joie de vivre*. Its entire bearing reveals the need to show off, to be noticed and admired. This lion is sitting up on its hind legs, its two forelegs raised and bent, its body straining forward, although the impression is of suppleness and dynamism. Its light-hearted pose is reminiscent of a dog sitting up and begging for a delicious titbit. The raised tail forms a perfect S and has a splendid plume of fur at its tip. This lion's superb curly mane forms numerous waves around its head and over its breast. Its eyes are wide open – even though we can only see one because it is shown in profile – and it is looking straight ahead, as if staring at someone. Lastly, another distinctive feature that makes us think of a begging dog: its tongue is lolling from its mouth. This likeable, cheerful creature is the epitome of the tame animal.

The third decan of Leo, from about 13 to the 23 August: this is the most mysterious and most intense of the three lions. Firstly, it is standing still, its head and eyes fixed on us, but it is facing in the opposite direction to the first two lions described above. It looks as if it was about to turn right before it came to a standstill and looked us straight in the eyes. It is standing with its two forelegs apart, its left hind leg almost centrally placed beneath its body, its right hind leg behind its hindquarters, all four placed firmly on the solid ground, as if to emphasize that this lion has roots. Its body is

slender, well-muscled and feline, its tail, passed through its two hind legs and beneath its stomach, forms a loop whose plumed end proudly points skywards. There is something supernatural about its mane, which seems to form a compact aura around its head. This latter looks like a mask, which bears some resemblance to the one made for Jean Marais in Jean Cocteau's film *Beauty and the Beast*. The fascinating and disturbing eyes, nose and mouth of this lion seem almost human. The bottom part of its mane could even resemble a curly beard. This is the Plutonian world of the *bête humaine* ('human beast'), so to speak, of raw power and the domination of base instincts, because with this lion, the division between man and animal is very thin.

Virgo

People often ask whether this sign represents the wise virgin or foolish virgin. The three decans of Virgo progress gradually from wisdom to folly. Is it foolish to be wise? Is it wise to be foolish? The answer to these two questions is yes and no, depending on the circumstances. Virgos – who often tend to pay close attention to detail, to notice or find the smallest proverbial spanner in the works, even when it has been missed by others, however attentive or persistent they were – have a fondness for analysis that springs from a kind of quiet, reasonable obsessiveness but sometimes borders on fanaticism.

Those born under the sign of Virgo are sometimes so sensible, so well-organized and logical, that they need to indulge in wild or reckless fantasies to compensate. Alternatively, they may feel as if their personality is so poorly structured or disorganized, their thoughts so muddled, that they cannot help doubting themselves and identifying with anything that allows them to focus on petty detail or something specific, anything that allows them to create order.

Thus, Virgos are sometimes wise and sometimes foolish in their approach to life and their behaviour. As everyone is, it might be objected. This is true, but Virgos are a little more extreme in this respect than most. The reason for this is that Virgo is the sixth zodiac sign and, psychologically, corresponds to what is called the differentiation stage, in other words, the period in a child's development when it feels its independence from its mother, that it is an individual in its own right. Because they are at this stage, Virgos try to be different and to stand out from others by being wise to be foolish or foolish to be wise, as the case may be.

The first decan of Virgo, from about 23 August to 1 September: the image of this first decan is a mythical figure, an angel. Although it is sometimes said that angels are sexless, this symbolic representation is clearly an angelic woman, with luxuriant plaited hair and two magnificent, outstretched wings. This woman, who is also an angel, is sitting on the ground in a field covered with sheaves of wheat, her legs probably tucked under the folds of her flowing dress. In her right hand she holds a splendid sheaf, which she is obviously in the process of assembling because she is holding several freshly gathered ears in her left hand. Her radiant face and gentle eyes are looking straight at us. She seems to be holding herself very still, as if posing for a painter or photographer. This Virgo is very good with her hands, which is obviously a sign of intelligence, because of the correlation between the hands and the mind, as can be seen by verbs such as 'to grasp', meaning 'to learn', 'to understand' and 'to seize'. This woman is also an angel, because the main emphasis is placed on the keen, vibrant intellect that can be seen shining from her face and eyes.

The second decan of Virgo, from about 2 to 13 September: it is rather surprising that a woman with a naked torso, revealing her ample breasts, should be used to symbolize a decan whose keynotes are modesty and shyness. After all, it is strange that a shy, modest woman should make an exhibition of herself and dare to walk openly and publicly half-naked through the countryside. This is precisely because this is the world of the Virgo who is sometimes wise and sometimes foolish, or who, being too sensible (although her nature is deeply, albeit discreetly, emotional) can fall victim to attacks of folly that cause her to break her own rules, even if she is bound to feel guilty afterwards. Whatever the case, this is a woman whose beauty is a little wild and unkempt and who seems to be walking confidently and quickly, her breasts naked and the rest of her curvaceous body covered

with a clinging skirt. Her face is cheerful, friendly and welcoming. In her right hand, she is holding the veil that should have covered her torso and that appears to have just been removed. However, make no mistake: there is nothing provocative or challenging about this woman's actions – she is simply stripping off her clothes. People born in the second decan of Virgo, which she represents, long to strip away their inhibitions, break their self-control, banish their critical lucidity so that they can give themselves up to their feelings and emotions.

The third decan of Virgo, from about 14 to 22 September: the symbolic figure of the third decan of this sign is the wisest of them all. But again, can we trust to appearances? It is difficult to know from the look of this woman, who is standing up, slightly to one side, showing her right profile. She is wearing a beautiful dress that conceals her entire body and disguises her shape. However, everything suggests that she is pregnant. This can be seen from her rounded stomach, her tranquil serenity and the impression of fulfilment radiating from her face. She is not holding any ears of wheat or sheaves, but her hands are stretched out before her in a gesture of helpfulness or offering. She is, however, wearing a magnificent crown of wheat ears, filled with plump, ripe grains, whose golden colour merges with the long blond hair that tumbles over her shoulders and down her back to her ample waist. Although she is standing still, she is not frozen in one position. Everything in her bearing and expression suggests that she feels at home in her setting and is attentive to everything happening around her,

although she is also fully self-aware and focused. All these qualities are clearly defined in the third decan of the sign of Virgo, whose ruling planet is Mercury and which is known as the 'altruism' decan.

Libra

Although the words indecisive, irresolute and tentative are often used to describe people born under the sign of Libra, the figures illustrating the three decans of this sign suggest a different vocabulary. In astrology, as in other fields, generally accepted ideas die hard, not least because, since the 17th century and particularly over the past three decades, a lot of nonsense has been put forward in the guise of astrology. As a result, numerous commonplaces and clichés exist with regard to the key characteristics of each of the 12 zodiac signs. For instance, Librans have been described as being confused and uncertain, wavering continually between two options, two possible choices, never being able to make up their mind or choose a specific course of action. If this were really the case, Miguel de Cervantes would never have created the character of Don Quixote, Giuseppe Verdi would never have composed his magnificent operas, Auguste and Louis Lumière would never have been regarded as the inventors of cinematography and, more recently, neither John Lennon nor Sting would have become famous songwriters. For all these talented, creative people were born under the sign of Libra.

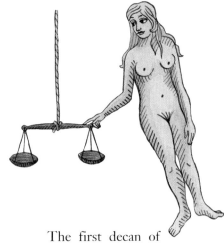

Furthermore, although it is true that this sign is closely associated with the qualities of justice, one important point should be made: justice is not as important as correctness in this context. Librans are less interested in the law and the established order than in a need for stability and harmony that can be obsessive and may mean that they are excessively perfectionist or pernickety.

That is why they devote a great deal of care and attention to adjusting, adapting and specifying different aspects of their life and, in so doing, they lay down the law and impose their own order which, in their view, is the natural order of things.

This sign is therefore identified with the values associated with Justice, the VIIIth card of the Major Arcana of the divinatory Tarot. However, this card does not represent the basic principle of this sign and Libra does not possess all the characteristics attributed to Justice as they appear in this Arcana: the scales, naturally, but also the two-edged sword of Justice. This is because the law does not just pass judgement – it also has to ensure that it is carried out.

Thus, it follows that Librans tend not to dispense justice, but do what they believe is right.

The first decan of Libra, from about 23 September to 2 October: the image illustrating the first decan of this sign bears certain similarities to the mythical figure of Proserpine-Persephone, whose legend clearly illustrates the dialectics of this sign that prioritizes the art of reaching a compromise and striking a happy medium. It depicts a beautiful woman, who is completely naked but not at all provocative. Her naked body radiates innocence and purity. She is leaning to the left as we look at her, in other words to her right, her left arm straight at her side, her open hand placed along her thigh. Her right arm is slightly bent and held away from her body and, with her fingertips, she is lightly touching or caressing the horizontal bar of a fairly basic set of scales, with no beam, that just has two wooden pans or dishes and is suspended on a piece of string. The setting for this woman and her scales is completely blank, so we do not know why or how she is leaning over like this without falling or what the latter is suspended from. Whatever the case, this is the world of the first decan of Libra, whose ruling planets are the Moon and Venus, characterized by sensitivity and the feminine properties of gentleness and receptivity. This Libran does not weigh or judge – she values, a word that has the dual meaning of loving and measuring.

The second decan of Libra, from about 3 to 13 October: this time, we are shown a proper balance scale with two metal pans that are perfectly stable and on the same level. It has its beam as well as three perpendicular knife-edges or steel prisms. It conveys an impression of perfect balance that appears to be unshakeable. We have the feeling that this set of scales is a proper weighing tool for measuring different

quantities – which is, after all, its primary function. However, nothing indicates what is about to be weighed. It is simply a set of scales, a basic symbol. As we have already said, it does not represent the scales of Justice but the search for perfect equilibrium or the desire to preserve it at any cost. There is no likelihood here that one of the two pans will be tipped, creating confusion or questioning everything that has been learned, established or instituted. There is nothing around this immobilized set of scales. This is the ascetic world peculiar to Saturn, the ruling planet of this second decan.

The third decan of Libra, from about 14 to 22 October: the symbol illustrating the third decan of this sign is much more light-hearted, even though this is the 'justice' decan. It is another set of scales, again shown in a bare setting but this time with a life of its own, so to speak. The right pan is clearly tipping to the right while, naturally enough, the left one is higher. What is more, this set of scales appears to be entirely wooden, giving it a more homely appearance, since it has none of the metallic rigidity and coldness of the balance scale representing the previous decan. Its two pans are suspended by three short pieces

of rope on wooden hooks at either end of the horizontal bar. Furthermore, it has one particular feature that is not unimportant: the horizontal bar passes through a slot cut in a piece of wood. A vertical needle, on top of the horizontal bar, is following the movement of the right pan, which is heavier and tipping to the right. A needle that can swing from right to left, depending on whether the right or left pan is heavier, is similar to the metronome used by musicians. Here we have an unstable situation that alludes to a type of perpetual motion, swinging from right to left and left to right. It is also the world of rhythm and, what is more, that of justice: food for thought indeed.

Scorpio

The three living symbols for this sign indicate that first-decan Scorpios are instinctive, second-decan Scorpios are indomitable and third-decan Scorpios are sentimental. This zodiac sign is famous for its bad reputation. Why? Because those who set great store by astrological commonplaces and clichés will tell you that Scorpios are often anti-social and destructive.

This naturally raises the question whether there is any such thing as a good or a bad sign. Can or should one make value judgements in relation to the signs of the zodiac? We do not think so: there is nothing fundamentally and definitively positive or negative in the structure of the zodiac. It simply presents an interplay of contradictory and complementary qualities – here quality should be understood in the sense of a distinctive attribute that makes an individual what he is – that mirror our true selves. For this reason, if the qualities attributed to the sign of Scorpio, especially its weaknesses or negative aspects, bother us more than those attributed, for example, to Taurus, its opposite sign, this is because, such as we are, we find it easier to accept the values associated with the sign of Taurus rather than those attributed to Scorpio.

Nevertheless, in line with the universal principle of the opposing and complementary forces that prevail over life, these qualities are interdependent.

Concentrating exclusively on one set of values to the detriment of the others obviously creates a general lack of balance – which might now be described as psychological, but which would once have been seen as a spiritual malaise – to which certain individuals are more susceptible than others. This lack of balance could therefore be at the root of certain compensatory, violent and extreme subconscious outbursts. After all, we are well aware that every time we lean too far in one direction, we create an imbalance whose repercussions are felt sooner or later.

For example, as regards the axis drawn between the fixed signs of Taurus and Scorpio, which in itself is not lacking in intensity, if we focus on certain existential qualities inherent in the former (possession, attachment, conformism, security), while trying to overlook, ignore or reject those that relate to the latter (dispossession, detachment, nonconformity, destruction), instead of experiencing the latter knowingly, we fall under their influence. This is the true reason for Scorpio's bad reputation: as a rule, especially nowadays, we refuse to make sacrifices, we do not want to wait until the future to reap what we have sown today. We cling to a conformist, reassuring interpretation of reality that makes us weaker the more it excludes the forces of regeneration revealed by the eighth sign of the zodiac.

The first decan of Scorpio, from about 23 October to 2 November: the first of Scorpio's three arachnids is perfectly representative of the ruling planet of this decan, which is also the sign's ruling planet: Mars. This scorpion is seen from above. It has a very elongated body, with eight legs. Its claws are extended in front and slightly raised above its body as a sign of aggression. Its tail forms a semicircle, the stinger facing forward, ready to attack, ready to sting. In this picture, there is nothing to indicate that the scorpion in question is about to attack – it merely suggests that it would be better to steer well clear of it. This is the world of irrepressible, instinctive and basic impulses that cannot be governed by reason and involve a certain animalistic

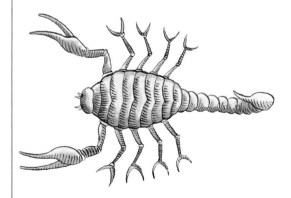

single-mindedness that generally frightens us and that, although we push it away or reject it, also fascinates and attracts us. First-decan Scorpios are full of these compelling contradictions.

The second decan of Scorpio, from about 3 to 11 November: this stylized illustration is rather childlike in execution. This scorpion looks more evasive and elusive than aggressive; it is no longer waiting motionless, ready to attack, but an untameable creature that will outrun its own shadow. This scorpion is also seen from above: its two claws, which are closed this time, are not stretched out in front, but to the side, parallel with its eight legs and the same size as them, which makes it look as if it has ten legs and emphasizes its speed and agility. Furthermore, its crudely drawn body is thin and lightweight, particularly in

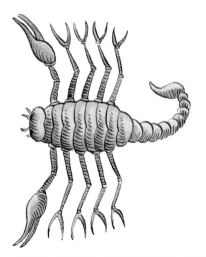

comparison to the creature represented in the previous decan. Finally, its tail is much shorter and its stinger is not raised above its body, ready to sting, but curved to the right, forming a loop. This scorpion symbolizes nonconformity, the provocative, disconcerting and disturbing spirit of rebellion that characterizes those born in the second decan, who are often impulsive and independent, qualities that spring from Uranus, the ruling planet of this decan.

The third decan of Scorpio, from about 12 to 21 November: the fixed, intense symbol of the last decan of this sign is a scorpion that gives no indication of any aggressiveness but which, in many respects, is reminiscent of the crayfish of the first decan of Cancer (see page 262). The first thing that catches our attention is its oval, protuberant body and the fact that, unlike the first two, it is facing right as we look at it – as if, again, we were situated above it. Its short legs, which are bent backwards, become increasingly shorter along the length of its body. Its tail, curved to one side, is long and thin and its stinger appears to be completely harmless. This scorpion has another distinctive feature: its round, open eyes are directly in line with its two

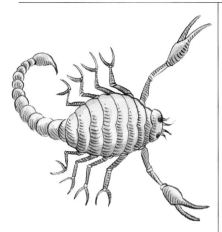

claws, which resemble open arms rather than instruments of war, either on the defensive or ready to attack. This scorpion, which seems to be immobile and receptive, is entirely representative of people born in this decan, who are endowed with considerable mental powers. Its ruling planet (Venus) also suggests that they place great emphasis on their feelings and emotions.

Sagittarius

Sagittarius, which means 'archer', from the Latin *sagitta* ('arrow'), is represented by a centaur, a mythical, fantastic creature. The direction in which he is aiming his arrow tells us a great deal about the character of each particular decan. Like the dragon, the Gorgon, the hydra, the unicorn or the angel, the centaur is a fabled creature from the world of myths invented by man, a product of his imagination, his psyche, even his subconscious mind, in more modern parlance. Centaurs have for us the same fascination as those ancient gigantic animals, the dinosaurs, because they embody our primordial, basic instincts and because, in a way – since it is thought they may have brought about their own ruin by being too greedy – we subconsciously identify with them.

Horse, man, bow and arrow. What should we focus on when looking at this fantastic, unreal animal symbolizing the ninth sign of the zodiac: horse, man, bow or arrow? The centaur has the body of a horse and a man's torso, head and arms. It is therefore half-man, half-animal. If this creature is ruled by its head, then man is obviously the dominant partner. On the other hand, if the centaur's actions are governed by the horse's body, represented in its entirety minus

the head, then the animal half of this hybrid creature is in control. In the last analysis, the arrow makes the difference. The direction in which the centaur is pointing its bow – straight ahead, behind or at the sky – tells us which part of its body is taking the initiative. This mythical creature, whose body and head have great symbolic significance, embodies the following moral: mental or physical concentration on something can, respectively, elevate it or devalue it. As for the origin of this image, we probably need look no further than the pictograms that preceded writing. The basic principle of this system of signs was the pictorial representation of any animal or object that the writer wanted to name or to list, if there were several or if they were different. Thus, by combining the man/ horse pictograms, the writers may have been referring to riders, or perhaps naked men riding on horseback, who were so at one with their mounts that people ended up thinking that they were fantastic creatures. However, what is so surprising is that ancient images like this, products of man's imagination, can strike genuinely relevant psychic resonances in our contemporary minds.

The first decan of Sagittarius, from about 22 November to 1 December: the horse's body of this first centaur is facing left, although the man's torso is twisted round to the right so that he can look behind. He is holding a drawn bow with the arrow aiming at something behind him, the arrowhead in line with his back and plumed tail. He is standing very still, ready to shoot his arrow. While it is true that, in the case of the centaur, horse and man are as one, forming a single entity, the picture of this centaur creates the overriding impression that he is actually at one with his bow, even his arrow – as well as the target that he can see even if we cannot. Because his target is behind him, he is turning to face the past. However, this is an ambitious past, so to speak, symbolically designated and brought up to date by his arrowhead. The first decan of the sign of Sagittarius, governed by Mercury, is the 'wisdom' decan. Jupiter and

Neptune, which are the ruling planets of this sign, make this an environment characterized by simplicity and inspiration, both of which tend towards wisdom.

The second decan of Sagittarius, from about 2 to 11 December: this centaur is resolutely galloping forward, his bow drawn and held in front of him. For this reason, unless he is exceptionally skilful, it is unlikely that he will be able to hit his target. However, we can assume that he will be shooting more than one arrow, since he has a quiver on his back, held in place by a leather strap looped around his naked torso, which is full of sharpened and feathered arrows. The motion of his horse's body exudes a sense of spirit, brio and power, while the muscles of his torso are as taut as his bow. If the centaur of the previous decan was resolutely facing the past, this one is firmly rooted in the present, even though this is a dynamic present, full of motion and action, not an instant that is forever fixed. Time is not standing still – it is flying, moving forward. This is the decan, not of adventure, but 'adventures', symbolized by the numerous arrows contained in the centaur's quiver. These he shoots here and there as he passes by, widening his field of action as he advances.

The third decan of Sagittarius, from about 12 to 21 December: like the centaur representing the first decan of this sign, this one is standing still, its hoofs braced against the ground. Its legs are locked and straight, lacking the often-characteristic delicacy of horses' legs. The man is leaning backwards slightly, his left arm pointing at the sky, his eyes focused along the shaft of his arrow, which is also aimed at the sky. If the arrow symbolizes the mind, ideas, aspirations and man's destiny, then we can presume that the mind, ideas, aspirations and destiny of this centaur are ambitious and noble. Sagittarians born in this decan are inclined to shoot their arrows further than they could possibly go. That is, the target, within the framework of this decan, is an ideal. And this is, in fact, the world of firm convictions, represented here by the hooves of this centaur, which is at one with the earth. These hooves provide firm support for Sagittarians so that they can deepen their knowledge of the world and of life and aim their arrows at an idealistic or humanitarian target, a noble and altruistic cause, something that drives third-decan Sagittarians towards the future.

Capricorn

The three decans of the sign of Capricorn are represented by two fishtailed goats and an ibex. Although Saturn is undoubtedly the ruling planet of the sign of Capricorn, nevertheless, according to Greek mythology, Zeus/Jupiter was responsible for placing this phantasmagoric creature with the tail of a fish and the head and body of a goat in the heavens as a constellation. 'Capricorn' literally means 'horned billy-goat' or, more accurately, if we go back to the Greek origin of this noun, *aigokereus*, a 'goat-horned' animal.

To understand the symbolic meaning of this sign and the mythical animal that represents it we must examine the combined symbols of the goat and the fish. Firstly, it is important to

highlight an important if subtle difference between the interpretations given to these two animals. The Greeks saw the goat as the mythical she-goat, Amaltheia, whose horn symbolized plenty, fertility and riches. However, in Europe, in the Middle Ages, under the influence of the Inquisition, the attributes of this goat, which once favoured good harvests and prosperity, were identified with those of the devilish billy goat, representing lewdness, vice and evil. The fish was associated with the fertile living forces at the origin of all life because it swam in the deep primordial waters of the oceans covering most of the earth's surface. Similarly, today, in psychoanalysis, it represents the deepest, often regenerative, levels of the personality.

The symbols of the goat and the fish therefore shed some light on this sign, which is not necessarily regarded with a great deal of sympathy, but which is always seen as a more or less beneficial indicator of fertility and riches; it is as if the most fertile and regenerative riches were to be found at the darkest, coldest and most barren level of the living world. This may well be the underlying message conveyed by the sign of Capricorn: the greatest riches are found in the midst of utter deprivation, while light spills from the heart of darkness.

The first decan of Capricorn, from about 22 to 31 December: the first symbol is represented by the fabulous animal with the head and body of a goat and a fishtail. However, this goat possesses a type of grace, a sort of delicacy. Lying down, its legs tucked under its body, its bony, immobile head facing straight ahead, radiating a certain strength, pride and nobility, it seems to be staring at a point on the horizon. It would almost be possible to draw a perfect semicircle above its slender body and behind its thick, powerful neck, from the tip of its muzzle to the point of its smooth horns that curve slightly downwards. Its body seems to become thinner and narrower towards its hindquarters, which end in a superb fishtail. This latter is looped under its body on the ground and its caudal fin, pointing towards the sky, resem-

bles a flower with three beautiful upturned petals. Its recumbent position, its forelegs tucked under its body – it has no hind legs, since the body ends in a fishtail – can be regarded not only as a sign of humility but also of patient, expectant waiting. The immobility of this fantastic animal's head and its eyes fixed on the horizon indicate clearsightedness, a piercing gaze that is not taken in by appearances. However, its fishtail suggests that it is also identified with the fertile, magnanimous and expansive principle and that, as a result, the presence of Jupiter, the ruling planet of the first decan, can be felt alongside the austere, lucid influence of Saturn, the ruling planet of this sign.

The second decan of Capricorn, from about 1 to 9 January: given that Mars governs this decan, we can expect to see a much more primitive hybrid creature, half-goat, half-fish. This is in fact the case. This is a wild goat, whose

body might have been cut in two in the middle and grafted on to the tail of a serpent or sea dragon. This time, the mythical animal representing this decan is not kneeling or lying down. Its two forelegs are stretched out in front, its head is slightly bowed, the tips of its horns are slightly curved upwards, its neck is thickly covered with hair and its long undulating fishtail is looped under its body and pointing sky-wards. This posture and these characteristics radiate an impulsive, resolute strength and an active, focused power that are wholly representative of the dual presence of Mars, the ruling planet of this decan, and Saturn, the ruling planet of this sign.

The third decan of Capricorn, from about 10 to 19 January: the image representing the third decan of the sign of Capricorn is much more modern. This is a mountain goat or chamois, at least as regards the long, slender and well-muscled legs that are clearly supple, strong and agile. These qualities are all the more obvious because this animal is shown rearing up on its two hind legs, not as if it were about to leap, spring, climb or jump over an obstacle, but as if it were about to stand upright like a man. There is something human and intelligent about the bearing of its head, which is slightly bowed and tilted to one side, and its expressive eyes. However, the shape of its long, powerful ridged horns leaves no room for doubt: this is not a goat or a chamois, but an ibex that lives in mountain ranges and is famed for its agility in jumping from rock to rock on the mountainside. Although the goat has had a very bad reputation since Herodotus (this Greek historian referred to the sex cult associated with an Egyptian god represented by a goat, particularly in the city of Mendes) in central Europe and Asia, the ibex is regarded as a sacred animal, the guardian of the world (in ancient times, the mountains often formed the boundary of a territory or country; even today, they are natural borders). The goat had the power to ward off sorcery and, because the mountainside is its home, it lives in close contact with the sky and heavenly powers, the world of Uranus, the ruling planet of this third decan and personification of heaven. Uranus is regarded as a fertile element, because he was the husband of Gaia, the earth, and he covered her as the billy goat covers the she-goat to impregnate her.

Aquarius

'Originality', 'inspirations' and 'utopias' are the three magical names of the three decans of Aquarius, whose living symbols combine dream and ambiguity, realism and imagination. 'Aquarius' comes from the Latin word meaning 'of water', which is used as a noun to mean water carrier. Some think it may be a simple translation of the Greek *hudrokhœus* – which initially meant 'who pours water', followed by 'rainy' – since etymologists agree that this sign governed a rainy period of the year.

However, in our view, this Greek word could not refer to such a period, because, in Greece, icy winds are more common in February than rain. It should also be remembered that the zodiac was not a product of Greek thought but was devised by the Mesopotamians, who lived in a region with a very different climate: as can be imagined, rain was rare and, for that very reason, seen as regenerative and fertilizing.

The eleventh sign of the zodiac is linked with both wind and water or, in other words, the two inseparable primordial elements of water and air. This singular combination of elements gives rise to a wide variety of original and unconventional interpretations and factors that make their presence felt in the living symbols of the three decans of this sign.

The first decan of Aquarius, from about 20 to 30 January: this decan is called 'originality' and its ruling planet is Venus. It is not altogether surprising therefore that the 'water carrier' representing the first ten degrees of this sign has a certain physical appeal. There is something effeminate about this young man's bearing and physique. Yet, although he could almost be an androgyne or an angel, he is definitely a young man. He is standing up, his right

leg forward, his right foot flat on the ground and his right knee slightly bent. His left leg is further behind, the tip of his left foot braced against the ground with his heel raised and his left knee decidedly more bent. He is dressed as a medieval page and is wearing a cape, which falls to just below his waist and floats in the wind behind him. The upper half of his body is bending forward slightly. In his left hand, he holds a water pitcher upside down by the handle and is pouring the contents into a basin already filled with water. As can be seen, both wind and water make an appearance in this illustration, the former suggested by the movements of his cape and his dishevelled hair, the latter, obviously, by the stream of water flowing from his pitcher. He seems oblivious to everything around him, concentrating on his right hand, which is resting on the base of the pitcher. It should be remembered that the chief ruling planet of Aquarius is Saturn. Thus, his power of concentration and his ability

to focus are of great significance. But why is he pouring the water from a pitcher into a basin already containing water that has been placed on the ground? Because he is symbolically pouring out his original thoughts and feelings in this way, although he is not interested in allowing them to spread. As a result, the basin contains and preserves the water of his thoughts, ideas and feelings, which are in no danger of trickling away. First-decan Aquarians are often renowned for their pragmatism.

The second decan of Aquarius, from about 31 January to 8 February: this world is less ambiguous than the first decan, but just as intense and more primitive. The figure represented at the heart of the sign of Aquarius is also standing up, but is completely naked. It might be more correct to say that he is as naked as prehistoric man. Although his body resembles that of a child who has grown up too fast, or that of a slightly misshapen adult whose body still retains its childlike plumpness and posture, he has an abundant growth of hair under his arms, on his torso and along his thighs. He therefore calls to mind an individual of primitive instincts, whose animal nature still dominates. His thick hair is tousled and floats in the wind. With his right hand, level with his face, he holds a basin upside down and pours out a stream of water resembling a river winding through a valley. We can assume that the stream of water is being stirred by the wind, as it is wavy. The primitive appearance of this figure, who radiates a blend of brutality and gentleness, is typical of the Black Moon, which governs this decan. As for the water rippling in the wind, it alludes to the qualities of inspiration, aspiration and divination attributed to this decan.

The third decan of Aquarius, from about 9 to 18 February: the last illustration is the one most often used in relation to the sign of Aquarius. This figure has his right knee on the ground. His left foot is securely placed on the ground and his left leg is bent.

He is posed like this on the bank of a tumultuous river. His powerful arms are supporting and encircling a heavy, impressive pitcher that is resting on his left shoulder. A wide, seemingly endless stream of water is pouring out; the pitcher in question appears to be bottomless. This obviously calls to mind the horn of plenty, or the infinite resources of the imagination and the mind. This decan, governed by Neptune, combines faith and utopianism. It encapsulates great potential emotional riches, vast reserves of inspiration and a profusion of dreams and utopias which give man reason to hope and are essential for his self-belief and personal development.

Pisces

Three pairs of fish represent the three decans of the last zodiac sign. Each symbolizes in its own way the ambivalent nature of this complex sign. Pisces has a bad reputation in most people's minds, second only to Scorpio. The blame must be laid on damaging commonplaces and clichés – but these are also found in many other fields; astrology does

not have the monopoly in this respect. Be that as it may though, the harm has been done.

Let us reposition this sign in the zodiac, therefore, while realizing that it is not the last sign – except from the point of view of a symbolic chronology established by our forebears, there is no first or last sign – but the one that coincides with the end of a natural cycle and ushers in a new one. This may well be its most important function. By following

the wheel of the zodiac, we discover the recommended, even mandatory, path to self-fulfilment that is everyone's final goal.

This path takes us through the gate of Capricorn, traditionally called the founder of the world, and on to Aquarius, the liberator of the world. Eventually, we enter the sign of Pisces, regarded by our forebears as the world saviour. In other words, it could be said that when man reaches Capricorn, he acquires knowledge and learning, when he draws level with Aquarius, he frees himself from all physical, moral, emotional, social dependencies, and when, lastly, he enters Pisces, he is saved, meaning that he escapes, he flees and thus leaves the eternal cycle of rebirth and the seasons that punctuate life on earth. From a pictorial viewpoint, the three pairs of fish representing this sign are very alike – they generally differ only in terms of their position and the direction in which they are swimming.

The first decan of Pisces, from about 19 to 29 February: the first pair consists of two identical fish, although this is true of all three pictures symbolizing the three decans of this sign. However, the main difference between the two fish in this decan and the two other pairs is their position in relation to each other. The first is perfectly horizontal, heading to the left; the second is below it, its head and body the other way round, as if they were head to tail or swimming in a sea or river at opposite ends of the world. However, although these two fish are identical, there is no apparent link between them and nothing prevents us from imagining that the one on top could have been the one below and vice versa. This thirty-fourth decan of the zodiac is the 'clairvoyance'

decan, and first-decan Pisceans are either perceptive and far-sighted or anguished and despairing. They may veer from one extreme to the other, without any transition, sometimes from morning to evening, or from one moment to the next.

The second decan of Pisces, from about 1 to 9 March: aesthetically speaking, this is the most attractive and most harmonious pair of fish featured in the final zodiac sign. Each of these two splendid long fish with beautiful scales has a slender, finely chiselled head, two ventral and dorsal fins and a caudal fin that are all well-developed but in proportion to the rest of its body. Each radiates a certain tranquillity tinged with confidence as well as delicacy and strength: attributes that allude as much to their superficial appearance as their inner beauty. These two fish are one above the other, the one on top swimming to the left, its body straight. A cord links its caudal fin to that of its fellow

creature or twin brother, which is swimming in the opposite direction below. Thus, each seems to want to choose the route, although they are linked together, united. This link symbolizes the subtle elements that connect two apparently contradictory yet complementary tendencies in Pisceans born in this decan. Here, even if body and soul are not in harmony, they are at least in constant touch with each other.

The third decan of Pisces, from about 10 to 20 March: the two fish representing this last decan of the zodiac are in constant motion and in their prime. Their bodies are also covered in scales, but this time these are larger, more noticeable. Their dorsal, ventral and caudal fins seem flattened by the force of the water. They are clearly being used, as these fish are swimming very fast. The one on top is no longer in a horizontal position, as was the case with the two previous decans. Facing right, its body forms a 45-degree angle above

the horizon. It might be thought that its head, pointing up towards the sky, is emerging from the waves. The head of its twin is pointing downwards, its body also forming a 45-degree angle, but below the horizon. This second fish is therefore in the process of diving to the depths. One is surfacing, the other diving, but they are linked by a cord, each holding one end in its mouth. This represents the ambivalence that often character-izes Pisceans born in this decan. They sometimes long to burst out of the shadows to express themselves and tell the world what they have sensed and seen, and sometimes they want to escape from the world, withdraw into themselves and dive into the inmost depths of their soul and their consciousness.

Index